Ancient Civilizations
AND THE BIBLE

A Biblical World History Curriculum - Volume One

TEACHER'S GUIDE

FROM CREATION TO CHRIST

Ancient Civilizations

AND THE BIBLE

A Biblical World History Curriculum - Volume One

TEACHER'S GUIDE

FROM CREATION TO CHRIST

DIANA WARING
HISTORY ALIVE!

Scripture quotations are taken from the New King James Version, Copyright © 1979, 1980, 1982 by Thomas Nelson, Inc., Publishers. Used by permission.

Ancient Civilizations & The Bible: Creation to Jesus Christ: Teacher's Guide
Copyright ©2004 Diana Waring
All rights reserved

Cover Design by Alpha Advertising
Interior Design by Pine Hill Graphics
Photos courtesy of freestockphotos.com
Maps courtesy of Geography Matters
Original layout design: Isaac Waring

ISBN 1-930514-26-3

Printed in the United States of America.

"And He has made from one blood every nation of men to dwell on all the face of the earth, and has determined their preappointed times and the boundaries of their habitation, so that they should seek the Lord…" Acts 17:26-27

TABLE OF CONTENTS

Sometimes, people work for a paycheck.

> *"Not enough to get tired,*
> Just enough to not be fired."

Ho-Hum.
In the same way, students often work for a grade.

> *"Not enough to really learn,*
> *Just enough to get the grade and move on."*

Ho-Hum.

But is that what God intended?

> *"And whatever you do, do it heartily, as to the Lord and not to men . . ."* Col 3:23

> *"Whatever you hand finds to do, do it with your might . . ."* Eccl 9:10

> *" . . . not with eye service, as men-pleasers, but as servants of Christ, doing the will of God from the heart, with good will doing service, as to the Lord, and not to men."* Eph 6:6-7

Rather than a ho-hum approach to life and learning, He created us to be passionately involved:

> *Love the Lord your God with all your heart, with all your soul, with all your mind and with all your strength!!!!*

Recognizing that we can not crawl inside the student's mind and heart, throw a switch, and create a passion for learning, how on earth do we get them involved in the process? How do we help them move beyond spectator to active player?
The solution we and many others have discovered is a new model:

> *We must work with the design of God.*

Our Creator uniquely designed each of us with strengths and styles of learning, so we must respond to this by developing an educational approach which gives opportunities for these differences. Realizing that our students are made in the image and likeness of God, and recognizing that we are working under God, we begin to comprehend that our labor in ministry is nurturing handcrafted masterpieces, not assembly-line, Dollar Store merchandise!
A basic, practical and attainable method for accomplishing this is to provide variety in the learning environment. With that in mind, the Ancient Civilizations & The Bible curriculum was designed with a broad variety of opportunities for pursuing information. Without the teacher having to analyze every student or to create a dozen different activities, the program offers suggestions for creating that variety.

In approaching this multi-sensory, interdisciplinary study of history, we encourage you to:

#1) *Honor and respect your students.* Allow them to be whom they were designed by God to be - physical? - verbal? - interactive? - daydreaming? - hands-on? - logical? - artistic? - musical? - quiet? - attention-getter? - leader?

The many-faceted suggestions within each section of the curriculum allow students to actively and personally pursue learning—no more *spectator* education! The students will purposefully be involved in setting the direction of each Unit through their exploration, discovery, discussion, hands-on activity, and creative expression. Engaging them this way honors and respects the unique approach to learning which God has set into each student. This impacts the entire course—not just by providing real opportunities for the students, allowing them to joyfully and actively learn the content, but by also providing real structure, a valid paradigm of structure and organization, enabling teachers to move forward within the content of the course. By approaching lessons this way, teachers are given the opportunity to be partial to every student (rather than partial to the linguistic and math/logical students whose successes normally dominate the classroom); to be fair and just in assessing student accomplishment through giving opportunities and honoring all the different types of learners; to be creative in the areas which appeal personally to them; to keep all the students motivated and moving along in their studies. This curriculum encourages each learner to become self-motivated: through choosing specific learning activities; through choosing how to creatively share what has been learned; through team projects as well as individual accomplishments; through visual, auditory, and kinesthetic learning opportunities; through the integration of multidisciplinary learning (which sometimes appeals to the student beyond the actual subject of history).

> *"Learning is not always FUN. Most of it is very hard work, but it does not also have to be unpleasant. Gardening in spring is delightful - it's hard work, but pleasant. Only a fool would try to carry out the same activities in winter. Why add unpleasantness to something already difficult? But we do that in learning all the time. Something hard but satisfying often unnecessarily becomes something both hard and unpleasant."* Rosalie Pedder

Our intent is keep learning delightful, even if demanding and challenging. We have endeavored to present a rich variety of creative activities for you to access for your students.

Teaching History From A Biblical Perspective

- Letting them learn history in ways that honor and respect their individual design;
- Letting them be inspired by the greatness of who God is and what He has done;
- Letting them meet the great heroes of world history and see the great villains;
- Letting them be mesmerized by the incredible adventures and cliffhanging tight spots;
- Inspiring them to jump in with both feet and discover whatever is unexplained, curious, awe-inspiring, funny, fascinating to THEM!

. . . IS TEACHING HISTORY FROM A BIBLICAL PERSPECTIVE.

#2) Teach history as HisStory. A *biblical perspective* in history means seeing God as central to our understanding. In this curriculum, we do not add a few Hebrew dates into an otherwise typical presentation of history and label it "biblical." Instead, we want to see history from His point of view; to view all of history—all cultures and events—in the light of God's revelation of Himself and of His ongoing redemptive purpose pursued throughout the world's existence. Encountering God in the affairs of men, distinguishing the good leader from the bad leader—the hero from the villain—and making those determinations based on the Bible, is teaching history from a *biblical perspective*. (See Appendix, Page 291 for an illustration of this principle.)

To gain this perspective, the student is frequently asked to consider, *"What was God doing in this moment of history?"* The answers are found and explored in the Bible, the archaeological record, the writings of experts, and historic source documents. This overlapping of what are often described as "secular" history and "sacred" history gives us a front row seat to observe the incredible events, the amazing people, and the fascinating imprints of God's interaction in our world. This provides not only insight into history but revelation of the Maestro of HisStory. With this perspective, students will not only gain academic understanding of history, but more importantly, they will grow in their personal understanding of God's faithfulness and wisdom.

The highest purpose and ultimate goal of this curriculum is to see the lives of students change as they come face to face with the reality of God's amazing faithfulness throughout all time.

May you find great joy in this study!

In Jesus,
Diana Waring

➤ *Structural Overview*

The Course of Study...

Unit One: *Creation & The Flood*
Unit Two: *The Rise of Civilizations*
Unit Three: *Egypt & The Exodus*
Unit Four: *The Children of Israel*
Unit Five: *Assyria & Babylon*
Unit Six: *The Persians & Medes*
Unit Seven: *Greece & The Hellenists*
Unit Eight: *The Rise of Rome*
Unit Nine: *Jesus Christ, Immanuel*

The Scope

The Structure of Each Unit...

The Sequence

Week One: Introduction

- *Discuss Key Concepts*
- *Read the Unit Article*
- *Listen to the appropriate recordings*
- *Consider and discuss opinions*
- *Choose interesting books or Internet search*

Week Two: Exploration & Discovery

- *Research a topic of your choice*
- *Learn the Words to Watch*
- *Construct the Timeline*
- *Report findings on your Research*

Week Three: Hands-On

- *Geography mapping*
- *View Art & Architecture*
- *Art projects*
- *Science Experiments*
- *Music suggestions*
- *Cook the recipe*

Week Four: Expression

- *Choose from these possibilities:*
- *Linguistics: Journalism, Prose, Poetry, Playing with Words*
- *Art: Painting/Drawing, Graphic Design, Sculpting, Cartooning*
- *Music: Compose, Practice Performance*
- *Drama: Comedy, Tragedy, Reality, Reader's Theater, Puppetry*
- *Movement: Pantomime, Dance, Action*
- *Conceptual Design*

Explanation of Structure

Based on the Myers-Briggs definitions of Learning Styles - Feeler, Thinker, Sensor, Intuitor (for more explanation, see Appendix), Ancient Civilizations & The Bible has been designed so that each Unit proceeds through a four-week cycle of one week per learning style. This means that every student will have the opportunity to learn history in their own style, as well as from other approaches.

Complementing this approach is the opportunity for students to learn new information from a combination of visual, auditory, and kinesthetic presentations. This insures that your students have the occasion to learn in the way they learn best. This "Digging Deeper" Study Guide has already designed this multi-modality approach into every unit. Hopefully, you will access aspects of each one in every unit.

Week #1 will appeal greatly to the *Feeler* Learning Style, as students gain the *"people* perspective" by listening with *you* to auditory recordings, reading the scriptures and other history materials, and *discussing together* what they are learning. The *discussion* suggestions range from open-ended questions with many possible answers to discovery questions which require both content and studied consideration.

Week #2 is designed to capture the interest of the *Thinker* Learning Style by appealing to the *authoritative* and *factual* perspective through chronological work with a *timeline*, vocabulary *drill*, and *research &* reporting projects. Since the students are allowed to each select their own *research project* and the manner in which they will report what has been learned, there is an intrinsic motivation factor—they choose what they want to learn about!

Week #3 provides the often neglected *hands-on* learning opportunities which will allow the *Sensor* Learning Style to thrive. This week focuses on the geography of a historic time through *mapmaking*, and gives place to the fine *arts*. Students are given exposure to great art, architecture, and music, and given *hands-on* experiences with *creating* art and *preparing* food. Science *experiments* round out this week, connecting the historic moment in time with its scientific inventions, explorations and discoveries.

Week #4 gives the *idea-loving Intuitor* Learning Style a platform and an audience for *creative expression*. The *possibilities* include creative writing, journalism, poetry, short stories, political cartooning, posters, illustrating, sculpting, skits, puppetry, music performance, role playing, pantomime, dance, conceptual design, and *more*. Each student has the opportunity to be *creatively involved* as deeply or as casually as their interests and time constraints take them.

GOALS FOR THE TEACHER:

Through this flexible, multidisciplinary, learning-style-centered approach to history, teachers will be enabled to:

- impart history instruction in ways that will be retained and comprehended;
- facilitate and guide the students' *active participation* in learning;
- recognize the value of each student's unique design of God in learning;
- validate the particular thread of history which the student is interested to learn;
- provide encouragement as needed;
- offer a safe atmosphere for discussion and creative problem-solving;
- help students choose appropriate projects and resources;
- give opportunities for students to demonstrate what has been learned;
- evaluate students progress based on direct experiences and actual learning.

GOALS FOR THE STUDENT:

Through this in-depth look at human history from Creation, the beginning of history, to Jesus Christ, the centerpiece of history, students will learn to:

- understand and trust God's faithfulness;
- view other cultures and peoples from His perspective;
- gain an understanding of some of God's intimate and overarching work in human history through nations and individuals;
- understand the importance of worldviews in interpreting history;
- gain a solid foundation in apologetics, using the Bible as literal history;
- comprehend the relevance of ancient times to today's headlines;
- understand the chronology, as well as the cause and effect of world history;
- have a critical and in-depth understanding of each of these cultures through various disciplines, such as art, science, literature, geography, music, warfare, agriculture, religion, family life, government, economics, architecture, communications, and history;
- understand these civilizations' unique impact on other cultures;
- learn how to approach, appreciate and apply the study of history.

➢ *Icon Key*

Intro Icon: As you cycle through the phases of each unit, you will see this symbol, referring your attention to pages in the Introduction. The instructions guiding your approach to various activities have been gathered into a single presentation in the Introduction, instead of repeating in each unit. The page number in the icon will indicate the page to which you should refer for guidance on the activity. Once you are familiar with the content of the Introduction, the icons will serve as helpful reminders.

Icon Teacher Tip: From time to time in each unit, there are suggestions or ideas which can make your work as a teacher easier, more creative, or more successful. This icon highlights these suggestions and ideas.

Icon Motivate: In the Research and Reporting stage of Phase Two, we have suggested alternative creative approaches for the reporting. The intention for including these suggestions is that they might provide students a greater motivation for digging into the material and allow them to more thoroughly present what has been learned. This icon leads you to these ideas.

Icon Question: Several questions have been provided for you to ask your students during the course of each unit. This icon emphasizes these questions—which can help spark more stimulating class discussions.

Icon Spiritual: Since this curriculum seeks to understand history in light of what God has done—tracing the history of redemption—and, since the object of the curriculum is to not only gain knowledge of the content but also an understanding of God's character and nature, there are opportunities in each unit to engage your students on a spiritual level. This icon can include areas for prayer and discussion, and suggestions for activities with a spiritual purpose.

Icon Evaluation: At the end of each Phase, there is a quick review of the projects that were covered during the week to which you could refer for formative assessments, along with suggestions directing you to the likely sources of summative assessments to evaluate what your students have done. This icon reminds you of these opportunities.

➤ *Phase One -*
The Introductory Week

1) Informally Discuss the Key Concepts

Pretests to discover what students already know, depending on the learning style of a student, generate either excitement or panic! Instead of a formal pretest, simply engage your students in an informal discussion by asking them what they've read, heard or thought about these concepts. This is not intended to make them feel stupid or ignorant but to activate their interests and generate ideas, so keep the session open and non-threatening. Avoiding the common shame-based questioning is critical in this opening exercise. Feel free to read excerpts of the expanded concepts to the students, after they have shared their own knowledge, if it will help generate more discussion.

Discussing the Key Concepts is not the same as exhaustive learning. It is merely an introduction—a chance for students to share what they know and to have their interest piqued concerning the information they will encounter through the rest of the unit.

Feel free to choose a small sampling of these concepts to discuss, or even, if the discussion is interesting, focus on only one. The students will be introduced to all of the concepts as the unit progresses.

2) Read the article

3) Listen to the Audio-Recordings, in class or on their own

Because some students receive new information better by seeing it, the articles have been included. Because other students receive new information better by hearing it, the audio recordings have been produced. Some students receive new information best by moving, so we encourage you to allow students the opportunity to quietly walk or do some other inconspicuous movement during the audio portion, if that will assist them.

4) Read the Scripture

$\mathcal{R}emember$:

Students learn:
10% of what they READ
20% of what they HEAR
30% of what they SEE
50% of what they SEE and HEAR
70% of what they SAY
90% of what they SAY and DO

$\mathcal{T}herefore$:

Encourage them to make mind maps or outline.
This is not to be graded!

---

5) Recap (process & review) Activity

After the students have read the article, listened to the appropriate recordings, and read the Scriptures, it is vital that they have an opportunity to process and review. God has designed many different types of learners, so offer the students a choice of several alternatives for process and review. Though it is more comfortable for us to regulate and control and officially streamline our students' activities, we must honor and respect God's design in each student (which may be quite different than our own design). We can do this in the Recap Activity by setting up eight different stations—one for each of the eight suggestions provided. Each activity represents one of the Eight Intelligences. (For more information, consult the Appendix, page 289.) Allow each student to choose which station would be most helpful.

> ### Remember:
> the point is to process and review, so don't encumber this session with other goals, or make it an instruction time for new material.

In order to facilitate all eight stations for the Recap Activity, you will need to occasionally gather a few materials, such as poster board and colored marking pens.

6) Opinion Column and Critical Puzzling answers on their own.

It is important to give students a chance to think about their answers to these questions before discussing them in class (see Step #7). Though some students generate answers spontaneously and verbally, other students require time to internally process answers before speaking. For this reason—to honor the different ways learners think—we ask that you give all the students time to ponder, consider, seek the Scriptures, and think about the possible answers prior to a class discussion. Give the students the assignment to write out their answers, whether partially or thoroughly, which will help them during the class discussion. These answers are not to be graded, although you could certainly give credit for having completed the assignment.

7) Class Discussion

It is important to create a safe environment for good class discussions. Prior to beginning, set the ground rules for each student, including taking turns, no sarcasm, etc. Students must realize that people each see from their own point of view, and, though someone's idea may seem dumb at first, if we give the person a chance to speak without fear of ridicule, we may hear some treasures! If someone's idea is not clearly stated, respectfully ask questions until the meaning is understood.

Good class discussion is quite different from a good lecture! As the teacher, see yourself as the moderator of the discussion, seeking to keep it positive, interesting, and creative; allowing students to interact; encouraging further thought without giving lengthy answers. In pursuing this activity in the Introduction Phase, we are still developing a sense of wonder that will propel the students through the rest of the unit.

TEACHER TIP

8) Choose books of interest/Internet search

This is one of the places in this unit where students have the opportunity to explore the specific areas in which they have an interest. Not everyone will find the same subjects fascinating, so allow the students as much leeway as possible as they explore potential topics.

SPIRITUAL

One of the greatest drawbacks to using the Internet for research, apart from the obvious dangers of pornography, is that many of the articles are filled with such arrogance (even some of the ones written by Christians). Our students may find themselves in a quandary trying to manage conflicting interpretations and even conflicting facts! My encouragement is to teach the students to beware of arrogance and embrace humility. Arrogant writers might or might not have correct knowledge, but they will certainly be lacking God's wisdom:

> *"But the wisdom that is from above is first pure, then peaceable, gentle, willing to yield, full of mercy and good fruits, without partiality and without hypocrisy." James 3:17*

If students can simply be made aware of the arrogance, it will help them considerably in understanding some of the raging debates among Christians. Teaching students to remain humble and teachable even while expressing their opinions earnestly, means that, if they examine an argument and choose one side, then later hear something which sheds new light on the issue, they can graciously let go of the wrong idea. It is always a good idea to embrace humility, as God "opposes the proud but gives grace to the humble." James 4:6

Evaluation

You might choose to evaluate your students based on their *participation* in the Class Discussion and in their *participation* in the Recap Activity. For further ideas on assessment and evaluation, please see pages 30-34.

≫ *Phase Two -*
The Exploration & Discovery Week

1) Choose topic and begin research

Students may conduct research in a variety of ways, including library research, internet research, interviewing experts, field trips, etc. If a student has a difficult time finding materials or information on a chosen topic, you can either help with the search, or suggest another topic for research.

Students may report what they have researched by writing a research paper or doing an oral report. However, for some students, having a creative alternative for reporting what they have discovered could make the difference between enthusiastically digging in and merely complying with the assignment.

2) Words To Watch - Vocabulary Practice

Vocabulary is important in that it allows students an opportunity to gain a better grasp of some of the concepts in a time period—concepts which are expressed in particular terms. We must not turn vocabulary practice into an arduous chore which breeds a hatred and contempt for the magnificence of language. Therefore, we have included in each unit of the Teacher's Guide a suggested activity highlighting one of the eight intelligences. This allows students a greater enjoyment of the process of learning the pertinent vocabulary, and results in improved retention and comprehension.

3) Construct the Timeline.

The point of doing a timeline is not to burden the student with needless labor. Instead, it is to begin to create a mental bulletin board on which to organize the people, the events, and the flow of history. Encourage your students to see this exercise as the start of a jigsaw puzzle, which will eventually display for them a very clear understanding of the chronology of history, which will in turn help them discover for themselves some of the cause and effect relationships between actions and subsequent reactions. Also, it will give the Christian student a much broader understanding of God's interaction with the people and nations of history.

Students using the timeline provided in the Student Manual may utilize their preferred system for marking people, events and dates. Some commonly suggested systems: use a bullet point to mark the date, then write the event or name; create a series of symbols for entering dates to distinguish between biblical and non-biblical, and to distinguish events versus persons versus locations; draw a sketch of the person or event; cut out a magazine photo to represent an event or date; use some other system which appeals to the artistic style of the student.

4) Research projects shared in class and/or turned in.

Remember that timing is everything! Do NOT criticize a student immediately after their presentation, unless, of course, you desire that they would never again make the attempt to share their thoughts, except in a safe, boring, mediocre way. If there is a criticism to be given, wait until a later moment to give it, as the moment of sharing is a tremendously vulnerable time, and we have the power to crush our students if we do not honor the value of what they have labored to accomplish.

Remember the Rule of Sandwich:

#1) Applaud, honor, appreciate

#2) Kindly give any pertinent critique

#3) Finish with appreciation and honor

Evaluation

You may wish to evaluate your students based on their *efforts* in the Research and Reporting projects and their active *participation* in the Vocabulary and Timeline exercises. For further ideas on assessment and evaluation, please see pages 30-34.

➤ *Phase Three -*
The Hands-On Week

These activities, though not strictly within the normal confines of a history or Bible class, will allow the students who learn best through hands-on and sensory activities to thoroughly learn cultural material relevant to this Unit. The teacher does not need to be well-versed in art, architecture, music, or science in order for the students to learn deeply during this phase. Every student will find new insights and understanding about the time period of this unit, so we recommend that all students participate, regardless of learning style. With all the options provided, students should be able to find something that looks interesting. The teacher need only facilitate the experience—the students will do the work.

1) Create a map and discuss the issues in teams

It is amazing to discover how greatly the geography of a location has impacted the history of that location. Help your students recognize that they won't understand their subject as well if they don't know where it is and what it is like geographically! A huge mountain range can have a daunting effect on invasion armies, a river can be a source of irrigation in a dry place, a swamp can affect the health of the settlers, and more.

If students have good, sharp colored drawing pencils, they may enjoy making artistic maps, showing, for instance, mountain ranges as a series of peaks, rather than functional maps, indicating mountain ranges merely with words.

2) Examine and discuss art masterpieces & architectural structures

There are no right and wrong answers to the questions listed in the Student Manual and the Teacher's Guide concerning these art forms. Give the students permission to have their own ideas about what they are seeing, rather than herding them into conformity—even a "Christian" conformity.

3) Arts in Action

Give one day for the start of any one of the art projects suggested, and then encourage the students to complete their art project on their own time. Depending on your resources, you may be able to offer students their choice of all of these art projects, or maybe only a few. If students find interesting art suggestions that you are not able to offer, encourage them to access the needed materials and accomplish the projects on their own for credit and for enjoyment.

Remember, some students will be naturally talented in art projects, but this is not an art class, so evaluate them based on effort rather than on the level of skill evidenced.

4) Do a science project or field trip

Science is seldom seen in its historical moment of time but is instead relegated to a strict area of experimentation, vocabulary, and rules. However, if students can discover the interrelationship between science and history, each subject area will be enhanced and enriched. Science-loving students might discover that history is worth knowing and history-loving students might embrace science as a fascinating subject!

TEACHER TIP

Though it should be obvious that this small amount of scientific experimentation is not a substitute for a thorough science curriculum, yet, it is presented for the obvious motivation that it can help students, especially the kinesthetic learners, enjoy their history studies more and possibly spark a greater understanding. In other words, it's worth doing!

5) Listen to and discuss the music

For students with strong intelligence in music, this exercise will help make the connection for them into history. It is, again, worth the effort, especially for those students.

6) Cook the food

For some students, smelling and tasting food related to the unit will be the difference between boring and memorable. If you are in a classroom setting, you may either bring in a sample of the food for the students to taste, or encourage them to make it at home. For students in a homeschool setting, be sure to take the time to make the recipe (or something similar). Make it part of the celebration of what has been learned thus far!

Evaluation

You may wish to evaluate your students based on their class *participation* in these Hands-on activities. For further ideas on assessment and evaluation, please see pages 30-34.

➤ *Phase Four -*
The Expression Week

Students may want to select their expression early in Phase One, in order to have adequate time to prepare their presentations.

TEACHER TIP

1) Choose area of expression and begin work either individually or in teams

This week is the culmination of the unit. Allow students the freedom to choose which area(s) they prefer to use as the expression of what they have learned. It may be that one selection will take a student the entire week to accomplish. On the other hand, a student might appreciate the opportunity to do several selections during the week. Students may work together in teams or individually—though this decision should be made at the beginning of the week for those wanting to do a selection from the drama or movement areas.

Linguistics

There are many possibilities of creative expression within the linguistics area. Some students who are intimidated by writing a paper might find delight in being able to express what they have learned in this phase through humor. Others will delight in the opportunity to write a first person narrative, or a children's book. Remember that this is *creative expression,* so be careful to not quench their exploration of creativity.

Art

Students who are attracted to painting, drawing, sculpting, graphic design, illustrating or cartooning will have the opportunity to share their enjoyment of art AND their insights into the history topics studied. This might provide spatially intelligent students the rare experience of successfully expressing what they have learned, since, traditionally, students are required to share what they know solely through linguistics. Provide a warm, welcoming atmosphere for these artistic students!

Music

To have the opportunity to use music to express what has been learned in history is another unusual form in traditional settings. However, if musically intelligent students can be released to share their knowledge of history through their instruments, it might motivate many other students to actually "dig deeper!" Be sure they take adequate time for practice, so that the performance is as polished as possible.

Drama

Encourage any students who wish to use drama as their means of expression to use the "Prop needs/Costume ideas/Role-player/Set suggestions" worksheet in their Student Manual to adequately prepare for their presentation. Although it is cute for five-year-olds to put on an "instant play" for guests, it is not appropriate for upper elementary through high school students. If students are planning to do solo presentations, encourage them to work carefully on writing their lines and memorizing them. If a team of students is going to work together, have them write out their lines and memorize them. Be sure to give adequate time for practice!

Movement

For students who are strong in the Bodily-Kinesthetic intelligence, this area will prove to be a tremendous blessing in allowing them to express what they have learned in the way they were designed. Encourage students to work in a team if they are going to do the Action selection. Again, it is not worthy of a student's effort to do an unrehearsed, poorly planned presentation. Remind the students to practice until the movements communicate effectively, and until the students have memorized the actions.

Conceptual Design

Some students will excel if given a chance to create something that has never been seen before. Encourage these students to reflect on what they are creating, and to work on it until it is of very high quality.

Create Your Own Expression

There may be some other avenue of expression which your student will decide best expresses what has been learned. Have students submit their ideas to you to ascertain the appropriateness and difficulty level. Encourage them to reach a high standard in their creative expression!

2) Share creative expressions in class.

Create a safe environment for the presentations. Set ground rules prior to the presentations for all the students, so that they know each one will be honored and respected in their work by all those observing.

Remember that timing is everything! Do NOT criticize a student immediately after their presentation, unless, of course, you desire that they would never again make the attempt to share their endeavors, except in a safe, boring, mediocre way. If there is a criticism to be given, wait until a later moment to give it, as the moment of sharing is a tremendously vulnerable time, and we have the power to crush our students if we do not honor the value of what they have labored to accomplish.

Remember the Rule of Sandwich:

#1) Applaud, honor, appreciate

#2) Kindly give any pertinent critique

#3) Finish with appreciation and honor

Evaluation

You may wish to evaluate your students based on their effort in the Creative Expressions, either as individuals or in teams. For further ideas on assessment and evaluation, please see pages 30-34.

PHASE ONE: *Introduction Week*

Learning Style Emphasis: Feeler

Students will be introduced to the time period and to the Scriptures relating to the Unit.

Teachers can choose to have students do one or two activities, rather than the entire week's schedule. Please use what works for you in your unique setting.

Monday:
  1) Informally discuss the Key Concepts

Tuesday:
  2) Read the article
  3) Listen to the audio recording(s)
  4) Read the Scripture listed in Read For Your Life (could be done on their own)

Wednesday:
  5) Recap Activity
  6) Opinion Column and Critical Puzzling answers on their own

Thursday:
  7) Class Discussion

Friday:
  8) Choose books of interest/Internet search

PHASE TWO: *The Exploration & Discovery Week*

Learning Style Emphasis: Thinker

Students will explore topics of interest through research and reporting, learn new vocabulary, and construct a timeline relating to the Unit.

Teachers can choose to have students do one or two activities, rather than the entire week's schedule. Please use what works for you in your unique setting.

Monday-Tuesday:
  1) Choose topic and begin research

Wednesday:
  2) Vocabulary Practice

Thursday:
  3) Construct the Timeline.

Friday:
  4) Research projects completed; share in class or hand in.

PHASE THREE: *The Hands-On Week*

Learning Style Emphasis: Sensor

Students will gain cultural understanding through sensory activities as they explore interrelated subject areas relating to the Unit.

Teachers can choose to have students do one or two activities, rather than the entire week's schedule. Please use what works for you in your unique setting.

Monday:
  1) Create a map and discuss the issues in teams.

Tuesday:
  2) Examine and discuss art masterpieces & architectural structures.

Wednesday:
  3) Arts in Action—Do an art project.*

Thursday:
  4) Do one science project or field trip.**

Friday:
  5) Listen to and discuss the music.
  6) Cook the food listed in the recipe, if desired.

*Art project will need to be planned ahead of time to acquire materials.
**Field trip will require extra planning time.

PHASE FOUR: *The Expression Week*

Learning Style Emphasis: Intuitor

Students, through creative self-expression, using one or more creative activities, will present some aspect of what they have learned in the past three weeks. Areas of expression include linguistics, art, music, drama, movement and conceptual design.

Teachers can choose to have students do one or two activities, rather than the entire week's schedule. Please use what works for you in your unique setting.

Monday - Thursday
  1) Choose area of expression and begin work either individually or in teams.

Friday
  2) Share creative expressions in class.

Alternative Calendar

For teachers confined to one semester for this course, we suggest that you complete for each Unit the Introductory Phase plus either the Exploration & Discovery Phase or the Hands-On Phase. This would allow you to finish Ancient Civilizations & The Bible in eighteen weeks.

Alternatively, you could choose to use only one or two activities per Phase, accomplish two Phases per week, complete an entire Unit in two weeks, and the entire course in eighteen weeks.

*For Homeschooling Parents:

If you are going to go through each of the four Phases in every unit, we suggest that you do Math, Language Arts, etc., in the mornings prior to starting Ancient Civilizations & The Bible. This will allow your children the freedom to dig into the material to their hearts' content, without concern for wrecking the schedule by following interesting rabbit trails. (We discovered, in conversation with a math teacher, that it is not only possible but beneficial to do mathematics on Monday, Wednesday, Friday, which leaves Tuesday and Thursday for language arts. This schedule worked well for our family, and our university-aged children have thrived in both areas, as well as in history!)

Evaluation & Assessment

For Classroom Teachers

"I have often asked a teacher what it means if their student receives 13 out of 20 - what was missing? What would a 14-out-of-20 assignment look like? Where is the assessment key the student worked from? It has horrified me that so many teachers have no idea what an assessment key is, and are marking a student's assignment more on the basis of how recently they had a good meal and a cup of coffee, than on the basis of an unchangeable set of criteria.

"This is an issue of justice we need to address. Many of our students have come from educational systems that are unjust. We must be different, and providing students with a clear set of expectations is a demonstration of justice. As students mature, the guidelines can become more headlines than details, leaving room for personal interpretation and expression that a student can be expected to defend.

"Much of a poor assessment practice can be attributed to the fact that the teacher often doesn't really know what he wants as he sets the assignment and can fall into the trap of letting the most interesting or visually attractive answer set the standard. This is completely unjust to everyone else. Everyone needs to know and be able to reach the unchanging target."

From Thinking Well by Rosalie A. Pedder

Proverbs 20:10 says, *"Diverse weights and diverse measures, they are both alike, an abomination to the Lord."* What does that mean to us as we consider the serious issue of evaluating and assessing what students have learned in this course? With a nontraditional curriculum like this, which allows students a wide range of choice and creative expression, in what is traditionally such a staid subject, what activities are available to teachers for assessing measurable growth and for evaluating a student's work for a grade? Combining the obligation of providing an evaluation that is not "diverse weights and diverse measures" with the reality that God has designed students as unique learners who do not display their knowledge in exactly the same ways, how do we find a system that is both just and manageable?

I have asked Dr. Julia Harper, a professor of education at Azusa Pacific University—and the mentor of Rosalie Pedder, my own mentor—to share what she has learned about evaluation and assessment through her many years of teaching in the classroom, as well as her doctorate studies and graduate level instruction. Her wisdom in this area is experienced, practical, and eminently usable.

"Evaluation, at the heart, is judgment, making decisions based on values. It is our decision-making about student performance and about appropriate teaching strategies.

"Assessment is an integral part of the teaching-learning connection. Teachers should make it very clear for students how their work will be assessed. And, when students are allowed to be creative in the process, it means you as a teacher must be prepared to think through even more clearly how that should be assessed. Otherwise, students will be inhibited in what they do or create. As you think about the evaluation process there are two types of assessments to think through—formative and summative.

"Formative evaluations are measurements that help teachers understand what students are learning and how they can adjust the teaching and learning environment to meet student needs. The purpose of formative evaluations is twofold: improving instructional practices and monitoring learning. As a type of ongoing evaluation, formative assessments also give students feedback on how they are doing.

"Summative evaluations are measurements that show what students have learned over time. They can also be used to help determine the effectiveness of a program. The research and reporting project could be your summative assessment for a unit of study, but it is also a performance assessment.

"You want both formative and summative assessments through out the course of study. As you think about the various options that students take to learn material, your assessments should be identified as either formative or summative, depending on how you are using the assigned tasks. For instance, as a formative assessment for Unit 1—Creation and the Flood, you could observe a student's participation in the Class Discussion or the Recap Activity to let the teacher know what the students are learning. As a summative assessment for Unit 1—Creation and the Flood, along with the research report, you could develop a test to assess the key concepts to measure their basic knowledge and understanding for that unit. The research report would allow for maximum divergence among students, even as they comply with a specific protocol of completeness which would be expressed in a rubric. Other activity choices accomplished within that unit may serve as formative assessments of how students are learning the key concepts for that unit. These key concepts will finally be measured in an objective test at the end of the unit. The objective test is a summative assessment that lets you as a teacher know how well the students are learning. The formative tasks let them learn in a way that is most meaningful for them.

"That is why it is so important to think formative and summative as you plan your assessment process. Formative allows you to assess your students and then make changes in what YOU do so the student can learn better; you can make course corrections based on your formative assessments. If you learn to read and interpret your formative then students should not find summative evaluations difficult either, because they will know what they know and will know what they don't know realistically.

"A scenario comes to mind when I think of this principle.

"In a rural part of the country where there was a high rate of poverty and low achievement, I got a job as the Title I teacher (5th and 6th grade). My training had been as a Talented and Gifted teacher, so I knew how to individualize with students, and how important it was to get them engaged in the learning. I devised formative assessments based on the individual learners and worked with them as individuals because their problems were not the same. As they were charting their learning in folders that contained their goals for learning, they began to see that they could make measurable change by using their own thinking, while learning new skills with me as the teacher. These students began to recognize what they needed to learn and take responsibility for themselves. But everybody took the same summative exam for the different content areas that I taught. It was really fun and exciting. I was able to see, through sustained gains testing when they were in high school, that they were scoring in the 80-90% on our standardized test. We had four elementary schools and one middle school and high school. When the State Department came down to our town, they discovered that the students scoring in the 80-90% came from one elementary and from one particular teacher—my class. These students, who had been marginal learners, were now thriving in their learning and outperforming the norm.

Formative and summative assessments can be developed with objective kinds of assessments or performance types of assessments. Creating a quiz or multiple choice test would be considered more objective. They can be used in either formative or summative evaluations. Performance assessments are used when there are different ways of demonstrating learning. Developing criteria for how a project is assessed gives the learner more freedom in the process. Rubrics are tools to give form and structure to more creative or performance types of learning.

Valley View Christian School
Creation & the Flood Team Research Project

Name: _____   Teacher: <u>Mrs. Smith</u>_____

Date Submitted: _____   Title of Work: _____

Criteria					Points
	4	**3**	**2**	**1**	
Introduction	All questions were answered completely and rationales for the answers **were** clearly stated.	All questions were answered completely, but rationales for the all the answers **were not** clearly stated.	Not all questions were answered completely, or greater than 2 rationales for the all answers **were not** clearly stated.	All questions **were not** answered completely.	
Task	All areas of the task were addressed and handled with a high degree of sophistication. The plan followed by the team demonstrated a great deal of thought.	At least one area of the task **was not** addressed. The plan followed by the team demonstrated a great deal of thought.	At least two areas of the task **were not** addressed. The plan followed by the team demonstrated a moderate level of thought.	The task is incomplete and/or it is apparent that little effort went into the development of the task.	
Process: Teamwork	It is evident that a mutual effort and cohesive unit created the final product.	The team worked well together, but could have utilized each other's skills to a better degree.	The team had problems working together. Little collaboration occurred.	The final product is not the result of a collaborative effort. The group showed no evidence of collaboration.	
Process: Originality	The ideas expressed by the body of work demonstrate a high degree of originality.	The ideas expressed by the body of work are mostly original. The group may have improved upon a previous idea.	The ideas expressed by the body of work demonstrate a low degree of originality.	There were no original ideas expressed in this project.	
Grammar, Format, and Spelling	The final body of work was free of grammar, spelling, and formatting errors.	The final body of work had 1 error related to either grammar, spelling, and formatting errors.	The final body of work had 3-5 grammar, spelling, and formatting errors.	The final body of work had major grammar, spelling, and formatting errors.	
				Total⟶	

"Rubrics: As you let students make decisions on types of projects to demonstrate their learning, you may want to set up a rubric to help the student identify performance expectations. These rubrics will also assist you in the assessing of these different types of projects. Creative projects can be very risky for students when they don't understand how the grading will be worked out. Remember too, creativity is at the top of the critical thinking structure. Creativity requires a transformational action which allows them to go from what has been learned, apply it in a creative process, and end with a new product. This is also where students make meaningful and personal connections to the learning, and it is very exciting and motivating. So there is a need for flexibility within the process but also a need for form that helps guide the process. Here is a website for you as a teacher to use for developing rubrics for many kinds of projects that students may come up with. It also lets you develop the criteria and the different elements that you may want to put into that project. http://teach-nology.com/web_tools/rubrics/general/

"The chart shown on Page 32 is another rubric maker that you can use to develop performance assessments for creative projects.

"Remember assessment and evaluation should be a celebration of what students know and demonstration of what they have learned. If we keep those two elements in mind students will gladly participate in the process and be proud to show what they know."

In addition to Dr. Harper's comments, I would like to encourage teachers to recognize that there are several areas in which students can be evaluated and grades assigned:

- Participation in Class Discussion and Recap Activity in Phase One
- Effort in Research and Reporting Project and Participation in the Vocabulary & Timeline exercises in Phase Two
- Participation in the Hands-On Activities in Phase Three
- Effort in the Creative Expression in Phase Four

Each of these could have their own rubric to determine point values. These point values would be used to determine letter grades.

In addition, teachers might choose to create a final summative assessment. For instance, they might give a final essay test on the key concepts, giving students the opportunity to each choose one concept and relate what they have learned and how this knowledge is applicable to their lives. Or, a teacher might choose to give an open-ended essay test, allowing students to pick two of the most important people or events of the unit and describe their significance; or they could choose to compare and contrast some aspect of what has been studied (for instance comparing and contrasting a secular and sacred approach to King Nebuchadnezzar); or look at how some events or people of the past unit influenced events or people of this unit. A teacher might also choose to include *identifications*, listing several names or events from the unit and asking the students to select two or three to identify. These are the types of test which allow students to show what they know rather than what they don't know, so teachers need to clearly express the required length of response, the extent of the information, and the nature of the content a student is expected to present in order to attain a certain grade.

As you are creating your system, please keep in mind that this curriculum encourages students to select areas of research, projects, and creative expressions that are interesting to them, which results in students learning dissimilar areas of information--all within the overarching framework of a particular period in history. It is all legitimate history, and the expression of what has been learned will be legitimate, through, perhaps, slightly unorthodox. Also, since we approach history with the knowledge that it is a vast, nearly limitless subject, we would be unreasonable to demand that every student know every aspect of what every other student learns. Therefore, a standard history test of names, dates, and places will not be adequate for this curriculum, nor will it display the particulars and the depth of what each student has learned. For this reason, we have not attempted to create a one-size-fits-all, detailed evaluation form, nor have we devised an objective final exam. Teachers will need to create their own systems of formative and summative assessments, based on the needs and structures of their own classrooms.

For Homeschool Parents:

We have found, in our twenty-plus years of homeschooling, that evaluations can and should be informal rather than formal. Tutors do not need the same type of testing procedures for one or two students as teachers need for thirty students. One on one interaction will speak volumes regarding what has been learned (and what has NOT been learned). I discovered this when I studied French with a tutor during my university years: Sister Consuelo knew immediately if I had not prepared for my lesson, as there was no one to hide behind!

As you provide the enthusiastic audience for what your children are learning, what they are reading, what they are thinking, what they are creatively sharing, you will readily discover what they have learned in this course. As you watch them interact with new ideas, grapple with their own questions, use higher level thinking skills to apply what has been learned to a creative expression, you will have a firm grasp of their measurable growth in this subject.

Assigning grades to our own children can be a daunting task. My husband and I looked for mastery of content in conversations and reporting projects, for effort as they worked on maps and art projects, for participation in discussions like the ones around the dinner table, and for the level of creativity they exhibited in their final projects. Because this course was, in general, so much fun for my children, they dug deeply into the areas that interested them and devoured the information. So we gave them "A"s on their high school transcripts for the subjects covered in this course. Our children then demonstrated their competence in history as they went on to study politics, international relations, New Testament history, and more at university. And, the retention continues--it amazes me to listen to them today discuss issues they learned many years ago during these studies. When we enjoy what we are learning, we remember far more far longer.

CREATION & THE FLOOD

UNIT 1

God's handiwork

Enthusiasm and delight are the best way to capture a student's interest and jump-start motivation, so:

1) ***For the Auditory Students:*** Consider playing dramatic music, such as Holst's **The Planets**, to introduce the new unit as the students come to the first class;

2) ***For the Kinesthetic Students:*** Have the students warm up as class begins by doing some active movement that is fun (have them sit down and stand up as fast as they can for 10 seconds—see who had the most!);

✗ 3) ***For the Visual Students:*** Bring a visual object to stimulate their interest in the new unit, like a poster of Earth from space;

4) ***For the hearts of all:*** Pray with them at the beginning of the unit, that God would help them discover what He has for each one to learn in that unit.

Pray with the students at the beginning of each unit.

PHASE 1

The Introduction Week

During this week, students will be introduced to the first nine chapters of Genesis. You may follow this suggested schedule or adapt it to meet your students' needs:

Monday:

1) Informally discuss the Key Concepts

Tuesday:

2) Read the article
3) Listen to the audio recording(s)
4) Read the Scripture listed in Read For Your Life (could be done on their own)

Wednesday:

5) Recap Activity
6) Opinion Column and Critical Puzzling answers on their own

Thursday:

7) Class Discussion

Friday:

8) Choose books of interest/Internet search

> *Teachers can choose to have students do one or two activities, rather than the entire week's schedule. Please use what works for you in your unique setting.*

INTRO - PG 18

1) Informally Discuss the Key Concepts

Listed in the Student Manual on page 21.

KEY CONCEPTS BACKGROUND INFORMATION

These are the main objectives of the unit. As you proceed through the four weeks, your students will be given various ways of understanding each of these objectives.

A Biblical View of the Beginning—EXPLANATION

TEACHER TIP

To get an informal discussion started on this key concept, ask a simple, leading question, such as, *"Why do you think it makes a difference whether a person believes in evolution or creation?"*

If we hold to the Judeo-Christian worldview, we recognize that man is neither the center nor the source of life. "All things were created **through** Him and **for** Him." (Col 1:16) It is crucial that students grasp that God is the foundation of all things, the Creator, the Designer, the Redeemer, the Giver of Life, the Savior, the Judge, the

Eternal. Therefore, as we begin the study of history, a thorough groundwork must be laid for history's place and meaning beginning and ending with God. If they miss this, they've missed the whole point.

I encourage you to pray for God's wisdom and grace in this endeavor, that He would show you how to help your students go beyond a mental assent of the truths of Genesis to a life-giving heart response as they work through this unit. Remember, at the end of the day, it's not how much information they know, it's how they apply God's truth to their lives that will count: ***"But be doers of the word, and not hearers only, deceiving yourselves." James 1:22***

SPIRITUAL

CREATION & THE FLOOD

UNIT 1

God's handiwork

KEY CONCEPTS:

- A biblical view of the Beginning

- The wonder of Creation

- The impact of the Fall of man

- Early man as an intelligent, capable creature

- The Flood and its cause

"In the beginning God..."

Our study of human history begins at the very beginning of all things—Page One, if you will—with the focus and emphasis on the Creator. Many people who study history in our day do not start on that page. They begin with prehistoric man, just after he "evolved" from the ape—our supposed evolutionary predecessor! They have drawings of Neanderthal, photos of cave paintings, imaginative descriptions of the

The Wonder of Creation— EXPLANATION

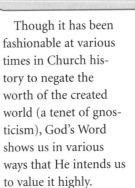
TEACHER TIP

To get an informal discussion started on this key concept, ask a simple, leading question, such as, *"What do you enjoy most about going out into the woods, the mountains, the deserts, or out on the ocean?"*

Though it has been fashionable at various times in Church history to negate the worth of the created world (a tenet of gnosticism), God's Word shows us in various ways that He intends us to value it highly.

"I will praise You, for I am fearfully and wonderfully made; Marvelous are Your works, and that my soul knows very well." Psalm 139:14

This article can be found in its entirety in the Appendix (see pg 296).

"O Lord, how manifold are Your works! In wisdom You have made them all. The earth is full of Your possessions ..." Psalm 104:24

"Where were you when I laid the foundations of the earth? Tell Me, if you have understanding. Who determined its measurements? Surely you know! Or who stretched the line upon it? To what were its foundations fastened? Or who laid its cornerstone, when the morning stars sang together, and all the sons of God shouted for joy?" Job 38:4-7

SPIRITUAL

If we can approach this aspect of Unit One with the wonder, the majesty, the joy of what God has done in creation, our students may develop a lifelong appreciation of created things. This would include good stewardship of their own bodies, their wisdom in environmental issues, their delight in the natural world. Some students who are strong in the naturalist intelligence will anchor their appreciation for history through this concept. Therefore, look for opportunities to go out into the great outdoors, look under a microscope or through a telescope, visit a zoo or a planetarium, gather books and videos that do a great job of communicating how marvelous His work is in Creation. Let your students help generate ideas of how to discover the wonder of Creation. All in all, enjoy the process!

PHASE 1

KEY PEOPLE:

Adam & Eve 4004 BC
—First people
6000 - 4000 BC

Cain 3874 BC
—First murderer

Seth 3769 BC
—The godly line

Tubal-Cain 5000 BC
—Instructor of metal craftsmen

Jubal
—Father of musicians

Noah ~~xxxxxxxxxx~~
—Ark builder
2948 BC
entered ark:
2349 BC

➤ Listen to this!

• **What in the World's Going on Here? Volume One**

— Creation & the Flood

• **True Tales from the Times of Ancient Civilizations & The Bible**

— Dates for Creation

— Early Man

• **An In-depth Study of...Noah's Ark**

➤ Read For Your Life

• **Scriptures on Creation**

— The Main Story: Genesis 1- 4

— Other Helpful Verses: Job 38:4–41:34, Psalm 8:3-9, Psalm 19:1-6, Psalm 65:5-13, Psalm 89:11-14, Psalm 95:1-7, Psalm 100, Psalm 104, Psalm 136:1-9, Psalm 148, Isaiah 40:12-31, Jeremiah 32:17, Matthew 19:4-6, John 1:1-5, Romans 1:20, Colossians 1:15-17, Hebrews 1:10, 11:3

• **Scriptures on the Flood**

— The Main Story: Genesis 5–10

— Other Helpful Verses: Matthew 24:37-39, Hebrews 11:4-7, 1 Peter 3:20, 2 Peter 2:5

30 / Unit One: *Creation & the Flood*

Key People:

The people listed in this column are the main characters, if you will, of this unit. They are listed in the Student Manual, along with a brief identifier, so that the students can familiarize themselves with these people.

The Impact of the Fall of Man—EXPLANATION

To get an informal discussion started on this key concept, ask a simple, leading question, such as, *"Can you think of anything in the world around you that was changed by the fall of Man in the Garden of Eden?"*

There are dimensions of our existence that do not make sense if we do not comprehend how life was changed at the Fall of Man. God designed humans to live in full relationship with Himself, with each other and with the created world, with no taint of sin. We were not designed to get sick and die, we were not designed to war with others, we were not designed to destroy. All of this, and much more, is a direct result of the actual space-time event known as the Fall.

As your students consider the information presented in this unit, watch for opportunities to help them apply the impact of the Fall to their questions and concerns. Pray daily for your students, that this truth (that there was an historic Fall), would combine with the even more powerful truth of God's redemption and then permeate their very being. Ask the Lord that He would reveal, in the midst of the tragedy of the Fall, His great love which brings us to victory, and that they *"being rooted and grounded in love, may be able to comprehend with all the saints what is the width and length and depth and height—to know the love of Christ which passes knowledge; that they may be filled with all the fulness of God." (Eph 3:17-19)*

Early Man as intelligent and capable—EXPLANATION

To get an informal discussion started on this key concept, ask a simple, leading question, such as, *"What kinds of stories have you heard about earliest man? Does early man in those stories seem intelligent or stupid?"*

Evolutionists would have us believe that, since man is continuing to evolve to a higher level, the further back in history you go, the less intelligent and capable man should be. However, archaeology has blasted that theory by uncovering numerous artifacts of highly developed technology and civilization concurrent with earliest times. We are not told that, however. We are treated to charts and diagrams showing tens of thousands of years of primitive man, with poor quality pottery, living in scattered villages before the rise of civilizations. It is up to those with a Biblical worldview to present the archaeological information within the Biblical framework, and then the facts speak for themselves.

Since this information is not readily available (at least, the Biblical interpretation is not readily available) in public libraries and secular history books, the students will need to look to the Creationist publications for their information. Many titles are listed in this curriculum, but there are new ones being printed every year, so encourage your students to become sleuths in tracking down truth.

The Flood and its cause—EXPLANATION

To get an informal discussion started on this key concept, ask a simple, leading question, such as, *"What do you think were some of the actions that brought about the Flood?"*

The Bible reports the Flood as a watershed event, you might say, in the history of mankind. Modern secular writers scoff at the idea of a worldwide flood. That scoffing, however, proves the Bible is accurate!

"Knowing this first: that scoffers will come in the last days, walking according to their own lusts, and saying, "where is the promise of His coming? For since the fathers fell asleep, all things continue as they were from the beginning of creation." For this they willfully forget: that by the word of God the heavens were of

old, and the earth standing out of water and in the water, by which the world that then existed perished, being flooded with water." 2 Peter 3:3-6

Our students need to understand both the geological and sociological implications of the Flood, and that:

1) The Flood really occurred in space and time history;
2) The Flood was God's promised and publicly proclaimed judgment on man's evil.

Look for opportunities to engage your students in discussion about the reality of God doing what He promised, even if it seems like it is taking forever!

2) Read the article

Begins on Page 21 of Student Manual

The article for Unit One is designed to help students think about the reality of Genesis, and to consider its implication for people today. The topics covered in the audio recordings provide an expanded version of the article, and contain other historic information beyond that, as well. In the article and recordings, along with introducing the basic understanding of history, we are also bringing in the biblical worldview.

You may choose to have your students read the article first and then listen to the audio recordings, or vice versa.

3) Listen to the audio recording(s)

Listed on Page 30 of the Student Manual.

• The main concepts and chronological flow are contained in **What in the World's Going On Here?**

• Fascinating stories of various ancient cultures' dating of Creation are discussed in **True Tales From the Times of…Ancient Civilizations & The Bible**
   - Several descriptions of OOP Arts are also discussed in this recording.

• A specific look at ancient stories of the Flood, as well as an interview with one veteran Ark hunter, Bob Cornuke, is contained in **An In-Depth Study of…Noah's Ark**

4) Read the Scripture listed in Read For Your Life

Listed on Page 30 of the Student Manual. You might choose to have the students read the Main Story verses either corporately or privately.

The Scriptures are central to our understanding, our character, and our decisions. Therefore, we must give the greatest weight possible to them. Help your students gain this perspective as they watch you handle the Scriptures with reverence and awe.

Though students are not **required** to look up all the verses (it IS a long list), the teacher might look them up, and choose a few to add in to the class discussion, or to assign to selected students for their input into the discussion.

The "Other Helpful Verses" listed contain much insight about the unit. Again, we want our students to move from a "Genesis myth" mentality to a "Genesis truth"—that it really happened in space and time history. It is critical to recognize that, when Jesus spoke of Adam & Eve in Matthew 19:4-6, He was describing their creation as an actual event, rather than relegating it to mythical status.

SPIRITUAL

5) Recap (process & review) Activity

In different parts of the room, set up stations for the Eight Intelligences Recap Activities. Then allow students to work alone or together in small groups to accomplish the following suggestions. At the start of the next class, ask for 3-4 groups of volunteers to share. <u>For homeschoolers, rather than set up all eight stations, allow the student(s) to choose which of these activities they would most enjoy, and do that.</u>

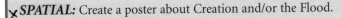

Recap Suggestions:

INTRO·PG 19

SPATIAL: Create a poster about Creation and/or the Flood.

BODILY-KINESTHETIC: Have one student toss a Koosh ball to the next student while stating a fact from this unit. How fast can they go?

INTERPERSONAL: In groups of 2-3, plan how to present this information to six year olds.

MUSICAL: Write lyrics about the information to the tune of "Row, row, row your boat."

LINGUISTIC: Create a ten-word slogan that communicates the message of this unit.

MATH-LOGICAL: Make a step-by-step chart of the events of Creation and/or the Flood.

INTRAPERSONAL: In small groups, share something new that was learned that had personal impact.

NATURALIST: Using materials found outside, assemble a "show & tell" for the class. (ex. "This stick represents the olive branch that the dove brought back to Noah on the Ark.")

OR…Activity of Your Choice: What would you like to have your students do for a review activity concerning this week's introduction to Creation & the Flood?

6) Opinion Column and Critical Puzzling answers on their own

Listed on Page 31 of the Student Manual. Students may begin these questions after completing their Recap Activities listed above.

7) Class Discussion

Using the questions listed on Page 31 of the Student Manual to get the students primed, create a discussion environment in the classroom. You may also want to draw from the open-ended questions listed below.

QUESTION

Why do you think God gave us the description of pre-flood technology? Based on your answer, consider some of the implications of an intelligent "early man." For instance, if Thomas Edison had lived in pre-flood times, with a life span similar to what is described in Genesis, what might he have invented?

QUESTION

Talk about the things Noah did, according to Genesis:

• He built an ark, or boat, before it ever rained. How far from the water do you think Noah might have lived?

• He labored for many years on an object that made no sense to the people of his day, since they had never seen it rain. Do you think he would have been ridiculed? Why or why not? Read Hebrews 11:7. Describe what the scoffing and hostility Noah and his family had to endure might have been like.

• He was a preacher of righteousness in a time when no one wanted to listen. How difficult, or even dangerous, do you think that might have been?

Phase 1

➢ *Talk Together*

• **Opinion Column:**

— What did you find to be the most interesting aspect or the most fascinating person you encountered in your introduction to Creation & The Flood?

— Adam was given the immense work of naming the animals. Talk about brain drain! If it was your task, what would the challenges be? What would the pleasures be?

— Noah labored for many years on the Ark, which must have seemed highly unusual to the people around him. Imagine yourself in his setting and consider what issues and difficulties he might have faced as he obeyed God.

• **Critical Puzzling:**

— Look in a Bible handbook or commentary to discover more information about where scholars believe the Garden of Eden was located. What factors should one take into account when considering the possible location?

— Read Genesis 3. Ponder the choice Adam and Eve made to disobey God and eat the forbidden fruit, and then write your thoughts on these issues:

- *Name some of the results of their choice.*

- *What is the ongoing impact of their choice on every person born after them?*

- *Considering the whole of Scripture, which events did God set in motion to restore us to relationship with Him?*

- *How has your own experience with God been affected by Adam and Eve's choice?*

— One of Cain's descendants was Tubal-Cain, who was an instructor of every craftsman in bronze and iron. (Genesis 4:22) This

Consider:

Look in the Bible for these terms:
• creation
• rest
• first Adam / second Adam
• redemption
• grace

Unit One: Creation & the Flood / 31

• He had to figure out how much food for people and animals was needed on the ark, acquire it and store it. How do you think he was able to find out what kind of food the animals needed? Also, discuss how he might have been able to calculate the amount, and give your thoughts on much would it have cost!

• Read about Lot getting his family out of Sodom and Gomorrah. How hard do you think it might have been for Noah to convince his family to get on the ark with him?

• He had to learn how to live after the Flood with a different type of climate, a different type of soil and terrain. Genesis tells us that he planted a vineyard. Where do you suppose he got the grape vines? How did he learn about post-flood agriculture? Where might he have gotten the tools?

Phase 1

Code:

AA (all ages)

RA (Read aloud)

E+ (elem & up)

UE+ (upper elem & up)

MS+ (Middle School & up)

HS (high school)

man demonstrates that pre- Flood man had obtained a much higher level of technology than we have been led to believe by evolutionists. What are the implications of pre-flood technology and intelligence? (If you can find *The Puzzle of Ancient Man*, use this as a source for your answer.)

➤ *Reviewed Resources for Digging Deeper:*

Choose a few books that look interesting, or find your own.

Creation:

Unlocking the Mysteries of Creation
by Dennis Peterson

This is an eye-opening book about Creation! Divided into three sections, it deals with evidences for a young earth, the questions about fossils and dinosaurs, and fascinating discoveries showing the astonishing accomplishments of early man (early civilizations). **AA**

Adam & His Kin by Ruth Beechick

A speculative, but fascinating look at what life might have been like during the first several chapters of Genesis. **RA UE+**

The Great Dinosaur Mystery and the Bible by Paul S. Taylor

Children often want to know, "What about the dinosaurs?" when we talk about Creation. This is a great picture book to introduce the answers on a child's level (though I learned a lot too!). **E+**

Understanding The Times
(abridged edition) by David Noebel

This book (especially Ch. 15 through 18) will greatly help to clarify the worldview positions of evolutionists and creationists. We think it is absolutely critical to understand the issue of worldview, and of its impact on every branch of learning. Dr. Noebel has written an excellent resource. **HS**

Darwin on Trial by Phillip E. Johnson

"The controversial book that rocked the scientific establishment! Why? It shows that the theory of evolution is based not on fact but on faith—faith in philosophical naturalism." This fascinating book was written by a professor of law, and is laid out so simply that the nonscientist can follow the arguments. It is very helpful for understanding the fallacies in the evolutionist argument. **HS**

Why do you think pre-Flood man ignored the lessons from Adam and Eve's experience? Why did they all choose to turn away from their Creator, except for Noah and his family? What can we learn from this time in human history?

QUESTION

Reading through the Old Testament, and studying the Church throughout history shows us the tendency for later generations to forget God and His wonderful works. Is there an antidote to this forgetfulness? What do you think? (Read Deuteronomy 6 to find some helpful suggestions.)

QUESTION

For the complete list of books from the Student Manual, refer to the Appendix (pg 299).

8) Choose books of interest/Internet search

A list of possible books for further reading is listed in the Student Manual beginning on Page 32. Encourage your students to look for books or videos on Creation & the Flood from this list and from other sources. You may want to gather a selection of further resources prior to beginning Unit One, or you may encourage the students to be treasure hunters and find them on their own.

Please recognize that since Unit One is a specifically Judeo/Christian look at Creation & the Flood, the public library may have very limited resources available. Christian school libraries, homeschool support group libraries, churches, online book suppliers and Christian bookstores will probably be your best bet.

TEACHER TIP

The Internet has a wealth of information concerning Creation & the Flood, though the articles available vary widely in dependability, worldview and attitude. Help your students learn to recognize the differences.

Remember:

Beware of Arrogance, Embrace Humility!

EVALUATION Review & Evaluation

In this Phase of Unit One, your students should have had the opportunity to explore Creation and the Flood through reading, listening, thinking and discussing. They will have:

1) informally discussed the Key Concepts;
2) read the article;
3) listened to the audio recording(s);
4) read the Scripture listed in Read for Your Life;
5) explored the Recap Activities;
6) completed the Opinion Column and Critical Puzzling answers on their own;
7) participated in Class Discussion;
8) chosen books of interest or searched the Internet.

You may wish to evaluate your students based on their *participation* in the **Class Discussion** and on their *participation* in the **Recap Activity**.

Learning Style Emphasis: THINKER

Students will explore topics of interest through research and reporting, learn new vocabulary, and construct a timeline relating to the first nine chapters of Genesis.

Monday-Tuesday:
1) Choose topic and begin research

Wednesday:
2) Vocabulary Practice

Thursday:
3) Construct the Timeline.

Friday:
4) Research projects completed; share in class or hand in.

> *Teachers can choose to have students do one or two activities, rather than the entire week's schedule. Please use what works for you in your unique setting.*

1) Choose topic and begin research

Allow the students the freedom to choose one of the topics listed on Pages 36-37, or to suggest their own area which they would like to research.

Motivating Suggestions:

Especially for Non-Linguistic students, and those who are not motivated by written or oral reports, here are suggestions for alternative ways of reporting what has been researched.

Creation/Flood
1) Act out the various stories of Creation, ending with the narration of Genesis 1.
2) Draw pictures for each of the stories of Creation found in tribal cultures, writing the appropriate Bible verse from Genesis beneath each picture.

Creation in Scripture
1) Create a chart showing the differences between Creationism and Theistic Evolution.
2) Find two selections of music which represent each of these systems of belief. Play excerpts for the audience, then explain how they show the differences between the two systems of belief.

MOTIVATE

Intelligent Design

1) Organize a debate, with one team representing Intelligent Design and one team representing evolution.

2) Create a poster for Creation, showing the days of Creation and the order of events. Create a second poster for evolution, showing the order of events. Display the two posters side by side for others to examine.

The Amazing Body

1) Choose one organ of the body, and show—through movement—the actions and functions of this organ. *The louder and messier, the better!*

2) Write a dialogue between different organs of the body which shows their interrelationships.

Metallurgy

1) Create a piece of copper art, and then explain some of the principles of working with metal.

2) Make a chart showing the chronological development of metallurgy in ancient times—which metals were used when and where.

Music

1) Videotape an interview with an instrument repairman, including questions which show the level of difficulty in making, playing, or repairing instruments.

PHASE 2

Exploration & Discovery Week

➢ *Research & Reporting*

Your mission, if you choose to accept it, is to explore one of these areas, and to discover something significant!

• **Creation/Flood:**

Investigate the various Creation and Flood stories in ancient or tribal cultures, including the Epic of Gilgamesh. Compare and contrast at least two of these versions with the Biblical account.

• **Creation in Scripture:**

Read Genesis and the New Testament scriptures about Creation, as well as any of the Creation books available to you. Do the writers of the New Testament, as well as the words of Jesus, indicate they believed the Bible account of Creation was literal history? Do theistic evolutionists? Using what you discover, write a defense of your position.

• **Intelligent Design:**

Find one of the books listed, or a book of your choice, for basic information on this branch of Creation versus evolution. Report your findings.

• **The Amazing Body:**

Do a research paper, with pictures, on the amazing intricacies of the eye, the brain, the heart, or any other part of the human body. Include the function of the organ, and its interrelation with other organs. Relate this to your study of Creation.

• **Metallurgy:**

Research the science of metallurgy. What is required to manufacture bronze? Iron? Explain how this demonstrates technological advancement. Consider how this contrasts with the theory of cave men and evolutionary development.

• **Music:**

Investigate what is necessary to create and play musical instruments. If possible, interview someone who makes or repairs instruments. Ask about the technology involved and the difficulties involved in this art. Interview someone who teaches a musical instrument. Find out what is involved in learning to play the instrument well. Ask at your music store for a video about instrument manufacturing. Explain how this demonstrates a sophistication of cultural development. Again, how does this contrast with the traditional theory of cave men?

• **Genealogy:**

Read the genealogies in Genesis 10, Matthew 1, and Luke 3. Research the term "genealogy." Collect the names and statistics of your family's ancestry, either through interviewing members of your family or researching through the library, Internet, other organizations. (Save this information for the Family Tree Project in Cycle Three.)

Genealogy

1) Do a class presentation of how people can find their genealogical roots, describing resources which can be used.

2) As a team, have 2-3 students work together to create their own family trees.

Order of Events

1) Write and illustrate a children's book which would help six year olds remember the order of events for Creation.
2) Write a song which would help teens and adults remember the order of events for Creation.

Floods

1) Gather video clips of flooding, then show examples of how devastating the flooding of one river can be. Afterwards, discuss together some of the impact of a worldwide flood.
2) Write a journalistic piece about one person's experience with a flood (whether from interviewing personally or from reading a first person account.)

Cavitation

1) Show a video clip of cavitation at a hydroelectric dam. Then discuss the similarities between the effect of that small cavitation damage and what may have happened on a much larger scale at the Grand Canyon.

2) Using color to demonstrate cavitation, create a picture of the impact of cavitation on a dam.

MOTIVATE

How Deep is Deep?

1) Create a graph showing different theories of the water level of the Flood. Label the different theories.
2) Give an oral presentation of the various theories about the Flood and the geological changes which occurred.

Phase 2

- **Order of Events:**

  Make a chart listing the order of events during the Creation week.

- **Floods:**

  Research the powerful and devastating impact of floodwaters. If a community nearby has recently been flooded, interview someone who experienced it first hand.

- **Cavitation:**

  Research cavitation and its danger at hydroelectric dams. Locate a video showing the catastrophic damage of cavitation.

- **How Deep is Deep?:**

  Read and report on the theories concerning how deep the water was at the Flood. Was it above Mt. Everest? Was Mt. Everest even there yet? Chart the various theories of the water levels.

- **Animal husbandry:**

  A necessary science on the ark! Find out some of the requirements for caring for reptiles, birds, and mammals. Comment on the difficulties of caring for a vast combination of animals.

- **Mt. Ararat:**

  In the library or on the Internet, research any information about the mountains of Ararat and the search for Noah's Ark. Also, compare the varying opinions of the creationists concerning where they believe Noah's Ark is located.

➤ *Brain Stretchers*

- **The Amazing Body, Part 2:**

  Find out how scientists explain the complexity of the eye, heart, etc. in light of their belief in a mindless evolutionary process. Compare/contrast this with the scriptural account of Creation.

- **Metallurgy, Part 2:**

  Research what it would take for your family to make bronze. Give an inventory of the necessary equipment and facilities, the cost involved, and the value of the product. Is it feasible? Visit your town's blacksmith shop, machine shop, or foundry. Report what you discover and relate what it suggests about pre-Flood times.

- **Cavitation, Part 2:**

  Research and report the effect of the Flood's cavitation on Planet Earth.

- **Buoyancy:**

  Research the requirements for ship stability in the water. Buoyancy is an important scientific principal that allowed the Ark to float. Write (include drawings) a description of the engineering and construction techniques required to build the Ark.

Create Your Own Research Topic:

_____
_____
_____

Brain Stretchers:

Brain Stretchers, listed on page 37, are intended for advanced students. Those who attempt the Brain Stretchers for their Research and Reporting can use the above list for ideas on how to report their findings.

Animal Husbandry

1) Bring an animal for "show and tell," describing the requirements for keeping that animal healthy. The more exotic the animal, the better!

2) Put on a short skit where students actually become some of the animals of the Ark, and have one person, playing Noah, explain the care and upkeep of these animals.

Mt. Ararat

1) Create a chart showing the various modern day attempts to locate the Ark. Label the explorers and the locations of their searches.

2) Analyze the different searches for the Ark. What do they have in common? What are their differences? What are their successes? What are their failures? What are the logistical difficulties? What are the political difficulties?

2) Words To Watch - Vocabulary Practice

Listed on Page 38. You may find other words in this unit that are especially appropriate for younger children. Feel free to substitute another vocabulary list for the one provided.

Here is one idea for making vocabulary study interesting and fun: ***Have students do Charades with the vocabulary list—acting out the words with their bodies.***

Phase 2

➣ *Words to Watch*

Remember—The easiest way to learn a subject is to master its terms:

prehistoric	deceive	cubit
technology	origins	catastrophic
banish	Sabbath	agriculture
antediluvian	altar	buoyancy
metallurgy	worldview	uniformitarianism
repentance	rebellion	animal
evolution	naturalism	husbandry
genealogy	religion	hostility
ancestor	ark	rebellion
creation	pitch	covenant
redemption	cavitation	descendant

Recognize that there is a distinction between the usage of some of these words in the Biblical context and their meaning in everyday common usage. Help your students understand both uses of the words.

3) Construct the Timeline.

Read the information listed with the "Key Dates" on Page 41. Dialogue with your students about the issues involved. Help them recognize that dating antiquity is not an exact science. For ease of reference, the timeline is included in the Appendix on Page 302.

Find the dates for the key people and events listed. In this unit, there will be a wide selection of possible dates for Creation, the Flood, Tower of Babel, etc. Though it may seem frustrating to both teacher and student to not be able to find the definitive date for each event, it IS educational to discover that there are differing viewpoints on this issue. Students may choose to:

- Take the date listed in their Bible;
- Take the date listed in Bishop Ussher's chronology;
- Take the date listed in a resource book they are using;
- Notate several different possibilities on their timeline, showing whose suggestion is whose;
- Choose a basic date, like 5,000 B.C. for Creation and 3,000 B.C. for the Flood;
- Have a debate in class about why one date should be chosen over another date (very good for developing critical thinking skills!).

*people -p. 38
creation 6000-4000BC
Flood ~~4000 5000BC~~ 2349 BC
Tower of Babel ~~3500 3000~~ 2242 BC*

4) Research projects shared in class and/or turned in.

Create a safe environment for the presentations. Set ground rules prior to the presentations for all the students, so that they know how much time is available for each student, and so that they understand each one will be honored and respected in their work by all those observing.

Review & Evaluation

In this second phase of Unit One, your students should have had the opportunity to explore Creation and the Flood through researching, thinking, and reporting. They will have:

1) done a research project;
2) learned the vocabulary;
3) constructed a Timeline;
4) created a project report on what was researched.

You may wish to evaluate your students based on their *efforts* in the **Research and Reporting** projects and their active *participation* in the **Vocabulary** and **Timeline** exercises.

PHASE 3

The Hands-On Week

Learning Style Emphasis: Sensor

Students will explore interrelated subject areas through sensory activities relating to the first nine chapters of Genesis.

Monday:

1) Create a map and discuss the issues in teams.

Tuesday:

2) Examine and discuss art masterpieces & architectural structures.

Wednesday:

3) Arts in Action—Do an art project.*

Thursday:

4) Do one science project or field trip.**

Friday:

5) Listen to and discuss the music.
6) Cook the food listed in the recipe, if desired.

*Art project will need to be planned ahead of time to acquire materials.
**Field trip will require extra planning time.

> *Teachers can choose to have students do one or two activities, rather than the entire week's schedule. Please use what works for you in your unique setting.*

INTRO - PG 23

1) Create a map and discuss the issues in teams

The students each have an outline map on Page 43. They will be given assignments for drawing in rivers, mountains, cities, and regional boundaries, which are listed on Page 42. For details on where these things are, please consult a historical atlas, an encyclopedia, a study Bible, or any other source for geographic information. For ease of reference, the map is included in the Appendix on Page 303.

Upper elementary students might be satisfied to accomplish only this portion:

- *Physical terrain:* This part of the mapping exercise will help students locate and mark the geological dynamics of a region.

Middle school students might be satisfied to complete both the previous mapping exercise and this exercise:

- *Geo-Political:* This section of the mapping exercise will provide the students an opportunity to locate and mark the cities, nations and empires of history. It will require more digging, as this information may not be listed on current maps. For example, the land of Shinar eventually became the nation of Babylon, which is in modern day Iraq.

High school students might be satisfied to complete both the previous mapping exercises and at least one exploration topic of this exercise:

- *Explore:* Discuss some selection from this portion of the mapping exercise in teams.

PHASE 3

The Hands-On Week

➢ *Maps and mapping*

- **Physical Terrain:**

  — Label and color the Tigris and Euphrates rivers on the outline map.

  — Color the Fertile Crescent.

  — Locate and indicate the mountain ranges, deserts, and green areas.

  — Shade and label the Black Sea, the Caspian Sea, and the Persian Gulf.

- **Geo-Political:**

  — Mark the possible locations of Mt. Ararat and the appropriate countries (Turkey, Iran).

  — Locate the land of Shinar.

- **Explore:**

  — *Cradle of Civilization:* Because the Garden of Eden was sealed off from man's presence after Adam and Eve sinned, and since the Flood thoroughly altered the geography of the Earth, it is impossible to pinpoint today exactly where the events of Genesis 1-7 occurred. However, archaeologists believe the "cradle of civilization", or the place of earliest man, is located in the Fertile Crescent between the Tigris and Euphrates. What reasons do you find to locate the Garden of Eden's original site in this area?

  — *Mr. Ararat:* Consult a relief map to discover the terrain of Mt. Ararat (both Turkey and Iran). Is it geologically active (any volcanoes)? What type of climate is typical in that part of the world? How would the terrain and climate have affected the reestablishment of mankind, agriculture, etc. How was it suitable for God's purposes?

  — *Out from the Ark:* Read Genesis 11:2. Look at a relief map of the region and try to trace the route taken by the post-Flood people from Mt. Ararat to the land of Shinar.

Garden of Eden

Many Bible scholars locate the Garden of Eden in the Fertile Crescent, partially due to the reference in Genesis about the Euphrates. However, it is fascinating to learn that that name is used more than once in the Middle East, and may, in fact, only hearken back to the original Euphrates which was destroyed during the Flood. Something to think about!

QUESTION

Mt. Ararat

Though there is a mountain in Turkey called Mt. Ararat, it may have only been known by that name since the Middle Ages. That is part of the reason that some Ark hunters believe that the Ark is actually in Iran rather than Turkey. As students look up information about Mt. Ararat, have them look both at Turkey and at Iran.

QUESTION

Genesis 11:2

There is some disagreement about the exact meaning of this verse. Some hold that it means "from the East" and others believe it means "to the East." Challenge your students to consider what the implications are for each of these meanings.

QUESTION

2) Examine and discuss art masterpieces & architectural structures

Locate either a copy of these paintings or Internet sites for each of the items listed on page 44. Allow the students time to observe the paintings without any conversation, and then, when they are ready, engage them in some or all of the questions listed below or in the Student Manual.

QUESTION

Creation *by Michelangelo*

- Various artists throughout history have attempted to express visually the story of Creation. Michelangelo's painting on the ceiling of the Sistine Chapel is one of the best known. Ask the students what emotions are evoked; what thoughts are suggested by the picture of God and Adam reaching toward each other with outstretched hands.

- Dr. Francis Schaeffer, in *How Should We Then Live*, describes Michelangelo's work on the ceiling of the Sistine Chapel as combining, "biblical teaching and non-Christian pagan thought…" How would the students agree or disagree with that statement?

- You might ask the students if they think Michelangelo's art on the Sistine Chapel ceiling was influenced at all by the pain he may have endured while lying on his back all those years!

QUESTION

Earth as Architecture

- Consider holding a class discussion about the questions listed in the Student Manual concerning the architectural structure of the Earth.

Phase 3

Consider:

Michelangelo painted the Sistine Chapel while lying on his back on scaffolding for several years!

≫ Art Appreciation

- **The Sistine Chapel – Creation** *by Michelangelo*

— Do you think his painting reflects what the Bible describes?

— How does the painting differ from your own impression of this historic event?

- *For a captivating look at his experience, watch the video, "The Agony and the Ecstasy".*

- **Noah's Ark** *by Edward Hicks*

— What does this painting communicate to you about Noah's Ark?

— Edward Hicks (1780-1849) is one of the best known American folk painters. Is there any identifiable "American" aspect to his painting?

- *Read more about Hicks' beliefs, and how that influenced his choice of subjects for painting.*

Consider:

Did you know that God is the Original and Greatest Architect? Hebrews 11:10: *"For he waited for the city which has foundations, whose builder and maker is God."* Look up architecture in a study Bible, and discuss the scriptures listed, considering some of the implications of the concept: God is an Architect.

≫ Architecture

The earth is perfectly proportioned for its travel through space.

— Locate one of the photos taken of earth from space. Then consult a relief globe to discover the architectural design of the land masses and the corresponding bodies of water. Describe the design of the earth: Are the lines rigid and straight? Is there fluidity? There are significant "water features." How does that impact the design? Would you deduce that God is a fabulous architect?

44 / Unit One: *Creation & the Flood*

Noah's Ark *by Edward Hicks*

- As a Quaker, Edward Hicks was deeply committed to painting scenes which communicated the truth of the Scriptures. Ask your students if they think there is a relationship between the pacifism of Quakers and the gentleness of Hicks' paintings.
- Edward Hicks was born at the end of the American Revolution and lived in a somewhat settled time for Americans, both politically and philosophically. Ask your students to find other examples of American painting during this time, and then compare it to the style of European painters in the early - mid 1800's.

Phase 3

≫ *Arts in Action*

Select one, and let your artistic juices flow!

- **Family Tree:**

On poster board, draw a large tree with branches. At the roots, label the names of the children in your family. On the first two branches, write your mother's name and your father's name. From those branches, keep adding branches as far back as you can go. Another option is to use fallen tree branches, or hanging cards with the names on them. Try making it three dimensional. Go for the glitz!

- **Copper Working:**

Learning to work with copper is an interesting means of understanding what early craftsmen dealt with. Locate a hobby shop and browse through their copper crafts. Be sure to ask questions about working with this substance, trying to learn all you can. Then, when you are ready, try your hand at creating a copper "work of art." (Suggestion: If you have Visual Manna's *Teaching History Through Art*, you will have a piece of copper foil and some suggestions of how to create art with it!)

- **Jewelry:**

Visit a jewelry store to learn about their use of metals and precious stones. Ask them how they make various pieces of jewelry. Then try making some metal jewelry.

- **Imitation:**
  — Try your hand at creating *the Creation* with Michelangelo (trace, follow colors, etc.)

  — Create a *Noah's Ark* in the style of Edward Hicks

- **Creating at home:**

Read Edith Schaeffer's book, *Hidden Art*. It is based upon the concept that we reflect our Creator when we create. There are many practical ideas for possible projects. Choose what appeals to you and make it! Possible areas to consider are gardening, floral arranging, cooking, clothes design, and making furniture. (Suggestion: Find a book or an expert who can help you get started in your creative endeavors.)

- **Construction:**
  — Try an *Easy-to-Make Noah's Ark* by Dover.

  — Carve a soap boat

  — Use Legos to construct a big boat

  — Make a model wooden boat or a raft-size houseboat (a good backyard project!)

- **Carving:**

Start a yearlong project carving animals. Check in the library or with a local expert (perhaps your grandfather?) for how-to information.

- **Imagine:**

In whatever medium you prefer, create your version of the Garden of Eden. Be able to explain some of your color, texture and style choices.

Unit One: *Creation & the Flood* / 45

---

3) Arts in Action

INTRO - PG 23

Listed on page 45.

This particular unit, because it is focusing on Creation, is a very good time to help students discover that, because they are made in the image of the Creator, they, too, are creative. Some people are creative with color, some with shapes, some with textiles. Others are creative with tastes, with aromas, with sounds. Give each student opportunity to try their hand at various creative media and encourage their attempts with praise. Some will be extraordinarily gifted, and that may be the area God chooses to use them for their life's work. Others will gain a certain sense of joy and fulfillment from creating something that is enjoyable just for them. The point of this moment in the curriculum is to give them joy in creativity.

Family Tree

This project will only be possible if the student has prepared beforehand because it will require quite an extensive list of ancestors in order to look like anything more than a young sapling!

Copper Working

If there is access to hobby shops or the library, there are many different avenues which can be pursued in working with copper. However, if cost or lack of readily available information is a deterrent, perhaps the interested student could find helpful suggestions on the Internet.

Jewelry

Ideally, metal jewelry could be created. However, for younger students, large beaded jewelry can be made out of Play Dough, or a similar material.

Imitation

Have the students look again at Michelangelo's and Edward Hicks' paintings. Then, with art supplies of colored pencils, pastels, or paint, try to recreate what is seen.

Creating at home

This suggestion will require advance preparation for either student or teacher. Locate a copy of *Hidden Art* by Edith Schaeffer and choose one of her suggestions for creating art. Actually, an interested student could try several forms of art until finding the most satisfying one(s), though this will obviously take much longer than one day.

Construction

Of the four, the soap boat and the Lego boat are the most readily pursued. Again, for interested students, the raft-size houseboat would be an incredible opportunity to gain a better appreciation for what Noah might have faced in building the Ark. It is a more difficult option for teachers who keep their classes inside all of the time, but could be just the breath of fresh air that some students need!

Carving

Woodcarving is a skill that has been largely lost in the past few generations. However, for an interested student, the possibilities when the skill is learned are enormous. A good woodcarving student might actually be able to make an income with this art form.

Imagine

For this project, anything goes—from a Garden of Eden in a shoe box to a terrarium to a life-sized construction including potted plants and a backdrop. (Watch out for snakes!)

4) Do a science project or field trip

Located on page 46. Feel free to choose one of these projects. If students love science, they might want to consider doing all of them!

Do-It-Yourself Flood

This eye-opening experiment was shown to me by Dr. Gary Parker, a noted Creationist in the field of paleontology. Your students will be amazed to discover how quickly various "strata" are formed.

Phase 3

➤ Science

- **Do-It-Yourself Flood:**

  — Create a "flood in a bottle" by putting sand, dirt, leaves, grass, and water in a tall plastic jar with a lid. Shake vigorously and observe the settling process. Do you see how different layers can be formed very quickly? Try varying the substances—how about rocks and oil?

- **Do-It-Yourself Cavitation:**

  — Build a nice big sandbox dam and fill a big reservoir behind it. Watch the valleys it forms after you poke a hole in the dam.

- **Agriculture:**

  — Plant a grape vine (if not possible, try potting a fruit vine or a bush like raspberries, strawberries, etc.) Go on a field trip to a vineyard. Learn about the cultivation of grapes. Learn about fermentation. If you can, try making vinegar or drying grapes to make raisins.

➤ Music

Many composers have created a tone poem or programmatic music where a scene is conveyed through the music. One of our favorites is Pictures at an Exhibition *by Modeste Mussorgsky. If you can find this recording, listen especially to "The Ballet of the Baby Chicks in Their Shells." If you can find the artwork which inspired Mussorgsky, you may be surprised! Another wonderful example of a symphonic poem type of music is Beethoven's Sixth Symphony "Pastoral." Listen for the sounds of nature recreated by the orchestral instruments.*

Sing:

All Things Bright and Beautiful

How Great Thou Art

All Creatures of our God and King

Great is Thy Faithfulness

O Worship the King

I Sing the Mighty Power of God

46 / Unit One: *Creation & the Flood*

Do-It-Yourself Cavitation

Many Creation scientists believe that geologic structures such as the Grand Canyon were formed after the Flood by the action of cavitation. Again, seeing is believing.

TEACHER TIP

Agriculture

If you have access to a vineyard, it is worth the trip in order to learn first hand some of the difficulties faced in trying to plant a new vineyard and have it flourish (as Noah did). Options might include interviewing someone who is a knowledgeable gardener about what is involved in starting a new garden, in growing fruiting vines, in establishing perennial plants. Ask your students, after the trip or interview, to consider what Noah and his family might have had to overcome in planting their gardens. Ask them to consider what the options were for food supply.

5) Listen to and discuss the music

Listed on pages 46-47.

INTRO - PG 24

Listen

- Locate a recording of either Mussorgsky's *Pictures at an Exhibition* or Beethoven's Sixth Symphony, "Pastoral." If you are using Mussorgsky's work, play for your students the selection "The Ballet of the Baby Chicks In Their Shells." After playing the music, ask your students what they "saw" in the music. Did it paint an auditory picture for them of what the title suggests? Beethoven's entire Pastoral is an effort to present the sounds and moods of nature in a musical setting. Listen for storms, bird calls, etc.
- Now have them listen to a portion of Franz Joseph Haydn's *Creation* Oratorio. In what way does the sound of this music give the sense of Creation to the students?

QUESTION

Try This

If it is possible to go outside and hear the sounds of nature (depending on where you live), take the students out to simply listen to the music of nature. Have them identify the different sounds after listening carefully for several minutes. Have them discuss whether any of the sounds they heard in nature where portrayed in the music. Were those sounds present at the first week of Creation?

6) Cook the food

Located on page 47.

• **Listen:**

— Now listen to The "Creation" Oratorio by Franz Joseph Haydn. As you listen to this formal piece of music, try to hear the dynamics of Creation. Why do you think Haydn called it "The Creation"? Does the music convey mental pictures to you?

• **Try this:**

— Listen to the music found in nature: the birds' song, the melodic tone of wind, the rhythm of falling rain… If you have a tape recorder, try to capture some of these sounds (and others) on tape—a symphony of nature!

➢ Cooking

Apricots have an interesting history. They seem to have been transplanted in the Middle East during the time of Noah! This is a fun recipe (though I'm not sure they had blenders on the Ark!)

• **Apricot Whip**

1 pound dried apricots	1/2 cup sugar
2 1/2 cup water	1/2 tsp. almond extract
1/2 tsp salt	1 1/2 cup. heavy cream

Cook apricots in water & salt till tender (20 min.). Stir in sugar and flavoring. Puree in blender. Chill. Beat cream till stiff, fold into apricots, chill again. Serves 6

What kind of foods do you think Noah and his family might have had on the ark? Do you think they cooked food or ate it all raw? What would they have had to consider as they packed food for themselves on the ark?

EVALUATION Review & Evaluation

In this Phase of Unit One, your students should have had the opportunity to explore Creation and the Flood through various hands-on and creative sessions. They will have:

1) completed a Mapping section;
2) observed and discussed Art & Architecture;
3) worked on an art project;
4) experimented with a Science Project or taken a field trip;
5) listened to music;
6) tasted a food related to this unit.

You may wish to evaluate your students based on their *class participation* in these **Hands-on** activities.

Learning Style Emphasis: *Intuitor*

Students, through creative self-expression, using one or more creative activities, will present some aspect of what they have learned in the past three weeks relating to Creation & the Flood. Areas of expression include linguistics, art, music, drama, movement and conceptual design.

Monday - Thursday

1) Choose area of expression and begin work either individually or in teams.

Friday

2) Share creative expressions in class.

> *Teachers can choose to have students do one or two activities, rather than the entire week's schedule. Please use what works for you in your unique setting.*

1) Choose area of expression and begin work either individually or in teams

INTRO - PG 25

Linguistics:

Listed on page 48.

Journalism

Have the students who wish to write a journalistic piece look at several articles in newspapers and/or magazines to understand the framework for journalism. Encourage them to be as wildly imaginative as they wish to be, as long as they convey something of what has been learned in the unit.

Playing With Words

• For students interested in renaming different categories of animals, encourage them to look through lists of classifications to see some of the variety of creatures available for consideration.

• Show students some examples of puns and limericks in order to get their creative juices flowing and to help them understand the model of what they are attempting to create.

TEACHER TIP

Prose

- There are many written accounts of someone's first glimpse of a new land (such as William Bradford's *Of Plymouth Plantation*) or a new place (such as Colonel Jim Irwin's *Destination Moon*). Students could model their descriptions after one of these examples.
- A touch of realism could be added, for those interested in animal health and care, through reading stories by zoo vets or accounts of shipping animals by boat.
- If students wish to write books for young children, have them examine some children's books to see the level of vocabulary, the length of sentences, and the style of illustration.

Art:
Located on page 49.

Painting/Drawing

There may be one student who wishes to write a book while another would like to illustrate the book, which is the normal delineation in the publishing industry. Encourage the team to work together, coming early into agreement about which parts of the story should be illustrated so the artist has time to work.

Graphic Design

If the design is created on a computer, it may be possible to print the design and actually put it onto a T-shirt.

Cartooning

A student might wish to use humor or to create a more serious mood, as some political cartoons do.

Sculpting

Sculptures may range from very realistic, painted figures to imaginative, barely recognizable fabric sculptures. Give creative and artistic space to the artist!

PHASE 4

The Expression Week

➤ *In Your Own Way...*

We have seen God's glory in the Creation and His mercy in providing a way of redemption. And we have explored the causes and effects of Noah's Flood. Now, choose a selection of these activities, or create your own, which will best express what you have learned from this unit.

Linguistics:

- **Journalism:**
  - Write an article for the "First Word Times" called, "A Day in the Life of Seth." Be sure to find the human interest details.

  - You are a newspaper reporter for the "Enoch Free News." Your assignment is to interview Noah about this monstrosity he's building, and to write up his story for the newspaper feature, subtitled "Truth is Stranger Than Fiction."

- **Playing with Words:**
  - Can you imagine naming thousands and thousands of birds, reptiles, mammals, amphibians, and... BUGS? Not to mention dinosaurs! Adam was AMAZING!

  - Choose five from each category above, and give them *new* names. Search for solid, interesting names which reflect the characteristics of the animal.

  - Finish this limerick about Cain:
    "There once was a man from Nod,
    Who offered his veggies to God..."

  - Try your hand at writing puns. Like this:
    "Hey Mom, you know what you call a fly that has no wings?"
    "No, son, what do you call a fly that has no wings?"
    "A walk!"

- **Prose:**
  - Write a creative description of what the new world looked like after the Ark was opened and the people first came out.

  - Write a first person account of life on the Ark, from the viewpoint of a sea-sick giraffe.

  - Write a book for young children describing Noah, the Ark and the Flood. You could use Scripture, write poems or tell short stories.

TEACHER TIP

Music:
Listed on page 49.

Compose

Students may wish to form a team to compose and perform a song, or they may wish to do this selection on their own. We have found that humor in music makes up for a lack of tunefulness!

Phase 4

Art:

- **Painting/Drawing:**

  Illustrate the book for young children listed above. Create captions for the illustrations.

- **Graphic Design:**

  Design the T-shirt front and back, with logo and catchy saying, which Noah and his family would have worn to family reunions in years after the Flood.

- **Cartooning:**

  The possibilities for cartoons on this subject are almost endless! Create a one frame cartoon of one of the Days of Creation, or a multi-frame cartoon of Noah's neighbors, or design your own political cartoon about one of the topics of this unit.

- **Sculpting:**

  Sculpt Ark animals from your preferred material (Play-Dough, clay, etc.)

Music:

- **Compose:**

  — Compose a song, either vocal or instrumental, about Adam and Eve entitled, "You and Me and the Forbidden Tree."

  — Use a familiar tune and write new words about life on the ark.

- **Performance Practice:**

  If you study an instrument, then, with your teacher's help, select an appropriate piece of music which expresses some element from this unit. Prepare and perform the piece for an audience. Communicate with your audience the reason for your selection either in the *program notes* or in a short speech.

- **Create:**

  Make your own instrument. It doesn't have to be fancy, it just needs pleasing sounds. Consider an instrument made of natural materials, such as a dried gourd filled with large beads. Or create your own rainstick, or perhaps a washtub bass. A homemade flute or drum from a hollow log would be perfect! If there are more than one instrument makers/players, form a musical group. Then either compose an original piece of music or learn to play a tune, so you can share your "music" with others!

Performance Practice

For musical students, this selection may be a wonderful opportunity to express what they have learned. Make sure they have selected a piece that they have adequate time to prepare.

Create

There are many different types of instruments that are within the instrument-making ability of young people. Books out of the library, Internet searches, and the simple instruments made out of natural materials by tribal people are all possible sources for ideas. Encourage any students who choose to make an instrument to remember that they are to express some aspect of what they have learned from this unit, so that they can be thinking of that application as they pursue the creation of the instrument.

Drama:

Located on page 50.

Comedy

- If students can imagine what it would be like to watch someone on a blind date, they might find much valuable material for the skit on Adam and Eve meeting for the first time.
- Imagine being cooped up on the ark with all kinds of animals for months at a time. Out of that understanding, write a skit showing realistic euphoria!!!

Tragedy

Students might choose to use a stylistic presentation, rather than a realistic one for the Fall of Man. Either way, try to create a mood which makes it tragic rather than funny.

Puppetry

Puppets are fun to use! However, what seems workable behind the puppet stage might not be as effective for the audience, so have an objective third-party critique the puppets' actions *before* you stage the show for a live audience.

Phase 4

Drama:

- **Comedy:**
  — Act out a humorous introduction of Adam and Eve by God. Possible questions might include, "Excuse me, where did you say you were from?"

  — Create a skit about Noah's excitement when he realized the flood waters were receding. Variation: Show the animals' excitement!

- **Tragedy:**
  Reenact the Fall of Man. Include some of the tragic consequences. Finish your presentation with some of the prophecies of the coming Redeemer, because to Christians the story need not end in tragedy.

- **Puppetry:**
  Use puppets to tell young children the story of Noah and the Ark. Be sure to include realistic animal sounds!

Movement:

Located on page 51.

Pantomime

- Pantomimists might choose six specific actions for the six days of Creation, or they could portray an ongoing fluid story from Day One to Day Six. Be sure to rest on the seventh day!
- Work to create the sense of different animals which are being herded. How would you herd an elephant? How does that differ from how you would herd a monkey? Etc.

Dance

So many possibilities exist for choreographing Creation or the Flood. Choose one or two main concepts to convey through the entire dance.

Action

It might be helpful to use a rhythmic beat for staging the stylized conflict, as it will help the participants move in a synchronized manner.

Phase 4

Movement:

- **Pantomime**

  — Using movement only (no words!), show the six days of Creation.

  — Convince your audience that you are herding animals onto the Ark, two by two.

- **Dance**

  Choose a selection of music that expresses to you the Creation or Flood, then choreograph a dance which will depict some aspect of this unit. You may use ballet, modern, jazz, or improvisational dance. Make sure your moves communicate the appropriate emotion to the audience.

- **Action**

  Stage a stylized conflict between God's goodness and Man's rebellion. It is effective to have groups of two doing the same actions.

Conceptual Design:

- **Game-Making:**

  Using the first two chapters of Genesis, create a game for children which will give them practice in naming both the days of Creation and what was created on that day. You will need to decide if this is a board-game, an action game, a rhyming game, a musical-chairs game, etc.

Create Your Own Expression:

_____

_____

_____

Conceptual Design:

Listed on page 51.

TEACHER TIP

Game-Making

Games help students learn, so keep in mind that your object is to help children remember the events and days of Creation. In other words, keep it simple!

2) Share creative expressions in class.

INTRO-PG 26

The same rules apply as suggested in the reporting section of Phase Two.

Review & Evaluation

EVALUATION

In this Phase of Unit One, your students should have had the opportunity to express what they have learned about Creation and the Flood through one or more various creative selections of their own choosing. These include:

1) Linguistics;
2) Art;
3) Music;
4) Drama;
5) Movement;
6) Conceptual Design.

You may wish to evaluate your students based on their *effort* in the **Creative Expressions**, either as individuals or in teams.

THE RISE OF CIVILIZATIONS

Queen Pu-Abi's Headdress

Pray with the students

at the beginning of each unit.

Enthusiasm and delight

are the best way to capture a student's

interest and jump-start motivation, so:

1) ***For the Auditory Students:*** Consider playing dramatic music which shows conflict, such as **The Firebird Suite** by Stravinsky, to capture their attention at the very beginning of class;

2) ***For the Kinesthetic Students:*** Have the students warm up as class begins by doing some active movement that is fun (set a timer for 17 seconds, then, with students standing by their chairs, have them sit down when they think 17 seconds is up—the timer will be the standard!);

3) ***For the Visual Students:*** Bring a visual object to stimulate their interest in the new unit, like a photo of the Ziggurat of Ur, or the Standard of Ur;

4) ***For the hearts of all:*** Pray with them at the beginning of the unit, that God would help them discover what He has for each one to learn in that unit.

PHASE 1

The Introduction Week

Learning Style Emphasis: *Feeler*

Students will be introduced to chapters 10-25 of Genesis. You may follow this suggested schedule or adapt it to meet your students' needs:

Monday:

  1) Informally discuss the Key Concepts

Tuesday:

  2) Read the article
  3) Listen to the audio recording(s)
  4) Read the Scripture listed in Read For Your Life

Wednesday:

  5) Recap Activity
  6) Opinion Column and Critical Puzzling answers on their own

Thursday:

  7) Class Discussion

Friday:

  8) Choose books of interest/Internet search

Teachers can choose to have students do one or two activities, rather than the entire week's schedule. Please use what works for you in your unique setting.

INTRO-PG 18

1) Informally Discuss the Key Concepts

Listed in the Student Manual on page 53.

KEY CONCEPTS BACKGROUND INFORMATION

These are the main objectives of the unit. As you proceed through the four weeks, your students will be given various ways of understanding each of these objectives.

The descendants of Noah—EXPLANATION

TEACHER TIP

To get an informal discussion started on this key concept, ask a simple, leading question, such as, *"Why do you think we have different people groups, with different racial characteristics, all over the world?"*

History is filled with wars between nations, atrocities committed against other people groups, prejudices based on skin color or language, and pride because of a supposed racial superiority. Because of deep-seated, sin-based arrogance and prejudice, various leaders or people groups have tried to elevate themselves above other groups. This has been the case from our earliest recorded memories. The God's-eye-view which dissolves these prejudices, this misplaced pride, this hatred of people different from ourselves…is found in Genesis 10 and 11, and Acts 17:26. It is in these accurate descriptions of where we all come from that we suddenly realize that we are all children of the same parents, and that the differences between German speakers and Thai speakers, between Australians and Africans, between North American and South American people are extremely superficial. Yes, there are very different ways of thinking, based upon worldview, language and experience, but at the very heart of each person in the world is a God-shaped vacuum, waiting to be filled by relationship with Him. So, in truth, we are all distantly-related cousins from a set of grandparents who lived a while back.

That changes everything, doesn't it? Talk with your students about prejudice, about the fear of other people groups and nations. Do they struggle with people of another culture, seeing them as scary or weird or stupid? Allow the truths of Scripture, that we really are all related, to begin to work its way into their thinking processes. Pray together that God would begin to give each one His perspective on the peoples of the earth. The simple children's chorus says it quite clearly:

SPIRITUAL

"Jesus loves the little children,
All the children of the world,
Red and yellow, black and white,
We are precious in His sight,
Jesus loves the little children of the world."

With your students, ponder the implications of this verse:

"And He has made from one blood every nation of men to dwell on all the face of the earth, and has determined their preappointed times and the boundaries of their habitation, so that they should seek the Lord, in the hope that they might grope for Him and find Him, though He is not far from each one of us; for in Him we live and move and have our being..." Acts 17:26-28

THE RISE OF CIVILIZATIONS

UNIT 2

Queen Pu-Abi's Headdress

KEY CONCEPTS:

• The descendants of Noah

• The Tower of Babel

• Sudden civilization

• Archaeology— its uses and limits

• Abraham & Ur

The adventures of early mankind continue...

As Noah and his family came out of the Ark and began a new life in a vastly changed world, we see described in the Bible the foundations of nations, the emergence of many languages, and the first of the world empires. There is contained within those first post-Flood people the latent effect of pre-Flood problems: active rebellion, willful disobedience,

Unit Two:

This article can be found in its entirety in the Appendix (see pg 304).

The Tower of Babel—EXPLANATION

TEACHER TIP

To get an informal discussion started on this key concept, ask a simple, leading question, such as, *"What do you think it was like when the people at the Tower of Babel suddenly couldn't understand each other's language?"*

The first nine verses of Genesis 11 are short enough to be easily read in class as the students begin to ponder the realities of this historic moment. There are several issues, these four to begin with, which arise from this Scripture reading:

1) The power of a common language with no hindrance to understanding—something that gains tremendous meaning when you travel outside your own country and hear languages that have no connection to you!

2) The power of a common purpose, even when it is disobedient—in this case, the people gathering on the plain of Shinar to build a permanent city and a tower where they would remain, rather than being obedient to go and fill the entire earth as God had commanded their ancestors;

3) The power of advanced technology—the pre-flood knowledge of city building, brick making, and tower construction, rather than ten thousand years of experimenting with little villages progressing eventually to cities;

4) The cataclysmic event—the scattering of languages and people, something which was embedded deeply into the myths and legends of many ancient and tribal people.

PHASE 1

KEY PEOPLE:

Ham 4400 ~~2200~~ BC
—father of the people who traveled South

Shem 2446 BC
—father of the people of the Middle East

Japheth 2448 BC
—father of the people who traveled North

Nimrod
—builder of the first post-Flood cities

Abraham ~~2165~~ 1996 BC
—father of the Hebrew and Arab nations, and of all those who have faith in God

➤ Listen to This

• **What in the World's Going On Here? Volume One**

— Rise of Civilizations

• **True Tales from the Times of…Ancient Civilizations & The Bible**

— the Table of Nations

— the Discovery of Troy

— the Discovery of Ur

➤ Read for Your Life

• **The Holy Bible**

— The Main Story: Genesis 11–36

— Helpful Verses: Psalm 105:1-15; Romans 4; Galatians 3:5-14; Hebrews 11:8-21

Key People:

The people listed in this column are the main characters, if you will, of this unit. They are listed in the Student Manual, along with a brief identifier, so that the students can familiarize themselves with these people.

Just imagine what it was like for the people at the Tower of Babel when God scattered them! There has probably never been a storm, an earthquake, a volcanic eruption to compare with the devastation and fear which was caused by this event. And yet, we see in Acts 17:26 that God had something very good in mind for these rebellious people—He wanted to give them a hunger and a yearning for Himself. Pray for and with your students that they will have that hunger and yearning for God, that He will capture their attention, their hearts, and that they will walk in obedience to Him.

Sudden civilization—EXPLANATION

To get an informal discussion started on this key concept, ask a simple, leading question, such as, *"What have you been told about the causes for early civilizations?"*

It is amazing to pick up modern history books and have them, one and all, describe the same scenario:

1) Man evolves from apes;
2) Man hunts and gathers;
3) Woman tells man they need to settle down (!);
4) Little villages are formed, with the beginning of crop production;
5) Eventually, cities are formed.

Is that actually what happened? Or is that, instead, just the common drivel from the prevailing worldview of the "evolution of man and technology" which is spontaneously generating even now from Darwin's *Origin of the Species*, written in the late 1800's?

This direct quote, concerning Austen Layard's discovery of Ninevah in the mid-1800's, demonstrates the change in perspective:

> *"Layard recalled the siege of Lachish in Israel by Sennacherib's generals, which resulted from Hezekiah's refusal to pay tribute, recorded in the Old Testament. Here, he proclaimed, was archaeological proof of the historical veracity of the scriptures. Popular interest in the…discoveries reached fever pitch in a devout age, when many educated people still believed in the literal historical truth of the scriptures."*
>
> Dr. Brian Fagan, in his introduction to Layard's classic *Nineveh and Its Remains*

So what changed from the "devout age," where educated people believed the literal historic truth of the Scriptures, to the "skeptical age," where educated people believe the Bible is myth? In a nutshell, evolution, as proposed by Darwin, gave an alternative way of viewing ancient history to all those who were looking for a reason to disbelieve. Archaeologists and historians now assume, for the most part, that evolution is literally true, therefore the Bible is patently untrue, and that civilizations, just like species, evolved from very simple beginnings to increasingly complex states.

Is that the only explanation for what is seen in the archaeological record? No. Actually, when students begin to peruse the writings of scientists, archaeologists and historians, they discover a tremendous amount of unexplainable, mysterious, OOP Arts (out-of-place-artifacts). These artifacts deviate so greatly from the accepted time frame that the evolution scientists have no tidy place on their shelf to set them.

When we read the scientists, archaeologists and historians who believe the Bible is true—which gives them the foundation for making sense of the archaeological record—we find no artifacts out of place, because they, in fact, are properly placed in the biblical record of the flow of history. Bible-believing scientists don't see these things as mysterious or out of place, but rather, as clear evidence that what the Bible described is actually the way things happened. The stages of development come into an explainable focus:

1) Technologically advanced pre-Flood people;
2) Flood;

3) Eight people with the knowledge and skill of the pre-Flood time survive;

4) Their descendants come together in rebellion at the Tower of Babel;

5) God scatters them across the face of the earth—some with more technology than others;

6) Differing levels of civilization seen across the earth—with tremendous similarities between widely diverse geographic locations;

7) An archaeological *suddenness* to technically advanced civilizations.

SPIRITUAL

Pray for your students, that they will develop by God's power, a firm, biblical foundation for seeing history and all human knowledge within the framework of the Word of God.

Archaeology—it's uses and limits—EXPLANATION

TEACHER TIP

To get an informal discussion started on this key concept, ask a simple, leading question, such as, *"Does anyone know what an archaeologist does?"*

At the turn of the nineteenth century, Napoleon took his troops to Egypt as part of an attempt to export the French Revolution. Things did not go as he planned, but one discovery, which was made in the course of exploring the Egyptian terrain, had a dramatic impact on Europe and gave rise to the modern study of archaeology: the discovery of the Rosetta Stone. Up until this point, ancient civilizations were unknown outside the pages of the Old Testament and a few glimpses of Greek writers. This all changed when the door into ancient Egypt was opened by the Rosetta Stone. This black basalt slab contained Greek writing (c.200 B.C.), Egyptian demotic writing and the Egyptian hieroglyphics. Because the Greek writing was readily understood, it provided the keys to unlocking the demotic writing and the hieroglyphics. Once these languages were deciphered, the inscriptions on monuments, tablets and other sources of ancient Egyptian writing could be translated, resulting in an unprecedented understanding of ancient Egypt.

Nearly half a century after the discovery of the Rosetta Stone, a British officer named Henry Rawlinson laboriously copied and deciphered a giant inscription in three ancient languages: Old Persian, Elamite and Akkadian. This discovery, known as the Behistun Inscription, was found 500 feet up a mountain side on an old caravan route. The story of Rawlinson's incredible, inventive, and dangerous adventure in copying the inscription is one of the great stories of archaeology! Ultimately, his work broke the code to the language of the ancient Assyrians and Babylonians, opening the doors to understanding ancient Mesopotamia through its Akkadian writings.

In the mid-1800's, an amateur archaeologist, Austen Henry Layard, discovered the ancient city of Ninevah, which had been covered by the sands more than two thousand years prior. The tremendous excitement generated by his discoveries continued to validate and affirm the importance of modern day archaeology.

From this time of early discoveries, much has been learned about how to safeguard archaeological finds, how to carefully conduct the digs, how to evaluate the ages of the various levels found in the digs, how to read the languages of various inscriptions and tablets. All of this has given a profound insight into ancient civilizations, and is to be highly valued.

However, archaeology has limits. As is explained in the article for this chapter in the Student Manual, archaeology is like searching for the proverbial needle in a haystack—except the haystack is mountains of dirt and rubble. There is so much which remains unknown. There is even a question whether the things that have been found are representative of the overall time or culture. It's helpful, yes, but it's not perfect. Our students need to grasp the difference between a solid footing established on the veracity of the Word of God and the somewhat unstable information which has been unearthed through archaeology. One is completely dependable because it has come to us from God Himself. The other is not completely dependable, not only because it is merely a small slice of the actual remains of a civilization, but also because it is subject to various interpretations, which, again, depend on the viewpoint of the one interpreting the data.

Abraham & Ur—EXPLANATION

To get an informal discussion started on this key concept, ask a simple, leading question, such as, *"What do you know about Ur, the city which Abram left?"*

TEACHER TIP

At this point in history, we have the opportunity to help our students not only know that Abraham left Ur, according to the biblical record, but also to discover with our students more about the ancient city of Ur from the archaeological record.

This gives added impetus for placing Abraham firmly in recorded history rather than relegating him to some mythical tale of the "once upon a time" variety. He lived in a real place during a real time in history, which we can know more about, thanks to the archaeological discoveries.

If one delves very deeply into the civilization of Ur, one finds a religious center devoted to the worship of the moon god, Sin. There are rather horrifying accounts of royal burial pits which include not only a royal personage but numerous servants and musicians who evidently committed cheerful mass suicide. It becomes clear that God intended Abraham, the one through whom He planned to bless all the families of the earth, to leave that home and journey to a new location—one which, by the way, was in a far more strategic spot for disseminating this global blessing!

> **FASCINATING FACT:**
>
> *One curious point: at the British Museum, in the display case containing the Standard of Ur, there is a small statue of a large sheep caught in a bush. You might describe it as a ram caught in a thicket. The archaeologists date that piece of sculpture to a time shortly before Abraham. Discuss with your students whether they think it is possible that God gave a prophetic piece of art to the culture of Ur concerning the nature of the sacrifice He would provide for Abraham in Genesis 22.*

2) Read the article

Begins on Page 53 of Student Manual.

The article for Unit Two is designed to help students think about the reality of the historical events and people recorded in Genesis, and the implication for people today. The materials covered in the audio recordings offer another look at this time period, covering slightly different information. In the article and recordings, along with introducing the basic understanding of history, we are also bringing in the biblical worldview.

SPIRITUAL

You may choose to have your students read the article first and then listen to the audio recordings, or vice versa.

TEACHER TIP

3) Listen to the audio recording(s)

INTRO - PG 18

Listed on Page 60 of the Student Manual.

• The main concepts and chronological flow are contained in **What in the World's Going On Here?**

• Fascinating stories of the rise of civilizations are discussed in **True Tales From the Times of…Ancient Civilizations & The Bible**
  • Several descriptions of OOP Arts are also discussed in the above tape.

4) Read the Scripture listed in Read For Your Life

Listed on Page 60 of the Student Manual. You might choose to have the students read the Main Story verses either corporately or privately.

The Scriptures are central to our understanding, our character, and our decisions. Therefore, we must give the greatest weight possible to them. Help your students gain this perspective as they watch you handle the Scriptures with reverence and awe.

SPIRITUAL

The "Other Helpful Verses" listed contain much insight about Abraham's place in God's plan of redemption. These verses show that Abraham believed God, and THAT was counted as righteousness before the Law was given. There is much to thoughtfully discuss with your students, if you are willing.

> ## Talk Together

- **Opinion Column**

  — What did you find to be the most interesting aspect, or the most fascinating person, you encountered in your introduction to the rise of civilizations?

  — Why do you think God called Abraham out of Ur?

  — One of the things that sets the Bible apart from other religious books is that it describes people accurately—with all of their failures and faults, as well as their successes. Why do you think the Scriptures tell us that Abraham, a man who deceived two kings, was a friend of God?

  — Think about Abraham and his experiences with God. In your own life, when has it been easy to trust God and when has it been difficult?

- **Critical Puzzling**

  — Noah, his wife, his three sons and their wives were the eight people who survived the devastation of the Flood, so from them descend all of the people of the earth. How should that impact our attitude about other nations, cultures, people groups?

  — What are some of the possible reasons that the archaeological record shows that civilization seems to just "pop" onto the scene?

  — Consider what might have been necessary for humanity to rebuild cities, provide a dependable food supply, reestablish metal working, and any other industries vital for civilization.

  — Read about Nimrod, the great-grandson of Noah, in Genesis 10:8-10. He was a prolific builder of cities. How much of Nimrod's character can be known from the character of the cities he built?

Unit Two: The Rise of Civilizations / 61

INTRO · PG 19

5) Recap (process & review) Activity

In different parts of the room, set up stations for the Eight Intelligences Recap Activities. Then allow students to work alone or together in small groups to accomplish the following suggestions. At the start of the next class, ask for 3-4 groups of volunteers to share. For homeschoolers, rather than set up all eight stations, allow the student(s) to choose which of these activities they would most enjoy, and do that.

Recap Suggestions:

×SPATIAL: Create an advertisement for moving to the city—for the people of ancient times!

BODILY-KINESTHETIC: Set up different sections of a room to represent the stages of Abraham's journeys, and then, as a tour guide, take groups to these geographic locations.

INTERPERSONAL: In groups of 2-3, discuss a current political leader who might be compared to Nimrod.

MUSICAL: In a small group, list four songs, whether secular or Christian, that relate to this unit.

LINGUISTIC: Retell one of the events in this Unit and explain the point of it.

MATH-LOGICAL: Make a list of the areas of human life impacted by the Tower of Babel.

INTRAPERSONAL: Write a short reflection about the historical fact that we are all related.

NATURALIST: Allow outdoor-loving students to go outside and find a place of elevation (on top of stairs, on a tree limb, on a hill). Then have them in groups share what they learned about the "rise" of civilizations.

OR...Activity of Your Choice: What would you like to have your students do for a review activity concerning this week's introduction to the rise of civilizations?

6) Opinion Column and Critical Puzzling answers on their own

Listed on Page 61 of the Student Manual. Students may begin these questions after completing their Recap Activities listed above.

7) Class Discussion

Using the questions listed on Page 61 of the Student Manual to get the students primed, create a discussion environment in the classroom. You may also want to draw from the open-ended questions listed below.

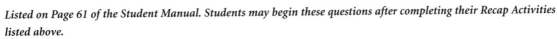

Why do you think early post-Flood people were intent on making a name for themselves in rebellion against God, rather than obeying and bringing glory to Him? How do you see this in evidence today in the cultures around you?

Consider with your students the implication of Matthew 28:19-20 in light of the Tower of Babel. God scattered the languages and the people, and Jesus tells us that now we are to go and make disciples of all the nations. What linguistic and relational challenges face us as we seek to obey this command?

Do you think it was difficult for Abraham to leave Ur? Why or Why not?

INTRO - PG 20

8) Choose books of interest/Internet search

A list of possible books for further reading is listed in the Student Manual beginning on Page 62. Encourage your students to look for books giving a Biblical perspective of ancient cultures, archaeology, cities, and general information about antiquity from this list and from other sources. You may want to gather a selection of further resources prior to beginning Unit Two, or you may encourage the students to be treasure hunters seeking to find them on their own.

The Internet has a wealth of information concerning the rise of civilizations, though the articles available vary widely in dependability, worldview and attitude. Help your students learn to recognize the differences.

For the complete list of books from the Student Manual, refer to the Appendix (pg 307).

> ## ℛemember:
> **Beware of Arrogance, Embrace Humility!**

Phase 1

➢ Reviewed Resources for Digging Deeper:

Choose a few books that look interesting, or find your own.

Biblical Perspective:

After the Flood by Bill Cooper

This is one of the MOST amazing books concerning the truth of the Scriptures! Mr. Cooper spent more than twenty years examining the accuracy of the Table of Nations in Genesis 10, and found the descendants of Ham, Shem and Japheth throughout the pagan king lists—which are the best chroniclers of families and chronologies in the ancient world. One of the watershed books of our time. Highly Recommended! **HS**

The Puzzle of Ancient Man
by Donald E. Chittick

Dr. Chittick has compiled an astonishing selection of OOP Arts (Out Of Place Artifacts) with a thoroughly biblical explanation. Worth searching for! **MS+**

The New Unger's Bible Handbook by Merrill F. Unger, Revised by Gary N. Larson

This book is one of my most-used reference books in the study of ancient history and the Bible. Highly recommended! MS+

Asia: A Christian Perspective
by Mary Ann Lind

Published by YWAM Publishing, this book is filled with information about Asia. Though our main focus in this study guide is the rise of civilization in the Fertile Crescent, Egypt and Greece, there are many other early civilizations found in the archaeological record. What I found particularly helpful about this book was the historical background of some of these civilizations such as India and China. This book tells about the rise of Confucianism, Hinduism, and Buddhism—a significant part of understanding Asian cultures and early Asian civilizations. **MS+**

Strongholds of the 10-40 Window
edited by George Otis, Jr.

Published by YWAM Publishing, this is an intercessor's guide to the world's least evangelized nations. It includes basic facts, historical background, Christian outreach and specific prayer requests from resident Christians. This book will help you turn *head knowledge* to *heart compassion* as you pray for the nations. **MS+**

62 / Unit Two: *The Rise of Civilizations*

Review & Evaluation

EVALUATION

In this Phase of Unit Two, your students should have had the opportunity to explore the rise of civilizations through reading, listening, thinking and discussing. They will have:

1) informally discussed the Key Concepts;
2) read the article;
3) listened to the audio recording(s);
4) read the Scripture listed in Read for Your Life;
5) explored the Recap Activities;
6) completed the Opinion Column and Critical Puzzling answers on their own;
7) participated in Class Discussion;
8) chosen books of interest or searched the Internet.

You may wish to evaluate your students based on their *participation* in the **Class Discussion** and on their participation in the **Recap Activity**.

PHASE 2

The Exploration and Discovery Week

Learning Style Emphasis: THINKER

Students will explore topics of interest through research and reporting, learn new vocabulary, and construct a timeline relating to Genesis 10-25.

Monday-Tuesday:
1) Choose topic and begin research

Wednesday:
2) Vocabulary Practice

Thursday:
3) Construct the Timeline.

Friday:
4) Research projects completed; share in class or hand in.

Teachers can choose to have students do one or two activities, rather than the entire week's schedule. Please use what works for you in your unique setting.

INTRO - PG 21

1) Choose topic and begin research

Allow the students the freedom to choose one of the topics listed on Pages 66-67, or to suggest their own area which they would like to research.

Motivating Suggestions:

Especially for Non-Linguistic students, and those who are not motivated by written or oral reports, here are suggestions for alternative ways of reporting what has been researched.

MOTIVATE

Early Civilizations

1) Make a chart listing the similarities and differences between each of the early civilizations examined during the research (for example, Sumer, Akkad, China, India)

2) To report on the "Rise and Fall of the Sumerian Civilization," use an ascending musical scale—one tone per fact—to sing the major points of the rise of Sumer, and a descending musical scale—one tone per fact—to sing the major points of the fall of Sumer. To envision what this might sound like, consider a liturgical service where the priest sings the words of the liturgy.

3) An artistic student could make masks (such as Greek comedy or tragedy masks) for the Indus Valley, China, and the Fertile Crescent. Use the masks during an oral presentation, or display the masks with written descriptions of these different civilizations.

4 Draw a map of the settling places of the three major groups of descendants of Noah. You might want to consult Josephus for this information.

5) Give a first-person presentation as Abraham, in which you are auditioning for a job as a tour guide of the Middle East. Be sure to include the high points of the beauty, mystery, temperature, and unusual political intrigues one would see if touring the area.

Cities

1) Make a flip-chart to show the structures or systems that every city requires—even the cities of antiquity.

2) To report the size of Nimrod's cities, map out a proportional area (i.e. 10:1 or 100:1, etc.) With the same proportional scale, show the size of a large city, or even a small town in your region, so that others can grasp the relative size of these ancient cities.

Architecture

1) Show photos of the three different structures—the Great Pyramid, the Ziggurat of Ur, and the Pyramid of the Sun in Mexico—and point out to the audience the differences and similarities.

2) Compose a song about one of these structures to a well-known tune.

Archaeology

1) Create a timeline of the Chronology of Archaeology, and show how various discoveries brought about a cause and effect reaction in archaeology.

2) Assemble a selection of items which represent the tools of the archaeologist's trade, and either write a short description of each or give an oral presentation.

PHASE 2

Exploration & Discovery Week

➤ *Research & Reporting*

Your mission, if you choose to accept it, is to explore one of these areas and to discover something significant!

• **Early Civilizations:**

— Find one of the books listed, or a book of your choice, to compare information on early civilizations. Key concerns will be: location, appearance, religion, writings.

— Research and report on the "Rise and Fall of the Sumerian Civilization."

— Research the rise of civilizations in the Indus Valley and China. Compare and contrast these civilizations with the civilizations in the Fertile Crescent.

— Investigate and report on the location of the descendants of Ham, Shem and Japheth.

— Find out about the climate, terrain and political situation of the Fertile Crescent during the time of Abraham. Describe (specifically) the changes in his life and situation after he left Ur for Canaan and Egypt.

• **Cities:**

— Research and report on what structural requirements are necessary in order to build a city. (Water, sewer, residences, roads, etc.) Then consider the technology required to accomplish building those structures.

— Try to discover what archaeologists know about the size of Nimrod's cities. Report your findings.

• **Architecture:**

In the library, or on the Internet, research the Great Pyramid, the Ziggurat of Ur, and the Pyramid of the Sun in Mexico. Report on your findings, answering these questions: What are the similarities between these three structures? What are some possible explanations archaeologists present to explain these similarities?

• **Archaeology:**

— Using the books listed on archaeology, or others you discover, research what archaeologists can determine about a civilization based on the ruins, and what they cannot. Can this tell you anything about the claims of non-Biblical archaeologists that attack the biblical record?

— List all of the tools, supplies, equipment and special needs an archaeology team must assemble before attempting an excavation. To go deeper, you may want to follow the story of an actual archaeological dig, from preparation to discovery.

Bible

1) Make a chart showing the flow of history from Adam to Abraham and Abraham to Jesus using different colors to represent the thread of redemption and the thread of rebellion.

2) Using action movements, show Abraham as both the recipient of God's promise and also as the father of Isaac. God promised to bless all the families of the earth through Abraham, and Isaac was the father of Jacob from whom the Hebrews descend. Abraham is the father of the line through which the Messiah comes—exactly as God had promised!

Culture

1) As a small team, create a newspaper or newsletter which contains the history of the Fertile Crescent from earliest times to the present.

2) Organize a debate which argues the question, "Is Ur preferable to Canaan?"

— The Chronology of Archaeology listed below gives dates and names. Research the events listed and report your findings.

• **Bible:**

In Scripture, discover the position of Abraham in regards to God's plan of redemption. Make a chart showing the flow of redemption from Adam to Abraham, Abraham to Jesus.

• **Culture:**

Investigate the history and culture of the Fertile Crescent from the time of Abraham to the present. Report your findings.

➤ *Brain Stretchers*

• **Genetics:**

Contact Institute for Creation Research to request information about the genetic and statistical explanation for the differences between people groups. Compare this to a secular evolutionary explanation. Report on your discoveries.

• **Early Travel:**

Look in the library for the books by Thor Heyerdahl, especially *Ra*. Report your findings on his theories of the ability of ancient people to travel across the earth. Compare his theories with Creationists, and notate the similarities and differences.

• **Language:**

Research the major language "families." Make a chart showing these language groups and their location in the world. What can you learn from this about the possible source, relationship, spread, and development of languages? You may want to consider investigating how this effects Bible translation work.

• **Mathematics:**

Discover the level of mathematical proficiency in early civilizations. (Consider: What was used for money? for calculating? for astronomy? An interesting place to start would be to trace the concept of "zero.")

Did you know?
During the excavation of Ur, a clay tablet was discovered with a mathematical theorem very similar to the Pythagorean theorem? Check it out!

Create Your Own Research Topic:

_____
_____
_____

Brain Stretchers:

Brain Stretchers, listed on page 67, are intended for advanced students. Those who attempt the Brain Stretchers for their Research and Reporting can use the above list for ideas on how to report their findings.

2) Words To Watch - Vocabulary Practice

Listed on Page 68. You may find other words in this unit that are especially appropriate for younger children. Feel free to substitute another vocabulary list for the one provided.

Phase 2

➤ Words to Watch

Remember—The easiest way to learn a subject is to master its terms:

Fertile Crescent	dispersion	archaeology
antiquity	clay tablet	babble
engineering	Ur	excavation
Tower of Babel	architecture	nation
Sumer	ziggurat	people group
civilization	cuneiform	protolanguage

TEACHER TIP

Here is one idea for making vocabulary study interesting and fun: *Set up a vocabulary relay race: two players per team, one says the word while the other looks it up and reads the definition. As soon as they finish one word, they move on to the next, switching roles. The first team to finish the race wins.*

3) Construct the Timeline.

The *Chronology of Archaeology,* found on Page 69, was compiled to give students a quick overview of some of the most significant archaeologists and their discoveries. You might discuss with your students the relative newness of the science of archaeology, the most significant discoveries in light of Scripture, and the current need for Biblical archaeologists.

Read the information listed with the "Key Dates" on Page 71. Dialogue with your students about the issues involved. Help them recognize that dating antiquity is not an exact science. For ease of reference, the timeline is included in the Appendix on Page 310.

➤ Chronology of Archaeology

Date	Name	Place
1760's	Karsten Niebuhr	Persepolis—Brought back bricks with cuneiform—His book was what Napoleon used on his trip to Egypt
1798	Napoleon/Denon	Egypt—First drawings of Upper & Lower Nile Dhautpoul—found Rosetta Stone, hieroglyphs
1802	Denon	Book Published
1802	Grotefend	German school teacher, first to understand how to decipher cuneiform
1821	Champollion	French scholar, deciphered Rosetta Stone
1837	Henry Rawlinson	English soldier, copied Behistun inscriptions
1843	" "	Translates inscriptions (Old Persian, Babylonian, Elamite)
1843–46	Paul Emile Botta	French consul, first to discover Assyria—Khorsabad, palace of Sargon II
1845+	Austen Layard	British (French born) adventurer, excavated Nimrud (biblical Calah)
1849+	" "	Uncovers Nineveh (Father of Assyriology)
1868+	Heinrich Schliemann	Uncovered Troy (against all odds)
1876+	" "	Excavated Mycenae (Agamemnon?—Opposed Troy)
1899-1913	Robert Koldewey	Excavated Babylon, discovered Ishtar Gate, walls of Babylon, Hanging Gardens, and perhaps the Tower of Babel
1900-26	Sir Arthur Evans	British, uncovered Minoan civilization (predecessor to Mycenaean civ.) - Palace of Knossos
1927+	Leonard Wooley	Excavated Ur of Abram
1964	Paolo Matthiae	Excavated Ebla (contemporary civilization of Sumer and Egypt)

Find the dates for the key people and events listed. In this unit, there will be some choices for dates for Abraham, based on the interpretation of Galatians 3:17, Genesis 15:13, and Exodus 12:40. Scholars who interpret the Old Testament scripture references through Galatians 3:17, believe that the Exodus 12:40 description of four hundred thirty years refers not only to the time spent by the Hebrews in Egypt, but to all the years from the moment God spoke His promise to Abraham until the Hebrews received God's Law at Mt. Sinai. As we will see in the unit on Egypt, this greatly affects the determination of which Pharaoh was drowned in the Red Sea during the Exodus. Student's may choose to:

• Take the date listed in their Bible;
• Take the date listed in Bishop Ussher's chronology;
• Take the date listed in a resource book they are using;
• Notate two different possibilities on their timeline, showing which Scripture is used as the source;
• Have a debate in class about why one date should be chosen over another date (very good for developing critical thinking skills!).

INTRO-PG 22

4) *Research projects shared in class and/or turned in.*

Create a safe environment for the presentations. Set ground rules prior to the presentations for all the students, so that they know each one will be honored and respected in their work by all those observing.

EVALUATION | ## Review & Evaluation

In this Phase of Unit Two, your students should have had the opportunity to explore the rise of civilizations through researching, thinking, and reporting. They will have:

1) done a research project;
2) learned the vocabulary;
3) constructed a Timeline;
4) created a project report on what was researched.

You may wish to evaluate your students based on their *efforts* in the **Research and Reporting** projects and their active participation in the **Vocabulary** and **Timeline** exercises.

Learning Style Emphasis: Sensor

Students will gain cultural understanding through sensory activities as they explore interrelated subject areas relating to Genesis 10-25.

Monday:
1) Create a map and discuss the issues in teams.

Tuesday:
2) Examine and discuss art masterpieces & architectural structures.

Wednesday:
3) Arts in Action—Do an art project.*

Thursday:
4) Do one science project or field trip.**

Friday:
5) Listen to and discuss the music.
6) Cook the food listed in the recipe, if desired.

*Art project will need to be planned ahead of time to acquire materials.
**Field trip will require extra planning time.

Teachers can choose to have students do one or two activities, rather than the entire week's schedule. Please use what works for you in your unique setting.

1) Create a map and discuss the issues in teams

The students each have an outline map on Page 73. They will be given assignments for drawing in rivers, mountains, cities, and regional boundaries, which are listed on Page 72. For details on where these things are, please consult a historical atlas, an encyclopedia, a study Bible, or any other source for geographic information. For ease of reference, the map is included in the Appendix on Page 311.

Upper elementary students might be satisfied to accomplish only this portion:

- *Physical terrain:* This part of the mapping exercise will help students locate and mark the geological dynamics of a region.

Middle school students might be satisfied to complete both the previous mapping exercise and this exercise:

- *Geo-Political:* This section of the mapping exercise will provide the students an opportunity to locate and mark the cities, nations and empires of history. It will require more digging, as this information may not be listed on current maps. For example, cities of Ninevah, Nimrud and Babylon are all ancient cities rather than contemporary cities.

TEACHER TIP

Encourage them to think for themselves, rather than parroting back information.

High school students might be satisfied to complete both the previous mapping exercises and at least one exploration topic of this exercise:

· *Explore:* Discuss some selection from this portion of the mapping exercise in teams.

QUESTION

Christian Outreach to countries in the Fertile Crescent.

If it is possible to either read a short biography of a missionary to Muslim lands, or to actually interview someone who serves the Lord in that region, students will be given realistic understanding of the issues involved.

QUESTION

Limited Archaeological Access in Bible Lands

Discuss with the students some of the issues related to the limited access archaeologists have in Muslim countries—particularly biblical archaeologists. Brainstorm with them possible means for opening some of these doors.

PHASE 3

The Hands-On Week

≫ *Maps and mapping*

· **Physical Terrain:**

— Label and color the Tigris and Euphrates rivers on the outline map.

— Color the Fertile Crescent.

— Draw in and color the mountain ranges.

— Look in a resource book to discover the areas which are desert and the areas which are fertile, and color them appropriately on your map.

· **Geo-Political:**

— Place Nineveh, Nimrud and Babylon on the map.

— What countries (both ancient and modern) are they located in?

— Draw the boundaries of Sumer (Mesopotamia), Egypt and Canaan on your map.

— What is the name of the country or countries that today occupy the same area as Sumer and Canaan?

— Mark the city of Ur.

— Trace Abraham's route from Ur to Egypt to Palestine.

· **Explore:**

· *Christian Outreach to countries in the Fertile Crescent:* What is the status of Christian outreach to these countries in the Middle East? Discuss the difficulties facing Christians seeking to serve God in these nations; brainstorm creative ways of overcoming these difficulties.

· *Limited Archaeological access in Bible Lands:* Discover the challenges which face archaeologists, especially Biblical archaeologists, in these countries, and then consider the impact this limited or restricted access has on our understanding of these ancient lands.

SPIRITUAL

Consider committing with your students to pray for either a specific people group or a specific missionary in the Fertile Crescent. You may want to actually keep a prayer journal to remember what is prayed, so that you can rejoice exceedingly as you see the specific ways God answers these prayers.

2) *Examine and discuss art masterpieces & architectural structures*

INTRO - PG 23

Locate either a copy of these art forms, or Internet sites for each of the items listed on Pages 74-75. Allow the students time to observe the art without any conversation, and then, when they are ready, engage them in some or all of the questions listed in the Student Manual or below.

Tower of Babel *by Pieter Bruegel, the Elder*

The Flemish Bruegel painters are known for their evocative style of painting.

QUESTION

- Give the students adequate time to look at this painting, and then engage them in discussion about how the Tower of Babel was portrayed.

The royal headdress of Queen Pu-Abi of Ur (displayed in the British Museum)

- Discuss with your students the level of artistry, beauty and elegance which this piece displays.
- Ask them if they find it incongruent that such an object of beauty would have come from a godless culture.

QUESTION

What other examples can the students think of that show this kind of juxtaposition of beauty and horror?

Phase 3

> *Consider:*
>
> Pieter Bruegel The Elder (circa 1530-1569 A.D.) was a Flemish painter who lived during the time of the Spanish war against the Netherlands. He was among the first artists to paint with an appreciation of landscape.

➤ Art Appreciation

- **Tower of Babel** *by Pieter Bruegel, the Elder*

Consider and discuss:

— Does the painting reflect what the Bible describes?

— How does the painting differ from your own impression of this event?

— How does Bruegel's painting reflect his own time period rather than antiquity?

- **The royal headdress of Queen Pu-Abi of Ur** *(displayed in the British Museum)*

— What does this show you about the culture of Ur?

— How does it display the craftsmanship of the time?

- *Leonard Wooley found this amazing piece of jewelry while excavating the royal burial grounds in Ur.*

- **The Royal Standard of Ur** *(displayed in the British Museum)*

— What activities are shown on the Standard of Ur?

— What facial expressions do you notice on the people?

- *Archaeological digs have brought to light beautiful ancient mosaics made from colored tiles, such as this one discovered in Ur.*

The Royal Standard of Ur (displayed in the British Museum)

QUESTION

This mosaic, which was found in pieces in the archaeological dig at Ur, is an amazing piece of art. If you look closely, you can see different expressions on the faces of the people!

- Talk with your students about what they observe in this mosaic. What are the people doing? How does this give a better idea of what day to day life was like in Ur?

The Ziggurat of Ur—Architecture

- How would your students describe this building? What similarities do they see between the ziggurat and a pyramid of Egypt? What are the differences? Do they have any ideas about why there are such similarities?

QUESTION

INTRO - PG 23

3) Arts in Action

Listed on Pages 75-76.

TEACHER TIP

Imitation

- Have the students look again at Bruegel's painting. Then, with art supplies of colored pencils, pastels, or paint, try to recreate some aspect of Bruegel's work.
- Have the students observe the details of how the people, animals, clothing, and other items are depicted in the Standard of Ur. Then, with art supplies of colored pencils, pastels, or paint, create a similar approach, with modern people, animals, clothing and other items for a Standard of... (the students' own hometown).

Mosaics

Students may choose to create a mosaic in the style of the Standard of Ur, or they may use their imaginations. There is a tremendous variety of materials which could be used for this project—the most magnificent being inexpensive tiles which are broken and then fitted together (and held together with a tile glue) on a wooden board as a mosaic.

Clay Pots

Clay pots are among the most common items found in archaeological digs. It makes sense when you consider that everyone has always needed some way to hold food and drink items. Clay pots can range from the simplest crude form to elaborately decorated and molded structures. Encourage your students to attempt whatever style of clay pot most appeals to them.

Phase 3

➢ Architecture

When the earliest cities in Mesopotamia, such us Uruk and Ur, were built, the buildings were constructed with the local materials available to the builders—mud, sometimes mixed with straw. From these mud bricks, temples, palaces, houses, and city walls were built. Unfortunately, mud bricks don't last as long as other building materials, so archaeologists have had to try to envision the design of ancient cities and their architecture. One of the most prominent features of these ancient Mesopotamian cities is the ziggurat, or temple tower. Ziggurats were pyramid-like, stepped structures, with the actual temple on a platform at the very top. Their architects used the technique of slightly curving the walls, so that the tall structures would not appear top heavy.

— Look for a photo of the reconstruction of the Ziggurat of Ur, as well as artists' renditions. How would you describe this building?

➢ Arts in Action

Select one, and let your artistic juices flow!

- **Imitation:**
  — try your hand at imitating Bruegel (trace, follow colors, etc.)

  — create your own Standard, like the Standard of Ur

- **Architecture:**
  Construct a small city from Legos, cardboard, etc. Where are the utilities? the parks? the transportation routes, the city/government center, the homes, the places of worship?

- **Mosaics:**
  There are many different kinds of materials to choose from in making mosaics. For this project you can make a mosaic using bits of colored paper or tiles glued to wood. Start with an outline for your design, then glue the pieces of paper within the outline. Check out the library for more information on how to create this art form.

Unit Two: The Rise of Civilizations / 75

FASCINATING FACT:

A book from the British Museum about Mesopotamia contains this fascinating tidbit: there were evidently cheap, throw-away pots used by laborers in Mesopotamia in ancient times. Archaeologists believe they were a one-use pot since they are so incredibly common—and they may have even be "manufactured" in a factory-style setting!

- **Clay Pots:**

  Find a book or an expert who can get you started with the simplest method—the coil pot. You will need a fair amount of clay for this project, depending on the size of your pot. You could also consider using Playdough.

- **Jewelry:**

  Try your hand at making ornate jewelry, in the style of the Sumerians. You might construct a headdress, arm bands, necklaces, or earrings. Check the library for a how-to book.

➢ Science

Archaeologists who excavated the ancient cities of Mesopotamia found that many sites had been continuously occupied for thousands of years. They discovered this by examining the artifacts found in the different layers, or strata, of earth. This allows them to separate and date the various artifacts to the proper time period.

- **Try this:**

  — Carefully dig a hole outside at least twelve inches deep by eight inches wide. The deeper you go, the more layers you may find. Examine the layers which are revealed in the hole. Do you see a difference in color and texture of the dirt? Measure the depth of each layer and record this in a notebook. How many layers did you find?

➢ Music

Though evolutionists believe that the advanced technology and complexity needed for musical instruments would require music to develop long after earliest man, the archaeological record does not show this. In fact, exquisite harps were discovered in the royal tombs of Ur, and archaeologists now know that there were also drums and double reed instruments in this early civilization.

Jewelry

The elaborate style of jewelry worn by the royal Sumerians can be a model for this project. Encourage the students to have lots of hoops, bangles, coins, etc. They may want to spray their jewelry with gold paint.

Architecture

Fashioning a small city with one's own hands can be an eye-opening learning situation. The student who attempts this project will suddenly be confronted with a myriad of decisions, and will better appreciate the technological know-how required of the early city builders.

4) Do a science project

INTRO - PG 24

Listed on Page 76. If students love science, they might want to consider doing all of them!

Archaeological Dig

The term used by archaeologists to describe the different layers of earth is stratigraphy. Archaeologists actually have a standardized chart for identifying the stratigraphy of a dig, which is called the Munsell Color Chart. This chart gives a uniform system for labeling soil colors all over the world. Check with your students to see if they carefully measured the depth of each layer and recorded it in a notebook. This is one of the first steps to a thorough, careful archaeological dig.

5) Listen to and discuss the music

Listed on Page 76-77.

Listen

Listen to a selection or a variety of selections of harp music. Afterwards, have the students talk about what they heard. What words describe the music? The harp has a unique and distinctive sound. Did the students enjoy the sound? How difficult would it be to learn to play the harp? If anyone knows a harpist, perhaps extend an invitation to perform or be interviewed to share with the class what is involved in learning to play the harp.

TEACHER TIP

Try this: Making a simple instrument can range from a comb kazoo to a washtub bass. If students are stymied by the possibilities, they could try blowing into pop bottles with varying amounts of liquid. Notice how the different levels create different tones. For the adventurous, try joining a small group of pop bottle players into an orchestra and playing a simple tune together.

- **Listen:**

  — There are many types of harp music available. Listen to a selection of different styles, such as Celtic, classical, and folk. As you listen, consider the level of difficulty in playing this ancient instrument. Does this show you anything about early man in post-Flood times?

- **Try this:**

  — Find a book in the library (or an instrument maker) that can show you how to construct a simple instrument: a drum, a bamboo flute, a whistle, a harp.

➢ Cooking

The Fertile Crescent was a remarkably productive area for crops. Located between the two great rivers, the Tigris and Euphrates, the Fertile Crescent was occasionally flooded, which brought rich, wonderful soil for the farmers. Here is a recipe that is typical of Middle East cooking.

- **Lentils with tomatoes**

1 cup brown lentils	1 tsp ground cumin
2 tbsp. oil	1/2 cup beef broth
1 large onion, minced	4 tomatoes, peeled and chopped
2 cloves garlic, minced	Salt & pepper

Soak lentils in cold water for 3 hours. Drain, then place lentils in pot of boiling salted water and cook over medium heat 30 min. Drain, reserve. Heat oil in large saucepan. Add onions and garlic, sauté about 5 minutes. Stirring constantly, add cumin and cook over high heat for 2 minutes. Add broth and lentils. Mix, then simmer, uncovered, over low heat until lentils are almost tender (15 minutes.) Stir in tomatoes and season. Continue simmering until tomatoes are tender, about 15 minutes. Serve immediately. Serves 4.

---

6) Cook the food

Listed on Page 77.

Lentils are among the fastest legumes to prepare—fast food for the ancients, if you will. Ask your students how the taste of this dish compares to their favorite fast food.

TEACHER TIP

Review & Evaluation

EVALUATION

In this third Phase of Unit Two, your students should have had the opportunity to explore the Rise of Civilizations through various hands-on and creative sessions. They will have:

1) completed a Mapping section;
2) observed and discussed Art & Architecture;
3) worked on an art project;
4) experimented with a Science Project or taken a field trip;
5) listened to music;
6) tasted a food related to this unit

You may wish to evaluate your students based on their *class participation* in these **Hands-on** activities.

PHASE 4

The Expression Week

Learning Style Emphasis: *Intuitor*

Students, through creative self-expression, using one or more creative activities, will present some aspect of what they have learned in the past three weeks relating to the Rise of Civilizations. Areas of expression include linguistics, art, music, drama, movement and conceptual design.

Monday - Thursday

1) Choose area of expression and begin work either individually or in teams.

Friday

2) Share creative expressions in class.

Teachers can choose to have students do one or two activities, rather than the entire week's schedule. Please use what works for you in your unique setting.

INTRO - PG 25

1) Choose area of expression and begin work either individually or in teams

Linguistics:

Listed on page 78.

TEACHER TIP

Playing With Words

Help students find some examples of words or phrases in various languages.

Journalism

Have the students who wish to write a journalistic piece look at several articles in newspapers and/or magazines to understand the framework for journalism. Encourage them to be as wildly imaginative as they wish to be, as long as they convey something of what has been learned in the unit.

Prose

• If a student wishes to write a short story, several short stories should be examined to gain an understanding of how long to make it, how to develop the story, and possible ways to capture the interest of the readers.

• Pretending to write a letter home can provide an informal approach to writing about what the student has learned. Encourage them to include the sorts of personal details that would be included in this sort of letter.

PHASE 4

The Expression Week

➤ *In Your Own Way . . .*

In this unit we have seen another major rebellion of mankind against God, the divine judgment which scattered people across the globe, and the resulting rise of civilizations in the archaeological record. We have also considered the reality of Abraham's time and his life in God's plan of redemption. Now, choose a selection of these activities, or create your own, which will best express what was most significant to you.

Linguistics:

• **Playing with Words:**

Have each student learn a few words in a separate foreign language, or create your own language (such as "grunt-grunt," gibberish, a tonal language, or a clicking language)—then try to communicate using these words that no one else understands! (A very small taste of the confusion at the Tower of Babel.)

• **Journalism:**

At the Tower of Babel, what would have been the impact of the sudden emergence of many different languages? Be a newspaper reporter at the Tower just after God confused the languages. Write the fast-breaking story!

• **Prose:**

— Write a short story about the farewell party in Ur for Abraham's family.

— You are on the archaeological team working with Leonard Wooley in 1922. Write a letter home to your church family describing the discovery of Abraham's hometown.

• **Poetry:**

Write a rhyming Ode to Archaeology. You could imitate Joyce Kilmer's famous poem,

*"I think that I shall never see
A poem lovely as a tree..."*

• **Script Writing:**

Write a "then and now" skit: Abraham leaves Ur while Leonard Wooley discovers Ur.

Poetry

TEACHER TIP

Encourage students to read some rhyming poems, especially the poem mentioned in the Student Manual. The poems could be either serious or comical.

Script Writing

The most difficult challenge of script writing is to create believable dialogue. Encourage the students to speak the lines out loud, and to work diligently until the lines sound natural and believable.

Art:

Located on page 79.

Painting/Drawing

TEACHER TIP

We have examined many aspects of the rise of civilizations. Students who wish to create a collage will have a wealth of images to draw from—the Ziggurat of Ur, the Tower of Babel, the scattering of the people, the three sons of Noah and their descendants, etc.

Graphic Design

Have students create an exciting poster to advertise the upcoming skit, "Then & Now."

Political Cartooning

Have students consider the facial expressions, the hurried actions, the abandoned tools and houses, the hasty departures from the Tower of Babel.

Sculpting

With the information about the separation into geographic locations of the three sons of Noah, have the sculptor create a piece which artistically informs the audience.

Music:

Located on page 79.

Compose

Students could form teams to compose and perform a song, or do this selection on their own. We have found that humor in music makes up for a lack of tunefulness!

Performance Practice

For musical students, this selection is a wonderful opportunity to express what they have learned. Make sure they have adequate time to prepare the piece they have selected.

Art:

- **Painting/Drawing:**

  Create a collage style drawing of your impressions of the people and events of this unit.

- **Graphic Design:**

  Design the poster for the "then and now" skit.

- **Cartooning:**

  Make a political cartoon showing the unanticipated results at the building of the Tower of Babel.

- **Sculpting:**

  Make a sculpture showing the separation of the three sons of Noah into their geographic locations.

Music:

- **Compose:**

  — Compose an original song entitled, "To Ur is Human; To Leave, Divine"

  — Write new lyrics to the tune of "Camptown Races" about Nimrod's rebellious cities. You could start like this:

  "Nimrod built a city wrong,
  doo dah, doo dah,
  Founded it on being strong,
  oh doo dah day..."

  Another option would be to use a familiar Beatle's tune.

- **Performance Practice:**

  If you are familiar with harps, prepare a short demonstration of the technical requirements for this instrument, referencing the discovery of harps in the burial pits of Ur in order to show the high level of advancement this discovery indicates.

Drama:

Located on page 80.

Comedy

- Think about what kind of things might be found in a garbage pit, even an old one. Then create a skit showing what the archaeologists find, and their pithy comments.
- To create the "Then and Now" skit, you might consider setting two separate stages, and intersperse the events and dialogues of one stage with the second stage.

Phase 4

Drama:

- **Comedy:**
  — Do a humorous skit about archaeologists sifting through a garbage dump that is 4,000 years old.

  — Act out the "then and now" skit listed above.

- **Tragedy:**
  Portray the imaginary story of Abram's best friend, Elimech, who would not leave his beloved Ur to travel to an unknown land on the word of an unseen God.

- **Puppetry:**
  Put on a puppet show describing Abraham and Sarah's adventures. Consider the age level of your audience as you decide which scenes to show.

Tragedy

If God told you to leave your home and travel to a distant land, how hard would it be to leave the people you love? Consider that carefully, then write the drama of Elimech who chose not to go with Abraham.

Puppetry

Abraham and Sarah had many different kinds of adventures, including leaving their homeland, settling in Canaan, traveling to Egypt (where Sarah was thought to be Abraham's sister), dividing land with Lot, rescuing Lot, witnessing the destruction of Sodom and Gomorrah, being told by God that they were going to have a baby long after child-bearing years, and more. Choose the ones you enjoy the most, or would be most easily staged with puppets.

Movement:

Located on page 81.

Pantomime

Leonard Wooley captivated the world with his reports of the biblical city of Ur. He was entranced at seeing this time period and this historic city come alive.

Dance

A dance of the Tower of Babel will necessitate confusion and dismay. Since the music will need to allow for the orderly progress of building and then transition to the confusion and wild scenes which occur after God confuses the language, students may choose either a single piece of music which allows this transition, or find two recordings and combine them.

Action

Dividing the earth could be either the separation of the continents, or the surveying and dividing the land for irrigation purposes.

TEACHER TIP

Conceptual Design:

Located on page 81.

Design-A-Tool

This is a time to let your imagination run wild. Will you create a simple tool or an incredibly complex one? Will it fit into your pocket or be the size of a truck? Will it be usable without power or will a power source be required? The student's idea could be a drawing, a cobbled together assortment of household items, a computer designed graphic, a Power Point presentation. The sky's the limit!

Phase 4

Movement:

• **Pantomime:**

Act out the discovery of Ur in 1922 without benefit of words. Be sure to show Mr. Wooley's excitement when he discovers it!

• **Dance:**

Find a piece of music which communicates the confusion of the Tower of Babel and create a dance showing the breakdown of languages and the division of people.

• **Action:**

Divide the earth as in the days of Peleg. You can choose your own interpretation of what "divide" means in this case.

Conceptual Design:

• **Design-A-Tool**

With what you have learned about archaeology in this unit, design a tool (on the drawing board) which would make life a lot easier for the archaeologist in the field.

Create Your Own Expression:

INTRO - PG 26

2) Share creative expressions in class.

The same rules apply as suggested in the reporting section of Phase Two.

EVALUATION ## Review & Evaluation

In this final Phase of Unit Two, your students should have had the opportunity to express what they have learned about the rise of civilizations through one or more various creative selections of their own choosing. These include:

1) Linguistics;
2) Art;
3) Music;
4) Drama;
5) Movement;
6) Conceptual Design.

You may wish to evaluate your students based on their *effort* in the **Creative Expressions**, either as individuals or in teams.

Teacher's Guide
EGYPT & THE EXODUS

The Sphinx

Enthusiasm and delight are the best way to capture a student's interest and jump-start motivation, so:

Pray with the students at the beginning of each unit.

1) **For the Auditory Students:** Consider playing dramatic music, such as, one of the songs from the soundtrack of **Prince of Egypt,** to capture their attention at the very beginning of class;

2) **For the Kinesthetic Students:** Have the students warm up as class begins by doing some active movement that is fun (try doing a mirror exercise—in groups of two, facing one another, one leads the action and the other follows, then switch leaders);

3) **For the Visual Students:** Bring a visual object to stimulate their interest in the new unit, like a photo of the Great Pyramid;

4) **For the hearts of all:** Pray with them at the beginning of the unit, that God would help them discover what He has for each one to learn in that unit.

PHASE 1

The Introduction Week

Learning Style Emphasis: *Feeler*

Students will be introduced to Genesis 39-50, the book of Exodus, and the history of ancient Egypt. You may follow this suggested schedule or adapt it to meet your students' needs.

Monday:
1) Informally discuss the Key Concepts

Tuesday:
2) Read the article
3) Listen to the audio recording(s)
4) Read the Scripture listed in Read For Your Life

Wednesday:
5) Recap Activity
6) Opinion Column and Critical Puzzling answers on their own

Thursday:
7) Class Discussion

Friday:
8) Choose books of interest/Internet search

> *Teachers can choose to have students do one or two activities, rather than the entire week's schedule. Please use what works for you in your unique setting.*

INTRO - PG 18

1) Informally Discuss the Key Concepts

Listed in the Student Manual on Page 83.

KEY CONCEPTS BACKGROUND INFORMATION

These are the main objectives of the unit. As you proceed through the four weeks, your students will be given various ways of understanding each of these objectives.

Ancient Egypt & God's plan—EXPLANATION

TEACHER TIP

> To get an informal discussion started on this key concept, ask a simple, leading question, such as, *"What do you know about ancient Egypt that would give a clue about God's purposes for it?"*

Often students are taught about ancient Egypt from a viewpoint which does not include the God of the Bible. They learn about mummies, pyramids, divine cats, pharaohs, the cycle of the Nile, Egyptian tomb painting, etc. These are all part of understanding the culture of ancient Egypt, but they do not give us insight into Egypt's true place in history. It is only as we gain God's perspective, through the Scriptures, that we begin to understand how Egypt was designed to function as a nation, and how far they fell from that design at the time of Moses. It is critical to give our students the understanding of Egypt as a place of refuge (Abraham, the sons of Jacob, Joseph with Mary and baby Jesus), and the way that it became a place of enslavement (the Hebrew people up to Moses). As the Egyptians became mighty, as the pharaohs became rich and powerful (thanks in part to Joseph's management), they became proud of heart, which has devastating consequences, according to Scripture (Proverbs 16:18).

One thing to remember is that Scripture indicates that there were non-Hebrews that came out of Egypt at the time of the Exodus (Exodus 12:38). Were some of these people Egyptians who had been convinced of the reality of the God of the Hebrews and chose to follow Him? Were there others who remained in Egypt yet became believers in this all-powerful God? It is interesting to consider that Akenaton, the Pharaoh who removed all the other Egyptian deities except for the god of the Sun, went against all the religious systems of his culture. Was his departure from the norm a trickle-down effect of the Exodus? No one knows for sure, but it may give some clues to the impact made upon the Egyptians by the plagues and the Exodus.

EGYPT & THE EXODUS

UNIT
3

The Sphinx

Let my people go...

"Go and gather the elders of Israel together, and say to them, 'The Lord God of your fathers, the God of Abraham, of Isaac, and of Jacob, appeared to me, saying, "I have surely visited you and seen what is done to you in Egypt; and I have said I will bring you up out of the affliction of Egypt to the land of the Canaanites and the Hittites and the Amorites and the Perizzites and the Hivites and the Jebusites, to a land flowing with milk and honey." Exodus 3:16-17

KEY CONCEPTS:

• **Ancient Egypt & God's plan**

• **Joseph's life**

• **Moses & The Exodus**

• **Possible routes**

Unit Three: *Egypt & the Exodus* / 83

This article can be found in its entirety in the Appendix (see pg 312).

Prayerfully share with your students the importance of a nation walking humbly before God. We can learn much from the example of ancient Egypt regarding the effects upon nations when leaders fail to heed the voice of God, and the need for God's people to beseech Him on behalf of our nations (2 Chronicles 7:14). This truth can transform our nations, but only as we humble ourselves before Him. Perhaps your students will be inspired to begin praying faithfully for the leaders of their nation, and seeking God for His merciful transformation of the culture.

Joseph's life—EXPLANATION

To get an informal discussion started on this key concept, ask a simple, leading question, such as, *"What do you know about Joseph's life?"*

Students may know the story of Joseph's life from Bible story books, from musicals, from Sunday school. He is often held up as a model of good character traits and qualities, as well he should be. However, that can reduce him from being an actual human man living in a real moment of history to a fairy tale kind of character, like Rumplestiltskin. It is, therefore, important to engage the students in a discussion of the reality of what Joseph went through in his lifetime, particularly so that the glory of God becomes evident.

We also miss, at times, that Joseph became the second most important man in the most powerful nation of the time. Having the power of Pharaoh to enact legislation, the responsibility of providing food for an entire nation (plus all those who would come begging), and the necessity of building and overseeing the granaries of the cities were all part of his job description. Help the students to consider what it would be like to be the second most powerful political leader in one of the strongest nations of the world. That will help them comprehend Joseph's place in history.

Joseph faced such incredible difficulties and disappointments in his life, but God used them for good. Pray for your students, that they will discover God's faithfulness and His ability to work all things together for good in their lives as they follow Him (Romans 8:28).

The Exodus—EXPLANATION

To get an informal discussion started on this key concept, ask a simple, leading question, such as, *"What happened during the Exodus?"*

The Exodus as an historic event is one of those issues which separates Bible-believing students from secular, since secular historians and archaeologists deny that it ever happened. They say that there is no evidence in the Egyptian writings nor in the archaeological records. In visiting most museums, especially in the U.S., you will discover a presupposition that the Hebrews did not even exist in the archaeological record of Egypt and Palestine until much later than the Bible indicates, and if they were ever in Egypt, they drifted out peacefully without any commotion or any particular archaeological evidence. What do we do with this? I believe that we must not ignore it! Instead, we must answer it thoughtfully and carefully, much as creationists do in discussions with evolutionists.

Therefore, in this unit, students will have in the article an opportunity to read about the work of David Rohl, who is suggesting one of the best answers to the questions raised. He has challenged the conventional dates of the Egyptian chronologies through suggesting that, on many occasions, more than one pharaoh was ruling in Egypt (sometimes as many as four). This shrinks the traditional Egyptian chronology by more than three hundred years and allows archaeologists and Egyptologists to search for clues of the Hebrew presence in Egypt much earlier than previously recognized. And, as we might expect, there is a tremendous amount of evidence for the presence of the Hebrews, both in Egypt and in Palestine, during the revised time frame given by Rohl.

Though we will examine the Hebrew presence in Palestine more in depth in the next chapter, suffice it to say that there are issues raised about the Exodus by archaeology, and there are answers now being discovered, which verify the veracity and validity of the Biblical record.

Help your students to gain a heart perspective on the Exodus far beyond a mere mental understanding of the facts and figures which would allow them to converse knowledgeably with nonbelievers. Instead, pray that, through examining this historic event, they receive a revelation of God's goodness and His ability to deliver His people out of bondage. As they grasp the reality of this, it will change their lives and enable them to trust God in a much deeper way. He really does hear our cry!

SPIRITUAL

Possible Routes—EXPLANATION

TEACHER TIP

To get an informal discussion started on this key concept, ask a simple, leading question, such as, *"What does the Bible tell us about where God parted the waters during the Exodus?"*

PHASE 1

KEY PEOPLE:

Menes
— First Pharaoh to unite Egypt

Khufu (Cheops) 2700-2200 BC
— The Great Pyramid was built for his tomb

Hatshepsut
— The best known woman pharaoh

Tutankhamen 1333 BC
— His tomb was found intact

Rameses II 1304-1237 BC
— Fought the Hittites at Battle of Kadesh

Joseph 1745 BC
— Hebrew vizier of Egypt

Moses 1525-1270 BC
— Leader of the Hebrews

➤ Listen to This

• **What in the World's Going On Here? Volume One**

— Egypt & The Exodus

• **True Tales From the Times of…Ancient Civilizations & The Bible**

— The Rosetta Stone

• **More True Tales From The Times of…Ancient Civilizations & The Bible**

— The interview with Bob Cornuke about his search for the real Mt. Sinai

— The Seven Wonders of the Ancient World (short version)

• **An In-Depth Study of…The Sevens Wonders**

— The Great Pyramid

➤ Read for Your Life

• **The Holy Bible**

— The Main Story: Genesis 39–50, Exodus 1–15, Acts 7:1-38 (the short version of the story)

— Helpful Verses: Deuteronomy 32:1-12; Psalms 66, 78, 95, 136; Isaiah 19, Ezekiel 29-32; Hebrew 11:8-29

Key People:

The people listed in this column are the main characters, if you will, of this unit. They are listed in the Student Manual, along with a brief identifier, so that the students can familiarize themselves with these people.

The traditional route of the Exodus takes the Hebrews to the Sinai Peninsula, to receive the Ten Commandments at Mt. Sinai and to wander forty years in the wilderness of the Sinai. It was accepted that they crossed the Red Sea in this endeavor. In the last century, a new idea was circulated which said that the Hebrews went through the Sea of Reeds instead of the Red Sea. (There are some difficulties with the translation and the original language, but it is not necessarily solved through use of "Sea of Reeds.") Most of the scholars promoting this notion believe that the Sea of Reeds was actually the Bitter Lakes region of Egypt. There are several problems with this view, not the least of which is that the Bitter Lakes does not fit the Biblical description of the Exodus. However, those holding to this view tend to not accept the Bible as 100% historically accurate, so it has not been an issue for them.

For those who believe that the Bible is, in fact, absolutely correct in what it states, there are some other options than the Sea of Reeds. Though there is tremendous controversy on all sides of the issue, there are some researchers with compelling evidence who believe that the Hebrews traveled down the west side of the Sinai Peninsula (the "desert road"), crossed over into Arabia on a land bridge normally under shallow water near the southernmost point of the Peninsula, and went on to receive the Ten Commandments at a mountain inside of Saudi Arabia. It is valuable, again, for older students to be made aware of the possibilities, the evidences, and the problems of each point of view. They can then make an informed decision about what they believe. The main point is that the Hebrews did, in fact, flee Egypt, the Egyptian army followed hard on their heels, the Red Sea parted, the Hebrews were saved, and the Egyptian army drowned. Beyond that, students have the opportunity to become detectives piecing together the best clues to determine where it actually occurred.

SPIRITUAL

The main objective I have in presenting this information to students is to help them discover that the Exodus was a cataclysmic event that really occurred in history. Help them to recognize that it is not a small thing, not an insignificant event that does not matter. Instead, as one of the great miracles of world history, it powerfully demonstrates God's interaction, immanence, and care for His people.

2) Read the article

Begins on Page 83 of Student Manual

SPIRITUAL

The article for Unit Three is designed to help students think about the reality of the historical events and people recorded in Genesis and Exodus, and the implication for people today. The materials covered in the audio recordings offer another look at this time period in ancient Egypt, covering slightly different information. In the article and recordings, along with introducing the basic understanding of history, we are also bringing in the biblical worldview—which will be of great contrast to the normal view of ancient Egypt!

TEACHER TIP

You may choose to have your students read the article first and then listen to the audio recordings, or vice versa.

INTRO-PG 18

3) Listen to the audio recording(s)

Listed on Page 94 of the Student Manual.

• The main concepts and chronological flow are contained in **What in the World's Going On Here?**

• An amazing interview with Bob Cornuke who went to Saudi Arabia in search of Mt. Sinai is contained in: **More True Tales From the Times of…Ancient Civilizations & The Bible**

• A description of the incredible design of the Great Pyramid is found in: **An In-Depth Study of…The Seven Wonders**

4) *Read the Scripture listed in Read For Your Life*

Listed on Page 94 of the Student Manual. You might choose to have the students read the Main Story verses either corporately or privately.

The Scriptures are central to our understanding, our character, and our decisions. Therefore, we must give the greatest weight possible to them. Help your students gain this perspective as they watch you handle the Scriptures with reverence and awe.

The "Other Helpful Verses" listed contain much insight about God's heart towards the enslaved Hebrews (Deut 32:1-12), about the importance of remembering what God has done (Psalm 66, 78), about God's incredible mercy (Psalm 136), about prophecies concerning Egypt (Isaiah 19, Ezekiel 29-32), and the perspective of faith (Hebrews 11:8-29) There is much to thoughtfully discuss with your students, if you are willing.

SPIRITUAL

5) *Recap (process & review) Activity*

In different parts of the room, set up stations for the Eight Intelligences Recap Activities. Then allow students to work alone or together in small groups to accomplish the following suggestions. At the start of the next class, ask for 3-4 groups of volunteers to share. <u>For homeschoolers, rather than set up all eight stations, allow the student(s) to choose which of these activities they would most enjoy, and do that.</u>

Recap Suggestions:

INTRO-PG 19

SPATIAL: In a small group, create a mind-map of what has been studied in this unit.

BODILY-KINESTHETIC: Use 4-5 pipe cleaners to make a representation of some aspect of the Exodus.

INTERPERSONAL: In groups of 2, take turns sharing the most interesting fact you have learned so far from the unit.

MUSICAL: In a small group, create a rhythmic chant about Joseph's life.

LINGUISTIC: In a small group, debate Pharaoh's hardness of heart. Do you think he had a concern for the best interests of the Egyptian nation?

MATH-LOGICAL: Analyze the impact on Egypt of having their Pharaoh and their entire army drown.

INTRAPERSONAL: Consider and jot down whether the things you have heard in this unit thus far conflict with what you already believe.

✗*NATURALIST:* Put together a list of items necessary in a survival kit for a trek into the desert. Then talk together about which of these items the Hebrews had as they fled Egypt.

OR...Activity of Your Choice: What would you like to have your students do for a review activity concerning this week's introduction to the Egypt & the Exodus?

6) *Opinion Column and Critical Puzzling answers on their own*

Listed on Page 95 of the Student Manual. Students may begin these questions after completing their Recap Activities listed above.

7) *Class Discussion*

Using the questions listed on Page 95 of the Student Manual to get the students primed, create a discussion environment in the classroom. You may also want to draw from the open-ended questions listed below.

QUESTION

Why do you suppose that Abraham thought God needed help fulfilling the promise of an heir? What are the consequences even today of Abraham's momentary lack of trust?

QUESTION

The ten plagues of Egypt have been described as the toppling of each of the Egyptian sacred deities, which would have demonstrated to the Egyptians, as well as to the Israelites, that Jehovah God was the true God. What purpose do you think God would have in this? Why would He want the Egyptians to know who was the true God?

QUESTION

What do you think was accomplished by God when Pharaoh and his army were drowned?

Phase 1

➤ *Talk Together*

• **Opinion Column**

— What did you find to be the most interesting aspect, or the most fascinating person, you encountered in your introduction to Egypt and the Exodus?

— *"You intended it for evil but God intended it for good."* Knowing that God is always good—that His ways are always righteous and pure—what purpose did God accomplish for Joseph as he went through the difficult situations of being sold into slavery, being accused wrongly, and being thrown into prison? As you answer this question, consider the implications in your own life.

— Honestly, thinking about the reality of the situation, why do you think that Moses chose to identify with the Jews who were now slaves in Egypt, rather than to enjoy the pleasures of Pharaoh's court?

• **Critical Puzzling**

— From the Scripture readings and the audio recordings, what can you discover about the Egyptian culture in regard to their treatment of other peoples? What aspects of their culture would you consider to be warlike? Can you draw parallels to any modern cultures?

— How did God demonstrate His love to both the descendants of Jacob and the Egyptians?

— The article describes Egypt as intended by God to be a safe haven, a refuge. What examples of this do you find in Scripture?

Unit Three: *Egypt & the Exodus* / 95

---

8) *Choose books of interest/Internet search*

A list of possible books for further reading is listed in the Student Manual beginning on Page 96. Encourage your students to look for books on a Biblical perspective of ancient Egypt, the current books on Egyptian chronologies, the Exodus and general information from this list and from other sources. You may want to gather a selection of further resources prior to beginning Unit Three, or you may encourage the students to be treasure hunters seeking to find them on their own.

The Internet has a wealth of information concerning Egypt & the Exodus, though the articles available vary widely in dependability, worldview and attitude. Help your students learn to recognize the differences.

Phase 1

➤ *Reviewed Resources for Digging Deeper:*

Choose a few books that look interesting, or find your own.

Egypt:

Cultural Atlas for Young People—Ancient Egypt by Geraldine Harris

The Cultural Atlas books are among the most informative, best laid-out history books for young people. Highly recommended! **MS+**

Pyramid by David Macauley

An incredible look at the construction of a pyramid—you actually get the sense that you are inside a pyramid with the workers! **AA**

Growing Up in Ancient Egypt by Rosalie David

This is an excellent introduction to the many facets of living in ancient Egypt. Though it is written for children, the information and layout makes it valuable to all ages. **E+**

The Pharaohs of Ancient Egypt by Elizabeth Payne

Landmark books are always good value, and this is no exception. Excellent for younger students. **UE+**

Tut's Mummy Lost and Found by Judy Donnelly

For elementary students, this book shows the fascinating adventure of Howard Carter who found King Tut in 1922. **E+**

Look What Came From Egypt by Miles Harvey

What a wonderful picture book of Egypt! Filled with photos and simple descriptions, this will be a great introduction for elementary students. **E+**

Make it Work! Ancient Egypt by Andrew Haslam & Alexandra Parsons

This is one of a series of the most incredible hands-on books of projects I've ever seen! It shows how to construct clothing, make jewelry, create instruments, even make a chariot! **UE+**

The Riddle of the Rosetta Stone: Key to Ancient Egypt by James Cross Giblin

An absolutely fascinating book about the man who deciphered the Rosetta Stone. **AA**

Seeker of Knowledge—The Man Who Deciphered Egyptian Hieroglyphs by James Rumford

If you collect excellent children's books, this is one for your shelves. It is the story of Jean-François Champollion, told with exquisite style and illustrations. **E+**

For the complete list of books from the Student Manual, refer to the Appendix (pg 316).

Remember:

Beware of Arrogance, Embrace Humility!

EVALUATION ┃ **Review & Evaluation**

In this Phase of Unit Three, your students should have had the opportunity to explore Egypt & the Exodus through reading, listening, thinking and discussing. They will have:

1) informally discussed the Key Concepts;
2) read the article;
3) listened to the audio recording(s);
4) read the Scripture listed in Read for Your Life;
5) explored the Recap Activities;
6) completed the Opinion Column and Critical Puzzling answers on their own;
7) participated in Class Discussion;
8) chosen books of interest or searched the Internet.

You may wish to evaluate your students based on their *participation* in the **Class Discussion** and on their *participation* in the **Recap Activity**.

Learning Style Emphasis: THINKER

Students will explore topics of interest through research and reporting, learn new vocabulary, and construct a timeline relating to Genesis 39-50, the book of Exodus, and ancient Egypt.

Monday-Tuesday:
1) Choose topic and begin research

Wednesday:
2) Vocabulary Practice

Thursday:
3) Construct the Timeline.

Friday:
4) Research projects completed; share in class or hand in.

Teachers can choose to have students do one or two activities, rather than the entire week's schedule. Please use what works for you in your unique setting.

1) Choose topic and begin research

Allow the students the freedom to choose one of the topics listed on Pages 99-100, or to suggest their own area which they would like to research.

Motivating Suggestions

Especially for Non-Linguistic students, and those who are not motivated by written or oral reports, here are suggestions for alternative ways of reporting what has been researched.

Hieroglyphics
1) Do a one-man show acting out Jean François Champollion's discovery.
2) Create a diagram which shows how hieroglyphic writing works. Include the meaning of some of the symbols.

Math
1) Give a ten minute lecture explaining triangulation as used in surveying.
2) Draw a picture showing an ancient Egyptian surveyor surveying the land with the aid of triangulation.

MOTIVATE

Chronology

1) Make a chart showing the Egyptian dynasties. The student may choose to show both the traditional dating and David Rohl's dating of these dynasties.

2) Create flash cards for each of the Egyptian dynasties, with the highlights of each dynasty written on the back of the card.

Egyptian History

1) Analyze the factors leading to Egypt's dominion, assign them a descending order of importance, then list them in this order on a chart. Do a corresponding chart showing the factors that led to the decline of Egypt. (Don't forget the Exodus!)

2) Write a journalistic news piece on the history of Egypt.

Bible

1) Create a series of drawings or paintings showing the various stages of Joseph's life.

2) Pantomime the four stages of Moses' life: prince of Egypt, shepherd of Midian, confronter of Pharaoh, leader of the Hebrews.

3) Make a diagram showing the chronological events of the book of Exodus.

PHASE 2
Exploration & Discovery Week

➢ Research & Reporting

Your mission, if you choose to accept it, is to explore one of these areas and to discover something significant!

• **Hieroglyphics:**

Research and explain what hieroglyphic writing is, and how it was deciphered in modern times. (Consider: Look up the Rosetta Stone and Jean François Champollion.)

• **Math:**

Research and report on the use of triangulation in surveying ancient Egypt. Why was regular surveying required? Is triangulation still used in surveying?

• **Chronology:**

Compile a list of the major names, dates and accomplishments of Egypt's dynasties. Using David Rohl's research or Ted Stewart's research, how does this list compare with the events listed in the Bible?

• **Egyptian History:**

— Summarize the factors that led to Egypt's far- reaching dominion and the factors leading to their decline. Be sure to include the impact of the Nile.

— Investigate the history of Egypt from the earliest times to the present. Report your finding.

• **Bible:**

— Research the life of Joseph in the Scriptures.

— Research the life of Moses.

— Investigate the book of Exodus in the Old Testament. To whom did God speak? What were the messages? How did the people (both Egyptian and Israelite) respond? How did God deal with each of them?

• **Wilderness Living:**

Research and report on the weather conditions and ecosystems in Egypt and in Midian. How would this have affected the children of Israel as they wandered for forty years?

• **Deserts:**

— Compare and contrast the desert in Egypt with other deserts, such as the Sahara or Mojave. How did the Nile River impact the desert of ancient Egypt? How is this different today?

Wilderness Living

1) In the style of "The Crocodile Hunter," demonstrate what is necessary for survival in ancient Egypt and in ancient Arabia.

2) Listen to Keith Green's song, "So You Wanna Go Back to Egypt" and then create your own verses about wilderness living.

Deserts

1) Create a mural showing the Egyptian desert, the Sahara Desert and the Mojave Desert. Be sure to visually show the differences between each.

2) Use video clips from appropriate movies to show the lifestyle of the Bedouins. Then explain what similarities there would be to the ancient Hebrews living in the wilderness.

Passover

1) For a memorable report on the Passover, cook a passover feast and, with the help of a book such as *Celebrate the Feasts*, explain the significance of each item as it's being consumed.

Egyptian Afterlife

1) With two students participating, have one interview the other before a "live audience." The student being interviewed needs to be an ancient Egyptian (costumes are optional) who can explain the Egyptian beliefs about afterlife, and the procedures done at death to ensure the best possible afterlife.

2) Make a chart showing the step by step process of mummification.

MOTIVATE

Phase 2

— Using a recent cultural anthropology study or a missions resource, learn more about nomadic desert dwellers (like the Bedouins), their lifestyle and how they care for their animals. Write a report showing the lifestyle of the desert dweller, then, extrapolate what we can learn from this in regard to the Israelites in the wilderness.

• **Passover:**

Read Exodus 12. Now, using either **Celebrate the Feasts** or another book describing the Jewish feast of Passover, chart the similarities between the feast and the original historic event of Passover.

• **Egyptian Afterlife:**

Why were the ancient Egyptians so concerned about the afterlife? What are some of the ways they demonstrated their concern? What scientific techniques used in mummification remain a mystery to us?

• **Building the Great Pyramid:**

Discover how big the Great Pyramid is, and as much as is known about how it was built. What is the average weight of each stone? How much, approximately, does the Great Pyramid weigh?

➤ *Brain Stretchers*

• **Egypt & Israel:**

Compare and contrast the history of ancient Egypt and the history of ancient Israel. What cultural distinctives (i.e. religion, war, politics, class structure) continue in each nation throughout the centuries of antiquity?

• **The Sinai:**

Find one of the books listed at the beginning of this unit, along with the encyclopedia or other history resource book, for basic information on what would be needed in a hot, dry climate to sustain life for people, flocks and herds. Is it available on the Sinai Peninsula? Would it be available in the land of Midian (Arabia)? Make a chart listing the necessary requirements to sustain life, and show which of these requirements are fulfilled in each of these two locations.

Keep in mind that God made miraculous provisions for the Israelites.

• **Geography of the Exodus:**

Read Exodus and note the geographical descriptions of the flight from Egypt, the crossing of the Red Sea, the route to and depiction of Mt. Sinai (reference Gal. 4:25 also.) Next, find a description of the traditional site of Mt. Sinai and the Sea of Reeds. In what way do these sites support or conflict with the biblical text? Write a report explaining what you discover.

Create Your Own Research Topic:

_____
_____
_____

Brain Stretchers:

Brain Stretchers, listed on page 100, are intended for advanced students. Those who attempt the Brain Stretchers for their Research and Reporting can use the above list for ideas on how to report their findings.

MOTIVATE

Building the Great Pyramid:

1) Create a miniature version of the Great Pyramid (out of Legos, papier mache, etc.) and use that as a prop while explaining: the enormous dimensions of the Great Pyramid; how heavy the stones were; any pertinent facts which have been discovered in the process of researching this wonder of the ancient world.

INTRO - PG 21

2) Words To Watch - Vocabulary Practice

Listed on Page 101. You may find other words in this unit that are especially appropriate for younger children. Feel free to substitute another vocabulary list for the one provided.

TEACHER TIP

Here is one idea for making vocabulary study interesting and fun: *Start a dialogue between three people, seeing how many vocabulary words can be worked into a conversation. For real excitement, let the third person be someone who isn't aware of the vocabulary list— see how subtle the introduction of these words can be!*

Phase 2

➢ Words to Watch

Remember—The easiest way to learn a subject is to master its terms:

Midian	Mt. Horeb	irrigation
plague	exodus	triangulation
Goshen	pharaoh	survey
famine	Mt. Sinai	pyramid
sorcerers	quota	mummification
Nile River	hieroglyphics	afterlife
slavery	petroglyph	sphinx
magicians	Passover	

INTRO - PG 21

3) Construct the Timeline.

Read the information listed with the "Key Dates" on Page 103. Dialogue with your students about the issues involved. Help them recognize that dating antiquity is not an exact science. For ease of reference, the timeline is included in the Appendix on Page 319.

Find the dates for the key people and events listed. In this unit, as has already been discussed, there are traditional dates for Egyptian Chronology which show the Exodus occurring either in 1446 B.C. under Thutmose III or in circa 1225 B.C. under Rameses II. In the new Egyptian Chronology, the Exodus occurs in circa 1446 B.C. under Amenemhet IV of the Twelfth Dynasty (Ted Stewart's suggested pharaoh) or Dudimose I of the Thirteenth Dynasty (David Rohl's suggested pharaoh). The dates of the later dynasties will also change accordingly. A student may choose to:

• Take the date listed in their Bible;
• Take the date listed in Bishop Ussher's chronology;
• Take the date listed in a resource book they are using;
• Notate two different possibilities on their timeline, showing which version of the Egyptian chronology is used as the source;
• Have a debate in class about why one date should be chosen over another date (very good for developing critical thinking skills!).

4) *Research projects shared in class and/or turned in.*

Create a safe environment for the presentations. Set ground rules prior to the presentations for all the students, so that they know each one will be honored and respected in their work by all those observing.

Review & Evaluation

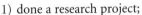

In this second Phase of Unit Three, your students should have had the opportunity to explore Egypt & the Exodus through researching, thinking, and reporting. They will have:

1) done a research project;
2) learned the vocabulary;
3) constructed a Timeline;
4) created a project report on what was researched.

You may wish to evaluate your students based on their *efforts* in the **Research and Reporting** projects and their active *participation* in the **Vocabulary** and **Timeline** exercises.

PHASE 3

The Hands-On Week

Learning Style Emphasis: Sensor

Students will gain cultural understanding through sensory activities as they explore inter-related subject areas relating to Genesis 39-50, the book of Exodus, and ancient Egypt.

Monday:
1) Create a map and discuss the issues in teams.

Tuesday:
2) Examine and discuss art masterpieces & architectural structures.

Wednesday:
3) Arts in Action—Do an art project.*

Thursday:
4) Do one science project or field trip.**

Friday:
5) Listen to and discuss the music.
6) Cook the food listed in the recipe, if desired.

*Art project will need to be planned ahead of time to acquire materials.
**Field trip will require extra planning time.

> *Teachers can choose to have students do one or two activities, rather than the entire week's schedule. Please use what works for you in your unique setting.*

INTRO-PG 23

1) Create a map and discuss the issues in teams

The students each have an outline map on Page 105. They will be given assignments for drawing in rivers, mountains, cities, and regional boundaries, which are listed on Page 104. For details on where these things are, please consult a historical atlas, an encyclopedia, a study Bible, or any other source for geographic information. For ease of reference, the map is included in the Appendix on Page 320.

Upper elementary students might be satisfied to accomplish only this portion:

• *Physical terrain:* This part of the mapping exercise will help students locate and mark the geological dynamics of a region.

Middle school students might be satisfied to complete both the previous mapping exercise and this exercise:

• *Geo-Political:* This section of the mapping exercise will provide the students an opportunity to locate and mark the cities, nations and empires of history. It will require more digging, as this information may not be listed on current maps. For example, Goshen and Midian will be a bit of a challenge to locate. The copper and turquoise maps of ancient Egypt were located on the Sinai Peninsula, in case that information is unavailable to your students.

High school students might be satisfied to complete both the previous mapping exercises and at least one exploration topic of this exercise:

- *Explore:* Discuss some selection from this portion of the mapping exercise in teams.

Christian Outreach to Egypt and Saudi Arabia.

If it is possible to either read a short biography of a missionary to Egypt or Saudi Arabia, such as *Borden of Yale* or to actually interview someone who serves the Lord in that region, students will be given realistic understanding of the issues involved.

QUESTION

PHASE 3

The Hands-On Week

➤ *Maps and Mapping*

- **Physical Terrain:**

  — Color and label the Nile River in Egypt.

  — Color the flood plain of the Nile (which is the fertile area of Egypt).

  — Color the desert area of Egypt.

  — Color the Mediterranean and the Red Sea.

- **Geo-Political:**

  — Draw the boundaries of Egypt (including the area of their copper and turquoise mines).

  — Divide Egypt into Upper Egypt and Lower Egypt.

  — Label the cities of Memphis, Thebes, the Valley of the Kings.

  — What modern day cities are close to these ancient cities?

  — Label the area of Goshen in the Nile delta.

  — Label and color the Sinai Peninsula.

  — Label the land of Midian.

  — What modern day country holds the land of Midian?

- **Explore:**

  — *Christian Outreach to Egypt and Saudi Arabia:* What is the status of Christian outreach to these countries in the Middle East? Discuss the difficulties facing Christians seeking to serve God in these nations, and brainstorm creative ways of overcoming these difficulties.

  — *God's Purposes in Earth's Structure:* How would the terrain and climate of Egypt, with the Nile River, the flood plain, the desert, the Upper & Lower portions of Egypt all have affected the Egyptian culture and God's purpose for it?

SPIRITUAL

Consider committing with your students to pray for either Egypt or Saudi Arabia, or for a specific missionary in those countries. You may want to actually keep a prayer journal to remember what is prayed, so that you can rejoice exceedingly as you see the specific ways God answers these prayers.

God's purposes in Earth's structure

QUESTION

If we recognize God as the Creator of Heaven and Earth, then we will begin to comprehend that just as He set the boundaries of the people groups (Acts 17:26), He also set geographical boundaries in locations. Discuss with the students the possible reasons God isolated and, at the same time, blessed Egypt with the desert, the Nile River, and their location at the top of Africa.

INTRO · PG 23

2) Examine and discuss art masterpieces & architectural structures

Locate either a copy of these art forms, or Internet sites for each of the items listed on Pages 106-107. Allow the students time to observe the art without any conversation, and then, when they are ready, engage them in some or all of the questions listed in the Student Manual or below.

QUESTION

The Deliverance of the Israelites *by Bernardo Luini*

- Bernardo Luini was a student of Leonardo da Vinci. As da Vinci spent a lot of time in Milan employed in military engineering, Luini was often left to his own devices and to learning from the previous Florentine masters. Is there anything in this painting that seems reminiscent of da Vinci's work? (Consider: the Mona Lisa).
- How would the students describe the scene? Is the sea turbulent? What aspect makes this a painting of dramatic deliverance?

QUESTION

Egyptian Tomb Painting

- A certain sameness of perspective and style was employed by the artists who created the Egyptian tomb paintings.
- Ask the students what purpose might have been served by this conformity in art? How might the Egyptians have viewed art? How does this differ from artists today?

QUESTION

The Great Pyramid - Architecture

- Consider holding a class discussion about the questions listed in the Student Manual concerning the overwhelming size and architectural structure of the Great Pyramid. Here are some facts to get the discussion started:

— 756 feet (230 meters) in length along each side;
— 450 feet (137 meters) tall;
— 2,300,000 blocks of stone, each averaging 2 1/2 tons in weight;
— the average distance between the stone blocks in the pyramid is 1/50th of an inch (.5 millimeters), and in places, they are as close as 1/500th of an inch (.05 millimeters)!
— 4 sides line up almost exactly with true north, south, east and west.

How did the Egyptians do this?

Phase 3

Consider:

Bernardo Luini (c. 1480-1532 A.D.) studied under Leonardo da Vinci, and was himself, a master artist. His style of painting was also influenced by the Florentine artists of an earlier time.

➤ Art Appreciation

- **The Deliverance of the Israelites** *by Bernardo Luini*

  — Does the painting reflect what the Bible describes?

  — How does the painting differ from your own impression of God's deliverance?

  — Does Luini's painting convey the epic nature of the destruction of Pharaoh and his army?

- **Egyptian Tomb Painting:** *Look in a book about Egypt, a book with historic art, or on the Internet for examples of Egyptian tomb painting.*

  — How would you describe the style of painting used by these Egyptian artists?

  — What kinds of scenes are depicted?

  — Does this style of painting make you think the Egyptian artists were sophisticated in their art? Do you consider them to be childish to the Western eye? Why do you think they painted in this style?

---

3) Arts in Action

Listed on Page 107.

Imitation

Have the students look again at Luini's painting. Then, with art supplies of colored pencils, pastels, or paint, try to recreate some aspect of Luini's work.

TEACHER TIP

Phase 3

➤ Architecture

The Great Pyramid is one of the Seven Wonders of the Ancient World. It was standing when Abraham ventured into Egypt—a long time ago. It still stands today! It is believed to weigh five million tons, and has more than two million blocks of stone. Napoleon thought there was enough stone in this pyramid, along with two other pyramids nearby, to build a wall ten feet high and one foot thick all the way around France!

— Look for a photo of the Great Pyramid of Khufu (or Cheops). What are some words that would describe this building?

Consider:

When it was originally built, the outside of this pyramid was covered with brilliant white Tura limestone, which would have made it even more impressive. Though most of it has been removed over the centuries, there is still enough in place that one can imagine the splendor of this architectural wonder of the world.

➤ Arts in Action

Select one, and let your artistic juices flow!

• **Imitation:**

Try imitating Luini, or the ancient Egyptian artists (trace, use colors, etc.)

• **Sphinx Carving:**

Try carving a Sphinx out of soap. Remember Michelangelo's advice: just carve away anything that doesn't look like the Spinx!

• **Egyptian Portraiture:**

Sketch a simple portrait of yourself or someone else, in the style of the Egyptian tomb paintings. (Notice how they usually paint flat profiles.) Then make a dry plaster

(a secco) painting: using very smooth plaster of Paris, brush a 1/8" layer of plaster over a piece of wood. When dry, lay your sketch over the wood and trace the outline with a nail. Use tempera to paint picture. Remember to keep it simple!

• **Egyptian Jewelry:** ✗

Egyptians liked to use jewelry in adorning themselves. (This came in very handy when the Israelites took their back wages out of the country!) Find a book showing the look of Egyptian jewelry, and try your hand at creating some. There are many, many possibilities for materials, colors, size, shape!

Sphinx Carving

Students may choose to carve a sphinx out of soap. Obviously, this is an intricate and somewhat difficult carving to do, so for younger students, or those who would become frustrated by the delicacy of the small motor skills required, encourage them to do one of the other art projects.

Egyptian Portraiture

Have your students study some of the ways Egyptian artists depict people—everyday people, pharaohs, slaves, etc. Then, encourage them to try creating a portrait in that same style. If they choose to work with the dry plaster mentioned in the student manual, it will give a very interesting texture to their work.

Egyptian Jewelry

It will be necessary to observe some pictures of Egyptian jewelry in order to discover the unique look of this style of jewelry. From there, the students can decide how to go about fashioning "authentic" Egyptian jewelry.

INTRO - PG 24

4) Do a science project

Listed on Page 108. Feel free to choose one of these projects. If students love science, they might want to consider doing all of them!

TEACHER TIP

Brick Making

   If necessary, purchase some potter's clay to use with water (and straw, if available) to make the kind of bricks the Hebrews made. If your soil has clay qualities, it will be suitable for this exercise. Have the students discover how long it takes for the bricks to dry. How hard are they? How difficult is it to build a small wall (very small!) with these bricks? What are the challenges? How would they solve the challenges presented?

FASCINATING FACT:

Many people in the world still make bricks in this way.

Levers & Pulleys

   There are books in the library describing simple machines and how to build them. If the library is not available to you, consider looking on the Internet for instructions. This is a really eye-opening experiment when students learn how great a weight can be lifted with the use of levers and pulleys.

Phase 3

➢ Science

• **Brick Making:**

— Using water, clay soil (or potter's clay), and straw, mix up a batch of "bricks." Make wooden rectangular forms to put the mixture into. Let it dry (it may take several days.) What's the difference between sun-dried brick and kiln-dried brick?

• **Levers & Pulleys:**

— Ancient Egyptians may have used levers and pulleys to build the pyramids. Construct a system of pulleys and ropes to try lifting a heavy object like a concrete block. Notice that, the more pulleys used, the easier. Consult the library for more info (see also "block and tackle").

➢ Music

In ancient Egypt, as we have seen in other early civilizations, people played various kinds of instruments, such as flutes, harps and drums. But they were not the only ones in Egypt with instruments! Exodus 15 tells us that Moses' sister, Miriam, played the timbrels (tambourine) during the triumphant song of deliverance after Pharaoh and his army were drowned in the Red Sea. One of the five elements of music, rhythm is the distinctive pattern of long and short notes in each piece of music. Along with the pattern of notes is the underlying pulse, or beat, of the music. The beat can be slow or fast or medium. We use the term tempo to mean the speed of music. So, slow music, like a lullaby, has a slow tempo, and fast music, like a march, has a faster tempo.

108 / Unit Three: *Egypt & the Exodus*

5) Listen to and discuss the music

Listed on Page 108.

INTRO - PG 24

Phase 3

- **Listen:**

  — Find a recording of a percussion ensemble, such as LUPÉ, or a recording of tribal drumming, to see just how creatively rhythm can be used.

- **Try This:**

  — Recite these children's verses:
  "Pat-a-cake, pat-a-cake, Baker's man..."
  "Twinkle, twinkle, little star..."
  "Hot cross buns..."

  — Now, try clapping (not saying) one of these verses. Can anyone guess which pattern you are clapping? That pattern is called the rhythm.

  — For a greater challenge, try clapping familiar tunes, such as Christmas carols or church songs.

  — Now, speed up the clapping, which changes the tempo. Next, slow down the clapping. Which speed allows the clearest presentation of the above verses?

  — Play a rhythm game where one person claps a short rhythm and everyone tries to repeat it. Take turns!

> *Consider:*
>
> Have you ever listened to a tambourine? Sometimes it is played consistently and regularly on the beat, but sometimes the tambourine player will make different patterns: a long, held-out "shimmering" sound, or a series of short, quick taps. The performer is creating a pattern of sounds, some longer and some shorter.

Try This

TEACHER TIP

- It is quite challenging to listen to someone clap and try to discover what song they are clapping! You could set this up in relay teams, disclosing to the leader of each team a list of songs to present. Then, the first pair of students to properly guess which song is being clapped passes the "baton" to the next pair of students. First team to finish, wins!

- Speeding up and slowing down the tempo, and making decisions about what tempo is appropriate can be a fine source of heated debate among students! Enjoy the fun.

INTRO-PG 24

6) Cook the food

Listed on Page 110.

Listed on Page 110.

FASCINATING FACT:

A Christian school teacher in New Zealand once told me that she loved teaching geography in the kitchen, where she helped students learn about the different parts of a region from the local ingredients and ethnic recipes. This enabled even her skeptical, standoffish students to get enthused about learning—they got to eat the results!

Phase 3

➤ Cooking

Since this unit looks at two different people groups, the Egyptians and the Israelites who fled Egypt, we will make two different recipes. Do you remember what the children of Israel complained about in the wilderness in regard to good ol' Egyptian food? (You may want to listen to Keith Green's "So You Wanna' Go Back to Egypt".) Sample the following and see what they were talking about! (Be sure NOT to complain!!)

• Stewed Beef with Okra (Egyptian)

2 tbsp oil	1/2 tsp. ground coriander
2 tbsp butter	1 pound tomatoes, peeled & sliced
1 1/2 pound stew beef (or lamb) cubed	1 tbsp tomato paste
2 onions, chopped	2 10 oz. pkgs. frozen okra
2 cloves garlic, minced	Salt & pepper

Heat oil and butter in casserole. Add meat cubes & saute until brown. Add onions, garlic, coriander, fry for one minute. Add tomatoes, paste, seasoning. Cover stew with water, bring to boil, reduce heat, cover, simmer 1 hour. Add okra, cook 30 minutes more.

• Unleavened Bread (The Exodus)

4 cups unbleached flour	1 tsp. salt
1 1/2 cup water, room temp.	

Combine flour and salt. Add enough water to make a dough that will clean sides of bowl and gather into a ball. Turn out onto lightly floured surface, knead 10 minutes. Shape into ball and cut in half. Cut each half into 8 pieces and form into 16 balls. Roll out each ball to form about a 7 " circle. Place on ungreased baking sheet and bake in 500 degree oven for about 5 minutes. Makes 16.

EVALUATION ## Review & Evaluation

In this third Phase of Unit Three, your students should have had the opportunity to explore Egypt & The Exodus through various hands-on and creative sessions. They will have:

1) completed a Mapping section;
2) observed and discussed Art & Architecture;
3) worked on an art project;
4) experimented with a Science Project or taken a field trip;
5) listened to music;
6) tasted a food related to this unit.

You may wish to evaluate your students based on their *class participation* in these **Hands-on** activities.

PHASE 4

The Expression Week

Learning Style Emphasis: *Intuitor*

Students, through creative self-expression, using one or more creative activities, will present some aspect of what they have learned in the past three weeks relating to Genesis 39-50, the book of Exodus, and ancient Egypt. Areas of expression include linguistics, art, music, drama, movement and conceptual design.

Monday - Thursday

1) Choose area of expression and begin work either individually or in teams.

Friday

2) Share creative expressions in class.

> *Teachers can choose to have students do one or two activities, rather than the entire week's schedule. Please use what works for you in your unique setting.*

---

1) Choose area of expression and begin work either individually or in teams

INTRO - PG 25

Linguistics:

Located on page 111-112.

Playing With Words

Help students understand the meaning of "pun," and then create one about Egypt.

Journalism

- Have the students who wish to write a journalistic piece look at several articles in newspapers and/or magazines to understand the framework for journalism. Encourage them to be as wildly imaginative as they wish to be, as long as their project conveys something of what has been learned in the unit.
- There are many magazine articles, newspaper articles and books concerning the lifestyles of royalty.

TEACHER TIP

Encourage students to read a few examples of this, along with descriptions of ancient Egyptian clothing and customs, so that they will have both the historical facts and the first-person sense of amazement in witnessing the splendor of royalty.

Prose

The student may wish to read a story about an orphan's experiences in order to gain insight into the kinds of issues important to orphans. This may be a very sobering account or it could be comical.

Poetry

- Many styles of rhyming poetry exist such as nursery rhymes, couplets, and rondelets and odes. Have students interested in writing rhyming poetry examine some examples of these in order to decide what style of poetry they wish to write. (Ogden Nash wrote rhyming poems in a most unusual manner. I highly recommend studying his style for students who enjoy humor and playing with words!)

- Encourage students to discover what an acrostic poem looks like. (Definition of "Acrostic:" a word, phrase, or passage spelled out vertically by the first letters of a group of lines in sequence.) Have them explore the variety of presentations possible in shape and word usage.

Art:

Located on page 112.

Painting/Drawing

- Many people have visited the Great Pyramid and have had their picture taken there. If a student can get a first hand description of the event, as well as a copy of the photo, it will prove invaluable. This is the time to start asking everyone you know whether they've been a tourist in Egypt!

- There are cinematic examples of the Exodus from Egypt (such as *Prince of Egypt*), as well as paintings (such as Arnold Friberg's *Parting of the Red Sea*). Students might look online to see examples of how other artists depict the drama of the event.

PHASE 4
The Expression Week

➤ *In Your Own Way . . .*

In this unit we have seen how the descendants of Abraham entered Egypt, a Biblical land of refuge. After God's powerful intervention through Joseph in what could have been utter devastation to both the Egyptians and the Hebrews, a generation arose who did not remember the past. Instead, they focused on the increasing might of the Hebrews, and out of fear for their own safety, they enslaved them. In one of the most powerful historic events of all time, God delivered the Hebrews, the descendants of Abraham, in the Exodus. In this, and through other Scriptures, we have discovered God's mercy and love to both the Egyptians and the Hebrews. Now, choose a selection of these activities, or create your own, which will best express what was most significant to you.

Linguistics:

- **Playing with Words:**

  Make a pun about Egypt. Like this:
  What do you call a pyramid that smells bad?
  A stynx!

- **Journalism:**

  — Be a newspaper reporter for the Palestine daily, "The Patriarch," and write the human interest story "Family Finds Long-Lost Son in Egypt."

— Imagine you were invited to a formal dinner at Nefertiti's palace. Write a detailed description of the guests, their outfits and the food served for the magazine, Lifestyles: Egyptian Royalty at Home.

- **Prose:**

  Write a fictional account of an Egyptian orphan who flees to a Hebrew family during the plagues, then comes with them on the Exodus.

Unit Three: *Egypt & the Exodus* / 111

Graphic Design

Encourage students to look at real estate advertisements to discover what kind of photos are shown, what kind of words are used to describe properties, and how the ads are laid out.

TEACHER TIP

Political Cartooning

The confrontation between Pharaoh and Moses must have seemed at first to be one-sided with the weight of power on Pharaoh's side. This was reversed by the end of their time. Remember that one man and God make a majority!

Phase 4

- **Poetry:**
  - Discover the connection these words have to the unit, and then write a rhyming poem using them: sea, flee, free; pharaoh, marrow, narrow; pulley, bully, fully; flood, blood, mud; slave, brave, save

  — Write an acrostic poem from the Hebrew perspective describing the night of the first Passover.

Art:

- **Painting/Drawing:**
  - Create a mural of the Great Pyramid, the Sphinx, and the surrounding Egyptian desert. If you have a current photo from which to draw, you might want to add the ubiquitous camels!

  — Paint the scene from the Exodus where God sends a wind to part the Red Sea. You might consider making it abstract to focus on the overall experience.

- **Graphic Design:**

  Design an ad for a real estate developer who has land for sale—just outside the flood plain of the Nile. Remember that the Egyptians described the land as either black (from the rich deposits of flooding) or red (the unrelieved desert ground).

- **Cartooning:**

  As a political cartoonist, draw a cartoon for the "Mt. Sinai Herald," showing the confrontation between Pharaoh and Moses.

Music:

- **Compose:**

  Exodus 15 contains the song that Moses and the children of Israel sang after their deliverance through the Red Sea. Select some portion of those verses and put them to music. If composing a melody is initially too overwhelming, start by creating a text-setting, which means setting a selection of text to rhythm. Try to get the most dramatic use of pauses and rhythmic emphasis.

- **Performance Practice:**

  There is a tremendous amount of drama in this unit. With your teacher, select an appropriate dramatic piece, with great contrast, to play at the end of this unit. Explain to your audience the way that the music represents what you learned about Egypt and the Exodus.

Music:

Located on page 112.

Compose

TEACHER TIP

Students may wish to form a team to compose and perform a song, or they may wish to do this selection on their own. The composition would do very well as a song of worship to the God who delivered the Hebrews.

Performance Practice

For musical students, this selection may be a wonderful opportunity to express what they have learned. Make sure they have selected a piece that they have adequate time to prepare.

TEACHER TIP

Drama:

Located on page 113.

Comedy

Portraying Moses' wife as slightly hard of hearing will provide Moses some opportunities for humorous misunderstand-ings—especially when he tries to tell her that God was speaking out of a burn-ing bush.

Phase 4

Drama:

• **Comedy:**

Do a humorous skit about Moses explaining to his wife that the reason he was late for dinner was because God was talking out of a burning bush!

• **Reality:**

Act out the Exodus. Use your imagination to create props, sets and costumes. Be sure to include realistic fear, as well as rejoicing! Add appropriate songs, worship choruses.

Puppetry:

Produce a puppet show on the life of Joseph. You could choose to begin with his time in prison. For inspiration, check out *Joseph and the Amazing Technicolor Dreamcoat.*

Reality

Bible scholars believe that between 300,000 and one million people fled Egypt during the Exodus. Since you won't have that many actors available, consider how you can create the effect of many people, of differing ages and conditions, traveling under somewhat terrifying conditions (at least, before the parting of the Red Sea).

Puppetry

Think about the main characters and main events in Joseph's life as you prepare the puppet show. What scenes might be appropriate to leave out without harming the overall story, and which need to remain?

TEACHER TIP

Movement:

Located on page 114.

Pantomime

• Remember that Joseph had been in prison a long time, and was quite possibly not in the best shape. He may need to stumble or weave a bit, to indicate lack of food and exercise.

• Consider all of the plagues of Egypt. Encourage your students to determine how one pantomimes frogs, water turning to blood, locusts, or hail.

Dance

The soundtrack from *Prince of Egypt* contains some music which powerfully communicates the bondage of the Israelites. You might want to listen and see if there are any songs which would be appropriate for your dance.

Action

Remember that Pharaoh and many of his officers were riding in chariots. How will you show the action of chariots? Consider what it was like for the Egyptian army to walk with the wall of water close to them—the wall of water which the Israelites had safely passed.

Phase 4

Movement:

• **Pantomime:**

— Pantomime Joseph's being called out of prison, cleaned up and dressed, to appear before Pharoah. Show how he listens to Pharoah's dream, interprets it, and is then honored with responsibility for the entire land of Egypt. If two students wish to do this together, one could portray Joseph and the other Pharoah.

— Pantomime the plagues of Egypt. Be sure to show how the Hebrews were saved out of them.

• **Dance:**

Dance the enslavement and bondage of Israel in the land of Egypt, showing how they cried out to God. Remember, after the Red Sea parted, Miriam danced to show her thankfulness to God.

• **Action:**

Perform a stylized action/dance of Pharoah and his army chasing the Israelites to the Red Sea, with the tragic end for the Egyptians and the victorious deliverance for the Hebrews.

Conceptual Design:

There are a tremendous number of possible explanations of how the pyramids were built, including poured concrete and the brute strength of slaves. Design an imaginative (it doesn't have to work in real life) pyramid building machine.

Create Your Own Expression:

_____

_____

Conceptual Design:

Located on page 114.

Anything goes for a pyramid-building machine. Remember, however, that the pyramids were MASSIVE and precisely set into their places.

TEACHER TIP

2) *Share creative expressions in class.*

INTRO-PG 26

The same rules apply as suggested in the reporting section of Phase Two.

Review & Evaluation

EVALUATION

In this Phase of Unit Three, your students should have had the opportunity to express what they have learned about Egypt and the Exodus through one or more various creative selections of their own choosing. These include:

1) Linguistics;
2) Art;
3) Music;
4) Drama;
5) Movement;
6) Conceptual Design.

You may wish to evaluate your students based on their *effort* in the **Creative Expressions**, either as individuals or in teams.

THE CHILDREN OF ISRAEL

UNIT 4

Menorah

Enthusiasm and delight are the best way to capture a student's interest and jump-start motivation, so:

Pray with the students at the beginning of each unit.

1) ***For the Auditory Students:*** Consider playing Jewish folk music, such as Itzhak Perlman's violin recordings of Israeli music, to capture their attention at the very beginning of class;

2) ***For the Kinesthetic Students:*** Have the students warm up as class begins by doing some active movement that is fun (such as, an action song, like "Hallelu-Hallelu-Hallelu-Hallelujah, Praise Ye the Lord!" with boys standing and girls sitting on the "Hallelu," switching quickly on "Praise Ye the Lord");

3) ***For the Visual Students:*** Bring a visual object to stimulate their interest in the new unit, like a drawing or three-dimensional depiction of Solomon's Temple;

4) ***For the hearts of all:*** Pray with them at the beginning of the unit, that God would help them discover what He has for each one to learn in that unit.

PHASE 1

The Introduction Week

Learning Style Emphasis: *Feeler*

Students will be introduced to Scriptures relating to the Conquest, the Judges, the United Kingdom and the Divided Kingdom of Israel, found in Joshua, 1 & 2 Samuel, 1 Kings. You may follow this suggested schedule or adapt it to meet your students' needs:

Monday:

1) Informally discuss the Key Concepts

Tuesday:

2) Read the article
3) Listen to the audio recording(s)
4) Read the Scripture listed in Read For Your Life

Wednesday:

5) Recap Activity
6) Opinion Column and Critical Puzzling answers on their own

Thursday:

7) Class Discussion

Friday:

8) Choose books of interest/Internet search

Teachers can choose to have students do one or two activities, rather than the entire week's schedule. Please use what works for you in your unique setting.

1) Informally Discuss the Key Concepts

Listed in the Student Manual on page 115.

KEY CONCEPTS BACKGROUND INFORMATION

These are the main objectives of the unit. As you proceed through the four weeks, your students will be given various ways of understanding each of these objectives.

Strategic Location & God's Purpose—EXPLANATION

To get an informal discussion started on this key concept, ask a simple, leading question, such as, *"Where is Israel located? What countries are around it?"*

The One who called the descendants of Abraham, Isaac and Jacob to be His own special people set the boundaries of their habitation. It was not an uninformed, thoughtless decision on God's part! He very carefully set them

---

THE CHILDREN OF ISRAEL

Menorah

This article can be found in its entirety in the Appendix (see pg 321).

KEY CONCEPTS:

- **Strategic Location & God's Purpose**

- **The Chronology**

- **The Glory**

- **The Divided Kingdom**

- **Application**

Into the Promised Land...

"So the Lord saved Israel that day out of the hand of the Egyptians, and Israel saw the Egyptians dead on the seashore. Thus Israel saw the great work which the Lord had done in Egypt; so the people feared the Lord, and believed the Lord and His servant Moses." Exodus 14:30-31

Out of Egypt! Deliverance and freedom! A new hope and a new future! Standing on the other side of the Red Sea, watching with incredulity the towering waters collapse on Pharaoh and his army, must have unleashed a torrent of emotions and thoughts in the escapees. Consider: first, the

Unit Four: *The Children of Israel* / 115

in a geographic location for the fulfillment of His plan's and purposes—to bless all the families of the earth (Genesis 12:3).

So what was so special about this land on the coast of the Mediterranean Sea? If your students look at a map, they will discover that Israel sits on the piece of land directly between Europe and Africa. People and goods traveling to Asia from these lands could also be routed through this strategically placed nation. At this point in history, Israel was not set in a backwater location to function in isolation. Instead, it was set in the best possible public place for disseminating the knowledge of God to all nations and people.

We know that the news about the Delivering God of the Hebrews was making the rounds throughout neighboring lands, because the people of Jericho were afraid of what they had heard:

"I know that the Lord has given you the land, that the terror of you has fallen on us, and that all the inhabitants of the land are fainthearted because of you. For we have heard how the Lord dried up the water of the Red Sea for you when you came out of Egypt, and what you did to the two kings of the Amorites who were on the other side of the Jordan, Sihon and Og, whom you utterly destroyed. And as soon as we heard these things, our hearts melted; neither did there remain any more courage in anyone because of you, for the Lord your God, He is God in heaven above and on earth beneath." Joshua 2:9-11

More than a thousand years later, the Messiah would tell His followers a truth that was a continuation of what had been God's intention for His people all along:

"You are the light of the world. A city that is set on a hill cannot be hidden. Nor do they light a lamp and put it under a basket, but on a lamp stand, and it gives light to all who are in the house. Let your light so shine before men, that they may see your good works and glorify your Father in heaven." Matthew 5:14-16

Pray that your students would begin to grasp the immeasurable goodness and love of God and His unrelenting plan that all the world would know.

The Chronology—EXPLANATION

To get an informal discussion started on this key concept, ask a simple, leading question, such as, *"Who can tell me what happened to the Israelites after the Exodus?"*

Sometimes the stories in the Bible become a mere collection of character-teaching tools or isolated moralistic stories to learn from. The impact of the realization that these were real people living in a real time is reduced when they are made to seem mythological or like something out of Aesop's Fables.

However, this is a tremendous opportunity to let our students see the history of Israel in its logical, chronological flow. This will allow them to comprehend that these events really happened, which will make a far greater impact on their lives than a fairy tale or myth!

The Glory—EXPLANATION

To get an informal discussion started on this key concept, ask a simple, leading question, such as, *"What was the most important part of Israel's history?"*

Many history books and museums minimize the history of Israel to a ragtag bunch of nameless people who are not worth studying. However, the Bible shows us that this is far from true! We see, instead, descriptions of a nation who, at the pinnacle of success, is distinguished in having the wisest man in the world as king. The wealth of the world flows to this nation as leaders seek the counsel of Solomon and the fame of the nation spreads far and wide.

This, however, is not the real glory of the kingdom. The real glory is God, Himself.

"Thus says the Lord: 'Let not the wise man glory in his wisdom, let not the mighty man glory in his might, nor let the rich man glory in his riches; But let him who glories glory in this, that he understands and knows Me, that I am the Lord, exercising lovingkindness, judgment, and righteousness in the earth. For in these I delight,' says the Lord." Jeremiah 9:23-24

This is one of those moments where we can learn that God's ways are not our ways and His thoughts are not our thoughts. Talk with your students about what constitutes the greatest treasure, the greatest glory in the world. Pray that their hearts would be illuminated by the Spirit of God to understand that He is our greatest treasure, our greatest glory, and that all else pales in comparison to Him.

The Divided Kingdom—EXPLANATION

To get an informal discussion started on this key concept, ask a simple, leading question, such as, *"Does anyone know why Israel divided into two kingdoms?"*

Peer dependence is not a new sociological phenomena. In fact, we see its folly demonstrated clearly in the son of the king, Solomon, who wrote, *"He who walks with wise men will be wise, but the companion of fools will be destroyed." (Proverbs 13:20)*

Rehoboam, son of Solomon, chose to not listen to the counsel of his father's advisors, instead, took the advice of his own friends, the young men. Through this shortsighted counsel, the kingdom was divided into the northern half—Israel—and the southern half—Judah. Even a cursory look at 1 & 2 Kings and 2 Chronicles shows the tragedy of the divided kingdom. The northern kingdom, from its earliest days, followed other gods and walked in utter disobedience to the word of the Lord. The southern kingdom had several godly kings who instituted reforms to bring the people back to an awareness of God as the One and Only God worthy to be worshipped, though there were also kings who led the people in disobedience and false worship. The following chapter will show the fruit of the rebellious north and sometimes rebellious south. Through it all, however, God preserved the line of David, and a remnant of faithful believers, for Himself.

Application—EXPLANATION

To get an informal discussion started on this key concept, ask a simple, leading question, such as, *"What do you think we might be able to learn from the history of Israel?"*

TEACHER TIP

The story of the children of Israel is truthfully told in Scripture, partly as an example so that we might see and learn:

"Then he spoke to the children of Israel, saying: 'When your children ask their fathers in time to come, saying, 'What are these stones?' then you shall let your children know, saying 'Israel crossed over this Jordan on dry land'; for the Lord your God dried up the waters of the Jordan before you until you had crossed over, as the Lord your God did to the Red Sea, which He dried up before us until we had crossed over, that all the peoples of the earth may know the hand of the Lord, that it is mighty, that you may fear the Lord your God forever.' " Joshua 4:21-24

"And what more shall I say? For the time would fail me to tell of Gideon and Barak and Samson and Jephthah, also of David and Samuel and the prophets... Therefore, we also, since we are surrounded by so great a cloud of witnesses, let us lay aside every weight, and the sin which so easily ensnares us, and let us run with endurance the race that is set before us..." Hebrews 11:32, 12:1

This means that we are not only learning the chronological flow of history, slotting each event into its proper place, but we are also being given the chance to observe the fruit of obedience and disobedience in real people's lives. If we are teachable, we can learn from their example that God is who He says He is, and that He does what He says He will do.

Pray for your students that they will, indeed, learn from this unit spiritual truths which they can apply to their own lives.

SPIRITUAL

2) Read the article

Begins on Page 115 of Student Manual

The article for Unit Four is designed to help students think about the reality of the historical events and people recorded in the Old Testament concerning the Conquest, the Judges, and the Kingdom of Israel—and the implication for people today. The materials covered in the audio recordings offer another look at this time period, covering slightly different information. In the article and recordings, along with introducing the basic understanding of history, we are also bringing in the biblical worldview which recognizes the centrality of the history of Israel in the redemption of mankind.

SPIRITUAL

You may choose to have your students read the article first and then listen to the audio recordings, or vice versa.

3) Listen to the audio recording(s)

Listed on Page 123 of the Student Manual.

• The main concepts and chronological flow are contained in **What in the World's Going On Here?**

• **More True Tales from the Times of…Ancient Civilizations**
  • The Hittites

4) Read the Scripture listed in Read For Your Life

Listed on Page 123 of the Student Manual. You might choose to have the students read the Main Story verses either corporately or privately. The "Short Version" is the rendering of the story into an encapsulated version by someone speaking in the Old Testament (such as Joshua), and brief glimpses of the most important events in the Kingdom of Israel. The "Longer Version" is for students who enjoy knowing the detail, and watching the events unfold moment by moment.

PHASE 1

➤ Listen to This

• **What in the World's Going On Here? Volume One**
  — Israel

➤ Read for Your Life

• **The Holy Bible**

  — The Main Story: (Short Version:) Joshua 24; 1 Samuel 12, 16-17; 2 Samuel 7; 1 Kings 3, 11-12. (Long Version) Joshua; Judges; 1 & 2 Samuel; 1 Kings; 2 Kings 1-14; 1 Chronicles: 2 Chronicles 1-27

  — Helpful Verses: Psalms, Proverbs.

➤ Talk Together

• **Opinion Column**

  — What did you find to be the most interesting aspect, or the most fascinating person, you encountered in your introduction to the children of Israel?

  — What do you think God's intention was for the children of Israel when He gave them the Ten Commandments? How do you think they function in our lives and our society today?

KEY PEOPLE:

Joshua 1470BC
—Leader who brought Israel into Canaan

Gideon 1199 BC
—An unlikely warrior

Deborah
—A woman who judged Israel

Samson 1175BC
—The strong man

King Saul 1100BC
—First king of Israel

King David 1055BC
—A man after God's own heart

King Solomon 1015BC
—The wisest man on earth

King Rehoboam
—A foolish son

King Jereboam
—Did not believe God's word

Key People:

The people listed in this column are the main characters, if you will, of this unit. They are listed in the Student Manual, along with a brief identifier, so that the students can familiarize themselves with these people.

The Scriptures are central to our understanding, our character, and our decisions. Therefore, we must give the greatest weight possible to them. Help your students gain this perspective as they watch you handle the Scriptures with reverence and awe.

The "Other Helpful Verses" listed are the Book of Psalms and the Book of Proverbs. Since King David wrote many of the Psalms, and, in fact, many of them reference the events of his life, we can discover why the Bible describes him as a man with a heart after God. If it is possible, read a few of the Psalms, along with their historical context, and discuss with your students David's response to God in the midst of his circumstances.

King Solomon penned much of the Book of Proverbs. The wisdom and insight contained in these books help us understand the greatness of King Solomon's wisdom, and why people from all over the known world came to him for advice. If possible, read a few pithy proverbs, discuss how they bring wise insight into living, and then talk about how King Solomon lost it all at the end of his days—how he refused to abandon his worship of other gods. Obviously, just knowing the right thing is not the same as doing the right thing.

Though students are not required to look up all the verses (it IS a long list), the teacher might look them up and choose a few to add in to the class discussion, or to assign to selected students for their input into the discussion.

5) Recap (process & review) Activity

In different parts of the room, set up stations for the Eight Intelligences Recap Activities. Then allow students to work alone or together in small groups to accomplish the following suggestions. At the start of the next class, ask for 3-4 groups of volunteers to share. <u>For homeschoolers, rather than set up all eight stations, allow the student(s) to choose which of these activities they would most enjoy, and do that.</u>

Recap Suggestions:

SPATIAL: Make a collage of the different periods of the history of Israel which have been studied in this unit.

BODILY-KINESTHETIC: In small groups, play charades depicting topics they have studied in Israel's history, with one student acting and the other(s) guessing.

INTERPERSONAL: In groups of 2 - 3, brainstorm a plan to present together a storytelling account of this time period.

MUSICAL: In a small group, sing a Jewish-style song of worship together.

LINGUISTIC: In a small group, talk about the pros and cons of King Solomon's decision to marry foreign wives.

MATH-LOGICAL: Make a simple chart showing the development of Israel as a nation during the time period of the unit.

INTRAPERSONAL: Have the students consider which of the history makers they would wish to be from this time period, and why.

NATURALIST: The Promised Land was described as flowing with milk and honey. Let the naturalists come up with several delicious possibilities utilizing milk and honey. Give everyone a sample of the best creation! (For example, make milkshakes with milk, honey, and ice.) Then, talk about what it would have meant to the children of Israel to live in such a place.

OR...Activity of Your Choice: What would you like to have your students do for a review activity concerning this week's introduction to the Children of Israel?

6) Opinion Column and Critical Puzzling answers on their own

Listed on Pages 123-124 of the Student Manual. Students may begin these questions after completing their Recap Activities listed above.

7) Class Discussion

Using the questions listed on Pages 123-124 of the Student Manual to get the students primed, create a discussion environment in the classroom. You may also want to draw from the open-ended questions listed below.

QUESTION

Why do you think God commanded the various feasts of Israel?

QUESTION

What can you discover in Scripture about the Israelites in regard to their treatment of other peoples? (Consider: Exodus 22:21) Remembering that God will never violate His character, why do you think God would instruct them to destroy the Canaanites? (Consider: Genesis 15:13-16.)

QUESTION

Why do you suppose David did not kill King Saul when he had the chance?

Phase 1

— Joshua was one of twelve men who had spied out the land promised by God to the children of Israel. But of the twelve, only Joshua and Caleb came back with an enthusiastic, God-fearing report. All of the others spoke glowingly of the natural resources but were terrified of the fierce people populating Canaan. They warned the people that if they tried to go into to the land, they would be destroyed. If you had been one of those delivered out of Egypt, what would you have thought about these conflicting reports?

• Critical Puzzling

— Considering the trade routes which pass through the Kingdom of Israel, what do you think God had in mind when He chose that geographic location for His chosen people?

— Consider whether God's "military strategy" was the normal strategy for besieging a city. What made it effective and do you think that it is repeatable today?

— During the period of the Judges of Israel, why do you think the nation suffered so many difficulties?

— In 1 Samuel 16, we see Samuel anointing a young, unknown man as king over Israel. Verse 7 tells us something significant about the difference between how we see people and how God sees people. What can you learn from this about God's ways?

— In the Psalms, David shares everything from dark despair to exultant victory. How did David's attitude toward God make a difference in his various situations?

— Why do you think King Solomon turned away from God after having received so much? What can we learn from this for our own lives?

124 / Unit Four: *The Children of Israel*

---

8) *Choose books of interest/Internet search*

A list of possible books for further reading is listed in the Student Manual beginning on Page 125. Encourage your students to look for general information on ancient Israel from this list and from other sources. You may want to gather a selection of further resources prior to beginning Unit Four, or you may encourage the students to be treasure hunters and find them on their own.

INTRO · PG 20

➤ Reviewed Resources for Digging Deeper:

Choose a few books that look interesting, or find your own.

Israel:

Halley's Bible Handbook

This book contains wonderful study helps and insights related to the Old and New Testaments. It includes archaeological explanations from a Biblical perspective. (However, the archaeologists' findings in the Fertile Crescent are interpreted to mean that the Flood was a localized event.) **UE+**

The New Unger's Bible Handbook
revised by Gary Larson

This is my preferred source for information and insight on the archaeological record from a Biblical perspective. It is filled with color pictures, timelines, notes, helps, and exciting tidbits! **UE+**

Victor Journey Through the Bible
by V. Gilbert Beers

With photos, maps, and charts and brief articles, this book gives an excellent enhancement to the reading of the Bible. **UE+**

Daily Chronological Bible

Reading this Bible was our basic introduction to the concept of studying ancient civilizations and the Bible. It is set up chronologically with

wonderful insights into the history of the Scriptures. **UE+**

Josephus

Since one of Josephus' purposes was to explain the history of Israel, this is an excellent (although difficult) resource for studying this subject. **HS+**

A Family Guide to the Biblical Holidays
by Robin Scarlata and Linda Pierce

A wonderful resource for celebrating the feasts of Israel in your family. Many helpful ideas and suggestions—an excellent addition to this study. **AA**

Dance, Sing, Remember—A Celebration of Jewish Holidays by Leslie Kimmelman

Written and illustrated for children, this is a delightful book. Discover recipes, games, history and more. **E+**

Student Bible Atlas

A Bible atlas is an indispensable tool in understanding the history of the children of Israel. This particular one is excellent for students. **AA**

ℛemember:

Beware of Arrogance, Embrace Humility!

The Internet has a wealth of information concerning the children of Israel, though the articles available vary widely in dependability, worldview and attitude. Help your students learn to recognize the differences.

For the complete list of books from the Student Manual, refer to the Appendix (pg 324).

EVALUATION | **Review & Evaluation**

In this Phase of Unit Four, your students should have had the opportunity to explore the Joshua, Judges and the Kingdom years through reading, listening, thinking and discussing. They will have:

1) informally discussed the Key Concepts;
2) read the article;
3) listened to the audio recording(s);
4) read the Scripture listed in Read for Your Life;
5) explored the Recap Activities;
6) completed the Opinion Column and Critical Puzzling answers on their own;
7) participated in Class Discussion;
8) chosen books of interest or searched the Internet.

You may wish to evaluate your students based on their *participation* in the **Class Discussion** and on their *participation* in the **Recap Activity**.

Learning Style Emphasis: THINKER

Students will explore topics of interest through research and reporting, learn new vocabulary, and construct a timeline relating to Joshua, Judges and the Kingdom years.

Monday-Tuesday:
  1) Choose topic and begin research

Wednesday:
  2) Vocabulary Practice

Thursday:
  3) Construct the Timeline.

Friday:
  4) Research projects completed; share in class or hand in.

> *Teachers can choose to have students do one or two activities, rather than the entire week's schedule. Please use what works for you in your unique setting.*

1) Choose topic and begin research

Allow the students the freedom to choose one of the topics listed on Page 127, or to suggest their own area which they would like to research.

Motivating Suggestions:

Especially for Non-Linguistic students, and those who are not motivated by written or oral reports, here are suggestions for alternative ways of reporting what has been researched.

The Ancient Kingdom
  1) Create a three-act play, showing the Conquest, the Judges, and the Kingdom.
  2) Draw a map of Israel, showing where each of the twelve tribes settled. (Consider: Remember the special provision for the Levites!)

Ancient Personalities
  1) Do a "live" interview with each of the people listed. Use the same questions for each.
  2) Make a chart showing the similarities and differences between each of the people listed in the three sets of ancient personalities.

MOTIVATE

The Temple

1) Make a flip chart for Solomon's Temple, then verbally instruct others using the chart.
2) Find or make a three-dimensional representation of Solomon's Temple, then label the different areas and write or tell an explanation for the labels.

Archaeology

1) Create a series of four posters, one for each archaeological site, showing (in photo or drawing) a sample of what has been discovered in each place. Give each of the posters a title which summarizes the significance of the site.
2) Set up four representational archaeological "digs" in a room or outside, with selected items (labeled) to represent the major finds in each dig. The student may conduct tours of the sites, answering questions.

Trade Routes

1) Draw a map showing the trade routes which went through the nation of Israel. Include the modes of transportation and the type of trade goods which would have typically been carried.
2) The student may create an ad for their camel caravans, in which they give merchants enticing details of the benefits of shipping with this particular caravan company!

PHASE 2
Exploration & Discovery Week

➢ *Research & Reporting*

Your mission, if you choose to accept it, is to explore one of these areas and to discover something significant!

• **The Ancient Kingdom:**

Find one of the books listed, or a book of your choice, for more information on the ancient kingdom of Israel. Report your findings.

• **Ancient Personalities:**

Compare and contrast Ruth and Rahab; Samson and Gideon; Samuel and Eli.

• **The Temple:**

Research the temple of Solomon. Report on the funding, the materials, the building of the temple, as well as the use or abuse of it in history.

• **Archaeology:**

Research and write about what archaeologists have uncovered in the digs of Jericho, Ebla, Jerusalem, and Tell el Amarna. Remember that there are differing interpretations of the actual finds.

• **Trade Routes:**

Research and report on the ancient trade routes of the Middle East. What modes of transportation were used in this area? What have archaeologists learned about trade goods imported and exported? What was used for money? How did this impact Judah and Israel?

• **Consequences:**

Explore in Scripture the consequences of obedience and disobedience in Israel's history. Can you extrapolate from this to your own society?

• **Phoenicia:**

Learn about Phoenicia: cities, export, navigation, trade routes, relation to Israel. What new process did the Phoenicians bring to writing? Hiram was king of Tyre during Solomon's reign. What did he do for Israel?

Consequences

1) Make a chart of the Scriptures that show the acts of obedience of this time period and the resulting consequences, and acts of disobedience and the resulting consequences.
2) Do a first person presentation, as a Hebrew, of what has been learned about obeying and disobeying the Lord.

Phoenicia

1) Report your findings as if you were a newspaper reporter.
2) Create a multimedia presentation highlighting the history of Phoenicia and its relationship to Israel, including music, drawings, photos, maps, video clips, newspaper or magazine articles, and anything else that would be helpful.

Brain Stretchers:

Brain Stretchers, listed on page 128, are intended for advanced students. Those who attempt the Brain Stretchers for their Research and Reporting can use the above list for ideas on how to report their findings.

Phase 2

≫ *Brain Stretchers*

• **North versus South:**

Do a research paper with photos or illustrations on the differences between the northern kingdom of Israel and the southern kingdom of Judah. Include geographical, political, economic, and religious differences. Using the Scriptures, determine why there are differences. What is the Scriptural explanation?

• **The Neighbors:**

Discover the geographical boundaries of the neighboring countries (such as Phoenicia, Philistia, Moab, Edom, etc.) What part did Egypt play in the politics of the area during the time of the Kingdom? Make a diagram showing the who, where, when, and how of these allies and enemies.

• **From Conquest to Current:**

Investigate, in the library or on the Internet, the history of Israel from the time of Joshua to the present. Use maps to show the dispersion throughout the world of the Hebrew people, and trace the persecution that often followed them. Consider what prophetic Scriptures have been fulfilled in their history.

Create Your Own Research Topic:

_____

_____

_____

2) *Words To Watch - Vocabulary Practice*

Listed on Page 129. You may find other words in this unit that are especially appropriate for younger children. Feel free to substitute another vocabulary list for the one provided.

Here is one idea for making vocabulary study interesting and fun: ***Make up a drama or dramatic reading using most or all of the terms.***

TEACHER TIP

Phase 2

≫ *Words to Watch*

Remember—The easiest way to learn a subject is to master its terms:

conquest	anoint	idolatry
temple	Philistines	talent
tabernacle	Jericho	shekel
tribute	Jerusalem	Pentateuch
alliance	Jordan river	Talmud
angel	Gilgal	Torah
monarchy	Gaza	tell (tel)
theocracy	Lachish	Ark of the Covenant
prophet	Canaan	

3) *Construct the Timeline.*

Read the information listed with the "Key Dates" on Page 131. Dialogue with your students about the issues involved. Help them recognize that dating antiquity is not an exact science. For ease of reference, the timeline is included in the Appendix on Page 326.

Find the dates for the key people and events listed. In this unit, the students have learned that the re-dating of Egyptian Chronology causes the archaeological evidences for the events listed in Scripture concerning the ancient nation of Israel to fall into place. The dating of this time period is clearly given in Scripture (1 Kings 6:1), though, again, secular historians would dispute this.

4) *Research projects shared in class and/or turned in.*

Create a safe environment for the presentations. Set ground rules prior to the presentations for all the students, so that they know each one will be honored and respected in their work by all those observing.

EVALUATION | Review & Evaluation

In this second Phase of Unit Four, your students should have had the opportunity to explore Joshua, Judges and the Kingdom years through researching, thinking, and reporting. They will have:

1) done a research project;
2) learned the vocabulary;
3) constructed a Timeline;
4) created a project report on what was researched.

You may wish to evaluate your students based on their *efforts* in the **Research and Reporting** projects and their *active participation* in the **Vocabulary** and **Timeline** exercises.

Learning Style Emphasis: Sensor

Students will gain cultural understanding through sensory activities as they explore interrelated subject areas relating to Joshua, Judges and the Kingdom years.

Monday:
1) Create a map and discuss the issues in teams.

Tuesday:
2) Examine and discuss art masterpieces & architectural structures.

Wednesday:
3) Arts in Action—Do an art project.*

Thursday:
4) Do one science project or field trip.**

Friday:
5) Listen to and discuss the music.
6) Cook the food listed in the recipe, if desired.

*Art project will need to be planned ahead of time to acquire materials.
*Field trip will require extra planning time.

Teachers can choose to have students do one or two activities, rather than the entire week's schedule. Please use what works for you in your unique setting.

1) Create a map and discuss the issues in teams

INTRO - PG 23

The students each have an outline map on Page 133. They will be given assignments for drawing in rivers, mountains, cities, and regional boundaries, which are listed on Page 132. For details on where these things are, please consult a historical atlas, an encyclopedia, a study Bible, or any other source for geographic information. For ease of reference, the map is included in the Appendix on Page 327.

Upper elementary students might be satisfied to accomplish only this portion:
- *Physical terrain:* This part of the mapping exercise will help students locate and mark the geological dynamics of a region.

Middle school students might be satisfied to complete both the previous mapping exercise and this exercise:
- *Geo-Political:* This section of the mapping exercise will provide the students an opportunity to locate and mark the cities, nations and empires of history. It will require more digging.

High school students might be satisfied to complete both the previous mapping exercises and at least one exploration topic of this exercise:
- *Explore:* Discuss some selection from this portion of the mapping exercise in teams.

Encourage them to think for themselves, rather than parroting back information.

Dissemination

Remind the students of God's promise to Abraham in Genesis 12:3. Considering His statement that Abraham was to be a blessing to all the families of the earth, discuss with the students the significance of the geographical setting for the nation of Israel.

Christian Outreach

Students may wish to locate information about Christian missions work in Israel. If it is possible to interview someone who has worked in that field, it will be even more helpful and insightful.

PHASE 3

The Hands-On Week

➢ Maps and mapping

- **Physical Terrain:**

  — Label and color the Jordan river.

  — Label and color the Sea of Galilee and the Dead Sea.

  — Draw in and color the mountain ranges, deserts, and green areas.

- **Geo-Political:**

  — Place Jerusalem, Bethlehem, Jericho, Tyre and Sidon on the map.

  — What countries (both ancient and modern) are they located in?

  — Color in the Kidron Valley, Hinnom Valley, Plain of Sharon and the Golan heights.

  — Draw the boundaries of the northern Kingdom of Israel and the southern Kingdom of Judah.

- **Explore:**

  — *Dissemination:* Israel is in a strikingly strategic geographic location when one examines the trade routes of antiquity. Consider together the different people groups who would travel through Israel. What would be the trickle down effect of the stories of the faithfulness and power of the Hebrews' God disseminating throughout different lands? Who do you think would hear these stories? How far away could this news travel, given the trade routes?

  — *Christian Outreach:* What is the unique position of Christianity to the people of Israel? What is the status of Christian outreach at this time? Discuss the difficulties and the potential solutions for Christians seeking to serve God in this land.

Scripture tells us clearly in Psalm 122:6 to pray for the peace of Jerusalem. With your students, begin to pray this prayer, with ever increasing insight as you discover more of the actual current needs and issues.

2) Examine and discuss art masterpieces & architectural structures

Locate either a copy of these art forms, or Internet sites for each of the items listed on Pages 134-135. Allow the students time to observe the art without any conversation, and then, when they are ready, engage them in some or all of the questions listed in the Student Manual or below.

Phase 3

Art Appreciation

Consider:

Peter Paul Rubens (1577-1640 A.D.) was highly educated, and was considered to be one of the most intellectual artists of the seventeenth century. He worked both as an international diplomat and an artist—quite an unusual combination! A wealthy and influential painter of the Baroque style, Rubens was a master of communicating movement in art.

• **The Judgment of Solomon** *by Peter Paul Rubens*

— What does this painting communicate to you about Solomon?

— How does the painting differ from your own impression of this historic event?

— How would you describe Rubens' use of color and movement in this scene?

• **The artwork in the Tabernacle** *(Read Exodus 25–27)* **Solomon's Temple** *(Read 2 Chronicles 3 & 4)*

— How would you describe the artistry of the Tabernacle, including the colors, textures, and design?

— How would you describe the artistry of Solomon's Temple, including the colors, textures, and design?

— What does this tell you about the value God places on beauty; on artistic endeavors?

The Judgment of Solomon *by Peter Paul Rubens*

Rubens was the quintessential Baroque painter, with a sweeping, vibrant motion visible in his paintings. Observe his use of color in this painting, as well as the snapshot feeling of movement in his characters.

• Ask the students to describe the style of costumes in this painting. Is it realistic to 1000 B.C.? If not, can they place the style in an historic moment of time? Why would Rubens have used this style, rather than reflecting ancient clothing?

The artwork in the Tabernacle (Exodus 25 - 27) & Solomon's Temple (2 Chronicles 3 & 4)

• Ask the students what purpose God might have had for such artistry in the Tabernacle and Temple. Do they think it was important to God to have beauty, or was it important to the worshippers, or was it important to both?

• Field Trip: To bring descriptions of the Tabernacle and Solomon's Temple to life, arrange a field trip to a fabric store and jewelry store to find samples of the different materials described in Scripture (alternately, bring samples to the students), so that the students can actually see and handle them.

The Temple—Architecture

• Discuss with the students the impact of such a visually stunning place of worship, with its overlay of gold, its columns of bronze, its enormous size and height.

• Ask the students if they think that such a magnificent building would have led people into a greater worship of the God to whom the building was dedicated, or, eventually would it have lowered their understanding of the God who set the stars in their courses and Who did not dwell in a habitation made by man?

3) Arts in Action

Listed on Pages 135-136.

Imitation

Have the students look again at Ruben's painting. Then, with art supplies of colored pencils, pastels, or paint, try to recreate what they see.

TEACHER TIP

Costuming

Since Biblical-style costumes are fairly easy to make, and because many churches have Easter or Christmas dramas, students should not encounter much difficulty in this project.

Psalm 23

Psalm 23 is filled with word pictures. Encourage the students to look at photos or paintings of green pastures, calm streams, sheep, etc., and then to make a collage or mural of the psalm.

Fabric Dying

Fabric dye can cause a mess, so be sure the students are well supervised and well covered! They may want to do this project first, and then make Biblical costumes with the dyed fabric.

Make the Temple

This could be a very complex, detailed project that takes a student months to complete, or it could be a very simple representation of the Temple.

➢ *Architecture*

The Temple in Jerusalem, which King Solomon built, was similar in its layout to the Tabernacle, but it was greatly increased in size and splendor. According to 2 Chronicles 3, the inside ceiling was fifty feet high, one hundred eighty feet long and ninety feet wide. The tallest point on the Temple was twenty stories high! The structure itself was rectangular, surrounded by open courtyards. It had the inner "Holy of Holies," with a large outer hallway in front containing two huge columns of bronze. The inner sanctuary and altar were overlaid with gold, as were the carved doors. It was one of the most monumental and impressive buildings of that time period, but when Nebuchadnezzar invaded Jerusalem nearly four hundred years later, Solomon's Temple was utterly destroyed.

— Look for an artist's rendition of Solomon's Temple online or in a book. How would you describe this amazing building?

➢ *Arts in Action*

Select one, and let your artistic juices flow!

• **Imitation:**

Try your hand at imitating Rubens (trace, follow colors, etc.)

• **Costuming:**

Try making Biblical costumes for your "reenacting" of Bible scenes. (I highly recommend **Bible Time Crafts for Kids** by Neva Hickerson, as it is filled with wonderful costumes, crafts, musical instruments, etc., that are easy to make!)

✗ • **Psalm 23:**

Depict King David's Psalm 23 through art. What expression does the shepherd have on his face? Try to capture all of the elements of this psalm.

• **Fabric Dying:**

The Phoenicians exported a purple dye that was extraordinarily expensive (one drop of dye from each mollusk!) Try dying fabric using a natural source, like beets or tea, for dye. Check the library for info.

Working with Wool

Some areas are rife with spinners, while other places are completely lacking. If it is possible to locate someone who spins, it will be a great chance for students to discover how complex something that looks very simple can be! With practice, spinning is a leisurely, extremely tactile hobby.

Knitting or crocheting a scarf is a great way to start beginners. Make sure that the wool is pleasant to handle, or it will quickly become an unfinished project.

Papier-Maché Map

An adventurous group of students in New Zealand spent weeks creating a detailed papier-maché map with all the nooks and crannies of Israel depicted. Their teacher told me that it was the most fulfilling project of the entire year!

4) Do a science project

Listed on Page 136. Feel free to choose one of these projects. If students love science, they might want to consider doing all of them!

INTRO - PG 24

Phase 3

- **Make the Temple**

  Make a model of Solomon's Temple. You could construct it from papier maché; fabric over a dowel; clay; bread dough, or whatever you prefer.

- **Working with Wool:**

  — See if you can find someone who spins wool. After observing, you may want to ask to try it. (It's not as easy as it looks!)

  — Once the wool is spun, it can be made into various articles of clothing through weaving, knitting or crocheting. This is a great time to learn how to do any of these. Check the library for how-to books and start with a VERY simple project.

- **Papier-Maché Map:**

  For an eye-opening adventure in geography, make a papier maché map of Israel including the Jordan River, the Sea of Galilee, the Dead Sea, the mountains and plains, plus the Desert of Zin, the Desert of Paran, and the Desert of Shur.

➤ Science

- **Sheep:**

  — Field Trip: Visit a farm with sheep, or a petting zoo. Ask lots of questions about the care of sheep, the way the wool is removed, what the wool can be used for. If you can touch the fleece, rub the wool in your fingers for a few minutes. What ingredient is in the sheep wool which makes your fingers soft?

- **Fermentation:**

  — Chemistry: Learn how grapes are grown and then turned into wine or vinegar. What is the process? Try an experiment with some type of fermentation (make sure Mom knows what you left in the pantry!).

Sheep

Field Trip: If you can arrange a trip to a farm or petting zoo with sheep, students will have the marvelous opportunity to see for themselves some of the characteristics of sheep which the Bible describes. Lanolin is the lotion-like substance contained in the unwashed fleece.

TEACHER TIP

Fermentation

There are many different fruits which can be used for fermentation. If a student or team of students wants to try an experiment with fermentation, it will take some time. However, everyone could try tasting the end result of fermentation. Try gathering some different types of vinegar—balsamic, malt, red wine, apple cider, white—and have the students sample them. Discuss why there are such different tastes to the different vinegars.

5) *Listen to and discuss the music*

Listed on Page 137.

Try This

Many hymns and worship choruses (especially older ones) come from the Psalms. With the students, consider how the words (many written by David) have tremendous meaning for our lives, yet how they also represent an actual historic moment in time. After singing some of the psalms together, discuss how the words were true for David and how they are also true for us.

Consider:

2 Chronicles 20:1-30 shows an amazing aspect of singing and praise in God's Kingdom. Talk with your students about what this story might mean for them in their own lives.

Phase 3

≫ Music

• Consider:

— The Bible is filled with references to musical instruments and singing in ancient Israel, both of which were used in the joyful worship of God. The Psalms were all meant to be sung. Many even have comments telling which instruments were to accompany! There were professional musicians employed in the worship at the Temple, and Scripture indicates that these musicians were to be skilled.

One of the most incredible stories in the Old Testament is found in 2 Chronicles 20:1- 30. It tells of a very unique task for musicians—to go into battle, before the army, worshiping and praising God! Read this account out loud for the whole class or family, and then stand and sing together the Doxology.

• Try this:

— Do you know any worship hymns or choruses using Psalms? Have each student look through the Psalms, and when anyone recognizes the words to a familiar song, sing it. Some you may know: Psalm 125, Psalm 89, Psalm 63, Psalm 34.

— You may also want to try singing your own melody, such as a folk tune or Christmas carol, with a Psalm. Start with one line or verse.

This is a family favorite (to the tune of "Short'ning Bread"):

You have dealt well with Your servant,
O Lord, according to Your word. Psalm 119:65

Doxology

Praise God from whom all blessings flow,

Praise Him all creatures here below,

Praise Him above, ye heavenly host,

Praise Father, Son and Holy Ghost.

➢ Cooking

God told His chosen people that He was taking them to a land filled with milk and honey. In order to really understand how wonderful milk and honey are, we are going to make Yogurt Cake with Honey Frosting. Thank you, Lord!

• Yogurt Cake & Honey Frosting

1 cup butter	3 cups flour
2 cups sugar	1/4 tsp salt
4 eggs, separated (room temp)	4 tsp. baking powder
1 cup yogurt (plain)	3 tsp. lemon extract

Cream butter and sugar together until light and fluffy. Add the egg yolks one at a time, beating until creamy and light. Stir in yogurt. Add flour, salt, baking powder, lemon extract. Mix well. Beat egg whites until stiff but not dry, and mix 1/3 into batter. Fold in remaining egg whites. Turn into a 10" tube pan and bake in preheated 350 degree oven for about 60 minutes, or until done.

Frosting:

1/2 cup honey	1/4 tsp salt
2 egg whites, room temp.	1/8 tsp cream of tartar

Bring honey to boil in saucepan. Beat egg whites until frothy, add salt and cream of tartar, continue to beat. When egg whites hold soft peaks, slowly add honey in a thin stream. Continue to beat until meringue is stiff and glossy. Frost cake when cool.

6) Cook the food

INTRO - PG 24

Listed on Page 138.

TEACHER TIP

When we read that God took His people to a land flowing with milk and honey, it might not hold any particular sensation. However, when they actually taste milk and honey , the students will connect the reality of the marvelous richness of the land with the fragrant richness of the flavors.

Review & Evaluation

EVALUATION

In this third Phase of Unit Four, your students should have had the opportunity to explore Joshua, Judges and the Kingdom years through various hands-on and creative sessions. They will have:

1) completed a Mapping section;
2) observed and discussed Art & Architecture;
3) worked on an art project;
4) experimented with a Science Project or taken a field trip;
5) listened to music;
6) tasted a food related to this unit.

You may wish to evaluate your students based on their *class participation* in these **Hands-on** activities.

PHASE 4

The Expression Week

Learning Style Emphasis: *Intuitor*

Students, through creative self-expression, using one or more creative activities, will present some aspect of what they have learned in the past three weeks relating to Joshua, Judges and the Kingdom years. Areas of expression include linguistics, art, music, drama, movement and conceptual design.

Monday - Thursday

1) Choose area of expression and begin work either individually or in teams.

Friday

2) Share creative expressions in class.

> *Teachers can choose to have students do one or two activities, rather than the entire week's schedule. Please use what works for you in your unique setting.*

INTRO · PG 25

1) Choose area of expression and begin work either individually or in teams

Linguistics:

Located on page 139.

TEACHER TIP

Journalism

Have the students read some journalistic "insider" writings from a recent war, such as the Iraq war, and then base their writing on that style.

Playing with Words

- The Alphabet Game: This is a fun way to go through a tremendous amount of information. Students or families may wish to set ground rules at the beginning, like, eliminating the letter "x."
- Show students some examples of limericks in order to get their creative juices flowing and to help them understand the model of what they are attempting to create.

Prose

- Encourage the students to really consider what it must have been like after five days of silently marching around a city. Did the people feel silly? …doubtful? Were they possibly mocked by the people inside Jericho? Was it an eery experience or simply humdrum, everyday walking?
- Sometimes journaling will allow a student to freely express what has been locked in his heart and mind up to this point. It is important in journaling that a student feel secure in sharing, so let the heart of what is being expressed be evaluated, rather than the grammatical construction.

PHASE 4

The Expression Week

➢ *In Your Own Way...*

We have seen the amazing way God cared for His people in the land of Israel, even when they walked in rebellion. Now, choose a selection of these activities, or create your own, which will best express what you have learned from this unit. Finally, pray for the peace of Jerusalem, and for your own nation.

Linguistics:

• **Journalism:**

Be a newspaper reporter for the "Desert Sun Times," and give the exclusive inside scoop on the spies who came back from Canaan.

• **Prose:**

— Write a fictional account of an Israelite named "Benjamin the Skeptic" on the sixth and seventh day of the march around Jericho.

— Consider journaling in the style of the Psalms. Let God know what is on your heart, but remember, as David did, God's faithfulness.

• **Playing with Words:**

— The Alphabet Game: One person starts with the letter "a." They must name a word that pertains to this unit beginning with "a" (such as "Ark of the Covenant".) The next person gives a word beginning with "b" (like "Benjamin"). Keep the game going through all of the letters, extra credit given for "X" & "Z". How did you do? (Variation: In a family or small group of students, have each one use the same letter, and then everyone advances to the next letter.)

— Finish this limerick about Hiram: *"There was a great king from Tyre, Who sent out his craftsmen for hire…"*

• **Poetry:**

In the style of David, compose a psalm of thanksgiving to God. (Psalm 100 is an example.)

• **Script writing:**

— Write a script that highlights the most important events during these 600 years of Israel's history, using vignettes of characters to tell the story.

— Write a funny monologue for Solomon, entitled "Life with Seven Hundred Wives."

Poetry

TEACHER TIP

Encourage your students to examine several of David's psalms in order to see the structure (or, at least, what the structure looks like in English.) That should give them a good start toward writing their own poem.

Scriptwriting

• To show the development of the history of Israel, students may choose to do a narrative with the players instructed to do movements rather than use dialogue, or students may prefer to create brief vignettes with dialogue.

• Students should read a selection of monologues to gain the flow and construction of this interesting verbal art form. A suggestion would be to examine some of Shakespeare's monologues—either comedy or tragedy.

Art:

Located on page 140.

TEACHER TIP

Painting/Drawing

Students may wish to view scenes from *The Ten Commandments* or *Prince of Egypt* to get ideas for their painting.

Political Cartooning

Have students examine some different styles of political cartoons until they have grasped the elements that make for a good one.

Set Design

The Feast of Tabernacles gives artistic students who enjoy three-dimensional art an opportunity to create a booth in the manner of Leviticus 23:40. You may have to substitute some of the types of branches and leaves, but be creative!

Music:
Located on page 140.

Compose

Students may wish to form a team to compose and perform a song, or they may wish to do this selection on their own.

Sing Ethnic

It is powerful to learn the music of a people group as it gives a fresh window of appreciation into their culture. Encourage your students to enjoy the experience!

Performance Practice

For musical students, this selection may be a wonderful opportunity to express what they have learned. Make sure they have selected a piece that they have adequate time to prepare.

Drama:
Located on page 141.

Comedy

Consider how God told Gideon to choose his army. Then look up how He told them to conduct their battle!

Puppetry

Using the first scriptwriting activity listed on Page 139, think about the ten most important events in ancient Israel's history from the Exodus to the Captivity. What scenes would work best for puppets? Remember that if you do a puppet show for younger children, they will lose interest fairly quickly, so don't make the show too long, and keep it moving!

Phase 4

Art:

- **Painting/Drawing:**
  Create an artistic rendering of the scene where Moses receives the Ten Commandments.

- **Political Cartooning:**
  Show Rheboam's decision to make life more difficult for the twelve tribes—and the unfortunate results.

- **Set Design:**
  The Feast of Tabernacles is an incredibly artistic holiday! Make Succoth booths outside, prepare festive food, and invite your family, friends, and church over to help you celebrate God's wonderful provision for His people.

Music:

- **Compose:**
  Write lyrics to a tune of your choosing about the Queen of Sheba coming to visit King Solomon. A good starting place might be the tune, "She'll be coming round the mountain."

- **Sing Ethnic**
  There are some wonderful Jewish songs which could be learned and then sung. "Hava Nagila" is an example.

- **Performance Practice:**
  With your teacher's help, select an appropriate piece of music written by a Jewish composer like Mendelssohn, or with Jewish content. Prepare and perform the piece for an audience. Communicate with your audience the reason for your selection either in the program notes or in a short speech.

Phase 4

Drama:

• Comedy:

Do a humorous skit about Gideon and his army.

• Puppetry:

Using puppets, act out the script listed above, using a narrator, worship songs, and quick scene changes.

• Reality:

Act out the story of the twelve spies. Use your imagination to create props, sets and costumes. Be sure to include the results for the twelve and the results for the two!

Reality

What did the twelve spies see in Canaan? What experiences did they have? As you look up the scriptural story, consider how to best act this out, especially the end of the story—which was tragic.

TEACHER TIP

Movement:

Located on page 142.

TEACHER TIP

Pantomime

The Bible tells us that David danced for joy as the ark was brought to Jerusalem, so much that his wife despised him.

Dance

Once you have learned the dance, plan to demonstrate, then teach it to others. There is such a sense of celebration when everyone joins in these folk dances.

Action

You might consider using stylized action or "living statues" which freeze between movements. Both of these would work well with a narration of the events.

Phase 4

Movement:

• Pantomime:

Pantomime the scene with King David bringing the Ark to Jerusalem.

• Dance:

Learn a Jewish folk dance, like the Horah.

• Action:

With a small group, design an action scene showing how Gideon was able to defeat the enemies of Israel. You may want to start from the scene where Gideon is in the winepress!

Conceptual Design:

• Game Design:

Design a board game to teach younger children about the history of Israel, from the time of Joshua through the division of the Kingdom. Your game board could show the geographic features of Israel, such as the mountains, the Jordan River, the Sea of Galilee, the Dead Sea, the Plain of Sharon, and whatever features would be useful in learning the history of this ancient people.

Create Your Own Expression:

_____

_____

Conceptual Design:

Located on page 142.

Game Design

A board game for younger children needs to have simple rules and interesting moves. Once you have created it, you might want to consider giving this game as gifts to children you know!

INTRO · PG 26

2) *Share creative expressions in class.*

The same rules apply as suggested in the reporting section of Phase Two.

EVALUATION | **Review & Evaluation**

In this final Phase of Unit Four, your students should have had the opportunity to express what they have learned about the Joshua, Judges and the Kingdom years through one or more various creative selections of their own choosing. These include:

1) Linguistics;
2) Art;
3) Music;
4) Drama;
5) Movement;
6) Conceptual Design.

You may wish to evaluate your students based on their *effort* in the **Creative Expressions**, either as individuals or in teams.

Teacher's Guide

ASSYRIA & BABYLON:
THE MESOPOTAMIAN CONQUERORS

UNIT
5

Winged Bull of Assyria

Enthusiasm and delight

are the best way to capture a student's

interest and jump-start motivation, so:

1) ***For the Auditory Students:*** Consider playing music from the **Star Wars** soundtrack, or other music which would communicate an overwhelming conqueror, to capture their attention at the very beginning of class;

2) ***For the Kinesthetic Students:*** Have the students warm up as class begins by doing some active movement that is fun (such as a contest for creating a soldier's marching step);

3) ***For the Visual Students:*** Bring a visual object to stimulate their interest in the new unit, like a photo of Assyrian bas relief sculpture, or a photo of the Ishtar Gate of Babylon;

4) ***For the hearts of all:*** Pray with them at the beginning of the unit, that God would help them discover what He has for each one to learn in that unit.

Pray with the students

at the beginning of each unit.

PHASE 1

The Introduction Week

During this week, students will be introduced to the Mesopotamian Conquerors, Assyria and Babylon, and their place in Scripture—2 Kings 17-20 & 24-25, Daniel 1-5, 7-8, Jonah, Nahum, Habakkuk, and Micah. You may follow this suggested schedule or adapt it to meet your students' needs:

Monday:
1) Informally discuss the Key Concepts

Tuesday:
2) Read the article
3) Listen to the audio recording(s)
4) Read the Scripture listed in Read For Your Life (could be done on their own)

Wednesday:
5) Recap Activity
6) Opinion Column and Critical Puzzling answers on their own

Thursday:
7) Class Discussion

Friday:
8) Choose books of interest/Internet search

> *Teachers can choose to have students do one or two activities, rather than the entire week's schedule. Please use what works for you in your unique setting.*

1) Informally Discuss the Key Concepts

INTRO- PG 18

Listed in the Student Manual on Page 143.

KEY CONCEPTS BACKGROUND INFORMATION

These are the main objectives of the unit. As you proceed through the four weeks, your students will be given various ways of understanding each of these objectives.

Jonah & Assyria—EXPLANATION

TEACHER TIP

> To get an informal discussion started on this key concept, ask a simple, leading question, such as, *"What do you know about the story of Jonah?"*

By the mid-eighth century B.C., Assyria's reputation for cruelty and conquests was legendary—one of their rulers, Shalmaneser III, had killed more than 16,000 enemy soldiers in one battle—and all the people in the Middle East quaked in fear of this terrible foe. Into this setting, God spoke His word to the Hebrew prophet, Jonah:

"Arise, go to Ninevah, that great city, and cry out against it; for their wickedness has come up before Me."
Jonah 1:2

God intends to warn these non-Jewish people that He is going to bring judgment against them, but Jonah wants no part in it. At the end of the book of Jonah, we discover his reason for his disobedience:

"Ah, Lord, was not this what I said when I was still in my country? …You are a gracious and merciful
God, slow to anger and abundant in loving kindness, One who relents from doing harm." Jonah 4:2

Knowing that God might forgive these terrifying conquerors, Jonah refused to go. He fled on a ship bound for Tarshish (Spain), rather than heading five hundred miles northeast to Ninevah. Isn't it interesting that the mercy of God, when directed to us and our friends, is good, but when directed to our worst enemies, might seem bad?

Through his watery adventure, Jonah finally came to a place of repentance. God then directed the great fish to spit Jonah onto dry land, and from that unknown spot, Jonah had to start hiking at least five hundred miles. When he arrived at Ninevah and spoke the word God had given him, the inhabitants responded in an unparalleled manner:

ASSYRIA & BABYLON:
THE MESOPOTAMIAN CONQUERORS

UNIT 5

Winged Bull of Assyria

KEY CONCEPTS:

• Jonah & Assyria

• Judgment of Israel

• Discovery of Nineveh

• Prophets & Babylon

• Babylonian Captivity

Into captivity...

From the northeast part of Mesopotamia, on the banks of the Tigris River, arose a mighty nation of conquering warriors who would eventually become both a watchword among the nations for cruelty, as well as participants in the greatest revival ever witnessed.

In the southeast part of Mesopotamia, on the banks of the Euphrates River, came a king from a powerful empire both to triumphantly destroy

This article can be found in its entirety in the Appendix (see pg 328).

Unit Five: *Assyria & Babylon: The Mesopotamian Conquerors* / 143

"Let neither man nor beast, herd nor flock, taste anything; do not let them eat, or drink water. But let man and beast be covered with sackcloth, and cry mightily to God; yes, let every one turn from his evil way and from the violence that is in his hands..." Jonah 3:7-8

God saw their repentance, that they actually turned from their evil ways, and He relented from destroying them. When we stop and consider, we will discover in this Old Testament history that God was concerned with all the people of the earth—even the most vicious—and not just with His Chosen People.

"For My thoughts are not your thoughts, nor are your ways My ways," says the Lord. "For as the heavens are higher than the earth, so are My ways higher than your ways, and My thoughts than your thoughts." Isaiah 55:8-9

SPIRITUAL

Pray that your students will begin to get a glimpse of God's heart from this account, and they will allow Him to mold their own understanding of nations and people groups around the world, regardless of their reputation.

Judgment of Israel—EXPLANATION

TEACHER TIP

To get an informal discussion started on this key concept, ask a simple, leading question, such as, " *Does anyone know why God sent judgment on the northern kingdom of Israel?"*

Standing in our moment of history, we can look back at the judgment of Israel and wonder why on earth the northern kingdom never listened to God's warnings and repented of its idolatries. It might be obvious to us that God's judgment on the sins of Israel allowed the Assyrians to conquer them, but we wonder why they didn't take the prophets seriously. Amos and Hosea, two of the prophets to Israel, told them clearly what was soon to come.

Ah, but that is human nature. Consider the situation in Israel at the time: Life was comfortable, even affluent, under the reign of Jeroboam II (793-753 B.C.). In fact, he brought the northern kingdom of Israel to its greatest military strength and economic prosperity. His successful foreign policy, like invading Damascus, was possible because the local bullying empire, Assyria, was in decline at this point. Into this pleasant time (in the natural realm), unpleasant words were spoken by the prophet Amos:

"Woe to you who put far off the day of doom, who cause the seat of violence to come near; who lie on beds of ivory, stretch out on your couches, eat lambs from the flock and calves from the midst of the stall, who chant to the sound of stringed instruments, and invent for yourselves musical instruments like David; who drink wine from bowls, and anoint yourselves with the best ointments, but are not grieved for the affliction of Joseph. Therefore they shall now go captive as the first of the captives, and those who recline at banquets shall be removed." Amos 6:3-7

Though it seemed impossible at the time, due to the ease and wealth, God's word was absolutely accurate. In 722 B.C., Sargon II of Assyria did indeed brutally capture Samaria, the capital city of Israel, and took nearly 30,000 of its people captive. We would do well to remember that, when God's justice seems delayed, it is coming nonetheless.

Discovery of Ninevah—EXPLANATION

> To get an informal discussion started on this key concept, ask a simple, leading question, such as, *"What have you heard about the ancient city of Ninevah?"*

A most amazing adventurer discovered the most incredible finds, beginning in 1845 on the banks of the Tigris River. Austen Henry Layard was an Englishman with a fascination for the dimly known ancient civilizations of Mesopotamia. On an overland trip to Sri Lanka in 1841 (which he never finished), near the city of Mosul in modern day Iraq, he discovered mounds of sand. Local legend equated the mounds with the city of Ninevah, known to Bible readers because of the adventures of Jonah. Layard was gripped with a ravenous hunger to know if palaces and temples, lost cities and civilizations were waiting, poised under the sand for someone to discover.

This was during a time when enlightened Europeans scoffed at the idea of an Assyrian civilization as described in the Bible. They were quick to point out to believers that, since no other ancient manuscripts spoke of the Assyrians and no ruins were visible, it was merely another one of the Bible's many mistakes.

That was about to change. When Layard and his workers began to dig into the mounds of sand, they discovered the city of Ninevah, the city of Nimrud ("Calah" in the Bible), and the palace of King Sargon. With the breathtaking and horrifying bas-relief sculpture of Assyrian conquests, the massive winged bulls as guardians, the palaces, and the massive library of Ashurbanipal, Assyria was firmly set in its rightful place of antiquity. The scoffers, for the moment, were silenced.

Prophets & Babylon—EXPLANATION

> To get an informal discussion started on this key concept, ask a simple, leading question, such as, *"Why do you suppose God kept sending His prophets to tell the people bad news?"*

Have you ever known someone who has an ongoing lifestyle of backsliding? One who goes their own direction until it gets them in trouble, then cries out to God in tears? As soon as life calms down, back to willful, determined sin they go. It can be the same way with nations. Listen to God's heart as He spoke to Judah:

" 'You have forsaken Me,' says the Lord, 'You have gone backward. Therefore I will stretch out My hand against you and destroy you; I am weary of relenting.' " Jeremiah 15:6

Though He had purposed to do good to this nation, He was weary of their constant unfaithfulness, their continual worshipping of other gods. He gave this analogy in Jeremiah 18:

" 'Arise and go down to the potter's house, and there I will cause you to hear My words.' Then I went down to the potter's house, and there he was, making something at the wheel. And the vessel that he made of clay was marred in the hand of the potter; so he made it again into another vessel, as it seemed good to the potter to make. Then the word of the Lord came to me, saying: 'O house of Israel, can I not do with you as this potter?' says the Lord. 'Look, as the clay is in the potter's hand, so are you in My hand, O house of Israel! The instant I speak concerning a nation and concerning a kingdom, to pluck up, to pull down, and to destroy it, if that nation against whom I have spoken turns from its evil, I will relent of the disaster that I thought to bring upon it. And the instant I speak concerning a nation and concerning a kingdom, to build and to plant it, if it does evil in My sight so that it does not obey My voice, then I will relent concerning the good with which I said I would benefit it.' "

He went on to tell the people of Judah that He was planning to bring destruction on them, but if they would turn from evil and do good, disaster would be averted. They replied,

"That is hopeless! So we will walk according to our own plans, and we will every one do the imagination of his evil heart." Jeremiah 18:12

And, so, judgment in the form of King Nebuchadnezzar came to Judah.

His ways are overflowing with mercy, His loving compassion is everlasting, but God is a Holy God, not a fool. He calls us to walk obediently before Him.

Babylonian Captivity—EXPLANATION

TEACHER TIP

To get an informal discussion started on this key concept, ask a simple, leading question, such as, *"Why do you think God sent the people of Judah into captivity?"*

"By the rivers of Babylon, there we sat down, yea, we wept when we remembered Zion. We hung our harps upon the willows in the midst of it. For there those who carried us away captive required of us a song. And those who plundered us required of us mirth, saying, 'Sing us one of the songs of Zion!' How shall we sing the Lord's song in a foreign land?" Psalm 137:1-4

Key People:

The people listed in this column are the main characters, if you will, of this unit. They are listed in the Student Manual, along with a brief identifier, so that the students can familiarize themselves with these people.

PHASE 1

KEY PEOPLE:

Jonah 760 BC
—Reluctant Prophet to Assyria

Tiglath-Pileser
—Assyrian king who took part of Israel captive

Shalmaneser
—Assyrian king who took the rest of Israel captive

Sennacherib 701 BC
—Assyrian king who challenged God…and lost!

Hezekiah 701 BC
—Good king of Judah

Josiah 640 BC
—Good king of Judah

➤ Listen to this!

- **What in the World's Going On Here? Volume One**
  — Assyria & Babylon

- **True Tales from the Times of…Ancient Civilizations & The Bible**
  — Austen Layard and the Discovery of Nineveh

- **An In-Depth Study of…Seven Wonders of the Ancient World**
  — Hanging Gardens of Babylon

➤ Read For Your Life

— The Main Story: Jonah; 2 Kings 17-18; 2 Chronicles 32:1-22; 2 Kings 20, 24-25; Daniel 1-5, 7-8.

— Other Helpful Verses: Nahum; Genesis 10:8-12; Isaiah 10:5-15; Isaiah 19:23-25; Isaiah 36-37; Micah 5:4-6; Zephaniah 2:13-15; Hosea 11:1-12; Psalm 137; Habakkuk, Micah.

154 / Unit Five: *Assyria & Babylon: The Mesopotamian Conquerors*

Refugees ache for home, yearning to return. Think about what it was like for these captives, brought from Jerusalem to Babylon. Consider with what grieving tears they remembered God's warning to them, and how they had ignored it. What might they have experienced as they recognized that their captivity was due to their disobedience…and it could have all been averted.

This could be a profound time to share together about the difference between the blessed wisdom of obedient actions and the heartbreaking remorse over foolish actions. How much better to recognize ahead of time that a foolish action can bring about devastation, and, though we weep bitter tears over the results, there is no going back in time to fix the problem. Pray that the Holy Spirit will illuminate this truth for your students, that they might walk in the fullness of blessing He longs to pour out on their lives.

2) Read the article

Begins on Page 143 of Student Manual

The article for Unit Five is designed to help students think about the reality of the historical events and people recorded in the Old Testament, as well as other sources, concerning the Assyrian and Babylonian civilization. The materials covered in the audio recordings offer another look at this time period, covering slightly different information. In the article and recordings, along with introducing the basic understanding of history, we are also bringing in the biblical worldview.

You may choose to have your students read the article first and then listen to the audio recordings, or vice versa.

TEACHER TIP

3) Listen to the audio recording(s)

Listed on Page 154 of the Student Manual.

- The main concepts and chronological flow are contained in **What in the World's Going On Here?**

- An amazing story about one of the first archaeologists—the man who found Ninevah—is contained in this audio-recording: **True Tales from the Times of—Ancient Civilizations & The Bible**

- Discover some incredible facts (and theories) about the Hanging Gardens in: **An In-Depth Study of…Seven Wonders of the Ancient World**

4) Read the Scripture listed in Read For Your Life

Listed on Page 154 of the Student Manual. You might choose to have the students read the Main Story verses either corporately or privately.

The Scriptures are central to our understanding, our character, and our decisions. Therefore, we must give the greatest weight possible to them. Help your students gain this perspective as they watch you handle the Scriptures with reverence and awe.

SPIRITUAL

The "Other Helpful Verses" listed are some of the prophets to Israel and Judah, such as Nahum, Zephaniah, Hosea, Habakkuk, Micah, and Isaiah. If it is possible, read through one of these prophets with your students, so that they can hear God's heart as He warns the people of impending judgment. Personally, they broke my heart.

Though students are not required to look up all the verses (it IS a long list), the teacher might look them up, and choose a few to add in to the class discussion, or to assign to selected students for their input into the discussion.

5) Recap (process & review) Activity

In different parts of the room, set up stations for the Eight Intelligences Recap Activities. Then allow students to work alone or together in small groups to accomplish the following suggestions. At the start of the next class, ask for 3-4 groups of volunteers to share. <u>For homeschoolers, rather than set up all eight stations, allow the student(s) to choose which of these activities they would most enjoy, and do that.</u>

INTRO-PG 19

Recap Suggestions:

SPATIAL: In a small group, create two poster-board sized murals—one to show Assyria as conqueror of Israel, and one to show Babylon as conqueror of Judah.

BODILY-KINESTHETIC: Design a style of walking which would be appropriate for a captive of Assyria, and, if it seems appropriate, a separate style for a captive of Babylon.

INTERPERSONAL: In pairs, take one minute to consider what are the three most important points to remember about this unit so far, and then share for one minute with your partner. Then the partner takes one minute to consider and one minute to share.

MUSICAL: Think of an appropriate dirge-like song to sing about the disobedience of God's children, writing new lyrics to an old song if necessary.

LINGUISTIC: Using one Assyrian and one Babylonian name, create a short rhyming poem that will help students remember the main points in this unit.

MATH-LOGICAL: Answer the question: What made Assyria so good at conquering cities?

INTRAPERSONAL: Journal a heart-to-heart talk with God about the importance of obeying Him.

✗ NATURALIST: Choose an animal to represent either Assyria or Babylon, or both, which has as many characteristics in common with these civilizations as possible. Be prepared to explain why that particular animal was chosen.

OR...Activity of Your Choice: What would you like to have your students do for a review activity concerning this week's introduction to Assyria & Babylon?

6) *Opinion Column and Critical Puzzling answers on their own*

Listed on Pages 155-156 of the Student Manual. Students may begin these questions after completing their Recap Activities listed above.

7) *Class Discussion*

Using the questions listed on Pages 155-156 of the Student Manual to get the students primed, create a discussion environment in the classroom. You may also want to draw from the open-ended questions listed below.

Phase 1

➤ *Talk Together*

• **Opinion Column:**

— What did you find to be the most interesting aspect, or the most fascinating person, you encountered in your introduction to Assyria & Babylon?

— Imagine you live inside Jerusalem during the reign of King Hezekiah. What will you think and what will you do when King Sennacherib of Assyria begins to threaten your city?

— Considering what you know about the life of Daniel and the three Hebrew companions, what do you think it would have been like to be one of the Judean captives taken to Babylon?

— Why do you think that God kept showing King Nebuchadnezzar the future, and why did God allow him to see the three Hebrew children with the fourth "like the Son of Man" in the fiery furnace?

— When the prophet Jeremiah told the people to settle down in Babylon, build homes and plant vineyards, they knew their time in captivity would not be short (Jer. 29:4-7). Imagine you are a Jewish mother or father of children born in Babylon. How would you describe what your homeland in Jerusalem had been like? What reasons would you give for the captivity?

— Why do you think that King Belshazzar ordered the vessels of gold from the Temple at Jerusalem to be used for his drunken party? What was the result?

KEY PEOPLE:

Major & Minor Prophets
— Warned Judah & Israel of coming destruction

Hammurabi
— Early Babylonian king who reformed laws

Nebuchadnezzar
— Babylonian king who took Judah captive

Daniel
— Hebrew advisor to King Nebuchadnezzar

Imagine you are trying to share the truth of Scripture with someone in the 1800's. They scoff at you in derision and say, "The Bible couldn't possibly be true. Look at the way it describes empires like Assyria, which everyone knows never existed!" What would you say to that person after Austen Layard's discovery of Nimrud and Ninevah?

How is your view of God and of nations affected after reading Isaiah 7:17-20 and after considering Assyria's role in the history of Israel and Judah?

Key People:

More of the main characters in this unit. They are listed in the Student Manual, along with a brief identifier, so that the students can familiarize themselves with these people.

QUESTION The Scriptures tell us that 185,000 soldiers were killed in one night by the Angel of the Lord. Would this number have been sufficient to threaten the safety of Jerusalem? (Consider: Compare modern battles to determine your answer.)

QUESTION What differences, if any, do you see between the Babylonians' treatment of other people, especially captives, compared with the Assyrians' treatment?

QUESTION How do you reconcile the thought that God would call King Nebuchadnezzar, "My

---

Phase 1

- **Critical Puzzling:**

  — Why do you think God sent Jonah to Nineveh, and how did the "revival" at Nineveh impact the Assyrian nation?

  — Referring to Isaiah 7:17-20, what do you think God's purpose was at that time for the Assyrian people?

  — The relief sculptures on the palace walls at Nineveh show the king hunting lions. How is this similar to the Biblical description of Nimrod? How might this indicate the attitude of the rulers towards their people?

  — Why do you think God called King Nebuchadnezzar, "My servant"? What does that tell us about the kind of people God can use for His purposes?

  — Read Habakkuk 3:16-19. What kind of response did Habakkuk have at the time of the invasion of Jerusalem, and how can you apply this to your life right now?

  — Babylon was the most magnificent city of antiquity, filled with the worship of false gods. What do you think it would have been like to be a worshipper of Jehovah living in this city?

  — Using the themes presented in Nahum 1:8 and Matthew 26:52, explain the connection you observe between Assyria's ways of warfare and its demise.

Servant" (Jeremiah 25:9)? Does that impact your view of current events? Does this hold true for all political leaders? Why or why not? (Consider: Daniel and the three Hebrews who refused to bow down.)

INTRO - PG 20

8) Choose books of interest/Internet search

A list of possible books for further reading is listed in the Student Manual beginning on Page 157. Encourage your students to look for general information from this list and from other sources on Assyria and Babylon. You may want to gather a selection of further resources prior to beginning Unit Five, or you may encourage the students to be treasure hunters and find them on their own.

The Internet has a wealth of information concerning Assyria and Babylon, though the articles available vary widely in dependability, worldview and attitude. Help your students learn to recognize the differences.

Remember:

Beware of Arrogance, Embrace Humility!

Phase 1

➤ *Reviewed Resources for Digging Deeper:*

Choose a few books that look interesting, or find your own.

For the complete list of books from the Student Manual, refer to the Appendix (pg 332).

Archaeological Finds of Assyria:

Secrets of the Royal Mounds
by Cynthia Jameson

This delightful book is the story of Austen Layard, a British adventurer in the mid-1800's, who was the first to discover the cities of Assyria. It's certainly worth the trouble to find, as it is written in a capture-your-interest style. **UE+**

Nineveh And Its Remains
by Austen Layard

Read a first hand account of the unbelievable discovery of Nineveh in the mid-1800's. It is an amazing read for older students, and has recently been reprinted! **HS+**

The Assyrians by Elaine Landau

It is difficult to find books on the Assyrian time period which are appropriate for younger students. This is the best we have seen! **UE+**

Discoveries Among the Ruins of Nineveh
by Austen Layard

This is a fascinating first-person account of Layard's second dig at Nineveh. It was published in the mid-1800's, so may be difficult to locate, but again, it's certainly worth the trouble. **HS+**

The Assyrians Activity Book
by Lorna Oakes

Published by the British Museum, this is a book with great suggested activities, interesting articles to read, and fascinating pictures to color. **UE+**

Then and Now by Perring and Perring

One chapter of this great archaeological resource deals with Nimrud (known as Calah in the Bible) which was once the capital city of Assyria. **UE+**

Review & Evaluation

EVALUATION

In this Phase of Unit Five, your students should have had the opportunity to explore the Mesopotamian Conquerors, Assyria and Babylon through reading, listening, thinking and discussing. They will have:

1) informally discussed the Key Concepts;
2) read the article;
3) listened to the audio recording(s);
4) read the Scripture listed in Read for Your Life;
5) explored the Recap Activities;
6) completed the Opinion Column and Critical Puzzling answers on their own;
7) participated in Class Discussion;
8) chosen books of interest or searched the Internet.

You may wish to evaluate your students based on their *participation* in the **Class Discussion** and on their *participation* in the **Recap Activity**.

PHASE 2

The Exploration and Discovery Week

Learning Style Emphasis: THINKER

Students will explore topics of interest through research and reporting, learn new vocabulary, and construct a timeline relating to Mesopotamian Conquerors, Assyria and Babylon.

Monday-Tuesday:

1) Choose topic and begin research

Wednesday:

2) Vocabulary Practice

Thursday:

3) Construct the Timeline.

Friday:

4) Research projects completed; share in class or hand in.

> *Teachers can choose to have students do one or two activities, rather than the entire week's schedule. Please use what works for you in your unique setting.*

INTRO·PG 21

1) Choose topic and begin research

Allow the students the freedom to choose one of the topics listed on Pages 160-162, or to suggest their own area which they would like to research.

Motivating Suggestions:

Especially for Non-Linguistic students, and those who are not motivated by written or oral reports, here are suggestions for alternative ways of reporting what has been researched.

MOTIVATE

Assyria

1) Create a mural of the history of Assyria, using the motif of a roller coaster—ups and downs.
2) Analyze the different categories which contributed to Assyria's domination (such as, culture), and the categories which contributed to their ultimate downfall (such as, pride going before destruction). Then make a chart showing these categories.

Siege Warfare

1) In a small team, pantomime the various techniques of siege warfare used by the Assyrians when capturing a walled city.
2) Find music which captures the sense of a city under siege. After playing a recording, share how this music demonstrates the Assyrians abilities in this area, or what it might have been like to be inside a walled city under siege by the Assyrians.

Assyrian Conquest

1) Interview a "slave" captured in Samaria by the Assyrians. Ask them about their treatment at the hands of their captors, their thoughts on slavery in general, and any advice they would give other Assyrian slaves.

2) Organize a debate with this question to consider: "Is deportation an effective and appropriate way to bring conquered lands under control?"

Old Testament

1) Do a one-man show of Amos or Hosea, explaining what conditions are like in Israel, and what God has asked you to do.

2) Create a children's book about Isaiah's and King Hezekiah's Great Adventure.

3) Imagine you were living in Judah during the time of Micah, or the time of Zephaniah and Habakkuk. Write a first-person account describing how their words would have influenced you.

Samaria

1) In a team of 2 or 3, discuss the reasons for Samaria's blended religion, and then decide how to best present the material to others. Make your presentation come alive!

2) To illustrate the problems with this blended religion, select several pieces of different styles of music, then make an audio-recording of disjointed bits and pieces.

PHASE 2

Exploration & Discovery Week

➢ *Research & Reporting*

Your mission, if you choose to accept it, is to explore one of these areas, and to discover something significant!

• **Assyria:**

Find one of the books listed, or a book of your choice, for basic information on the history of ancient Assyria. Summarize the factors that led to Assyria's far-reaching dominion and the factors leading to their decline. Report your findings as "The Rise and Fall of the Assyrian Empire."

• **Siege Warfare:**

The Assyrians were remarkably adept at capturing fortified cities. Research and report on what kind of techniques and machinery they used for this purpose.

• **Assyrian Conquest:**

Not much is known about the daily life of the common people in Assyria, though it appears that their lives were significantly controlled by the "government". However, there is much information about the captives and slaves of Assyrian conquest. Investigate what you can discover about this culture in regards to their treatment of other peoples. Be sure to include the issue of deportation.

• **Old Testament**

— Investigate the books of Amos and Hosea in the Old Testament. Report on such questions as:

- *To whom were these prophets speaking?*

- *What was the message?*

- *How did the people respond?*

- *How did God deal with them?*

— Research and report on the lives of Isaiah and King Hezekiah. Use the whole of Scripture.

— Investigate the books of Micah, Zephaniah, and Habakkuk in the Old Testament. Report on such questions as:

— *To whom were these prophets speaking?*

— *What was the message?*

— *How did the people respond?*

— *How did God deal with them?*

MOTIVATE

Cuneiform

1) Gather or create your own examples of cuneiform writing, and then create a display which explains how this style of writing works, and how it was deciphered in modern times.

2) Put on a skit of a librarian at Ashurbanipal's library in Ninevah. You may want to deal with issues of noisy patrons, misfiled books, impatient customers, etc. Remember to include your research on the variety of books that were discovered in this most ancient library.

Assyrian/Biblical Chronology

Create a poem for two voices, in the style of *Joyful Noise* by Paul Fleischman, showing the differences, the similarities, and the interaction between Assyria and the Hebrews.

Assyria in Today's News/Babylon in Today's News

1) Compare and contrast the wars of ancient Assyria and/or Babylon with the modern wars of Iraq. Display this information on a chart.

2) Using video clips, first person interviews, and newspaper or magazine articles, etc. create a multimedia collage of what it is like in Assyria and Babylon today.

Modern Day Assyrians

1) Learn the cultural dances of the Assyrian people and do a demonstration. Appropriate costumes would greatly enhance the performance.

2) Set up a photo display of modern day Assyrian people. Include descriptions of their cultural practices, religious beliefs, and maps of their locations across the globe.

Sennacherib

Using items from nature as three-dimensional analogies, explain Sennacherib's actions, attitudes, and assassination. (For instance, "They say that a rolling stone gathers no moss. This smooth rock, with no moss, illustrates the fact that Sennacherib rolled across the Middle East, conquering as he went.")

Phase 2

• **Samaria:**

Research and write about the cause for Samaria's blended religion. Include comments regarding the impact this had on the conversation in John 4.

• **Cuneiform:**

Research and explain what cuneiform is, and how it was deciphered in modern times. Explain the significance of the discovery of the library of Asshurbanipal in Nineveh in understanding cuneiform.

• **Assyrian / Biblical Chronology:**

Compile a list of names, dates and accomplishments of Assyria's key leaders. Make a chart which shows this list in comparison with the events listed in the Bible, including the time of Jonah, the captivity of Israel, the siege of Judah, and the destruction of Nineveh.

• **Assyria in Today's News / Babylon in Today's News:**

In the library or on the Internet, research any information from current events relating to the kingdom of Assyria or the kingdom of Babylon. (Hint: Especially, research the Persian Gulf War or the Iraq War.)

• **Modern Day Assyrians:**

There are Assyrian people today, from the land of Iraq, who have moved to various parts of the world. Research and report on their belief system, their cultural practices, their integration into other cultures.

• **Sennacherib:**

Investigate Sennacherib in the history of Assyria. Report on his significance in Assyrian history and how the empire was affected by his death.

• **A Scriptural View:**

— Summarize, either in written or verbal form, what you know about:

  1) the role of Jonah in Assyrian history;

  2) God's timing in sending Jonah;

  3) the effect of Israel's not obeying God, nor receiving His correction;

  4) the truth of Scriptural prophecies in relation to Assyria's destruction.

— Summarize, either in written or verbal form, what you know about:

  1) the disobedience of Judah;

  2) the warnings of the prophets;

  3) the chastisement delivered by Nebuchadnezzar;

  4) the confrontation by God in Nebuchadnezzar's life;

  5) the fall of the Babylonian Empire.

A Scriptural View

1) Hold a trial for Jonah, who has been accused of going AWOL, with God as the Judge. You may have witnesses, prosecutor and defense attorneys, as well as the accused.

2) As an on-the-spot television reporter, interview one of the three Hebrews who has just emerged out of the fiery furnace. If you can manage it, interview King Nebuchadnezzar as well.

The Hanging Gardens

1) Plant a miniature version of the Hanging Gardens. Show what you've planted and tell the theories about how the Hanging Gardens were built.

2) Paint a scene from the Hanging Gardens, including some aspect of the watering system.

Babylon

1) Make two posters, one for Babylon under Hammurabi, one for Babylon under Nebuchadnezzar. Using a collage style, illustrate some of the high points and low points of each reign.

2) Create a resumé for Daniel, which he will hand to King Darius, showing his work in the Babylonian Empire.

Hammurabi

Hammurabi's Code was discovered on a black stele. In whatever materials seem best, create a stele with the Ten Commandments written on it. Be prepared to explain the similarities and differences between the original two codes.

Judah's Captivity

MOTIVATE

1) Choreograph a dance which shows the three stages of Judah's captivity. If you have enough students to set up three groups, you could show how some of the people were left in Jerusalem while others were taken to Babylon until the final destruction of Jerusalem.

2) Make a chart showing the events of each of the three stages. Include dates and causes for each stage.

Phase 2

- **The Hanging Gardens:**

Research the Hanging Garden of Babylon. How and why do archaeologists believe the Hanging Garden was built? Compare and contrast the difficulty in normal irrigation and the type of irrigation the Hanging Garden would have required.

- **Babylon:**

Find one of the books listed, or a book of your choice, for basic information on the two kingdoms of Babylon, both the early one under Hammurabi and the later under King Nebuchadnezzar. Summarize the factors that led to the far-reaching dominion of the later kingdom of Babylon, and the factors leading to its decline. Subtitle your report "The Rise and Fall of the Babylonian Empire." Be sure to include the importance of Daniel's role in the later government of Babylon.

- **Hammurabi:**

Research and report on King Hammurabi, the code of laws he gave, and his impact on the early city of Babylon.

- **Judah's Captivity:**

Investigate in Scripture the three stages of captivity Judah experienced. What were the causes of each stage? What was the effect of each stage? What was the final result?

- **Pottery:**

Read about pottery in antiquity, and how it is used in modern times by archaeologists to understand ancient cultures. Discover what some of the potential difficulties are with this system.

- **A Biblical View of Babylon:**

Babylon is mentioned from Genesis to Revelation. List the verses relating to this city, and chart what the Bible says about Babylon (chronologically).

- **Nebuchadnezzar:**

Research and report on the life of King Nebuchadnezzar. How significant was this leader in Babylonian history? How was that empire affected by his death? Be sure to include what Daniel says about the attitude of the king in his last days.

- **Archaeological Finds of Babylon:**

Research and report on Robert Koldewey, the German archaeologist who excavated Babylon from 1899–1913.

Pottery

1) Illustrate on poster board the different stratas of earth which help archaeologists to date remains. Then, add to it the most common types of pottery found in the Middle East and in which strata they are commonly found.

2) Try throwing a pot on a potter's wheel, or, if that proves insurmountable, create a coil pot. Give a demonstration of what you learn, and discuss some of the similarities in ancient pottery.

A Biblical View of Babylon

1) Create a rhythmic chant of the different stages of Babylon (from the Tower of Babel to Revelation) which would help others remember the main moments.

2) List the attributes which are found in the Scriptural description of Babylon. Place them in order of importance, at least, in your own understanding of their importance.

Nebuchadnezzar

1) Write an epitaph for King Nebuchadnezzar. He accomplished many works, experienced unusual phenomena, and ruled a mighty empire, so use enough words.

2) Hold a political forum during the time of King Nebuchadnezzar's insanity to decide if he should be permanently removed from the throne.

Archaeological Finds of Babylon

In costume, give a first person presentation of Robert Koldewey describing his accomplishments.

Phase 2

≫ *Brain Stretchers*

• **Iraq & Israel:**

Compare and contrast the history of Iraq (Assyria & Babylon) and the history of Israel. What cultural distinctives continue throughout the centuries in each nation, i.e. religion, war, politics, class structure?

• **Assyria and Babylon to the Present:**

Investigate the history of Iraq from the time of Nimrod and the building of the city of Babel, through the time of the Assyrians and the Babylonians, and up to the present. Be sure to include Alexander the Great's use of Babylon. Report your findings.

• **Empires:**

We will be looking at five major empires over the next several units. Consider starting an ongoing project to uncover any universal factors contributing to the rise and fall of empires.

Create Your Own Research Topic:

_____

_____

_____

Brain Stretchers:

Brain Stretchers, listed on page 163, are intended for advanced students. Those who attempt the Brain Stretchers for their Research and Reporting can use the above list for ideas on how to report their findings.

2) Words To Watch - Vocabulary Practice

Listed on Page 164. You may find other words in this unit that are especially appropriate for younger children. Feel free to substitute another vocabulary list for the one provided.

Here is one idea for making vocabulary study interesting and fun: **Design a crossword puzzle with the vocabulary words.**

Phase 2

➢ *Words to Watch*

Remember—The easiest way to learn a subject is to master its terms:

deportation	soothsayer	lyres
irrigation	empire	tribute
chastise	administrator	cuneiform
scourge	siege	stylus
judgment	engines	pottery
remnant	bas-relief	

---

3) Construct the Timeline.

Read the information listed with the "Key Dates" on Page 167. Dialogue with your students about the issues involved. Help them recognize that dating antiquity is not an exact science. For ease of reference, the timeline is included in the Appendix on Page 335.

Find the dates for the key people and events listed.

Help the students recognize the significance of God's timing in Jonah's journey to Ninevah, the Assyrian capture of Israel, the fall of Ninevah to the Babylonians and Medes, and the fall of Babylon to the Persians and Medes. It will build their trust in God as they see His amazing ability to work situations out at just the right moment to accomplish His purposes. You might want to draw out what your students will share about current situations in their lives which need the timing and power of God, and then to pray with them.

4) Research projects shared in class and/or turned in.

Create a safe environment for the presentations. Set ground rules prior to the presentations for all the students, so that they know each one will be honored and respected in their work by all those observing.

EVALUATION **Review & Evaluation**

In this second Phase of Unit Five, your students should have had the opportunity to explore Mesopotamian Conquerors, Assyria and Babylon, through researching, thinking, and reporting. They will have:

1) done a research project;
2) learned the vocabulary;
3) constructed a Timeline;
4) created a project report on what was researched.

You may wish to evaluate your students based on their *efforts* in the **Research and Reporting** projects and their active *participation* in the **Vocabulary** and **Timeline** exercises.

PHASE 3

The Hands-On Week

Learning Style Emphasis: Sensor

Students will explore interrelated subject areas through sensory activities relating to the Mesopotamian Conquerors, Assyria and Babylon.

Monday:
1) Create a map and discuss the issues in teams.

Tuesday:
2) Examine and discuss art masterpieces & architectural structures.

Wednesday:
3) Arts in Action—Do an art project.*

Thursday:
4) Do one science project or field trip.**

Friday:
5) Listen to and discuss the music.
6) Cook the food listed in the recipe, if desired.

*Art project will need to be planned ahead of time to acquire materials.
**Field trip will require extra planning time.

> *Teachers can choose to have students do one or two activities, rather than the entire week's schedule. Please use what works for you in your unique setting.*

1) Create a map and discuss the issues in teams

INTRO - PG 23

The students each have an outline map on Page 169. They will be given assignments for drawing in rivers, mountains, cities, and regional boundaries, which are listed on Page 168. For details on where these things are, please consult a historical atlas, an encyclopedia, a study Bible, or any other source for geographic information. For ease of reference, the map is included in the Appendix on Page 336.

Upper elementary students might be satisfied to accomplish only this portion:
- *Physical terrain:* This part of the mapping exercise will help students locate and mark the geological dynamics of a region.

Middle school students might be satisfied to complete both the previous mapping exercise and this exercise:
- *Geo-Political:* This section of the mapping exercise will provide the students an opportunity to locate and mark the cities, nations and empires of history. It will require more digging.

High school students might be satisfied to complete both the previous mapping exercises and at least one exploration topic of this exercise:
- *Explore:* Discuss some selection from this portion of the mapping exercise in teams.

Encourage them to think for themselves, rather than parroting back information.

QUESTION

Christian Outreach

Students may wish to locate information about Christian missions work in Iraq. If it is possible to interview someone who has worked in that field, it will be even more helpful and insightful.

QUESTION

Babylonian Ecosystem

There is a dramatic contrast between the hills of northern Mesopotamia and the sun-baked plains of southern Mesopotamia. This created different responses. The Assyrians were more prone to conquer, since they lacked many natural resources. The Babylonians, with much more space, had to irrigate in order to eat. Knowing more about the ecosystems of these two empires may provide greater insight into their histories.

PHASE 3

The Hands-On Week

➢ *Maps and mapping*

- **Physical Terrain:**

  — Label and color the Tigris and Euphrates rivers on the outline map.

  — Color the Fertile Crescent.

  — Locate and indicate the mountain ranges, deserts, and green areas.

- **Geo-Political:**

  — Locate and label the land of Assyria and the Assyrian Empire. What is today's name of that country?

  — Label Nineveh and Nimrud on the map. What modern day cities are close to these ancient cities?

  — Discover the terrain and climate of ancient Assyria.

  — Locate and label the Babylonian Empire on the map. What is today's name of that country?

  — Label the city of Babylon on the map. What modern day city is close to this?

  — Discover the terrain and climate of ancient Babylon.

- **Explore:**

  — *Christian Outreach:* What is the status of Christian outreach to the modern country where Assyria and Babylon were located? How has Christian outreach been affected by recent wars? Discuss the difficulties and remarkable opportunities facing Christians in that area of the world today.

  — *Babylonian Ecosystem:* What kind of terrain and ecosystem is in the land of ancient Babylon? How did the Babylonians grow food? What does this indicate about the level of technology available to this ancient people? Contrast this with Assyria's terrain and ecosystem.

  — *Climate:* What type of climate is typical in the Mesopotamian region? How would the terrain and climate have affected the Assyrian culture and the Babylonian culture? Does this give you any insight into God's purpose for it?

QUESTION

Climate

Help students to think through the implications of a long growing season, especially if the farmers can irrigate. Contrast this with harsher climates, such as Siberia. Again, consider the impact this would have on the cultures and the warfare.

2) *Examine and discuss art masterpieces & architectural structures*

Locate either a copy of these art forms, or Internet sites for each of the items listed on Pages 170-171. Allow the students time to observe the art without any conversation, and then, when they are ready, engage them in some or all of the questions listed in the Student Manual or below.

Belshazzar's Feast *by Rembrandt*

QUESTION

At this early point in his career, Rembrandt's Baroque style is vivid and dramatic. Notice how he painted so that viewers would feel as though they were seated at the same table!

It might be interesting to consider with the students the impact of electricity on our lives. Notice how dark the night seems. People in earlier times obviously dealt with much more shadow and darkness in their evening get-togethers than we are used to.

• Ask the students whether they think this might affect our perspective of the darkness of this painting? If so, how might Rembrandt have painted if he were living in modern times?

Assyrian Bas Relief Sculpture in the British Museum

QUESTION

The Assyrians were among the best bas-relief sculptors in history. As you can probably tell, this was the height of their artistic ability, and they carefully crafted the scenes. Notice the muscles on the lions!

• Ask the students what they think was the motivation for creating these bas-relief sculptures, considering that it was used largely to decorate the palaces of the Assyrian kings.

Phase 3

➤ *Art Appreciation*

Consider:

Rembrandt (1606-1669) was one of the greatest Dutch painters, a master of the Baroque style. He used rich colors, light and shadow, and a revolutionary technique with the paintbrush to achieve his masterpieces. A prolific artist, Rembrandt created approximately 600 paintings, 1,400 drawings and 300 etchings!

• **Belshazzar's Feast** *by Rembrandt*

— Do you think this painting reflects what the Bible describes?

— How does the painting differ from your own impression of this historic event?

— How would you describe Rembrandt's use of shadow and light in this painting?

• **Assyrian Bas Relief Sculpture** *in the British Museum*

— How does this artwork help you understand more about the Assyrians?

— Do you think the people under siege by the Assyrians were frightened? How does this artwork inform your decision?

— How would you describe the animals depicted in Assyrian bas relief?

- *Assyrian palaces were decorated with bas-relief pictures of battles, lion hunts, and other scenes intended to impress the viewer with the power and majesty of the king.*

Hanging Gardens of Babylon as Architecture

This is an unusual architectural structure to study, since there are no remains, no photos, and not even a certainty of its location! However, there are many theories about how the Hanging Gardens were constructed and watered. One of my favorites is the one that described the Hanging Gardens appearing to a traveler as a tall green mountain in the midst of the sun-drenched plains.

• Ask the students what they think it might have been like to visit the Hanging Gardens.

INTRO · PG 23

3) Arts in Action

Listed on pages 171-172.

TEACHER TIP

Imitation

Have the students look again at Rembrandt's painting. Then, with art supplies of colored pencils, pastels, or paint, try to recreate what is seen.

Cuneiform

Students often enjoy creating codes for writing secret letters to friends. You might use that as an idea to inspire some students to try this project. Encourage them to use very simple marks to represent words, rather than 26 different marks for the letters of the alphabet—that would become very complicated in clay!

Repentant Prophet

It might be fun to spread out a roll of butcher paper, and then have each student lie down in the position they imagine Jonah would have been stuck in inside the great fish. Have someone then trace the student's position with crayons or markers. From that point, the student can surround his image with a drawing of a very large fish!

Phase 3

➤ Architecture

The Hanging Gardens of Babylon were one of the seven wonders of the ancient world. According to tradition, these gardens were created by King Nebuchadnezzar for his Medean queen, Amytis. No one knows exactly how the Hanging Gardens were built, or even where they were built. (A current theory is that the Hanging Gardens were actually built in Assyria!) However, it is possible to speculate that a well-watered garden, built on ascending levels, would provide a refreshing haven from the fierce Babylonian heat.

— Look for artists' renditions of the Hanging Gardens of Babylon. Are there any agreements about how this wonder was built?

➤ Arts in Action

Select one, and let your artistic juices flow!

• **Imitation:**

Try your hand at creating a scene from the book of Daniel in the style of Rembrandt

• **Cuneiform:**

Try making your own cuneiform book! Items needed: modeling clay, "stylus", knife. Roll clay into flat "slates." Your "stylus" could be a drinking straw cut lengthwise, a wedge-shaped stick, a pencil halved. Make up a simple code, then write a sentence. Show the code to your family or other students. Can anyone read the sentence? You could also imitate actual cuneiform markings by copying real examples from Assyria.

• **Repentant Prophet:**

Draw a picture of a large fish or whale. Now draw a Jonah's-eye-view of a huge fish stomach! Can you draw the ribs of the fish or whale? Is Jonah sitting, kneeling, lying down, standing up? What color is it inside the belly? What color is Jonah? (Consider: Many scholars believe that Jonah may have been bleached white inside the sea creature, and perhaps that is why the city of Nineveh took his message seriously!)

What do Jonah's clothes look like? Does the fish or whale look puzzled?

Unit Five: Assyria & Babylon: The Mesopotamian Conquerors / 171

Hanging Gardens

The idea behind this art project is to create a three-dimensional artistic rendition of the Hanging Gardens. Older students may choose to use artificial moss, miniature trees, etc., to create a stunning display. They might even include a few royal personages wandering among the trees!

Relief Sculpture:

Though this may sound like a messy project, it is fun! And it is very satisfying to actually sculpt in soft "stone."

The Four Empires

If you have the butcher paper, it could be used for this project as well. Have the students lie face up on the paper one at a time and outline their bodies from head to toe. Then, they can divide the drawing into four empires, and color them accordingly.

Painted Babylonian Walls

This project will take a while for the different sections to dry. It could be an ongoing project for a week, however, with short sessions each day.

Phase 3

- **Hanging Gardens**

Try making a miniature version of the Hanging Gardens. You could make it with papier maché, Legos, wood, styrofoam, or whatever your imagination suggests.

- **Relief Sculpture:**

Make a soft "stone" relief! Items needed: vermiculite; plaster of Paris; water; bucket; small board for each student; plastic spoon or old tool for carving; aluminum foil; masking tape. Make a "form" for each board with aluminum foil—bring the edges of the foil up 1/2" above the board, secure with masking tape. In a plastic bucket mix 3 scoops vermiculite, 2 scoops plaster of Paris, 2 scoops of water. Stir with a stick until very thick. Pour into aluminum foil form and wait 30 minutes or until hardened. Using plastic spoon, carve a relief sculpture. Possibilities: an animal, a person, a chair, a mountain, a city... (Fact: Much of what is known about the Assyrian civilization was learned from the relief carvings on the walls of the archaeological ruins. Find some photos of these carvings. Do you think they were good artists? Do you think the Assyrians would enjoy Western art?)

- **The Four Empires**

Draw a picture of Daniel's vision of the four empires. Using the interpretation given by Daniel in Daniel 2, portray the differing aspects of these four empires. Check what you learn about Babylon, Persia, Greece and Rome with the Biblical description.

- **Painted Babylonian Walls**

Make a "wall" of bricks to paint: On a piece of wood, roll out clay, or bread dough, or plaster, etc.. Mark lines in it while still soft to indicate bricks. After the wall dries, paint the wall blue using either tempera or acrylic to cover completely. After this layer dries, paint designs on selected bricks with bright colors. If you painted fierce animals, as the Babylonians did, would you be frightened to walk by this wall?

➤ Science

- **Container Gardening:**

— Contact the local County Extension office to learn about gardening in different kinds of soil, different climates, and irrigation. Then plant at least two different mini-gardens in containers. One should be for plants which thrive in hot, dry climates, another should be for moisture-loving, shade plants. What kind of obstacles would the architect(s) of the Hanging Gardens of Babylon have had to overcome?

172 / Unit Five: *Assyria & Babylon: The Mesopotamian Conquerors*

---

4) Do a science project

Listed on Page 172. Feel free to choose one of these projects. If students love science, they might want to consider doing all of them!

TEACHER TIP

Container Gardening

Consider planting a terrarium for the moisture-loving plants, as they will thrive in the humid environment. For the dry-environment plants, consider planting a small cactus garden. Be careful to not over water!

SPIRITUAL

Isn't God an amazingly versatile Creator? He not only created plants that luxuriate in the rain forests, He also created plants that thrive in dry and thirsty locations. The giant cactus of the American southwest is a notable example. Pray for your students that each of them will grow in the revelation that He designed them specially for His purpose for their lives, as well.

TEACHER TIP

Evaporation

A simple, fast experiment showing the cooling effects of evaporation might be to have the students splash water on their faces, then turn on an electric fan (or use handheld fans) to discover how cool their faces become as the water evaporates. (That's a good trick for the heat of summer!) For a less dramatic effect, the students could splash water on their faces and stand in a still place to feel the cooling sensation.

Phase 3

• **Evaporation:**

— One resource on the Hanging Gardens said that the rooms under the garden area were kept cool in the summer by the foliage of the plants and by the evaporating water. Discover what "swamp coolers" are, and how they function. Experiment with the cooling process of evaporation: 1) on a hot day, put room temperature water on your face and arms. As it evaporates, does it cool? 2) on a hot day, find some leafy trees or an arbor to sit under. 3) Try leaving one cup of room temperature water outside in direct sunlight and one cup in the cool leafy shade. See if there is a difference in the rate of evaporation. 4) Devise your own experiments.

➤ Music

In the archaeological digs of Assyria, many pictures were found of musicians and various types of musical instruments. One can observe different instruments being played at the same time, such as harps and flutes. In fact, one scene from Assyria is that of a king and his queen reclining in their chairs in a lovely garden, while several musicians play (softly?) in the background. Though we do not know what the music sounded like, we can listen to the soothing sounds of the harp and the lilting voice of the flute today.

You might think, "Well, it's obvious!—A trumpet doesn't sound like a voice. And a guitar doesn't sound like a piano or a banjo." That's a very good observation, and what you have just noticed is one of the five major elements of music. Timbre (sounds like TAM-ber) is the name we give this element. Timbre is the uniquely different quality of sound produced by different instruments.

How do you know which is which? How does the listener know which is the sound of the harp and which is the sound of the flute? If your friend is sitting around the corner, playing a guitar and singing, how do you know that it is a guitar being played rather than a piano or banjo? Or, how can you tell that your friend is singing instead of practicing trumpet?

Unit Five: *Assyria & Babylon: The Mesopotamian Conquerors* / 173

---

5) *Listen to and discuss the music*

Listed on Pages 173-174.

Listen

Peter and the Wolf by Prokofiev and *A Young Person's Guide to the Orchestra* by Benjamin Britten are fun to listen to, and will help students better understand the various timbres of symphony instruments. You could choose to enjoy but a short sampling of either of these, if time is of the essence.

Try This

- The suggestion for a musical gathering in the Student Manual is not intended to produce cacophony! Rather, think of an old fashioned family time on the front porch, with everyone sharing some sort of musical instrument, whether ensemble or solo. Excellence is not the goal—having FUN is the goal.

- Listening to the recordings, in order to identify various timbres, could be an opportunity for the students to share their own favorite recordings, as well as a time to introduce classical music.

Phase 3

- **Listen:**

  — *Peter and the Wolf* by Prokofiev and *A Young Person's Guide to the Orchestra* by Benjamin Britten are musical pieces written to help students become familiar with the different instruments in the symphonic orchestra. These are highly regarded as an introduction to the element of timbre.

- **Try this:**

  — To experiment with timbre, get your family and friends to gather as many musical instruments as you can find (piano, trumpet, recorder, violin, drum, etc). Add some non-musical instruments as well, such as metal pots and wooden spoons. While the rest close their eyes, let one person pluck, blow or tap an instrument. Try to determine which instrument is being played just by its sound. Let everyone have a turn.

  — Now listen to some recordings of various types of music. Can you identify any of the instruments being played? Listen for percussion, woodwinds, brass and strings. If there are singers, listen for the differences in men's, women's, and children's voices.

  Isn't it wonderful that God gave us more than one sound to use in music? Thank you Lord, for giving us different timbres.

INTRO · PG 24

6) Cook the food

Listed on Pages 175-176.

TEACHER TIP

Don't overlook the second recipe! The bread would be great with the soup.

Phase 3

➤ Cooking

The Assyrians used barley as one of their primary grains. Though this recipe was not found in the ruins (!), it will give you a taste of the foods of this culture.

• Barley Soup *Serves 8*

1 1/2 cups barley, soaked overnight in water	1 egg, lightly beaten
3 tbsp butter	2 cups water
1 tbsp. flour	1 tsp salt
4 cups chicken broth	1 cup onion, chopped fine
white pepper	4 cups yogurt, plain
	2 tbsp fresh coriander
	(or 1/2 tbsp dried)

Drain barley and place in saucepan with water and salt. Cover tightly and simmer until barley has absorbed all liquid, and grains are separated, about one hour. Add more water only if necessary. Cook onion in butter until soft but not brown. Stir in yogurt. Remove from heat. Mix egg and flour together and blend into the yogurt mixture. Bring the chicken stock to a boil in a large saucepan; stir in yogurt mixture and barley. Add pepper and salt. Pour into bowls and sprinkle with coriander.

Consider:

Those who were taken captive by Babylon had many changes to adjust to, including unusual and unfamiliar ingredients for basic food. It was undoubtedly a difficult time, but the routine of daily life had its own comforts. Try this unusual "comfort food" and rejoice in the goodness and dependability of the Lord!

Phase 3

• Ezekiel's Many-Floured Bread

2 tbsp yeast	1 tbsp. coriander seed
1 1/2 cup warm water	1/4 cup lentil flour
1 egg	1/4 cup barley flour
1/4 cup oil (plus 1 tbsp to brush top of bread)	1/4 cup fava (broad bean) flour
2 1/2 tsp salt	1/3 cup honey 1/4 cup millet flour
1 tbsp. cumin	2 cups whole wheat flour
	2 – 2 1/2 cups unbleached flour

Dissolve yeast in warm water. Mix in next 5 ingredients. Stir in all flours, except white flour, and beat well. Add enough white flour to make a dough that can be gathered into a ball. Turn onto lightly floured surface and knead 10 minutes. Place in greased bowl, turning over to grease surface. Cover with a cloth and let rise in warm place until double in bulk, about 1 1/2 hours. Punch down and let rise again about 1 hour. Shape into 2 round loaves and place on greased baking sheet. Cover and let rise 1 hour. Bake in 350 oven for about 30 minutes. Remove, brush with remaining oil. Makes 2 loaves.

Review & Evaluation

EVALUATION

In this third Phase of Unit Five, your students should have had the opportunity to explore the Mesopotamian Conquerors, Assyria and Babylon, through various hands-on and creative sessions. They will have:

1) completed a Mapping section;
2) observed and discussed Art & Architecture;
3) worked on an art project;
4) experimented with a Science Project or taken a field trip;
5) listened to music;
6) tasted a food related to this unit.

You may wish to evaluate your students based on their *class participation* in these **Hands-on** activities.

PHASE 4

The Expression Week

Learning Style Emphasis: *Intuitor*

Students, through creative self-expression, using one or more creative activities, will present some aspect of what they have learned in the past three weeks relating to the Mesopotamian Conquerors, Assyria and Babylon. Areas of expression include linguistics, art, music, drama, movement and conceptual design.

Monday - Thursday

1) Choose area of expression and begin work either individually or in teams.

Friday

2) Share creative expressions in class.

> *Teachers can choose to have students do one or two activities, rather than the entire week's schedule. Please use what works for you in your unique setting.*

INTRO - PG 25

1) Choose area of expression and begin work either individually or in teams

Linguistics:

Located on page 177.

TEACHER TIP

Journalism

- Have the students read some journalistic "exposé" writings. They might look at Watergate or a similar political scandal, and discover the way it was reported in the press.
- "The Babylon Babbler" is obviously a tabloid-style newspaper, focusing on sensationalism. Have the students consider how a Christian might write a sensationalistic piece without deceiving or lying. Quite a challenge!

Prose

- Students who wish to write about Jonah's hike might want to read some stories of explorers and adventurers who head into the wilderness alone and come back to tell about it. For a sense of what it was like to cross five hundred miles of desert,

and some of the things Jonah might have faced, students could watch *Lawrence of Arabia*.

- Encourage students who are interested in writing home from Layard's dig to look through some accounts of archaeological digs in order to discover the realities of day-to-day life.
- Students considering the short story should find an anthology of short stories so that they can read a few. They should examine the length and breadth of a typical short story, particularly those with a dramatic or horrifying conclusion.
- To retell the captivity of Judah with modern names and terms, students might want to write out the biblical version first, and then look up the current place names and consider modern day terms for some of the events.

Playing with Words

- There are excellent books for students showing how to create coded messages, which might provide ideas for students wishing to write their "cousin in Jerusalem."
- Show students some examples of limericks in order to get their creative juices flowing and to help them understand the model of what they are attempting to create.

Poetry

Examine some rhyming poems to discover how poets put words together. For an unconventional look at rhyming, consider Ogden Nash's poems.

PHASE 4
The Expression Week

➤ *In Your Own Way...*

We have seen God's grace and mercy towards the Assyrians and the Babylonians, and how He used them in the kingdoms of Israel and Judah. Mercy and justice combined under the wisdom of God for His eternal purposes.... Now, choose a selection of these activities, or create your own, which will best express what you have learned from this unit.

Linguistics:

- **Journalism:**
  — Be a newspaper reporter for the "Hebrew Times" and write an exposé on Sennacherib's defeat at Jerusalem.

  — Be a newspaper reporter for the "The Babylon Babbler" and write the fast-breaking story of "Three Engage in Civil Disobedience, Come Out Smelling Like a Rose?" or "Fourth Figure Found in Flaming Fiery Furnace!"

- **Prose:**
  — Write a fictional account of Jonah's experience hiking across the desert to Nineveh.

  — You are with Layard at the discovery of Nineveh. Write a letter "home" to tell your family about the happenings of the dig.

  — Write a short story from the perspective of one of the slaves commanded to bring the holy vessels from Jerusalem to Belshazzar at his feast.

  — Retell the captivity of Judah using modern names and terms.

- **Playing with Words:**
  — Imagine you are one of those Israelites taken into slavery by King Sargon II. Write a coded message to your cousin in Jerusalem.

  — Finish this limerick about Jonah's "pity party" after God forgave the Ninevites: *"There was a young man from Israel, Who honestly felt rather miserable..."*

- **Poetry:**
  — Discover the connection these words have to the unit, and then write a rhyming poem using them: *irrigation, evaporation, deportation (Babylon); demonstrate, illustrate, appreciate (Daniel); weep, reap, leap (Judah)*

Art:
Located on page 178.

Painting/Drawing

Have students look at some young children's illustrated books. Do they prefer a rich palette of colors with very few words? Instead, do they prefer simple stick figures in childlike drawings? Have them look at several examples in order to make a decision about their own style for this book.

Graphic Design

Students should look at tourist t-shirts to gain an appreciation for how outlandish some of this "junk" is. There are also gorgeous tourist t-shirts which are appropriate for a different crowd. Have the student choose the preferred style. Which do they think will sell the best?

Sculpting

Students may choose to do a miniature wall of Assyrian bas-relief, or they could choose to do a large scene. They should lay the clay on a board at the start of the project so it will have adequate support for the final display.

Political Cartooning

Have students examine some different styles of political cartoons until they have grasped the elements that make for a good one.

Phase 4

Art:

• **Painting/Drawing:**

Illustrate a book for young children showing Jonah's adventures.

• **Graphic Design:**

Design a T-shirt that King Nebuchadnezzar would sell to tourists showing who REALLY is in charge of Babylon.

• **Sculpting:**

Using bas-relief sculpture, tell the story of Assyria's major events.

• **Cartooning:**

As a political cartoonist for the local "Jerusalem News" in 701 B.C., draw your version of the Rabshakeh (messenger from Sennacherib), or of what recently transpired outside the city gates.

Music:

• **Compose:**

— Write a tongue-in-cheek Hymn of Tribute to King Nebuchadnezzar.

— In honor of Shadrach, Meshach and Abed-nego, compose a song called, "Just the Three of Us," but add a historically surprising fourth part.

• **Performance Practice:**

With your teacher's help, select an appropriate piece of music which expresses some element from this unit. Prepare and perform the piece for an audience. Communicate with your audience the reason for your selection either in the program notes or in a short speech.

Music:

Located on page 178.

Compose

Students should find some examples of tongue-in-cheek songs, such as *Clementine* or *Monster Mash* or *Little Boxes* or *So You Wanna Go Back to Egypt* (by Keith Green).

Performance Practice

For musical students, this selection may be a wonderful opportunity to express what they have learned. Make sure they have selected a piece that they have adequate time to prepare.

Drama:

Located on page 179.

Comedy

• Remember that many people of the early 1800's, who didn't believe the Bible was true, used to mock the idea that Assyria existed, since only the Bible described it and the ruins were unknown.

• Daniel tells us about the momentous event of King Nebuchadnezzar's insanity, its reasons, and its conclusion. Be sure to show a full-of-pride, swaggering king!

Reality

- What are the events included in the book of Jonah? How will you portray being inside the great fish? What attitude will you take when you tell the people of Ninevah that they are going to be destroyed? What attitude will you have when the vine which has shaded you is destroyed? What is your ending attitude?
- The people of Jerusalem knew that if God did not act on their behalf, they would experience what almost every other city experienced when Assyria attacked—they would be tortured and killed. Keep that kind of suspense throughout the scene.

Tragedy

How will you portray God's heart as we have seen in this unit? Consider using, as a narration, the words found in the Scripture to depict God's heart yearning for His people, while they turn away.

Puppetry

Think about the kind of rich food that might be set before the people at the king's table. In the puppet show, you might want to show several different courses of wild, exotic, probably-bad-for-you food, then contrast it with the food Daniel and his friends were eating.

Phase 4

Drama:

- **Comedy:**
  - Do a humorous skit about scoffers in the 1800's being confronted with Layard's discovery.
  - Do a humorous skit about Nebuchadnezzar, his pride, going crazy, and his eventual repentance.

- **Reality:**
  - Act out the book of Jonah. Use your imagination to create props, sets and costumes. (Good luck with the big fish!) Be sure to include realistic mourning and rejoicing!

  - Perform the scene with King Hezekiah, the prophet Isaiah, and the people of Jerusalem as they are attacked by the Assyrians. Set up the surprise ending!

- **Tragedy:**

  Act out God's heart as His people continually reject Him.

- **Puppetry:**

  Put on a puppet show showing the young men with Daniel who refused the king's rich food. Be sure to show the effects of the rich diet on other young men!

Movement:

Located on page 180.

Pantomime

- Jonah was spit up. We might think of it as being vomited out of the great fish! How will you pantomime this action? Practice the pantomime walk which, though in constant motion, doesn't move you anywhere.
- Austen Layard had some wild adventures in his discovery of Ninevah and Nimrud. There was always danger of wind storms, angry natives, greedy rulers, and disappointing finds.

Dance

The scene with the handwriting on the wall was a furiously wild, drunken party, with paralyzing fear of the Persians who were just outside the walls.

Miniature Action

The Lego version of Jerusalem should include as many Assyrian soldiers as possible—after all, the angel of the Lord killed 185,000 in one night!

TEACHER TIP

Conceptual Design:

Located on page 180.

Irrigate an Elevated Garden

Though the exact dimensions of the Hanging Gardens are not known, it had to have been an impressive place, so plan your own accordingly. How high will it be elevated? Will it be in a desert climate, so that irrigation will be essential? What kinds of trees and plants will you include?

INTRO-PG 26

2) Share creative expressions in class.

The same rules apply as suggested in the reporting section of Phase Two.

Phase 4

Movement:

• Pantomime:

— Pantomime Jonah's being swallowed, being spit out and walking for days across the desert.

— Pantomime Austen Layard's excitement when he discovered Nineveh. Include the huge mounds of sand, the excavations, and some of the surprising discoveries.

• Dance:

Choreograph a dance which portrays the incident of the handwriting on the wall in Babylon.

• Miniature Action:

Make a small "settlement" out of Legos or other building toys. Build a wall around the settlement. Now make a "siege engine" with a battering ram. Add soldiers to the scene. Now reenact either the captivity of Israel or God's deliverance of Judah.

Conceptual Design:

• Irrigate an Elevated Garden:

Design a hanging garden, of the same basic dimensions as the original, which would use high-tech engineering currently available, or future-tech engineering which you dream up.

Create Your Own Expression:

_____

_____

EVALUATION ## Review & Evaluation

In this final Phase of Unit Five, your students should have had the opportunity to express what they have learned about the Mesopotamian Conquerors, Assyria and Babylon, through one or more various creative selections of their own choosing. These include:

1) Linguistics;
2) Art;
3) Music;
4) Drama;
5) Movement;
6) Conceptual Design.

You may wish to evaluate your students based on their *effort* in the **Creative Expressions**, either as individuals or in teams.

Teacher's Guide

THE PERSIANS & MEDES

Pillar from Darius' Palace

Enthusiasm and delight

are the best way to capture a student's

interest and jump-start motivation, so:

1) ***For the Auditory Students:*** Consider playing the music of royalty, such as **Trumpet Voluntary** by Clark, to capture their attention at the very beginning of class;

2) ***For the Kinesthetic Students:*** Have the students warm up as class begins by doing some active movement that is fun (such as a "Simon Says" warm up, where one student leads the others in calisthenics);

3) ***For the Visual Students:*** Bring a visual object to stimulate their interest in the new unit, like a drawing of a gallows (on which Haman was hung!);

4) ***For the hearts of all:*** Pray with them at the beginning of the unit, that God would help them discover what He has for each one to learn in that unit.

Pray with the students

at the beginning of each unit.

PHASE 1

The Introduction Week

Students will be introduced to the Medo-Persian Empire and its place in Scripture—Ezra, Esther and Nehemiah. You may follow this suggested schedule or adapt it to meet your students' needs:

Monday:

1) Informally discuss the Key Concepts

Tuesday:

2) Read the article
3) Listen to the audio recording(s)
4) Read the Scripture listed in Read For Your Life (could be done on their own)

Wednesday:

5) Recap Activity
6) Opinion Column and Critical Puzzling answers on their own

Thursday:

7) Class Discussion

Friday:

8) Choose books of interest/Internet search

> *Teachers can choose to have students do one or two activities, rather than the entire week's schedule. Please use what works for you in your unique setting.*

INTRO - PG 18

1) Informally Discuss the Key Concepts

Listed in the Student Manual on Page 181.

KEY CONCEPTS BACKGROUND INFORMATION

These are the main objectives of the unit. As you proceed through the four weeks, your students will be given various ways of understanding each of these objectives.

The Persian Empire—EXPLANATION

TEACHER TIP

To get an informal discussion started on this key concept, ask a simple, leading question, such as, *"What do you know about the ancient empire of Persia or about King Cyrus?"*

   After the terror of cities besieged and battles lost to Assyrian and Babylonian armies—combined with the yoke of slavery and deportation—enslaved people found hope rising under the benevolent governing of the newly established empire of Persia. King Cyrus, the first and greatest king, was every inch a conquering monarch, but he did not use his power to oppress and terrify. Instead, Cyrus allowed foreign people in his dominion to return to their homelands—-and in the case of the Jews, they returned with his blessing and provision. Even the Greeks, notorious enemies of Persia and bitterly cynical about their rulers, had only good things to say about King Cyrus. The king's tremendous start in repatriation and benevolent rule gave Persia a forward momentum which lasted long past the rule of the first three good kings, unlike the short rule of Babylon as an empire.

THE PERSIANS & MEDES

UNIT 6

Pillar from Darius' Palace

Repatriation to Jerusalem...

"Thus says the Lord to His anointed, to Cyrus, whose right hand I have held, to subdue nations before him and loose the armor of kings, to open before him the double doors, so that the gates will not be shut; I will go before you and make the crooked places straight; I will break in pieces the gates of bronze and cut the bars of iron, I will give you the treasures of darkness and hidden

Unit Six: *The Persians & Medes* / 181

KEY CONCEPTS:

• The Persian Empire

• Daniel's vision

• Rebuilding the Temple

• Esther and Purim

SPIRITUAL

Talk with your students about the great impact leaders have on their nations and people. Proverbs 29:2 says, "When the righteous are in authority, the people rejoice; but when a wicked man rules, the people groan." We are commanded to pray for those in authority over us (1 Timothy 2:1-2). This is not a "religious" duty, this is God's wisdom for our nation and our time.

It is fascinating to consider that King Cyrus was mentioned *by name* in Isaiah at least eighty years before his birth. God's purposes for His people were about to be accomplished by one who did not even know the Lord (Isaiah 45:4).

After the reign of King Cyrus, both

This article can be found in its entirety in the Appendix (see pg 337).

Darius and Xerxes attempted to extend their empire to the European continent. Though it seemed unimaginable to these rulers with hundreds of thousands of soldiers and technological advancements, this tiny incursion into Europe, against an insignificant number of Greeks, would prove the cause of the eventual downfall of the Persian Empire.

Daniel's vision—EXPLANATION

TEACHER TIP

To get an informal discussion started on this key concept, ask a simple, leading question, such as, *"Daniel had a vision of four empires. What do you know about them?"*

The book of Daniel is filled with prophetic visions of the Gentile empires which were and were to come. Daniel's night vision, in which he saw the Babylonian king's dream, shows the flow and chronology of conquering empires until the coming of Messiah (Daniel 2:44).

The image in the vision had a head of gold (the Babylonian Empire); chest and arms of silver (the Persian Empire); belly and thighs of bronze (the Hellenistic or Greek Empire); and legs of iron (the Roman Empire).

This vision, along with other visions of Daniel, provide an exact description of events and characteristics of these four empires. Though much is still veiled from our sight about the book of Daniel, we can examine and study the things that have historically occurred.

SPIRITUAL

Give your students a sense of anticipation as they consider Units 5, 6, 7, and 8 (pertaining to the four empires of Daniel's vision), so that they begin to understand how accurate God's word is and how powerful He is to accomplish His purposes on earth—even through unbelievers who have no regard for Him. The implications of this for our own lives are breathtaking!

Rebuilding the Temple—EXPLANATION

TEACHER TIP

To get an informal discussion started on this key concept, ask a simple, leading question, such as, *"What do you know about the second Temple, the one that was built after Solomon's Temple was destroyed?"*

In Unit Five, we looked at the response of the people of Judah to God's word as delivered by the prophets. They said, "That is hopeless! So we will walk according to our own plans, and we will every one do the imagination of his evil heart." In this unit, we see an entirely different response to the prophets. Zerubbabel and Joshua, the High Priest, responded immediately to the Lord *in obedience.* One of the results of obedience was God's provision and help to finish the Temple, a visible and physical reminder of God's relationship to them.

Look at God's word concerning the moment of Zerubbabel's obedience:

"The hands of Zerubbabel have laid the foundation of this temple; his hands shall also finish it.
Then you will know that the Lord of hosts has sent Me to you.
For who has despised the day of small things?
For these seven rejoice to see the plumb line in the hand of Zerubbabel." Zechariah 4:9-10

When God calls His people to a task, we need not despise *the day of small things.* Remember, God's ways are not our ways—He sees things from a perspective altogether superior to ours. Even though the elderly men had wept in despair as the foundation for the Temple was laid, God was well pleased with the obedient hearts of His people.

" 'The glory of this latter temple shall be greater than the former.' says the Lord of hosts. 'And in this place I will give peace,' says the Lord of hosts." Haggai 2:9

This Temple, which outlasted Solomon's Temple by two hundred years, was the one in which the Prince of Peace, the Promised Redeemer, would declare that He was the light of the world (John 8:12).

Encourage your students to persevere with courage in the tasks God has given them. In the words of William Carey, the Father of Modern Missions, "Attempt great things for God. Expect great things from God."

SPIRITUAL

Esther and Purim—EXPLANATION

To get an informal discussion started on this key concept, ask a simple, leading question, such as, *"What do you know about the festival of Purim or about the biblical Esther?"*

TEACHER TIP

The story of Esther is both historical and educational: First, it is set in a verifiable moment of Persian history, and, second, it teaches us the lesson that God is able to deliver His people from implacable foes. We become better equipped to understand the lesson as the history comes to life.

Esther was queen to a Persian king. What that statement really involves is not readily seen, until we study more about the Persian culture and monarchy. Kings not only held the power of life and death, but further, their word was absolute law. Once proclaimed, not even the king could change the law. No one dared approach the throne unless summoned, on pain of death. The only exception to this summary execution was the rare moment a king would hold out his scepter in pardon.

Knowing that King Xerxes had banished his favorite wife, Queen Vashti, because of her choosing not to appear when summoned (which was not against the law), Esther might have assumed he would have more reason to execute a wife for choosing to appear when not summoned (which *was* against the law). She therefore sought the help of the Lord in fasting and prayer, to grant favor and wisdom at this moment of desperate difficulty.

How many of us, when confronted with diabolical plans of genocide, would have the wisdom and insight to hold a special banquet for the two who organized and authorized the genocide—two days in a row? When the king, at the end of the first banquet, asked Esther what her petition was, she deferred her terror and merely asked the two men to return the next day for another banquet. And, at the end of the second banquet, when the king offered to give Esther her petition, even up to half of the Persian Empire, she did not go into hysterics but simply asked him for her own life and the lives of her people. God obviously granted Esther wisdom from on high:

"But the wisdom that is from above is first pure, then peaceable, gentle, willing to yield, full of mercy and good fruits, without partiality and without hypocrisy." James 3:17

She didn't ask for Haman's head on a platter, which would have been understandable. Instead, she merely asked for life. But Haman's confirmed wickedness, along with his foolishness in falling across Esther's couch, secured his fate. The king was utterly convinced of Haman's evil ways, and had him hanged.

The edict of the king could not be reversed, but the Jews were commanded by a new edict, written by Mordecai and Esther, to arm and defend themselves on the day appointed for their destruction. God took the weapons of the enemy, intended for the annihilation of the Jews, and turned them the opposite direction: seventy-five thousand enemies of the Jews were killed, and many people became Jewish, as the fear of the Lord fell on them. The Feast of Purim is the celebration of this mighty deliverance.

Talk with your students about God's wisdom, as seen revealed in the Book of Esther. When terrible troubles and violent enemies rise up against us, our response needs to be the same as Esther's—we need to seek Him in fasting and prayer, and then do what He shows us to do. He will provide wisdom from above and He will work on our behalf, more than we can even imagine!

SPIRITUAL

2) Read the article

Begins on Page 181 of Student Manual

The article for Unit Six is designed to help students think about the Persian Empire, and the Scriptural understanding given in Ezra, Esther and Nehemiah. The materials covered in the audio recordings offer another look at this time period, covering slightly different information. In the article and recordings, along with introducing the basic understanding of history, we are also bringing in the biblical worldview.

You may choose to have your students read the article first and then listen to the audio recordings, or vice versa.

3) Listen to the audio recording(s)

Listed on Page 192 of the Student Manual.

• The main concepts and chronological flow are contained in **What in the World's Going On Here?**

Key People:

The people listed in this column are the main characters, if you will, of this unit. They are listed in the Student Manual, along with a brief identifier, so that the students can familiarize themselves with these people.

PHASE 1

KEY PEOPLE:

Cyrus 538 BC
—King of Persia

Darius I 521 BC
—Persian king who lost battle of Marathon

Xerxes 480 BC
—Persian king who lost battle of Bay of Salamis

Esther
—Hebrew queen who saved the Jews

Zerubabel 520 BC
—Jewish leader who rebuilt the Temple

Ezra 457 BC
—Jewish priest of repatriation

➤ Listen to this!

• **What in the World's Going on Here? Volume One**

— The Persians & The Medes

➤ Read For Your Life

• **The Main Story:**

— Ezra, Esther, Nehemiah

— Other Helpful Verses: 2 Chronicles 36:22-23; Isaiah 13:17-19, 44:24-28, 45:1-7; Daniel 2:39, 5:30-31, 6:1-28, 9:1-11:2; Haggai, Zechariah, Malachi.

➤ Talk Together

• **Opinion Column:**

— What did you find to be the most interesting aspect, or the most fascinating person, you encountered in your introduction to the Persians and the Medes?

— Isaiah 44:28 and 45:2 speak of a man by the name of Cyrus whom God described as "a shepherd." Considering the fact that the book of Isaiah was written sometime between 740–680 B.C., and King Cyrus appeared on the scene of history in the mid 500's B.C., why do you think God would speak to Isaiah about a non-Jewish king one hundred-fifty years before he showed up?

192 / Unit Six: *The Persians & Medes*

---

4) Read the Scripture listed in Read For Your Life

Listed on Page 192 of the Student Manual. You might choose to have the students read the Main Story verses either corporately or privately.

The Scriptures are central to our understanding, our character, and our decisions. Therefore, we must give the greatest weight possible to them. Help your students gain this perspective as they watch you handle the Scriptures with reverence and awe.

The "Other Helpful Verses" listed are the last three books of the Old Testament, as well as the prophetic descriptions of Cyrus (Isaiah 44 & 45), the Persian Empire as seen in Daniel and Isaiah 13, and the proclamation of Cyrus to rebuild the Temple (2 chronicles 36:22-23).

Though students are not required to look up all the verses (it IS a long list), the teacher might look them up, and choose a few to add in to the class discussion, or to assign to selected students for their input into the discussion.

5) Recap (process & review) Activity

In different parts of the room, set up stations for the Eight Intelligences Recap Activities. Then allow students to work alone or together in small groups to accomplish the following suggestions. At the start of the next class, ask for 3-4 groups of volunteers to share. <u>For homeschoolers, rather than set up all eight stations, allow the student(s) to choose which of these activities they would most enjoy, and do that.</u>

Recap Suggestions:

SPATIAL: Create a poster depicting the 2 or 3 most interesting facts from the reigns of Cyrus, of Darius, and of Xerxes, using drawings, cut up magazines, photos, etc.

BODILY-KINESTHETIC: Become a piece of "living" sculpture, exemplifying one person you have learned about in this unit.

INTERPERSONAL: In groups of 3, with one student acting the part of King Cyrus, one acting the part of a Jew enslaved in Babylon, and one acting the part of a negotiator, communicate back and forth the pros and cons of Cyrus releasing the Jew to return to Jerusalem.

MUSICAL: In a small group, decide what the appropriate sounds would be to reflect the rebuilding of the Temple. Then, organize and make the sounds, paying attention to rhythm, loudness, and pitch.

LINGUISTIC: Write a reelection speech convincing the people of Persia that King Xerxes is still right for the job, even after his defeat at the Battle of the Bay of Salamis.

MATH-LOGICAL: Make a prediction of what will occur in the non-Persian nations of the Persian Empire if Artaxerxes (successor to Xerxes) unsuccessfully attacks Greece.

INTRAPERSONAL: Brainstorm ways you might have helped Nehemiah in his task to organize the rebuilding of the city wall of Jerusalem.

NATURALIST: Using materials found outside, create a visual representation of the Persian Empire as Daniel saw it in one of his visions.

OR...Activity of Your Choice: What would you like to have your students do for a review activity concerning this week's introduction to the Persians and Medes?

6) Opinion Column and Critical Puzzling answers on their own

Listed on Pages 192-193 of the Student Manual. Students may begin these questions after completing their Recap Activities listed above.

7) Class Discussion

Using the questions listed on Pages 192-193 of the Student Manual to get the students primed, create a discussion environment in the classroom. You may also want to draw from the open-ended questions listed below.

QUESTION

Read Nehemiah 4:16-18 in which Nehemiah describes building the wall of Jerusalem. Why do you think city walls were so important? What role did Nehemiah play in the rebuilding of the wall and how necessary was his part?

QUESTION

Why do you think that some Jews chose not to return to Jerusalem? (Consider: What was it like in Jerusalem before the rebuilding took place? What was it like in Babylon? What was it like to live under Persian rule?)

— After reading the article at the beginning of this unit, imagine you are one among hundreds of thousands of Xerxes' foot soldiers. When you are told to cross the bridge over the Hellespont, what is your reaction?

— Read Ezra 8:21-23. Imagine you are one of the people returning to Jerusalem with Ezra. Considering that it was extremely dangerous to travel through enemy territory, what are your thoughts as Ezra chooses to seek God for protection rather than ask the king for military escort? Have you and your family ever chosen to trust God in prayer in a specific situation, rather than rely on human wisdom? What was the outcome?

— Why do you think it was so death-defying for Esther to present herself to the king?

• **Critical Puzzling:**

— The Persians followed a different policy of governing captured people than either the Assyrians or the Babylonians. Their policy was "repatriation," which allowed the people to return to their own lands. Why do you think they had this radically different policy than the Assyrians and Babylonians? What impact do you think this had on the Jews and what effect did it have on God's plan of redemption?

— Do you think Xerxes had any concept that he might be defeated by the Greeks at the Battle of the Bay of Salamis? Support your opinion.

KEY PEOPLE:

Nehemiah
— Jewish rebuilder of the walls of Jerusalem

Malachi
— Last prophet of the Old Testament

Unit Six: The Persians & Medes / 193

---

8) *Choose books of interest/Internet search*

A list of possible books for further reading is listed in the Student Manual beginning on Pages 194-195. Encourage your students to look for general information from this list and from other sources on ancient Persia. You may want to gather a selection of further resources prior to beginning Unit Six, or you may encourage the students to be treasure hunters and find them on their own.

The Internet has a wealth of information concerning the Persians and the Medes, though the articles available vary widely in dependability, worldview and attitude. Help your students learn to recognize the differences.

Phase 1

➤ Reviewed Resources for Digging Deeper:

Choose a few books that look interesting, or find your own.

Persia:

The Persian Empire by Don Nardo

It is difficult to find books appropriate for children on the Persian Empire. This is the best one we have found. **UE+**

Persian Leaders:

Cyrus the Persian by Sherman A. Nagel

This is a fascinating account of the life of Cyrus, written as historical fiction about the Babylonian, Persian and Biblical events. **UE+**

Behold Your Queen! by Gladys Malvern

Historical fiction concerning Esther, this wonderful book makes the details of the story of Esther come to life. **UE+**

Stories from Herodotus translated by Glanville Downey

This book is a children's version of the ancient Greek historian Herodotus. It details the invasion of Greece by the Persians in 490 B.C. and 480 B.C. We couldn't put it down. **UE+**

World Leaders Past and Present: Xerxes by Morgan Llwelyn

Written in a very interesting style, this is an excellent book about a fascinating leader! This gives a very thorough understanding of the most significant king of Persia. **MS+**

Within the Palace Gates—The King's Cupbearer by Anna P. Siviter

Originally published in 1932, it is a spellbinding story of Nehemiah, woven into the backdrop of the royal Persian Court. **UE+**

A Modern Day Daniel:

Imprisoned in Iran by Dan Baumann

A riveting true story about a Christian in Iran sharing the love of God while imprisoned and facing the death penalty in the land of ancient Persia. From YWAM Publishing. **UE+**

194 / Unit Six: *The Persians & Medes*

$\mathcal{R}emember$:

Beware of Arrogance, Embrace Humility!

For the complete list of books from the Student Manual, refer to the Appendix (pg 341).

EVALUATION | **Review & Evaluation**

In this Phase of Unit Six, your students should have had the opportunity to explore the Medo-Persian Empire through reading, listening, thinking and discussing. They will have:

1) informally discussed the Key Concepts;
2) read the article;
3) listened to the audio recording(s);
4) read the Scripture listed in Read for Your Life;
5) explored the Recap Activities;
6) completed the Opinion Column and Critical Puzzling answers on their own;
7) participated in Class Discussion;
8) chosen books of interest or searched the Internet.

You may wish to evaluate your students based on their *participation* in the **Class Discussion** and on their *participation* in the **Recap Activity**.

Learning Style Emphasis: THINKER

Students will explore topics of interest through research and reporting, learn new vocabulary, and construct a timeline relating to the Medo-Persian Empire.

Monday-Tuesday:
1) Choose topic and begin research

Wednesday:
2) Vocabulary Practice

Thursday:
3) Construct the Timeline.

Friday:
4) Research projects completed; share in class or hand in.

> *Teachers can choose to have students do one or two activities, rather than the entire week's schedule. Please use what works for you in your unique setting.*

---

1) Choose topic and begin research

Allow the students the freedom to choose one of the topics listed listed on Pages 196-197, or to suggest their own area which they would like to research.

Motivating Suggestions:

Especially for Non-Linguistic students, and those who are not motivated by written or oral reports, here are suggestions for alternative ways of reporting what has been researched.

Invasion of Greece
1) Conduct interviews with two soldiers after the Battle of Marathon—one from the Persian army, one from the Athenian army—to gain their perspectives on winning and losing, and the effect this has on their respective countries.
2) Analyze the effects of the Persian/Greek wars upon Persia and upon Greece. Make a chart which shows your conclusions.

Old Testament Prophets
1) Set the scene: Haggai prophesies to Zerubbabel concerning the rebuilding of the Temple. Then using pantomime, illustrate Haggai 1:6. Afterwards, you might discuss Zerubbabel's response to God's word.
2) On three separate poster boards, paint depictions of the essence of God's messages to His people as spoken through: #1) Haggai, #2) Zechariah, #3) Malachi.

MOTIVATE

Persian Highway

1) Construct a miniature Royal Road of Persia. Include stations, horses, travelers on foot, etc. Attach a list of facts which would be interesting to viewers.
2) Write a comparison between the Royal Road of Persia and the Pony Express of America in the mid-1800's.

Daniel's Vision

1) Give a first-person presentation, as the Persian Empire, concerning the way you were described in Daniel. If appropriate, defend yourself from Daniel's description of you as "inferior."
2) Make a chart showing a comparison between the major events in the reigns of King Nebuchadnezzar and King Cyrus.

Floating Bridges

1) Calculate the cost in today's money to build Xerxes' bridge across the Hellespont. Show on paper each item, the approximate quantity needed, and, using information gained from local or mail-order suppliers, the cost of each item.
2) Write a young children's book showing the step-by-step process of building this floating bridge.

PHASE 2

Exploration & Discovery Week

➢ *Research & Reporting*

Your mission, if you choose to accept it, is to explore one of these areas, and to discover something significant!

• Invasion of Greece:

Find one of the books listed, or a book of your choice, for basic information about the Persian invasions of Greece. What was the short term impact of these invasions upon the Medo-Persian Empire? What was the long term impact upon Greece? Report your findings.

• Old Testament Prophets:

Investigate the books of Haggai, Zechariah, and Malachi in the Old Testament.

- To whom were these prophets speaking?

- What was the message?

- How did the people respond?

- How did God deal with them?

• Persian Highway:

Do a research paper on the Royal Road of Persia between Sardis and Susa.

• Daniel's Vision:

Using the vision of the four empires listed in Daniel 2, research the way that the Medo-Persian Empire fulfilled the Biblical vision. Report your findings.

• Floating Bridges:

Discover the method used in creating Xerxes' floating bridge which spanned the Hellespont. What materials were used? How was it constructed? How stable would it have been? How many troops crossed it? What else crossed it? How long did it take? Was the bridge there when the army returned from Greece?

• Purim:

Research and write about the Feast of Purim, both the historical beginnings and the modern day celebration.

• The Whole Story:

Research and report on the "Rise and Fall of the Medo-Persian Empire." Who finally conquered this empire?

• Persia to the Present

Investigate, using the library or the Internet, the history of Persia and Media from the time of King Cyrus to the present. What is the modern name of this nation? You may wish to interview adults who remember the deposing of the Shah in the 1970's. Report your findings.

Purim

1) Learn some of the traditional games of Purim, and then teach them to others.
2) Prepare a last minute defense plea to King Xerxes on behalf of Haman, to ask for a change from the death sentence to life imprisonment. Then, create a rebuttal by the prosecuting attorney, showing why Haman's death is justified and necessary.

The Whole Story

1) Before beginning, decide how many reasons for the rise and fall of this empire will need terraces. Then, create a papier-mâché mountain. Create terraces, or steps, on two sides of this mountain. Then, using the terraces on one side, label the reasons for the rise of the Medo-Persian Empire. On the second side, label the reasons for the fall of the Medo-Persian Empire.

2) Write a musical folk ballad: *Ode to the Persian Empire.* In each verse, tell the story about a major event in the rise and fall of the Persian Empire. (For instance, the first verse could describe Cyrus' armies capturing Babylon in one night.)

Persia to the Present

1) Make a comparison chart, depicting the similarities and differences between the ancient Persian Empire and modern day Iran.

2) Create a photographic display which shows photos of ruins and art from ancient Persia interspersed with photos of people and events in Iran from the 1970's to the present. Be sure to title this display.

Phase 2

- **Persian/Biblical Chronology**

Compile a list of names, dates and accomplishments of Media's and Persia's key leaders. How does this list compare with the events listed in the Bible?

- **Xerxes and His Army:**

Look up Xerxes in your history resources. How significant was this leader in Medo-Persian history? Discover more about the immense army of Xerxes. Where did his soldiers come from? Describe Xerxes special fighting unit. How was Xerxes' army reprovisioned as they traveled? How many returned from the war in Greece? How was the empire affected by Xerxes' death?

- **Persian Law:**

Research and report on the way the ancient Persians viewed honesty. How is this magnified in the law of the kings? Can you make any modern comparisons or connections?

- **A Scriptural View:**

Summarize, either in written or verbal form, what you know about:

1) King Cyrus;

2) King Xerxes;

3) The invasions of Greece;

4) Esther;

5) Jews returning to Jerusalem;

6) Rebuilding the Temple;

7) Rebuilding the Wall;

8) Obedience to the Commandments.

- **Rebuilding the Temple:**

Research and report on the rebuilding of the Temple. Make a chart showing the history of the Temple from the time of Solomon until the present.

≫ *Brain Stretchers:*

- **Compare and Contrast:**

Research the differences and similarities between Xerxes' bridge across the Hellespont and modern floating bridges of today. Report your findings.

- **Battle of the Bay of Salamis:**

Discover the tactics of the Greeks in fighting the Battle of the Bay of Salamis. Where did Xerxes' ships come from? How did he get them to Greece? How did Xerxes' navy

lose the battle? Describe the differences between the Medo-Persian ships and the Greek ships.

Create Your Own Research Topic:

_____

_____

_____

Brain Stretchers:

Brain Stretchers, listed on page 197, are intended for advanced students. Those who attempt the Brain Stretchers for their Research and Reporting can use the above list for ideas on how to report their findings.

Persian/Biblical Chronology

Draw a picture of two roads, labeling one "Persia" and the other "Bible." At appropriate intervals, have the two roads intersect. Label each intersection with the person or event in Persian history which was also described in the Bible. In between the intersections, label the span of years, and the kings, events, or prophets which were most important, such as "Malachi—last book of the Old Testament."

Xerxes and His Army:

1) Make a map showing the regions which supplied soldiers to Xerxes, along with the route his armies followed as they went to war.

2) Write several first-person entries for the diary of a disgruntled soldier who served for one year in Xerxes' invasion army. Though you may draw on your imagination for details, be sure to include facts you have discovered in your research.

Persian Law

1) Create an acrostic for the Persian view of honesty, using the letters "H," "O," "N," "E," "S," "T," "Y."

2) Write a short story for children about the importance of honesty, using stories of Persia as your basis.

A Scriptural View

1) King Cyrus was an amazing historical figure. Story-tell his life as you would to young children.

2) Dramatize the story of Esther from the viewpoint of a worried Persian advisor-to-the-king, whether through first-person narration or a skit.

3) Write your personal understanding, based in part upon what you have researched in Scripture during this unit, of the value of obeying God's word.

Rebuilding the Temple

Construct a Temple out of materials found outside. You might choose to create a miniature version (measured in inches or cm) or a larger version (measured in feet or m). Conduct tours, explaining what the different areas were used for and what the original materials might have been.

2) *Words To Watch - Vocabulary Practice*

Listed on Page 198. You may find other words in this unit that are especially appropriate for younger children. Feel free to substitute another vocabulary list for the one provided.

Here is one idea for making vocabulary study interesting and fun: *Briefly explain instances in your life when you have come to understand the meaning of any of these terms.*

Phase 2

➢ *Words to Watch*

Remember—The easiest way to learn a subject is to master its terms:

repatriate	tactics	Marathon
invasion	Purim	Persepolis
trireme	Royal Road	gallows

---

3) *Construct the Timeline.*

Read the information listed with the "Key Dates" on Page 201. Dialogue with your students about the issues involved. Help them recognize that dating antiquity is not an exact science. For ease of reference, the timeline is included in the Appendix on Page 343.

Find the dates for the key people and events listed.

In this unit, the story of Esther is presented at its historical moment in time. Beyond the context of the Persian Empire, however, is the personal context of Esther's choice to risk her life on behalf of her people. "Yet who knows whether you have come to the kingdom for such a time as this? " (Esther 4:14) Encourage and pray for your students, that they would consider their own personal moment in time, and what God's call on their life might be. Are they willing to obey Him, to follow Him, even to risk for Him?

4) *Research projects shared in class and/or turned in.*

Create a safe environment for the presentations. Set ground rules prior to the presentations for all the students, so that they know each one will be honored and respected in their work by all those observing.

Review & Evaluation

In this second Phase of Unit Six, your students should have had the opportunity to explore the Medo-Persian Empire through researching, thinking, and reporting. They will have:

1) done a research project;
2) learned the vocabulary;
3) constructed a Timeline;
4) created a project report on what was researched.

You may wish to evaluate your students based on their *efforts* in the **Research and Reporting** projects and their active *participation* in the **Vocabulary** and **Timeline** exercises.

PHASE 3

The Hands-On Week

Learning Style Emphasis: Sensor

Students will gain cultural understanding through sensory activities as they explore interrelated subject areas relating to the Medo-Persian Empire.

Monday:
1) Create a map and discuss the issues in teams.

Tuesday:
2) Examine and discuss art masterpieces & architectural structures.

Wednesday:
3) Arts in Action—Do an art project.*

Thursday:
4) Do one science project or field trip.**

Teachers can choose to have students do one or two activities, rather than the entire week's schedule. Please use what works for you in your unique setting.

Friday:
5) Listen to and discuss the music.
6) Cook the food listed in the recipe, if desired.

*Art project will need to be planned ahead of time to acquire materials.
**Field trip will require extra planning time.

---

1) Create a map and discuss the issues in teams

The students each have an outline map on Page 203. They will be given assignments for drawing in rivers, mountains, cities, and regional boundaries, which are listed on Page 202. For details on where these things are, please consult a historical atlas, an encyclopedia, a study Bible, or any other source for geographic information. For ease of reference, the map is included in the Appendix on Page 344.

Upper elementary students might be satisfied to accomplish only this portion:
- *Physical terrain:* This part of the mapping exercise will help students locate and mark the geological dynamics of a region.

Middle school students might be satisfied to complete both the previous mapping exercise and this exercise:
- *Geo-Political:* This section of the mapping exercise will provide the students an opportunity to locate and mark the cities, nations and empires of history. It will require more digging.

High school students might be satisfied to complete both the previous mapping exercises and at least one exploration topic of this exercise:
- *Explore:* Discuss some selection from this portion of the mapping exercise in teams.

Encourage them to think for themselves, rather than parroting back information.

TEACHER TIP

PHASE 3

The Hands-On Week

➢ *Maps and mapping*

- **Physical Terrain:**

    — Label and color the Tigris and Euphrates rivers.

    — Locate and indicate the mountain ranges, deserts, and green areas of the ancient Medo-Persian Empire.

    — Shade and label the Persian Gulf.

- **Geo-Political:**

    — Draw the boundaries of ancient Persia and Media. What is today's name of those ancient countries?

    — Label the cities of Persepolis and Susa. What modern day cities are close to these ancient cities?

    — Discover the terrain and climate of Persia and Media.

- **Explore:**

    — *Christian Outreach:* What is the status of Christian outreach to the modern country where Persia was located? How has Christian outreach been affected in this country by the recent wars? Discuss the difficulties and remarkable opportunities facing Christians in that area of the world today.

    — *The Geography of Esther:* After reading the book of Esther, look in an atlas to discover where Shushan (Susa) was located. How far was it from Susa to Babylon to Jerusalem? How much territory was covered by the decree of the King of Persia to destroy the Jews?

Consider:

Read Dan Baumann's book, *Imprisoned In Iran*, and discuss what his experience shows about the possibilities for Christian outreach in this nation.

202 / Unit Six: *The Persians & Medes*

Christian Outreach

Students may wish to locate information about Christian missions work in Iran. If it is possible to interview someone who has worked in that field, it will be even more helpful and insightful. (Again, I recommend Dan Baumann's book, *Imprisoned in Iran*, by YWAM Publishing.)

QUESTION

The Geography of Esther

The students have been asked to discover the size of the area affected by the king's decree to destroy the Jews. Have them pencil in the names of the current countries included in this area and the current population of these countries. Scripture tells us that the Jews killed 75,000 of their enemies on

QUESTION

the day they were to have been annihilated, which appears to be a fairly small percentage of the people in the land. How does this number compare to the number of people living in these areas today? What percentage would it be?

2) Examine and discuss art masterpieces & architectural structures

Locate either a copy of these art forms, or Internet sites for each of the items listed on Pages 204-205. Allow the students to observe the painting or glazed tile relief without any conversation, and then, when they are ready, engage them in some or all of the following questions:

QUESTION

Daniel in the Lion's Den *by Henry O. Tanner*

It is interesting to consider that Henry O. Tanner lived most of his adult life in a country other than that of his birth. (He choose to live in France due to the racism he faced in America as an African-American painter.) The subject of this painting, Daniel, also lived most of his life in a country other than that of his birth.

• Ask the students whether they see any indication in this painting of a foundational sympathy towards another expatriate.

QUESTION

Glazed tile relief of ancient Persia

Notice the position of the faces on the glazed tiles. Isn't it interesting that the Persians, Babylonians, Assyrians, and Egyptians all painted the profiles of people?

• Ask your students if they have any theories as to why the ancient artists chose to paint in that manner.

QUESTION

Darius' Palace at Persepolis

Though the Persians did not create a new style of architecture, they elevated the borrowed forms of earlier civilizations to a new height. If possible, look at a photo of the artwork on Darius' monumental tomb!

Phase 3

Consider:

Henry O. Tanner (1859-1937 A.D.) was the first African American artist to win international acclaim. He spent most of his professional career in France, avoiding the increasing hostility and racism of that time period in America. Tanner traveled twice to the Holy Land, which provided inspiration and insight into his many religious paintings.

➢ Art Appreciation

• **Daniel in the Lion's Den** *by Henry O. Tanner*

— Do you think this painting reflects what the Bible describes?

— How does the painting differ from your own impression of this historic event?

— How would you describe Tanner's use of shadow and light in this painting?

• **Glazed tile relief of ancient Persia**

— How would you describe Persia's glazed tile relief artwork?

— Is it similar to other artwork we have previously observed?

— What can you learn about this culture from its art?

— From what you can discover, did the Persians and Medes create any art that was original to their culture?

---

3) Arts in Action

Listed on Pages 205-206.

≫ Architecture

The magnificent architecture of the Persians can be glimpsed in the remains of the palace King Darius constructed at Persepolis, beginning c. 518 B.C., which Alexander the Great later destroyed. It appears, from what can be seen of the ruins, that Darius intended the city of Persepolis to be the seat of government and the showplace of his fabulously wealthy empire. Alexander the Great, in 330 B.C., allowed his soldiers to loot the city, carting away so much treasure that it took 20,000 mules and 5,000 camels to carry it all. He then set fire to Darius' palace, utterly destroying it, except for the ruins which can be seen today.

— Look for photos of Darius' palace, especially the grand staircases decorated with reliefs, and the city of Persepolis. How would you describe these ruins? What are the similarities to Assyrian or Babylonian architecture?

≫ Arts in Action

Select one, and let your artistic juices flow!

• **Imitation:**

— try imitating Henry Tanner's use of light in the lion's den.

— try creating something in the Persian style of art

• **Relief Carving:**

Try making a relief carving on wax or soap. Or, if you prefer, try using a slab of clay rolled flat onto a board to carve a relief of a simple animal, such as a fish. Let it dry and mount it.

• **Sand Cast Candle:**

A wonderful bronze head (cast, not sculptured) was found in the excavations of Persia. Make a sand cast candle by pouring hot wax into a form made in the sand. You can make a hollowed out space by packing the sand very firmly around a can, a ball, your hands, etc., then carefully removing the object. This creates the form. If you are very adventurous, try making a plaster cast. Check the library or an expert for more info.

Imitation

Have the students look again at Tanner's painting or at the glazed tiles of Persia. Then, with art supplies of colored pencils, pastels, or paint, try to recreate what is seen.

Relief Carving

You might want to make a salt dough "clay" for carving with a plastic knife. Here is a recipe:

Salt Dough

1 cup salt
1 1/4 cup warm water
3 cups white flour

Dissolve the salt in the warm water. Add the flour, and stir. When it is too stiff to stir, knead the dough until it is smooth. Use immediately, or cover tightly and refrigerate for up to one week.

After the salt dough has been carved into a relief, bake it in a slow (250 degrees) oven. (If the student doesn't like what has been carved, simply roll it into a ball again, flatten, and start over.) It will take 1-2 hours to bake—it is finished when it is a golden color and baked through. After it cools, the student may wish to paint the relief.

Sand Cast Candle

Be VERY careful with heated candle wax. This art project should only be attempted under close adult supervision, and with proper information concerning candle making. Having said that, candles are wonderfully satisfying, no matter how they turn out!

Potato Stamp

Encourage the students to start simple in order to learn the technique. Once they have become comfortable with creating the potato stamp, they might want to make some elaborate designs.

Floating Bridge

Though this is a messy project, it could absolutely cement in a student's memory an understanding of this historic moment. Remember—*the greater mess, the better memory!*

INTRO · PG 24

4) Do a science project

Listed on Page 206. Feel free to choose one of these projects. If students love science, they might want to consider doing all of them!

Braided Rope

Ecclesiastes 4:12 says, "Though one may be overpowered by another, two can withstand him. And a threefold cord is not quickly broken." As the students are braiding various types of rope, ask them what they think this scripture means. In human friendships, who could be the third strand of this three-braided cord?

This is a wonderful time to ask the Lord to illuminate the students' hearts concerning the importance of His centrality in all of their relationships.

Phase 3

• Potato Stamp:

In the Book of Esther, the king gives to Haman and then to Mordecai his signet ring. A signet ring was extremely important because it was stamped on official documents (much like a signature today). Create a stamp using a potato! Cut a potato in half, then use a toothpick to poke a design into the exposed surface on one half. Next, carefully carve away about 1/4 inch of the rest of the potato half, letting the design stand out in sharp relief. Press the potato relief onto a rubber stamp ink pad, then stamp your relief design on paper.

• Floating Bridge:

Build a "floating bridge" out of balsa wood, Legos, Ivory soap bars, or other materials. Anchor ships across the span of a sink, wading pool, or small creek. Make miniature cables and string them across the tops of the ships. Build it up with planking, railing, etc., just as described at the crossing of the Hellespont.

➢ Science

The cables used in supporting Xerxes' bridge across the Hellespont were made of flax and papyrus that were braided together. The first bridge he attempted also used cables of flax and papyrus, but they were not braided together, and the bridge came apart in a storm.

✗ **• Braided Rope:**

— Experiment with braiding various short ropes, each made with only one substance (thread, string, horse hair, human hair, etc.) Test their strength by hanging weights from the end until the ropes break. Now try braiding different substances together and hanging weights from the rope. Which ropes are the strongest? Does it improve the strength of a rope to use more than one material? Compare all of these to the strength of a spider's web.

- **Variation:** *Try making a rope that is not braided, and one that is. Which is stronger? Read Eccl. 4:12 and discuss it in light of your experiment.*

- **Space Age:** *Learn more about the new fibers and textiles used in space age technology. Imagine the possibilities if Xerxes had had these materials!*

206 / Unit Six: *The Persians & Medes*

5) Listen to and discuss the music

Listed on Page 207.

INTRO - PG 24

Phase 3

➤ Music

After the plot of Haman was uncovered, the Jews were allowed to defend themselves on the day of attack. Their defense was successful, and the Jewish nation survived this attempted annihilation. In response, the people celebrated with feasting and joy. Though the Bible does not describe the music of the celebration, we know that the Jews had used music in celebrations in the past. Do you think the music would have been loud or soft? Or, perhaps would it have been a combination of loud and soft? The term used to describe the loudness or softness in music is dynamics. Dynamics is another one of the fundamental elements of music. A piece of music can be played all at a loud dynamic level, or it can be played at a soft dynamic level, but most music has a combination of various dynamic levels.

• **Listen:**

— A wonderful example of strong dynamic changes is the *Surprise Symphony* by Franz Joseph Haydn. He wrote strong contrasts of dynamics in this piece of music to address a problem. He was a diligent, hardworking, Christian composer who greatly respected the musicians in his orchestra. However, the rich people who came to hear the orchestra often fell asleep due to too much feasting and drinking. So he devised a solution! Listen carefully to the second movement, called the "Andante," to hear what he did. Imagine yourself sleeping like the rich patrons. Do you think his solution was effective?

• **Try this:**

— See how softly you can sing or tap or hum; then see how loudly you can sing or tap or hum; then determine how many different levels you can make. For instance, can you sing very, very soft? very soft? soft? medium soft? medium loud? loud? very loud? very, very loud? Musicians use Italian terms to indicate dynamic levels. "Piano" means soft, "forte" (FOR`-tay) means loud.

Listen

The *Surprise Symphony* by Franz Joseph Haydn is worth listening to. Don't tell the students what the surprise is (if you know it)! My suggestion is to set the volume fairly high.

TEACHER TIP

Try This

Let the students judge what is very, very soft all the way to very, very loud by voting for their opinion. This would be an appropriate time to inform them that listening to very, very loud music can damage their ears very, very severely, and they could end up wearing a hearing aid when they are still young! (A possible debate for your students: "Is it worth wearing a hearing aid when I'm thirty to listen to loud music today?")

INTRO-PG 24

6) Cook the food

Listed on Page 208.

TEACHER TIP

Cold soup may sound terrible if you are not used to it, but this is a very tasty way to experience the novelty. And just consider how refreshing it would be on a sun-baked Persian rooftop!

Phase 3

➢ Cooking

Our unit examines both the Medo-Persian Empire, the return of the Jews to Jerusalem, and the deliverance of the Jews recorded in the Book of Esther. When you learn about the climate of Persia, perhaps this soup will sound just right! (It is served cold.) And to help you celebrate Purim, we have included a delicious cookie—Rejoice!

• Persian Cucumber & Yogurt Soup

1 quart yogurt (plain)	3 small cucumbers, peeled,
1 cup buttermilk	seeded, chopped
1/2 cup walnuts, chopped	1/2 cup fresh mint, finely chopped
	(or chopped green onions)

Beat yogurt and buttermilk together until well blended. Stir in mint and cucumbers; salt and pepper to taste. Serve very cold, sprinkle with chopped walnuts. Serves 8.

• Hamantaschen Cookie Recipe (Purim)

1 cup whole wheat flour	1/4 cup butter, softened
1 cup white flour	2 eggs, slightly beaten
2 tsp. baking powder	1 tsp. almond extract
1/2 cup sugar	1/4 cup orange juice

(Traditional filling: poppy seed, prune. However, you can also use your imagination and come up with a sure-to-please-the-family filling.)

Combine and mix all dry ingredients. Cut in the butter. Add the eggs, almond extract, and juice. Mix dough into a ball, adding extra flour or water if needed for a workable dough. Roll out dough on a floured surface, 1/4" thick. Cut with cookie cutter in 3" circles. Place 1 tsp. filling in the center, and pinch dough up on three sides to form an open triangle. Bake at 350 degrees for 20 min., or until golden.

EVALUATION | ## Review & Evaluation

In this third Phase of Unit Six, your students should have had the opportunity to explore the Medo-Persian Empire through various hands-on and creative sessions. They will have:

1) completed a Mapping section;
2) observed and discussed Art & Architecture;
3) worked on an art project;
4) experimented with a Science Project or taken a field trip;
5) listened to music;
6) tasted a food related to this unit.

You may wish to evaluate your students based on their *class participation* in these **Hands-on** activities.

Learning Style Emphasis: *Intuitor*

Students, through creative self-expression, using one or more creative activities, will present some aspect of what they have learned in the past three weeks relating to the Medo-Persian Empire. Areas of expression include linguistics, art, music, drama, movement and conceptual design.

Monday - Thursday

1) Choose area of expression and begin work either individually or in teams.

Friday

2) Share creative expressions in class.

> *Teachers can choose to have students do one or two activities, rather than the entire week's schedule. Please use what works for you in your unique setting.*

1) Choose area of expression and begin work either individually or in teams

Linguistics:

Located on page 209.

Journalism

Have students examine the style of journalism used by war correspondents who write ongoing descriptions of an army's battles.

Prose

- It would add greater interest to the story if students spent time investigating some of the needs and troubles of sheep. There are several books written by Christians on that subject, since people are likened to sheep in Scripture. It is not a flattering comparison! (If students choose to illustrate the "Baa-aa-aa-Hum-Bug" account, they might consider using cotton balls on the sheep for added texture and fun.)

- There are many children's books in the library depicting wars and battles. It might be very helpful, to students interested in creating the book about Esther, to see how the preparations and experiences of war are shown for children.

TEACHER TIP

Playing with Words

Limericks are fun to write and easy to memorize. Encourage your students to write memorable limericks that will help others understand some aspect of this Biblical history.

Poetry

- Zerubbabel has such a great name, with possibilities of such great rhymes. My favorite little saying about him is, "Zerubbabel went to clean up the rub-a-ble." Of course, a student may choose to write a poem about him that does not rhyme. (But it would be a tragic waste of a great name!)
- For more serious poets, Esther's vigil the night before she went to the king is suitable for a powerful poem. Examine some dramatic, emotion-filled poems for inspiration, such as Curfew Shall Not Ring Tonight by Rose Hartwick Thorpe.

PHASE 4
The Expression Week

➤ *In Your Own Way...*

We have seen God's amazing timing and redemptive purposes in the Medo-Persian Empire, and how He saved the Jewish people from extermination through Esther's intervention with the king. Praise the Lord for His perfect timing, perfect provision and perfect purposes! Now, choose a selection of these activities, or create your own, which will best express what you have learned from this unit.

Linguistics:

- **Journalism:**

  Be a war correspondent accompanying Xerxes' invasion army. Write a series of news reports for the "Susa Sun" about the progress of the invasion of Greece.

- **Prose**
  — Write a fictional account of the journey from Babylon to Jerusalem, from the viewpoint of a sheep named "Baa-aa-aa-Hum-bug."

  — Write a book for young children showing the events of Esther's life. Include her someday-to-be husband going off to subdue those rebellious Greeks.

- **Playing with Words**

  Finish this limerick about Esther's uncle:
  *There once was an uncle named Mordecai
  Whose enemies wanted to hang him
  high...*

- **Poetry**
  — Write a poem with the first line, "From Babylon went good Zerubbabel."

  — Write a poem of Esther, with her prayer to God the night before she went unbidden to Xerxes.

Art:

Located on page 210.

Painting/Drawing

Students might wish to examine some of the works by Rubens and Rembrandt for ideas on color in a dramatic scene.

Graphic Design

- Many cities and towns hold annual celebrations. Have students find a selection of posters for these events in order to understand the visual elements which are used over and over again to promote attendance.
- Students who wish to create the enlistment poster should be encouraged to study what the military has used for the last hundred years to visually entice civilians to enlist. This might provide tremendous stimulus for the students' own ideas.
- Clothing stores and tourist shops often carry a line of "talking T-shirts." Students might wish to view a sampling of these T-shirts to gain ideas for their survival messages.

Illustration

Esther must have been a stunningly beautiful woman. Encourage students wishing to illustrate the book about her life to examine photos and paintings of some of the beautiful women of history, such as the *Mona Lisa* by Da Vinci.

Sculpting

To sculpt Daniel's vision, students could choose a medium that would be air dried or one that would be dried in the oven, and then painted the appropriate colors. Alternately, fabric of appropriate colors could be sewn together and stuffed with batting for a soft sculpture.

Political Cartooning

- When a cartooner depicts a scene which is controversial or heated, he uses certain techniques to increase the temperature. Encourage students to look for various examples of this to understand how it is done.
- Have students look at multi-frame cartoons to observe how the action progresses. They might want to add an occasional caption to their frames, or they might prefer to let the pictures tell the whole story.

Phase 4

Art:

- **Painting/Drawing:**

  Paint a scene from the rebuilding of the Temple. Focus on what colors best evoke the suppressed excitement and fear they would have felt as they worked in the midst of their enemies.

- **Graphic Design:**

  — Create an advertisement for the second annual Feast of Purim, held in downtown Susa.

  — Make an enlistment poster for soldiers to join Xerxes in his military invasion of Greece.

  — Design a T-shirt for those who went with Ezra back to Jerusalem. Start with "We survived…"

- **Illustration:**

  Illustrate the book for young children listed above.

- **Sculpting:**

  Using the materials you prefer to work with, suggesting the materials described in the vision, sculpt the four empires of Daniel 2.

- **Cartooning:**

  — Draw a political cartoon showing the folks who were angry about the wall in Jerusalem being built (Nehemiah 4:7-9) and Nehemiah encouraging the Jewish wall builders to arm themselves against these angry folks.

  — Make a multi-frame cartoon of Esther inviting King Xerxes and Haman to her house for a cozy meal, only to invite them again.

Music:

- **Compose:**

  Create a jubilant song of praise about the dramatic deliverance of God's people from their enemies, focusing on Esther and Haman. You could use the songs of Miriam or Moses as your model, or one of the psalms of David.

- **Performance Practice:**

  With your teacher's help, select an appropriate piece of music which expresses some element from this unit, such as the joy of the repatriated Jews. Prepare and perform the piece for an audience. Communicate with your audience the reason for your selection either in the program notes or in a short speech.

Music:

Located on page 210.

Compose

A Jewish motif would be appropriate (though not necessary) for this joyous music. Students might want to listen to exuberant, exultant praise music for ideas.

Performance Practice

For musical students, this selection may be a wonderful opportunity to express what they have learned. Make sure they have selected a piece that they have adequate time to prepare.

TEACHER TIP

Drama:

Located on page 211.

Comedy

It is obvious in Scripture that Haman hated Mordecai, and would have been fuming at having to carry out the king's instructions to honor him. How might you portray this fuming, especially since it would have been dangerous to be seen acting contrary to the king's desires?

Phase 4

Drama:

• Comedy:

Create a humorous skit about Haman having to honor Mordecai.

• Reality:

Act out the rebuilding of Jerusalem's wall. Begin with Nehemiah's conversation with King Artaxerxes. Use your imagination to create props, sets and costumes. Be sure to include realistic fear and rejoicing!

• Celebrate:

Celebrate the Feast of Purim. Learn about the traditions and rituals of this feast, prepare costumes and props to tell the story of Esther, and invite your family, friends, or neighbors to share this miraculous event.

• Reader's Theater:

Do a dramatic reading about the invasion of Greece by King Xerxes.

Reality

The wall of Jerusalem was a critical factor in the safety of the people, but no one had the courage to overcome the enemy's objections and to rebuild the wall. That is, until Nehemiah came on the scene. He is such a great character for a dramatic presentation, since he did so many dramatic things!

Celebrate

The Feast of Purim is still celebrated today, so there should be books in the library or information online to learn how to have a traditional celebration. If you have any Jewish friends who can help, that would add a tremendous blessing to the endeavor. Be sure to invite them!

Reader's Theater

This is one of the most amazing military events in history—and very similar to the story of David and Goliath. Be sure to find the best descriptions of Xerxes' bridge across the Hellespont, the pass at Thermopylae, the burning of Athens, and the Battle of the Bay of Salamis.

TEACHER TIP

Movement:

Located on page 212.

Pantomime

How will you portray the position Esther finds herself in? She has chosen to put her trust in God, though she knows it is quite possible, even probable, that Xerxes will be angry and have her killed for disobeying the law.

Dance

This will be a dance of joy—the repatriation of the people back to Jerusalem!

Phase 4

Movement:

- **Pantomime:**

  Pantomime Esther's anxiety as she goes to Xerxes, knowing that he may not extend his scepter.

- **Dance:**

  Choreograph a dance which depicts the ending of seventy years of captivity, and the royal proclamation of King Cyrus for the willing Jews to return to Jerusalem.

- **Action:**

  — Show the events of Haman's life in stylized action, including his swaggering pride.

  — Act out the fights between the Jews and Persians, after Xerxes' second proclamation.

  — What is the difference in mentality of the two groups? Consider representing this with different action styles.

Conceptual Design:

- **Prefabricated Bridge:**

  Using the concept of the prefabricated bridges used in World War II, design a pre-fabricated bridge with materials which would have been available in Xerxes' time. Improve the floating bridge used in the invasion of Greece at the Hellespont.

Create Your Own Expression:

Action

TEACHER TIP

Haman's actions, as described in Scripture, can be divided into specific scenes. Choose the appropriate actions for each of these scenes to best convey Haman's attitudes.

What was supposed to have been ethnocide and the complete destruction of the Jews, turned out to be a day of destroying the enemies of the Jews. The Bible says that many of the people who were not Jews, when they saw how God had protected them, decided to follow the Jewish God. Can you portray the various attitudes of the different people?

Conceptual Design:

Located on page 212.

TEACHER TIP

Prefabricated Bridge

During World War II, the Army Corps of Engineers created prefabricated bridges that could be quickly set up across rivers when the previous ones were bombed by the Germans. Crossing the Hellespont is a greater challenge than crossing a stream or river, but by learning about the prefabricated bridges, you may find a way to improve on Xerxes' plan.

2) *Share creative expressions in class.*

The same rules apply as suggested in the reporting section of Phase Two.

INTRO - PG 26

EVALUATION | Review & Evaluation

In this final Phase of Unit Six, your students should have had the opportunity to express what they have learned about the Medo-Persian Empire through one or more various creative selections of their own choosing. These include:

1) Linguistics;
2) Art;
3) Music;
4) Drama;
5) Movement;
6) Conceptual Design.

You may wish to evaluate your students based on their *effort* in the **Creative Expressions**, either as individuals or in teams.

GREECE & THE HELLENISTS

UNIT 7

Alexander the Great

Enthusiasm and delight

are the best way to capture a student's interest and jump-start motivation, so:

Pray with the students at the beginning of each unit.

1) ***For the Auditory Students:*** Consider playing Greek folk music, such as the soundtrack to **My Big Fat Greek Wedding**, to capture their attention at the very beginning of class;

2) ***For the Kinesthetic Students:*** Have the students warm up as class begins by doing some active movement that is fun (such as learning a simple Greek folk dance, or, if that is not possible, do jumping jacks or rhythmic jumping to the Greek folk music.);

3) ***For the Visual Students:*** Bring a visual object to stimulate their interest in the new unit, like a Greek vase or sculpture (a photo of the Parthenon would also be interesting);

4) ***For the hearts of all:*** Pray with them at the beginning of the unit, that God would help them discover what He has for each one to learn in that unit.

PHASE 1

The Introduction Week

Students will be introduced to ancient Greece and the Hellenists, along with the Scriptures in Daniel which refer to the Hellenistic Empire. You may follow this suggested schedule or adapt it to meet your students' needs:

Monday:

1) Informally discuss the Key Concepts

Tuesday:

2) Read the article
3) Listen to the audio recording(s)
4) Read the Scripture listed in Read For Your Life (could be done on their own)

Wednesday:

5) Recap Activity
6) Opinion Column and Critical Puzzling answers on their own

Thursday:

7) Class Discussion

Friday:

8) Choose books of interest/Internet search

> *Teachers can choose to have students do one or two activities, rather than the entire week's schedule. Please use what works for you in your unique setting.*

INTRO · PG 18

1) Informally Discuss the Key Concepts

Listed in the Student Manual on Page 213.

KEY CONCEPTS BACKGROUND INFORMATION

These are the main objectives of the unit. As you proceed through the four weeks, your students will be given various ways of understanding each of these objectives.

Golden Age of Greece—EXPLANATION

TEACHER TIP

> To get an informal discussion started on this key concept, ask a simple, leading question, such as, *"What have you heard or read about ancient Greece?"*

To study history from a Biblical perspective means we allow the Bible to show us what God's perspective is on a culture, a leader, a behavior. When it comes to the study of Greece, many curriculums and teachers focus on the fifty years of Greek history after the victory at the battle of the Bay of Salamis up to the defeat of Athens in the Peloponnesian Wars (480-430 B.C.). However, though the Bible very clearly speaks in the book of Daniel about Greece, it does not describe this time of man's achievement. Instead, it looks to the time of Alexander the Great and his empire.

Why then is there such a focus on this Golden Age, even among Christians? Part of the answer lies in the humanistic glory of Greek architects, historians, dramatists, and philosophers. In fact, during the Renaissance, it was the allure of man's achievements during this ancient time period that many longed to recreate in Europe. Though it is interesting to study this time period, we need to call important what God calls important.

Consider this: He may not be nearly as impressed with the ancient Greek accomplishments as we are.

Though Western Civilization looks back, in large measure, to the ancient Greeks to discover its values and philosophy, yet, as biblical Christians, we need instead to look back to the Garden of Eden—relationship to our Creator—to measure what is valuable and what is true.

Pray for your students during this unit, that they may know God's perspective on man's ways, since the very essence of humanism is found in ancient Greece.

SPIRITUAL

Greek intellectual achievements—EXPLANATION

To get an informal discussion started on this key concept, ask a simple, leading question, such as, *"How many have ever heard of the Pythagorean Theorem, or the Hippocratic Oath? Since these both come from the time of the ancient Greeks, why do you think theirs was a time of so much discovery?"*

TEACHER TIP

During the sixth century B.C., many Greek thinkers began to look at the world from a scientific perspective based on observation. Prior to that, many of the explanations of such issues as sickness and disease were thought to be found in the inscrutable work of the gods. This change from myth to science brought about tremendous practical discoveries in various arenas of learning: Euclid wrote about geometry, Eratosthenes measured the circumference of the world (very accurately!) and Archimedes discovered the principle of buoyancy, among other things. There were also influential philosophies developed by Greek thinkers, including Socrates, Plato, and Aristotle.

It is interesting to note that, while Hippocrates provided a valuable standard of medical ethics through the Hippocratic Oath, Aristotle (born shortly before Hippocrates died) in many ways actually hindered the development of medical knowledge: he did not believe in the value

> ### FASCINATING FACT:
>
> *One example of Aristotle's nonscientific attitudes which masqueraded as "medical science" had to do with his view on women:*
>
> *The female is a "monstrosity," "a deformed male," and "a deformity...which occurs in the ordinary course of nature." "The female sex has a more evil disposition than the male, is more forward and less courageous...The males are in every respect opposite to this; their nature is as a class braver and more honest, that of the female being more cowardly and less honest." (Quoted from the book,* Why Not Women? *by Loren Cunningham and David Hamilton.)*

of observation and experimentation. Rather, he felt that man should rely solely upon reason to understand many medical issues. Because he was considered the Father of the Scientific Method, and because his opinions on various scientific matters were so revered, the pioneers of the Scientific Revolution in Europe had to battle to convince others that the mighty Aristotle was wrong—that many of his opinions were not based on science but on human reasoning.

Influence of Greek worldview—EXPLANATION

To get an informal discussion started on this key concept, ask a simple, leading question, such as, *"What can you think of in the world today that is attributable to Greek influence?"*

When Aristotle was chosen by Philip II of Macedonia to tutor his son, Alexander, a philosophy and love of Greek culture was imparted that would have earthshaking consequences. When Alexander came to manhood, leading his troops to battle in far-flung nations of the earth, he took with him a belief in the superiority of all things Greek. Alexander saw nothing ethnocentric in imparting a Greek worldview to all he conquered, as he was convinced that it was the best way to think. Greek thinking, Greek language, Greek culture, and Greek religion permeated the conquered countries, bringing a widespread influence. Thus, the seeds of the Greek worldview were planted to bear fruit through the ages.

It would be interesting to discuss with your students any similarities they see between this distribution of Greek thinking during the ancient Hellenistic Empire, and the distribution of English thinking during British Colonialism of the eighteenth and nineteenth centuries, which introduced English attitudes, language, culture, and religion to much of the world.

Alexander the Great and His Empire— EXPLANATION

To get an informal discussion started on this key concept, ask a simple, leading question, such as, *"Why do you think people call Alexander, 'The Great'?"*

It is amazing to consider that one man could wage war on the most powerful empire of the world and conquer not only it, but every other

This article can be found in its entirety in the Appendix (see pg 345).

GREECE & THE HELLENISTS

UNIT **7**

Alexander the Great

The third kingdom of Daniel's vision emerges...

Just before the defeat of the Babylonians at the hands of the Medo-Persian army in 539 B.C., Daniel was given another startling, prophetic vision by God. In this vision, he saw a mighty, victorious ram that conquered to the west, the north, and the south, and was so powerful that no one could withstand it. Suddenly, from the west came a fierce male goat which attacked the ram, and this furious goat trampled the ram to the ground. Daniel saw that "there was no one that could deliver the ram from his hand."

When Daniel sought the meaning of this vision, the angel Gabriel came to him and explained that, *"the ram which you saw, having the two*

KEY CONCEPTS:

- **Golden Age of Greece**

- **Greek intellectual achievements**

- **Influence of Greek worldview**

- **Alexander the Great and His Empire**

- **Hanukkah's history**

---

city and nation he came to—all within ten years. This was done without benefit of motorized vehicles, airplanes, telephones, computers, satellites, or any other of the technological wonders our modern military relies on. How did he do it? There was such a drive in this man, such a passion to see and conquer new places, and such a power to motivate soldiers, that he was able to do what no European had previously done—conquer distant regions of Africa and Asia. In fact, legend reports that when Alexander was a boy, his great fear was that his father would conquer everything first, leaving nothing for him to do!

Consider that the Persians were the first Asian conquerors to try to conquer regions in Europe. Their incursion into Greek territory provided the excuse Alexander needed to justify his push into their lands. And because of his brilliant, military mind, he understood the vital need to protect his flanks, which gave him the excuse to take Egypt—and everything that lay between Egypt and himself! It may have been a lust for conquering or a curiosity for seeing India that drove him to attempt warfare in a place no European or Middle Eastern empire before him had conquered. However, at that point, his power to motivate soldiers dissipated, and they refused to go any further.

There have only been a few military conquerors in history to ever compare with him, but none have exceeded him. Perhaps that is why Daniel saw Alexander the Great in his visions—Alexander was a profoundly important, world-changing conqueror, single-handedly building an empire that God used to shape events in the chronological flow of HisStory.

Hanukkah's history—EXPLANATION

To get an informal discussion started on this key concept, ask a simple, leading question, such as, *"Does anyone know why the Jews celebrate Hanukkah?"*

Hanukkah is not just a festive holiday for the Jewish people. It represents a dramatic triumph over the humanism of Greek philosophy by the power and mercy of God. If we consider the motivation behind Antiochus Epiphanes' desire to eliminate the biblical forms of worship of the Jews, we can begin to understand that this was not a mere battle between humans. This was a battle between competing philosophies—one with man at the center, one with God at the center—and the genesis of the war was not on earth but in the heavenlies.

"For we do not wrestle against flesh and blood, but against principalities, against powers, against the rulers of the darkness of this age, against spiritual hosts of wickedness in the heavenly places." Ephesians 6:12

Pray that your students will grasp that they are in a battle, that they will hold firmly to their faith and not be seduced into the vain and humanistic philosophies of man:

"Beware lest anyone cheat you through philosophy and empty deceit, according to the tradition of men, according to the basic principles of the world, and not according to Christ." Colossians 2:8

2) Read the article

Begins on Page 213 of Student Manual

The article for Unit Seven is designed to help students think about the ancient Greek civilization, the Hellenistic Empire, and the implication for Christians today. The materials covered in the audio recordings offer another look at this time period, covering slightly different information. In the article and recordings, along with introducing the basic understanding of history, we are also bringing in the biblical worldview, which is especially critical in considering the fount of humanism!

You may choose to have your students read the article first and then listen to the audio recordings, or vice versa.

TEACHER TIP

INTRO · PG 18

3) Listen to the audio recording(s)

Listed on Page 225 of the Student Manual.

- The main concepts and chronological flow are contained in **What in the World's Going On Here?**
  - **More True Tales from the Times of…Ancient Civilizations & The Bible**
- The Seven Wonders (this is the short version)

- **An In-Depth Study of…The Seven Wonders of the Ancient World**
  - Colossus of Rhodes—Pharos of Alexandria
  - Temple of Artemis—Statue of Zeus at Olympia
  - Mausoleum at Halicarnassus

PHASE 1

➤ Listen to this!

- **What in the World's Going on Here? Volume One**
  - The Greeks & The Hellenistic Empire

- **More True Tales from the Times of Ancient Civilizations & The Bible**
  - The Seven Wonders of the Ancient World (short version)

- **An In-Depth Study of…The Seven Wonders**
  - The Colossus of Rhodes, the Temple of Artemis, and the Lighthouse of Alexandria

➤ Read For Your Life

- **The Holy Bible**
  - The Main Story: Daniel 8:5-8, 21, 11:3-4, Acts 17:16-34, Acts 19:23-41

➤ Talk Together

- **Opinion Column:**
  - What did you find to be the most interesting aspect, or the most fascinating person, you encountered in your introduction to Greece and the Hellenistic Empire?
  - Why do you think God gave Daniel such a clear vision of a Greek king who would quickly sweep through the world, and then be gone just as quickly?

KEY PEOPLE:

Pericles 443-429 BC
—Architect of the Golden Age of Greece

Herodotus
—the first historian

Socrates 469-399 BC
—the Greek philosopher

Plato 429-347 BC
—the disciple of Socrates

Aristotle 384-322 BC
—Plato's disciple and Alexander the Great's tutor

Alexander the Great 356-323 BC
—conquered the world in 10 years

Key People:

The people listed in this column are the main characters, if you will, of this unit. They are listed in the Student Manual, along with a brief identifier, so that the students can familiarize themselves with these people.

4) *Read the Scripture listed in Read For Your Life*

Listed on Page 225 of the Student Manual. You might choose to have the students read the Main Story verses either corporately or privately.

The Scriptures are central to our understanding, our character, and our decisions. Therefore, we must give the greatest weight possible to them. Help your students gain this perspective as they watch you handle the Scriptures with reverence and awe.

The verses in Acts will help students gain a better understanding of a Christian view of Greek philosophy and the Greek religion.

5) *Recap (process & review) Activity*

In different parts of the room, set up stations for the Eight Intelligences Recap Activities. Then allow students to work alone or together in small groups to accomplish the following suggestions. At the start of the next class, ask for 3-4 groups of volunteers to share. <u>For homeschoolers, rather than set up all eight stations, allow the student(s) to choose which of these activities they would most enjoy, and do that.</u>

Recap Suggestions:

SPATIAL: Create a mural, choosing colors for the background which speak to you of ancient Greece or the Hellenists, then draw images or cut up magazine photos to show some aspect of what you have learned about Greece.

BODILY-KINESTHETIC: Assign one corner of a room to be Greece, one corner to be Persia, one corner to be Egypt, and one corner to be India. Move from one corner to the next, in the appropriate order, with the appropriate level of enthusiasm and speed (marching, running, dragging, etc.) to depict the attitudes of Alexander's soldiers.

INTERPERSONAL: In teams of two, role play the High Priest of Jerusalem going to Alexander the Great, after his defeat of Tyre, to request safety for Jerusalem and favor for Judaism.

MUSICAL: Play the Greek folk music from the beginning of the unit, close your eyes if that will help your concentration, and think about what you have learned so far about ancient Greece and the Hellenists. Then list the four most important facts you have learned.

LINGUISTIC: Imagine and write a short sequel to Alexander the Great's conquest, wherein he does not die until he is seventy years old.

MATH-LOGICAL: Chart the sequence of major events in ancient Greek history through the time of Alexander.

INTRAPERSONAL: Consider and discuss in a small group what it would have felt like to have all of your debts forgiven under the rule of Solon. Imagine this both from the position of one who was greatly in debt, and one who had loaned money to many people.

NATURALIST: Compare the various events of ancient Greece to weather patterns, and then share which kinds of weather compares with which events.

OR...Activity of Your Choice: What would you like to have your students do for a review activity concerning this week's introduction to Greece and the Hellenists?

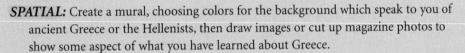

6) Opinion Column and Critical Puzzling answers on their own

Listed on Pages 225-226 of the Student Manual. Students may begin these questions after completing their Recap Activities listed above.

7) Class Discussion

Using the questions listed on Pages 225-226 of the Student Manual to get the students primed, create a discussion environment in the classroom. You may also want to draw from the open-ended questions listed below.

QUESTION

Considering the geographical location of Greece and what we learned in the last unit about the failed invasions of the Persians, why do you think the Greeks were so fiercely independent?

QUESTION

Why do you think Greece had its "Golden Age" after Xerxes' defeat?

QUESTION

Paul addresses the issue of art in Acts 17:29. What did he say about the Greek purpose in their religious art? How does that differ from a Biblical view of art?

QUESTION

Most of the seven ancient wonders of the world were "religious art" and were made either by Greeks or under the influence of the Greeks. Discuss this in light of Acts 17:29. (Consider: Did Paul try to destroy the statues? Did he walk away in disgust? What did he do? What can we learn from him?)

Phase 1

KEY PEOPLE:

Judas Maccabees
—leader of the Maccabean revolt

Antiochus Epiphanes
—Syrian ruler who stirred up the Jews

Ptolemy II
—Ordered the Hebrew scriptures translated into Greek— the Septuagint

Key People:

More of the main characters in this unit. They are listed in the Student Manual, along with a brief identifier, so that the students can familiarize themselves with these people.

— Imagine you are an Athenian. How would you describe Sparta to a foreigner?

— The statue of Zeus at Olympus was built about 430 B.C. as an object of worship. After reading Acts 17:29, imagine you were an Athenian, had seen the statue of Zeus, and were listening to Paul. How would Paul's words affect you? What response would you give?

• **Critical Puzzling:**

— Why do you think the Greek soldiers were so effective? What application of this can you make in your own life? (Ephesians 6:10-17)

— The Greek philosopher and teacher, Aristotle, was Alexander the Great's tutor, prior to Alexander's conquests. What kind of impact do you think this famous Greek thinker would have had upon this Macedonian prince?

— Paul, in Acts 17, built a bridge of communication to the Greeks, using familiar things from their culture (statues, poetry, etc.) Consider, in light of his example, what our response should be to people who are outside of the Christian worldview.

— Why do you think that four generals were needed to take over Alexander's empire, rather than just one?

— About 270 B.C., the Pharos (or Lighthouse) of Alexandria was built, and was considered to be one of the ancient wonders of the world. The Great Wall of China was finished about 220 B.C. Why do you think this wasn't selected as one of the seven ancient wonders?

— Ptolemy II had the Old Testament translated from Hebrew to Greek. Why do you think he was so interested in the holy book of the Jews? What benefit do you see that this might have had for the Jewish people?

---

8) *Choose books of interest/Internet search*

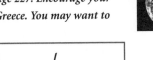

A list of possible books for further reading is listed in the Student Manual beginning on Page 227. Encourage your students to look for general information from this list and from other sources on ancient Greece. You may want to gather a selection of further resources prior to beginning Unit Seven, or you may encourage the students to be treasure hunters and find them on their own.

The Internet has a wealth of information concerning ancient Greece, though the articles available vary widely in dependability, worldview and attitude. Help your students learn to recognize the differences.

> *Remember:*
> **Beware of Arrogance, Embrace Humility!**

Phase 1

➤ *Reviewed Resources for Digging Deeper:*

Choose a few books that look interesting, or find your own.

> For the complete list of books from the Student Manual, refer to the Appendix (pg 350).

Ancient Greece:

The Greeks—Usborne Illustrated World History by Susan Peach and Anne Millard

Filled with short descriptions and great pictures, this is a wonderful, concise, fact-filled book about ancient Greece. **UE+**

Ancient Greece by Pamela Bradley

This Cambridge Junior History book is an excellent introduction to ancient Greece for pre-high school students. **UE+**

Growing Up in Ancient Greece by Chris Chelepi

Great overview! This series really helps explain many different aspects of life in ancient times. **E+**

Focus on Ancient Greeks by Anita Ganeri Published by Aladdin Books

If you can find it, this book is an excellent, multifaceted look at Greece. **E+**

Famous Men of Greece edited by Rob Shearer

An excellent, brief introduction to the important historical figures of Greece, written in biographical style. **UE+**

Golden Days of Greece by Olivia Coolidge

This is one of the best authors of short biographies that I've found. Her books are uniformly interesting and filled with the kinds of tidbits that make history memorable. **UE+**

Travelogue:

Herodotus by Henry Cary

This Greek historian was the first world traveler who kept track of the places he visited. Herodotus is one of the most important writers of antiquity, and his writings are still fascinating. **HS+**

Unit Seven: *Greece & the Hellenists* / 227

EVALUATION | **Review & Evaluation**

In this Phase of Unit Seven, your students should have had the opportunity to explore ancient Greece and the Hellenists, and their place in Scripture, through reading, listening, thinking and discussing. They will have:

1) informally discussed the Key Concepts;
2) read the article;
3) listened to the audio recording(s);
4) read the Scripture listed in Read for Your Life;
5) explored the Recap Activities;
6) completed the Opinion Column and Critical Puzzling answers on their own;
7) participated in Class Discussion;
8) chosen books of interest or searched the Internet.

You may wish to evaluate your students based on their *participation* in the **Class Discussion** and on their *participation* in the **Recap Activity**.

PHASE 2

The Exploration and Discovery Week

Learning Style Emphasis: THINKER

Students will explore topics of interest through research and reporting, learn new vocabulary, and construct a timeline relating to ancient Greece and the Hellenists and their place in Scripture.

Monday-Tuesday:
1) Choose topic and begin research

Wednesday:
2) Vocabulary Practice

Thursday:
3) Construct the Timeline.

Friday:
4) Research projects completed; share in class or hand in.

> *Teachers can choose to have students do one or two activities, rather than the entire week's schedule. Please use what works for you in your unique setting.*

---

1) Choose topic and begin research

Allow the students the freedom to choose one of the topics listed listed on Pages 231-233, or to suggest their own area which they would like to research.

Motivating Suggestions:

Especially for Non-Linguistic students, and those who are not motivated by written or oral reports, here are suggestions for alternative ways of reporting what has been researched.

Greece

1) Describe what you have learned about Greece (whether ancient or modern) as a Tour Guide. It would be helpful to include posters or photos of Greece as you tell your tour group about all the fascinating places they will visit.

2) Create a flip chart of the key Greek leaders to show their greatest strengths and/or weaknesses. Then present the information to a select group of Persian leaders who are trying to decide whether they should attack Greece for the third time.

3) Using drama, illustrate aspects of the Golden Age of Greece, showing how they influence culture and thinking today. You might use two settings—one in ancient times, one in modern times—going back and forth from one to the other to portray the continuing influence of Greece.

4) Interview a Greek slave owner to ask his opinions about the uses of slaves and their value, or worth, as people. Then interview a slave in Athens to discover his opinions about the Greek attitude towards other people groups, and about how they view slaves.

MOTIVATE

5) Create a newspaper article for everyday readers which highlights only the most intriguing, adventurous people and events of these six hundred years in Greek history.

Alexander the Great & His Empire

1) Create a salt dough map of Alexander the Great's conquests, then label the various regions, the sites of major battles, and major cities that were captured. You could include some miniature armies, horses, supply wagons, etc.

2) Paint a mural which depicts the major events of the rise of Alexander's empire, and the major events of the fall of his empire.

3) Create a multimedia presentation of the fall of Tyre, including narration from Zechariah 9:1-4, appropriate music and sound effects, pictures, maps, etc.

4) Put on a skit which shows the four generals under Alexander, the area of land they took, and the basic stance of each general toward the people of the land. (Three of the generals are easy to research—the Antigonids, the Ptolemies, and the Seleucids. If you can not find information on the fourth general—it IS difficult!—then indicate in the skit that, though there were originally four generals, one has mysteriously gone missing.)

PHASE 2

Exploration & Discovery Week

➤ *Research & Reporting*

Your mission, if you choose to accept it, is to explore one of these areas, and to discover something significant!

• **Greece:**

— In the library or on the Internet, research any information related about Greece. (Look at newspapers, magazines, books, videos, etc.) Write to the Greek Embassy to request information about the history, terrain, climate, agriculture, etc., of Greece. Give your overview from ancient Greece to the present.

— Compile a list of names, dates and accomplishments of Greece's key leaders. Include Themistocles and Xenophon, though they were studied in Persia.

— Research and report on the Golden Age of Greece. Discover the answers to these questions: Why was it considered the Golden Age? What was accomplished during this time? Who were the important and influential people? How has the Golden Age continued to influence the world?

— Research and discover the ancient Greek attitude in regards to their treatment of other people groups. What

purpose did the slaves fulfill? How did that impact the culture and lifestyle of the Greeks? Report your findings.

— Summarize the major events during this time period from approximately 800 B.C. to 200 B.C. Draw a chart to show these events, their location, dates and participants.

• **Alexander the Great & His Empire:**

— Do a research paper with diagrams showing Alexander the Great's military conquests. Discover such issues as: Where did he start? Where did he go before Persia? Where did his armies stop? What were his provisioning needs? What were the attitudes of his soldiers and his officers to him?

— Research and report on the "Rise and Fall of Alexander's Empire."

— Research Alexander's conquest of Tyre. Read Zech. 9:1-4 and explain how this prophecy from 150 years earlier was fulfilled.

---

5) Gather together a group of students who will depict the "rise and fall" through a stair-step movement. To show the "rise," have half the group begin by crouching on the floor. With one short and to-the-point sentence, each student in turn will rise slightly above the previous students as each cause is described. For the "fall," reverse the procedure by having the other half of the group standing, then each one bending their legs to shrink below the previous students as each cause is described.

Peloponnesian War

1) Two soldiers, one from Sparta, one from Athens, are to be interviewed on a late night television news show. Each has a very different point of view, and is expected to speak the party line. Be prepared for a violent confrontation.

2) Write a short story describing the imaginative results of Athens winning the Peloponnesian War.

Compare & Contrast

1) Make a chart showing the differences between Hellenists and Jews in the area of education, recreation and religion, and any other areas of difference you discover in your research.

2) Using analogies from nature, compare the treatment of the Jews under the Ptolemies to their treatment under the Seleucids (especially Antiochus Epiphanes). You may use geological, botanical, zoological, or meteorological analogies. If you can bring a physical specimen of your analogy, so much the better.

Science & Math

1) Create a flip chart for different branches of science and math which were either introduced or developed under the Greeks. Each chart should show the major personality and his discoveries or inventions.

2) Videotape an interview with a local physician concerning his/her views on the Hippocratic Oath and what it has meant to medicine. Be sure to discover his/her views on whether modern medicine is continuing to hold to the Hippocratic Oath.

3) Pythagorus was a complex and strange man. He discovered mathematical principles which are foundational to mathematics, yet he held odd philosophical ideas. Share what you discover about him as a "pro" and "con" presentation. "On the one hand…yet, on the other hand…"

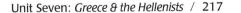
MOTIVATE

Phase 2

— After Alexander's death, his empire was divided between four generals. Research and report on what you discover about these generals. Answer such questions as: What country were the generals from? What did the Greeks think about "foreign" people? Who did the Greeks consider to be "barbarian"? Why? What opinion did the ruling generals have of foreigners in their lands? How does ethnocentrism fit this picture? Do you find evidences of racism as well?

— Research and report on the "Rise and Fall of the Ptolemies and the Seleucids."

• **Peloponnesian War:**

Find out who the Peloponnesian war involved, what issues were at stake, and the results (both short term and long term). Report your findings.

• **Compare & Contrast:**

— Research and report on the differences between the Greeks and the Jews during the Hellenistic period. (**Hint:** Find out about the forms of education, recreation, religion.)

— Research and report on the treatment of the Jews by the Ptolemies. How did the Seleucids differ? Does your research indicate any reason for this difference?

• **Science & Math:**

— Research and write about how science and mathematics were explored by the Greeks. What branches of science did the Greeks develop? What mathematical properties and concepts were discovered by the Greeks? Investigate the

scientific and mathematical discoveries of Archimedes, Euclid and Eratosthenes.

— Discover the beginnings of medical practice, including Hippocrates and the Hippocratic Oath. How has this influenced medical practice over the centuries? Report your findings.

— Research and explain who Pythagorus was, including his impact upon mathematics and music.

• **A Scriptural View:**

Read the eighth and eleventh chapter of Daniel, and then look in a Bible handbook or commentary to discover more information. How were the prophecies fulfilled? Report your findings.

• **Redemptive History:**

The hellenization of the known world had a unifying effect on the trade languages. Research and report on the effect this had upon the spread of the Gospel of Jesus Christ.

• **The Maccabean Revolt:**

— Find one of the books listed, or a book of your choice, for basic information on the Maccabean revolt. Discover the short term result of Antiochus Epiphanies' desecration of the Temple, as well as the long term result. Report your findings.

— Do a research paper on Hanukkah, its beginning, and the subsequent developments in its celebration.

A Scriptural View

1) Make a poster showing, on one half, the scriptural references to Alexander the Great and his empire, and listing, on the other half, the events which accomplish these prophetic scriptures. You might want to highlight with different colors to connect the appropriate scriptures to the appropriate events.

Redemptive History:

1) Make a map which shows the underlying languages that had Greek language superimposed upon them for trade purposes. Then, using the book of Acts and Paul's missionary journeys, discover the areas to which the Gospel was taken where Greek was the common language. This will give a visual demonstration of God's purposes in preparing much of the world for the coming of the Gospel.

2) To demonstrate the spread of the Gospel, learn a simple Christian song in several different languages—same tune, different language. Share with the class what has been learned about the spread of the Gospel to other languages and other people groups. This will show the fellowship Christians have—regardless of language and cultural differences—as we all worship the One who is worthy. The purpose of redemptive history is not to give us all the same language but to give us the same Savior!

- **Alexandria:**

  Look up and write about the people and events that contributed to Alexandria becoming a center of learning and influence.

- **Syria:**

  In the library, or on the Internet, research any information related about Syria. (Newspapers, magazines, books, videos) Give an overview from the time of the Seleucids to the present.

- **Seven Wonders:**

  Find out more about the wonders of the ancient world that were built during the Hellenistic period. How long did they last? Were they still standing in New Testament times? Were they seen by any New Testament figures?

➢ *Brain Stretchers:*

- **Compare & Contrast:**

  Compare and contrast the events in the Middle East during this time with the events in China and India.

- **Science:**

  Aristotle was not only Alexander the Great's tutor. He was one of the most influential scientists in world history. Research and report on Aristotle, his views on science, his long-lasting impact on medicine and other branches of science, and how the Scientific Revolution finally eradicated many of his theories.

- **Greek Education:**

  Plato wrote in his "Republic" about his utopian views of education. Research and report on the impact his influence had on educational practice in the Middle Ages through the *Trivium* and *Quadrivium*, and the extent of his influence on education today. Do you feel these are positive or negative foundations?

- **Western Civilization:**

  After reading about the Greek victories over the Medes and Persians, research the history of Western civilization. Make a simple chart showing the flow of Western civilization from the time of the Greeks to the present. Make another chart showing the history of the Middle East from the time of the Medes and Persians. Show the differences between the two charts, and explain what the impact of a Medo-Persian victory at Salamis would have had upon history.

- **Empires:**

  Continue your work begun in Unit Five on the universal factors contributing to the rise and fall of empires.

Create Your Own Research Topic:

_____

_____

_____

Brain Stretchers:

Brain Stretchers, listed on page 233, are intended for advanced students. Those who attempt the Brain Stretchers for their Research and Reporting can use the above list for ideas on how to report their findings.

The Maccabean Revolt:

1) Interview Judas Maccabee to discover why he thinks it is appropriate to revolt against the governmental authorities. What justification does he have for his actions?

2) Compose lyrics to a song about Hanukkah, and then perform the song. Be sure to include enough historical information in the lyrics that others can learn the most important points of this historic event and continued Jewish celebration.

Alexandria

1) Do a first person presentation as the keeper of the lighthouse at Alexandria. Explain to a group of school children on a field trip the importance of Alexandria, and who has contributed to its magnificence. You have great pride in your city's history, so make sure to share your enthusiasm and knowledge, especially any insider information about structure or function.

Syria

1) Make a timeline of Syria's history, from the Seleucids to the present. You may add pictures and illustrations to the timeline if you wish.

2) Using dance or pantomime, portray Antiochus Epiphanes and his desire to eradicate Judaism.

Seven Wonders

1) Create a chart listing each of the seven wonders: their location, when they were built, when they were destroyed (if known), what culture or person (if known) built them, and any connection to New Testament people or events.

2) Select seven different pieces of music to represent each of these wonders of the ancient world. Play the selection of music while displaying a photo or drawing of the place, then ask if any one knows what connection you saw between the music and the architectural monument. Be prepared to answer questions about each of the Seven Wonders.

2) Words To Watch—Vocabulary Practice

Listed on Page 234. You may find other words in this unit that are especially appropriate for younger children. Feel free to substitute another vocabulary list for the one provided.

Here is one idea for making vocabulary study interesting and fun: *Bring in items from nature or pictures of items which represent the meaning of the words.*

Phase 2

➢ *Words to Watch*

Remember—The easiest way to learn a subject is to master its terms:

democracy	architecture	guerrilla
sculpture	column	warfare
acropolis	capital	library
conquest	pedestal	translate
barbarian	circumference	Menorah
mathematics	geometry	colossal
spartan	buoyancy	hellenize
philosopher	fulcrum	assimilate
debate	desecrate	

3) Construct the Timeline

Read the information listed with the "Key Dates" on Page 237. Dialogue with your students about the issues involved. For ease of reference, the timeline is included in the Appendix on Page 353.

Find the dates for the key people and events listed.

SPIRITUAL

Pray for your students! At this point in history, we see a rapid development of structures which will permit the Gospel to go forth quickly to people groups whose minds and hearts have been prepared.

The literal explosion of the Gospel occurred because of the preparation of the people and the power of the Holy Spirit. Ask the Lord to help your students recognize that He is setting up circumstances in the earth today, all over the earth, for the final push of the Gospel into regions which have never known His name. Pray that their eyes will be opened, even as they read about current events, to see God's hand at work.

4) Research projects shared in class and/or turned in.

Create a safe environment for the presentations. Set ground rules prior to the presentations for all the students, so that they know each one will be honored and respected in their work by all those observing.

EVALUATION | Review & Evaluation

In this second Phase of Unit Seven, your students should have had the opportunity to explore ancient Greece and the Hellenists and their place in Scripture, through researching, thinking, and reporting. They will have:

1) done a research project;
2) learned the vocabulary;
3) constructed a Timeline;
4) created a project report on what was researched.

You may wish to evaluate your students based on their *efforts* in the **Research and Reporting** projects and their active *participation* in the **Vocabulary** and **Timeline** exercises.

Learning Style Emphasis: Sensor

Students will gain cultural understanding through sensory activities as they explore interrelated subject areas relating to ancient Greece and the Hellenists and their place in Scripture.

Monday:
1) Create a map and discuss the issues in teams.

Tuesday:
2) Examine and discuss art masterpieces & architectural structures.

Wednesday:
3) Arts in Action—Do an art project.*

Thursday:
4) Do one science project or field trip.**

Friday:
5) Listen to and discuss the music.
6) Cook the food listed in the recipe, if desired.

*Art project will need to be planned ahead of time to acquire materials.
**Field trip will require extra planning time.

> *Teachers can choose to have students do one or two activities, rather than the entire week's schedule. Please use what works for you in your unique setting.*

1) Create a map and discuss the issues in teams

The students each have an outline map on Page 239. They will be given assignments for drawing in rivers, mountains, cities, and regional boundaries, which are listed on Page 238. For details on where these things are, please consult a historical atlas, an encyclopedia, a study Bible, or any other source for geographic information. For ease of reference, the map is included in the Appendix on Page 354.

Upper elementary students might be satisfied to accomplish only this portion:
- *Physical terrain:* This part of the mapping exercise will help students locate and mark the geological dynamics of a region.

Middle school students might be satisfied to complete both the previous mapping exercise and this exercise:
- *Geo-Political:* This section of the mapping exercise will provide the students an opportunity to locate and mark the cities, nations and empires of history. It will require more digging.

High school students might be satisfied to complete both the previous mapping exercises and at least one exploration topic of this exercise:
- *Explore:* Discuss some selection from this portion of the mapping exercise in teams.

TEACHER TIP

Encourage them to think for themselves, rather than parroting back information.

QUESTION

Christian Outreach

Students may wish to locate information about Christian missions work in Greece, Macedonia, Syria, Egypt or other parts of the Hellenistic Empire. If it is possible to interview someone who has worked in that field, it will be even more helpful and insightful.

SPIRITUAL

Help your students to understand that many of the people of Greece belong to the Greek Orthodox Church, which makes it inconceivable to them that other branches of Christianity would want to evangelize their already "Christianized" nation. As one Greek Orthodox woman from Thessalonika remarked, "What do you have to tell me that the Apostle Paul did not already say to us?"

Talk with your students about the difference between an outward adherence to religious traditions (whether Greek Orthodox, Roman Catholic, or Protestant) and a vibrant, living relationship with Jesus Christ, which supersedes any particular tradition.

QUESTION

Greek Terrain

If it is possible to locate a relief map of Greece, it will help broaden their understanding of that mountainous land, and the influence of the sea.

PHASE 3

The Hands-On Week

➢ *Maps and mapping*

- **Physical Terrain:**

  — Label the mainland and islands of Greece.

  — Label the countries of Macedonia, Crete, and Rhodes.

  — Label Syria and Sicily.

  — Shade and label the Mediterranean Sea and the Aegean Sea.

  — Shade and label the Bay of Salamis.

- **Geo-Political:**

  — Label the cities of Sparta, Athens, Corinth, and Ephesus. What modern day cities are close to these ancient places?

  — Draw the boundaries of Alexander's empire. What modern day countries are located within this area?

  — Draw the boundaries of Ptolemaic Egypt (including the conquests), Syria (including the conquests), and Israel.

  — Label the cities of Alexandria, Damascus, and Jerusalem.

  — Locate and label each of the Seven Wonders of the ancient world that were either built by or influenced by the Greeks, including sites such as Mt. Olympus and Halicarnassus.

- **Explore:**

  — *Christian Outreach:* What is the status of evangelical outreach to Greece and the former Hellenistic Empire today? What opportunities and what difficulties face those who share the Gospel from an evangelical perspective in these nations?

  — *Greek Terrain:* How would the geographic location of Greece, the terrain, the climate, and the Mediterranean Sea, have affected the Greek culture and God's purpose for it?

  — *Palestinian Terrain:* How would the terrain and climate of Israel have affected God's purposes as seen in the Maccabean revolt?

> *Consider:*
>
> What was the type of warfare used by the Jews in the revolt, and how were such small numbers able to succeed over the larger Syrian army?)

When we consider God's purposes in a particular nation, we will obviously never be able to plumb the depths of His understanding, but if we will take into account the various geographical elements and the history, we might discover insights into His amazing ways. Remember, it is not enough to know about, or even to appreciate, an historic time. In order to truly understand a culture, we must search to understand God's heart for those people. Pray for modern Greece: for the leaders, the people, the missionaries, the Church.

2) *Examine and discuss art masterpieces & architectural structures*

Locate either a copy or an Internet site of this painting listed on Page 240. Allow the students time to observe the painting without any conversation, and then, when they are ready, engage them in some or all of the following questions:

Philosophy *(popularly known as* The School of Athens*) by Raphael*

Dr. Francis Schaeffer described this painting as a depiction of the two competing philosophies of man: Plato, with his upraised finger, begins with great universal truths to understand the individual particulars; whereas Aristotle, with his hand toward the ground, starts with the individual particular bits of knowledge and from them discovers universal truths.

Consider:

Raphael (1483-1520 A.D.) was one of the giants of the High Renaissance period. Leonardo da Vinci and Michelangelo were his principal teachers when he moved to Florence as a twenty-one year old—quite an amazing pair of teachers! Pope Julius II requested Raphael to come to Rome in 1508 in order to paint frescoes in his Papal apartment. In this setting, Raphael, the "prince of painters," created two of the masterpieces of Renaissance art and philosophy—the "Disputa" and the "School of Athens."

➤ *Art Appreciation*

• Philosophy **(popularly known as The School of Athens)** *by Raphael*

— At the center of this painting, two figures are shown walking together. They are Plato, who points heavenward, and Aristotle who gestures towards the earth. Other philosophers are seen in this painting as well, including Euclid and Heraclitus. Why do you think he focused on Plato and Aristotle?

— How would you describe this painting?

— Notice the use of perspective. Have you seen other paintings in this study that convey the same sense of perspective?

➤ *Architecture*

The Parthenon in Athens, Greece was constructed after the destruction of the city by Xerxes in 480 B.C. It is one of the most famous buildings in history, built between 447 and 432 B.C. The architects, Kallicarates and Iktinos, used meticulous measurements to create the appearance of exact alignment. All the horizontal lines are actually raised slightly in the middle in order to correct for the "sag" we would normally see in a long horizontal structure. They also made the columns bulge slightly outward one-third of the way up from the base. This was an amazing achievement for both the architects and the craftsmen, and it gave the Parthenon that particular sense of elasticity and life. Built entirely of marble, this Doric temple was dedicated to the goddess Athena. Her statue was sculpted in gold and ivory by Pheidias, the same sculptor who created the statue of Zeus at Olympia (one of the seven wonders of the ancient world).

— Look for a photo of the Parthenon in Athens. What still remains in this ruin? How would you describe this building?

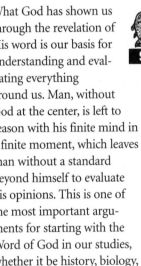

What God has shown us through the revelation of His word is our basis for understanding and evaluating everything around us. Man, without God at the center, is left to reason with his finite mind in a finite moment, which leaves man without a standard beyond himself to evaluate his opinions. This is one of the most important arguments for starting with the Word of God in our studies, whether it be history, biology, or geometry.

Ask your students what they think is the difference between the philosophy of "reason," as promoted by the Greeks and the theology of "revelation," which is the biblical perspective. What observations do they have about what Raphael was trying to communicate in his painting?

The Parthenon

QUESTION

Several descriptions of the Parthenon use the terms "living" and "elastic" because of the careful way the architects made mathematical adjustments to correct the visual perception of the long lines and columns. Later temples, by comparison, are described as "cold" and "lifeless." Have your students look at photos of the Parthenon and of other comparative temples to see if they agree with these descriptive terms.

INTRO · PG 23

3) Arts in Action

Listed on Page 241.

TEACHER TIP

Imitation

Have the students look again at Raphael's painting. Then, with art supplies of colored pencils, pastels, or paint, try to recreate what is seen, or create a piece in the style of Raphael's *School of Athens*.

Greek Vase Art

As it is more difficult to create a picture on a rounded vase or bowl than on paper, encourage your students to chose a very simple design. They might want to first sketch their design on paper and then carefully transfer the design to the vase or bowl.

Greek Columns

There were two main architectural styles for buildings in ancient Greece, the Doric Order (with an undecorated column top) and the Ionic Order (with two swirls on the column top). Less common in ancient Greece, but more popular in Roman times, was the use of the Corinthian column, which had a very ornate top.

Soft Stone Sculpting

This is a very satisfying sculpting material, if the students do not attempt sculpture that is too elaborate. They may want to create an abstract design, if they experience difficulties in making their first sculpture work!

Phase 3

➢ Arts in Action

Select one, and let your artistic juices flow!

• **Imitation:**

Try creating a vignette in the style of Raphael's *School of Athens*

• **Greek Vase Art:**

Buy a cheap white vase or try making a papier maché bowl. Paint a solid color, then when it is dry, paint your family on the vase. The only portraits done by Greeks were on vases!

• **Greek Columns:**

Draw or construct examples of the different Greek columns: Ionic, Dorian and Corinthian.

• **Soft Stone Sculpting:**

"Chisel" a sculpture made of soft stone: 3 scoops vermiculite, 2 scoops plaster of Paris, 2 scoops water. Stir in bucket until it is very thick. Pour into small carton to harden for 30 minutes. Peel off carton and "chisel" with a plastic spoon or knife. How is this different from the casting process?

• **Candle Making:**

The Festival of Hanukkah is also known as the Festival of Lights. To illustrate this, try making your own candles. Since melted wax can be dangerous (it is VERY hot!), adult supervision is required. Consult your library or local expert for more info. After they are made, light one candle in a dark room. Then read John 8:12 out loud.

• **Make a Lighthouse:**

Make a model of the Pharos Lighthouse of Alexandria. Legos would be a great building material, or papier maché, or modeling clay. Try setting up the Pharos on a harbor of blue construction paper, showing that the lighthouse was on an island and that Alexandria was on the mainland.

• **The Great Wall of China:**

If you have a young friend or sibling with a sandbox, conquer it for an afternoon. Then build a Great Wall to keep out the barbarians. Use a map of the Great Wall to get some of the contours.

Candle Making

TEACHER TIP

- Again, candle making can be VERY dangerous. It requires adult supervision. Having said this, you can use many different types of molds for candles, from purchased reusable metal molds to small waxed cardboard containers (like milk cartons). Another suggestion would be to make dipped taper candles by tying candle wicking to a pencil, then dipping the other end into melted candle wax. When it hardens, dip again. Continue this process until the candle is the thickness you prefer.
- If you prefer to not melt wax, you could investigate using beeswax sheets which can be rolled around a wick, creating a long-burning candle.

Make a Lighthouse

Some students may want to create an elaborate lighthouse, including a small light at the top. The more interest they have in creating an authentic Pharos, the greater the learning opportunity—so let them go for it!

The Great Wall of China

The Great Wall is the longest wall in the world, with the main section extending over 2,000 miles! Any student wishing to create the Great Wall should discover some of its peculiarities, such as the fact that it does not run continuously.

Phase 3

≫ *Science*

Aristotle is considered the Father of the Scientific Method. He emphasized:
- *the importance of making one's own discoveries*
- *collecting information*
- *analyzing the information*
- *classifying the information*

Consider:

Thales (thay-leez) was another Greek scientist and philosopher. He figured out how to measure the height of the Great Pyramid of Cheops, based on an observation. He knew his own height, and could measure the height of his shadow. He could also measure the height of the pyramid's shadow. With these three numbers known, it was possible to calculate the fourth unknown number (the height of the pyramid.)

- **Scientific Method:**

  — Find a definition of the current Scientific Method. Choose an animal or plant that you can find nearby. Observe your subject. Weigh it, measure it, poke it (if possible), smell it, test it every way you can think of. Write down everything you observe. Did you discover anything you didn't already know? What new ways could you classify the subject?

- **Measure:**

  — Try measuring a tall tree like this: On a sunny day, make a stake three and a half feet tall. Drive it into the ground so that it is three feet tall. Label this measurement "A." Now measure the length of the stake's shadow. Label this measurement "B." Measure the length of the tree's shadow. Label this measurement "C." You can now figure the height of the tree, which we will label "X". (A/B = X/C) Just solve for x.

- **Buoyancy:**

  — Experiment with the principle of buoyancy. You could try Archimedes' experiment by getting into the bath tub and seeing how high the water rises. Or, try dropping various materials of different weights into a jar of water. Record the different levels the water rises to. Do large items displace more water than smaller items? Do heavy items displace more water than larger items?

INTRO - PG 24

4) Do a science project

Listed on Page 242. Feel free to choose one of these projects. If students love science, they might want to consider doing all of them!

242 / Unit Seven: *Greece & the Hellenists*

TEACHER TIP

Scientific Method

One of the most impressive stories of observation I learned in university had to do with Professor Agassiz, a teacher who brought a fish into class one day and asked his students to observe the fish, noting their observations. After a short time, the students finished their cursory observation and wrote a few sentences. Professor Agassiz asked them to continue their observation for the rest of the class period, and they somewhat unwillingly complied. The next day the professor brought the same fish in, and asked that they would observe and record their observations again. This went on for an entire week. Just about the time that the students grew utterly sick of that fish, and certain there was nothing left to observe, they would suddenly notice something new. By the end of the week, the students had learned valuable lessons about the nature of observation and the patience required to plumb the depths of what is being observed.

That story was told to us as we began to use an inductive Bible study method, to teach us not to be satisfied with a cursory, superficial look at God's Word. Perhaps your students can discover the same valuable lesson as they conduct their observations.

Measure

Thales of Miletus calculated the height of the Egyptian pyramids by measuring their shadows, just as your students are using a tree's shadow to measure the height of the tree. Amazing!

Buoyancy

The story of Archimedes' discovery—when his king asked him to determine whether the gold smith who made the king's crown had actually cheated him by substituting a base metal—shows that it is the volume of an object that displaces the same volume of water. The end of the story? The goldsmith was caught red-handed.

≫ *Music*

Pythagorus, a Greek mathematician, was walking down the street one day when he heard the sound of four hammers beating on metal. Realizing that the sounds were pleasing to the ear, he recognized the golden opportunity to determine what made them so. The littlest hammer rang out with a higher sound than the others, while the biggest hammer produced the lowest sound. Pythagorus was hearing the "pitch" of the hammers.

Pitch is the musical term used to describe the highness or lowness of sound. It is one of the five elements of music. Sing the words, "Twinkle, twinkle, little star." Which word do you say when you are singing the highest sound? Which word do you say when you are singing the lowest sound? The highest sound is the highest pitch, and the lowest sound is the lowest pitch.

• **Try this:**

— Using a keyboard or other instrument, have someone play two different notes. With your eyes closed, tell whether the second note is higher or lower than the first. (Thumbs up if the second note is higher, thumbs down if it is lower.) Have each member of the class or the family try this experiment.

  - *Variation: Play three notes in one direction. Determine if the pitches are ascending or descending. How did you do? This is an excellent starting place for learning to distinguish pitch, and for developing a "musical ear."*

  *When we combine different pitches, the sound can be pleasing (**consonance**) or harsh sounding (**dissonance**). What Pythagorus heard was a pleasing sound (consonance) and he determined to research why these particular hammers sounded good together. What he found was that the hammer with the highest pitch was exactly one-half the size of the hammer with the lowest pitch. The other two hammers also*

---

5) Listen to and discuss the music

Listed on Pages 243-244.

Try This

If staying on pitch during the singing of the round is a problem, try strumming a guitar on one chord for the entire song. It will keep everyone in the same key!

Phase 3

had precise mathematical ratios with the lowest. Pythagorus came up with an explanation of which combinations of notes are consonant and which combinations are dissonant. But the amazing thing about Pythagorus was that he figured it out using mathematical ratios!

- **Try this:**

  — Sing together "Row, Row, Row Your Boat." Now, try singing it as a round with each new part entering when the previous part starts the phrase: "…gently down the stream." Listen to the sound. Can you hear the different pitches that are being sung at the same time? Is it pleasing, or harsh?

  — Play around with notes on the piano. Can you find pleasing consonant sounds and harsh dissonant sounds? Don't be discouraged if you can't. It takes practice!

➢ Cooking

Greek foods are one of my absolute favorites! There are so many recipes to choose from, but this one is one of the best.

- **Baklava** *Serves 8*

10 sheets filo pastry (freezer section)	1/2 cup honey
1/2 cup melted butter	1/2 tsp. ground cloves
1 1/4 cup finely chopped walnuts	1/2 tsp. grated orange peel
1/4 cup honey	1 tsp. lemon juice
1/2 tsp. cinnamon	

Cut pastry sheets in half (20 12x8 inch sheets). Brush 7 sheets of filo with butter and layer them into a buttered 12x8 metal baking pan. Combine walnuts, 1/4 cup honey, and cinnamon. Spread 1/4 of the mixture over filo in pan. Cover with 2 more sheets of buttered filo, then add another 1/4 of the mixture. Repeat until you have used a total of 13 sheets of filo and all of

244 / Unit Seven: *Greece & the Hellenists*

Try This

If a student has difficulty determining which is the higher note of two pitches, try using a series of three ascending or descending pitches to help them determine which direction the pitches are moving. This is an easier place to start, and is a good way to help students grow in their discernment of pitch.

6) Cook the food

Listed on Page 244 - 245.

Baklava is one of those pastries that you have to taste to believe. It is sweet, crunchy, nutty, and buttery all in one tiny bite. Though it may seem like a lot of work, the end justifies the means!

the mixture. Brush remaining 7 sheets of filo with butter, and place on top of sheets in the pan. With a sharp knife, cut pastry to form 16 diamond-shaped pieces. Top with remaining butter and bake in 350 oven for about 50 minutes, until top is crisp. While baking, combine remaining ingredients in a small pan. Bring to a boil, then lower heat and simmer for 8 to 10 minutes. Remove baklava from oven. Top immediately with hot syrup. Cool.

• **Potato Latkes**

4 large potatoes (peeled, grated)   2 Tbsp. flour
1 small onion (grated)   salt & pepper
3 eggs (beaten)

Drop by large spoonfuls into a hot, oiled fry pan. Cook until brown on both sides. Serve warm and topped with sour cream, applesauce or yogurt.

> Celebrate the miracle of Hanukkah with lots of oil! It is traditional to eat both potato cakes and fried doughnuts. (Thankfully, this feasting is not for every day!)

EVALUATION Review & Evaluation

In this third Phase of Unit Seven, your students should have had the opportunity to explore ancient Greece and the Hellenists and their place in Scripture, through various hands-on and creative sessions. They will have:

1) completed a Mapping section;
2) observed and discussed Art & Architecture;
3) worked on an art project;
4) experimented with a Science Project or taken a field trip;
5) listened to music;
6) tasted a food related to this unit.

You may wish to evaluate your students based on their *class participation* in these **Hands-on** activities.

PHASE 4

The Expression Week

Learning Style Emphasis: *Intuitor*

Students, through creative self-expression, using one or more creative activities, will present some aspect of what they have learned in the past three weeks relating to ancient Greece and the Hellenists and their place in Scripture. Areas of expression include linguistics, art, music, drama, movement and conceptual design.

Monday - Thursday

1) Choose area of expression and begin work either individually or in teams.

Friday

2) Share creative expressions in class.

> *Teachers can choose to have students do one or two activities, rather than the entire week's schedule. Please use what works for you in your unique setting.*

---

1) Choose area of expression and begin work either individually or in teams

INTRO-PG 25

Linguistics:

Located on page 246-147.

Journalism

If possible, have students find some journalistic writing which describes military bases, military training, and military preparedness. This will give them a model as they write about Sparta or about the Maccabean Revolt.

Prose

- The students may have noticed the use of alliteration in the "Annals of Aristotle's Assistant." They might enjoy writing this prose using alliteration simply for the start of each paragraph or of each chapter of a children's book, or they could use alliteration as frequently as possible throughout.
- There have been many people in history who have translated the Scriptures, including modern day workers, such as those with Wycliffe Bible

Translators. Encourage students to read a few descriptions of the challenges and difficulties of translating before they tackle this assignment.

- Many descriptive stories have been written by sailors, including *Two Years Before the Mast* by Richard Henry Dana, Jr. Have students examine some of these descriptive writings as they prepare to write their own story.
- Humor is a very effective writing tool, but it is not as easily done as one might think! One suggestion of a humorous series for students to study would be *Hank the Cowdog* by John R. Erickson.

TEACHER TIP

Playing with Words

The suggestions given for rhyming words might indicate a limerick to the student, or, all three sets of rhymes might be used in a poem about Greece.

Poetry

- If a student chooses to write a poem, "To the Unknown God," they might use a yearning voice of one Greek child who wonders if there is a God beyond the petty gods of their religion.

- The Festival of Lights is a joyful holiday in Jewish history and culture. Students would benefit greatly by reading poems of national or cultural celebrations, such as *Paul Revere's Ride* by Henry Wadsworth Longfellow.

Art:

Located on page 247.

Painting/Drawing

The Athenian citizens, since they were not allowed to conduct business or do manual labor, might have spent time reclining and eating as they pondered the deep Greek philosophies of life. If the student can capture the indolence and luxury of the time, and, if they choose, contrast it with the difficult labor of the slaves around them, it will communicate an important aspect of this culture.

Sculpting

If a student wishes to sculpt in modeling clay, have them look for helpful instructions in working with clay, so that, if they are not experienced, they will not become totally frustrated.

Cartooning

The Golden Age lasted a mere fifty years, yet it is often regarded as a foundational and influential time for all of Western Civilization. Encourage the students to show both the accomplishments (which were amazing) and the brevity of the period.

PHASE 4

The Expression Week

➤ *In Your Own Way...*

We have seen the Golden Age of Greece and its influence on the world, Alexander the Great's empire and it's hellenization of the known world, and the scientific and mathematical achievements of the Greeks. We have contrasted ancient Greek thinking with Biblical truths, discovered God's great deliverance of his people from the Seleucid army and learned about the origin of Hanukkah. Now, choose a selection of these activities, or create your own, which will best express what you have learned from this unit.

Linguistics:

- **Journalism:**

  — Be a reporter for the magazine, "The Modern Military." Your assignment is to visit Sparta before the outbreak of the Peloponnesian wars. Describe the training and tenacity of the Spartan army.

  — Be a war correspondent for the "Voice of the Maccabeans" and write the behind-the-scenes story of Judas Maccabees and his guerrilla army.

- **Prose:**

  — Write the annals of Aristotle's assistant, assigned to acquire all the animals for Aristotle's assessment.

  — Write a first person account about translating the Old Testament into Greek. Describe some of your Jewish translation buddies in Alexandria.

  — Imagine you are a sailor and describe the Pharos of Alexandria to folks at home who have never seen it.

  — Pretend you are a novelist in Ephesus, dealing with writer's block. Then Paul comes, as described in Acts 19, and inspires you to write the best-selling novelette, "A Funny Thing Happened on the Way to the Temple."

- **Playing with Words:**

  Discover the connection these words have to the unit, and then write a rhyming poem (or poems) using them: *culture, sculpture, picture; Pericles, Themistocles, Hippocrates; Parthenon, Marathon, Xenophon.*

Graphic Design

This poster was suggested by the Uncle Sam recruiting posters in the United States. Have students look at some of these posters, and then craft a somewhat similar poster using the weaponry and military outfits of the Greeks at the time of Xenophon.

Illustration

Hanukkah has both historical significance and contemporary traditions of celebration. Encourage students to investigate both aspects of Hanukkah as they seek to illustrate a picture book for children. Will they set the historical Hanukkah at the beginning of the book and current celebrations afterwards? Or, perhaps they might enjoy setting the historic events alongside the contemporary traditions.

Phase 4

- **Poetry:**

  — Compose a poem entitled, "To the Unknown God." (Reference Acts 17.)

  — Write a poem about the Festival of Lights (Hanukkah).

Art:

- **Painting/Drawing:**

  Paint or draw someone lounging in Greek fashion on a Greek couch, wearing Greek clothes and eating Greek grapes.

- **Sculpting:**

  Using modeling clay, try sculpting a bust in the Greek style.

- **Cartooning:**

  Draw a cartoon of the shortness & wonder of the Golden Age of Greece.

- **Graphic Design:**

  Create a poster recruiting Greek mercenaries to fight with Xenophon. "Uncle Xeonphon wants YOU!"

- **Illustration:**

  Create a picture book showing the history of Hanukkah, and how it is celebrated today.

Music:

- **Compose:**

  Write a song using the Dorian mode. (Dorian mode is found by playing a scale on the piano, beginning at "D," and using only white keys.) This is a Greek mode, but may not be the same today as it was to ancient Greek musicians. These modes are known as the "Church Modes" and they use Greek names, but we have no way of knowing what the Greek mode called "Dorian" actually sounded like. Dorian has a wonderful, haunting sound, however, that will be evocative of Greek music and culture.

- **Performance Practice:**

  With your teacher's help, select an appropriate piece of music which expresses some element from this unit. If possible, find a piece written for Hanukkah. Prepare and perform the piece for an audience. Communicate with your audience the reason for your selection either in the program notes or in a short speech.

Music:

Located on page 247.

Compose

Even a very simple melody composed in the Dorian mode will evoke a unique and haunting sound, so encourage students that they need not feel pressured to write an entire symphony! At the same time, for students who love to compose, give them the freedom to write as complex a piece of music as their heart desires. Even if it is not finished at the end of the week, have them share the completed section. Eventually it might become one of the great masterpieces of the world!

Performance Practice

For musical students, this selection may be a wonderful opportunity to express what they have learned. Make sure they have selected a piece that they have adequate time to prepare.

Drama:

Located on page 248.

Comedy

- If a student chooses to emcee the banquet for Greek superstars, they may wish to do a one-man show where they describe those who have been awarded honors. Or, they might

---

Phase 4

Drama:

- **Comedy:**

  — Aristotle, Pericles, Pythagorus, Thales, Themistocles, and Alexander are all going to receive an award at a Greek banquet. You are the emcee for the banquet. Introduce at length each of these famous Greeks to explain why they merit this award.

  — Do a humorous skit about Archimedes' discovery of buoyancy.

- **Tragedy:**

  The Greeks were the ones who drama-tized tragedy, using all male casts and masks. Create a tragedy, on the model of the Greek tragedies. If you have any females in the cast, dress them as boys who dress as girls!

- **Reality:**

  Perform the scene from Josephus about Alexander the Great coming to Jerusalem. Use your imagination for costumes, props, horses (!), etc.

- **Puppetry:**

  Using puppets, act out the scene in the Temple when the Menorah was kept miraculously lit. Use your imagination to create props, sets and costumes. Be sure to include realistic rejoicing!

---

prefer to join with several other students and have both the comments by the emcee as well as the acceptance speech by the honored Greek.

- If it is possible to obtain a children's wading pool for Archimede's sudden revelation, the skit would come alive! (A bathing suit, though required in the skit, is not historically accurate.)

Tragedy

If a team of students wishes to enact a tragedy along Greek lines, it would be helpful to inform the audience either before or after (or in program notes) of the specific features of Greek tragedy.

Reality

One gets the sense from Josephus' description of Alexander the Great coming to Jerusalem that it was a powerful and supernatural moment. The people with Alexander fully expected him to harm the Jews, and instead he honored them. Encourage the students who choose this reality skit to work to cre-ate a sense of holy awe.

Puppetry

Puppets can provide a vibrancy in drama through the use of unusual puppets (design, material, color), through the use of unusual sounds (recorded or live), and through interaction with the audi-ence. Encourage the students who are truly interested in puppetry to learn about puppet making, set design, sound effects, voices, etc.

Movement:

Located on page 249.

Pantomime

The story of Alexander riding Bucephalus is one of careful observation on the part of Alex, total surprise on the part of the audience, and complete pride on the part of Alex's father. Encourage students who choose to pantomime this scene to recreate these actions and reactions.

Dance

Eratosthenes, in 290 B.C., plotted the circumference of the earth to be 24,856 miles—he only missed it by 42 miles!

Miniature Action

No one had captured Tyre before Alexander the Great, and it was conquered at an astonishing cost in time, money and lives. Students who choose to build the city of Tyre, and to demonstrate Alexander's military plan for capturing it, should research the various strategic points of attack.

Phase 4

Movement:

- **Pantomime:**

  Create a pantomime showing little Alex begging his father, King Philip, to let him ride that big black horse (Bucephalus.) Be sure to include the look of surprise on everyone's face while he is riding!

- **Dance:**

  Choreograph a dance of Eratosthenes figuring out how to measure the world.

- **Miniature Action:**

  Using Legos, papier maché, clay or other medium, build a miniature version of Tyre. Demonstrate Alexander's successful techniques for capturing this heretofore unconquered city.

Conceptual Design:

- **Game of Conquest:**

  Create a game which will show the extent and the speed of Alexander the Great's conquests. This may be a board game, an action game, or a computer game.

Create Your Own Expression:

_____

_____

Conceptual Design:

Located on page 249.

Game of Conquest

There are some military strategy games that students could look through to make their own game, such as *Axis and Allies*, *Risk*, and *Stratego*.

INTRO·PG 26

2) Share creative expressions in class

The same rules apply as suggested in the reporting section of Phase Two.

EVALUATION | **Review & Evaluation**

In this final Phase of Unit Seven, your students should have had the opportunity to express what they have learned about ancient Greece and the Hellenists and their place in Scripture, through one or more various creative selections of their own choosing. These include:

1) Linguistics;
2) Art;
3) Music;
4) Drama;
5) Movement;
6) Conceptual Design.

You may wish to evaluate your students based on their *effort* in the **Creative Expressions**, either as individuals or in teams.

Teacher's Guide
THE RISE OF ROME

Statue of Caesar

Pray with the students

at the beginning of each unit.

Enthusiasm and delight

are the best way to capture a student's

interest and jump-start motivation, so:

1) ***For the Auditory Students:*** Consider playing music by the Italian composer Respighi, such as **Pines of The Appian Way**, to capture their attention at the very beginning of class;

2) ***For the Kinesthetic Students:*** Have the students warm up, as class begins, by doing some active movement that is fun (such as, marching like Roman soldiers—through the class, out the door, outside?)

3) ***For the Visual Students:*** Bring a visual object to stimulate their interest in the new unit, like a drawing, or three-dimensional representation, of the aqueduct at Nimes or of the Colosseum;

4) ***For the hearts of all:*** Pray with them at the beginning of the unit, that God would help them discover what He has for each one to learn in that unit.

PHASE 1

The Introduction Week

Learning Style Emphasis: *Feeler*

Students will be introduced to the Roman Republic and Empire, along with the appropriate Scriptures from Daniel and Luke. You may follow this suggested schedule or adapt it to meet your students' needs:

Monday:
1) Informally discuss the Key Concepts

Tuesday:
2) Read the article
3) Listen to the audio recording(s)
4) Read the Scripture listed in Read For Your Life (could be done on their own)

Wednesday:
5) Recap Activity
6) Opinion Column and Critical Puzzling answers on their own

Thursday:
7) Class Discussion

Friday:
8) Choose books of interest/Internet search

> *Teachers can choose to have students do one or two activities, rather than the entire week's schedule. Please use what works for you in your unique setting.*

INTRO · PG 18

1) Informally Discuss the Key Concepts

Listed in the Student Manual. on page 251.

KEY CONCEPTS BACKGROUND INFORMATION

These are the main objectives of the unit. As you proceed through the four weeks, your students will be given various ways of understanding each of these objectives.

The rise of Rome—EXPLANATION

TEACHER TIP

> To get an informal discussion started on this key concept, ask a simple, leading question, such as, *"What have you heard about ancient Rome?"*

It is important to recognize the characteristics of the Roman Republic and how it led to the Roman Empire. The Republic began in 510 B.C. when the Romans expelled their last king and constructed a governmental system called a Senate. The Senate provided for rule by many leaders rather than just one king. In the early days of the Republic, this fledgling country had to fight for its life against all of the neighboring kingdoms who disliked upstart republics. Eventually, through many hard lessons, Rome became the most powerful city-state in Italy. During these developmental years, much thought was given to honor and virtue, which came to be very highly esteemed.

The Punic Wars against Carthage (200's - 100's B.C.) provided Rome with the opportunity and necessity of building a navy. After emerging victorious in the Punic Wars—largely due to their navy—Rome rose to the height of military prowess in the Mediterranean. Despite the victories over enemies abroad, at home there was an ongoing struggle between the rich and poor, between the patricians and plebians, resulting eventually in a single leader receiving too much power, rather than sharing power among a number of leaders. This focus of power led to an increasing thirst for wholesale murder of perceived enemies. From Maurius and Sulla, to Pompey and Julius Caesar, the traditional Senatorial rules of the Republic began to shift to a tyrannical dictatorship. Julius Caesar, perhaps the best of the dictators, was on his way to creating a more workable system of government when the senators, fearful of his becoming king, assassinated him.

From that point, the struggle for supreme power in Rome—in the midst of chaos, war, mob-rule, and treachery—devolved into a struggle between two men—Octavius and Mark Antony. Octavius, rightful heir of Caesar and dutiful son of Rome, was set against Mark Antony—illegally married to Cleopatra, and totally given to ruling the world with her by his side. In the final battle, the Battle of Actium, Antony and Cleopatra fled the scene leaving the day to Octavius and his troops. He emerges in history in 30 B.C. as the First Citizen of the most powerful, largest empire in world history. He took the name of Caesar, since it was rightfully his through Caesar's will, and the Senate voted him the name "Augustus." Caesar Augustus, first Emperor of the new Roman Empire, was the world leader who would demand that people across his empire return to their ancestral homes in order to be taxed…including the people of Palestine.

The leaders of Rome—EXPLANATION

To get an informal discussion started on this key concept, ask a simple, leading question, such as, *"Do you know anything about rulers in Rome, such as Julius Caesar?"*

TEACHER TIP

Two stories highlight the differences in Rome's leaders. In the first, we learn of Romulus and Remus, raised by a she-wolf, trying to decide which would have the honor of building a city and naming it after himself. The argument grew so heated that Romulus killed his brother and named his city Rome. If the beginning of a nation contains within it the seeds of its destiny, its DNA if you will, then Rome's beginning was founded on betrayal and bloodshed. Many of the later leaders (such as Maurius and Sulla) showed a profound link back to this first story, vengefully killing all of those who opposed them, even all those who might ever have proven a threat!

In the second story we learn of Cornelia's jewels. Cornelia was a patrician woman of a powerful Roman family. When a guest in her home noticed her lack of finery, she asked in amazement, "Cornelia, where are your jewels?" Her eyes brimming with tears, Cornelia called her two boys to her side and proclaimed, "These are my jewels." These two boys, the jewels of Cornelia, were the grandsons of Scipio, the Roman general who had defeated Hannibal's troops in the Second Punic War. When the boys, Tiberius Gracchus and Gaius Gracchus, grew to manhood, they went into politics, trying to right the wrongs of the system. Tiberius, a tribune in 133 B.C., proposed that the wealthy return their unlawfully gained land in order to distribute it to the poor. This led to a patrician-incited riot in which Tiberius was killed. His brother, Gaius, also a tribune, initiated more land reform in 123 B.C., and was killed for his stand for justice, as well.

Thus we see that Rome had different types of leaders: those who sought to serve the people of the Republic with just and moral laws, and others who sought to serve themselves, willing to murder anyone who got in their way.

The engineering feats of Rome—EXPLANATION

TEACHER TIP

To get an informal discussion started on this key concept, ask a simple, leading question, such as, *"Has anyone seen photos of Roman arched bridges in Europe or of the aqueducts they built to bring water down from the hills to the cities? Can you describe what they looked like?"*

Though previous empires had constructed highways, such as the Royal Road of Persia, Rome's accomplishments in this regard were far greater than all who had come before. In fact, beyond the quality and durability of Roman roads was the immense quantity of them: by 300 A.D., they had over 53,000 miles of major paved highways. When you add to that the smaller roads branching out from the main roads, the mileage total was in the hundreds of thousands!

Along with roads, the Romans built aqueducts to bring clean water from the high hills down to the cities. With the ease of access to clean water for thousands of people, coupled with the ease of transporting trade goods (especially food) on the Roman roads, cities supplied by these aqueducts and roads began to grow extensively in many places of the Empire.

It is astonishing to consider that the Roman roads and bridges were so carefully constructed that many are still in use today—2,000 years later! Truly, the artistry of Rome was evidenced in the practical, durable, efficient construction of roads, aqueducts and bridges.

This article can be found in its entirety in the Appendix (see pg 355).

THE RISE OF ROME

UNIT

8

Statue of Caesar

KEY CONCEPTS:

• The rise of Rome

• The leaders of Rome

• The engineering feats of Rome

• God's plan for Rome

The largest empire begins...

"After this I saw in the night visions, and behold, a fourth beast, dreadful and terrible, exceedingly strong. It had huge iron teeth; it was devouring, breaking in pieces, and trampling the residue with its feet. It was different from all the beasts that were before it..."
Daniel 7:7

Unit Eight: *The Rise of Rome* / 251

God's plan for Rome—EXPLANATION

> To get an informal discussion started on this key concept, ask a simple, leading question, such as, *"Rome is the fourth empire which Daniel saw in his vision. Do you have any ideas on why God might want to use this empire as part of His plan?"*

TEACHER TIP

In the book of Daniel, God gave Daniel vision and understanding of four empires which would arise, beginning with Babylon. Each of these empires had a part to play in God's unfolding plan of redemption, though they were not Hebrew kingdoms and did not offer the God of the Universe worship due Him. Though we can not fully comprehend God's ways in HisStory, we can be assured that Rome rose to prominence, even outliving Hannibal's menacing invasion, because God purposed to use it.

Rome, at the time of Caesar Augustus, was the largest empire to have yet existed on the face of the earth. Caesar placed upon his empire the Pax Romana, or Roman peace, which brought about a safety and security for travelers, and a quietness within the far reaches of empire. This quietness did not last long, and the people chafing under the yoke of Rome's might began struggling to throw it off, but for a short time, much of the world was under the rule of one man—one man who wanted it peaceful, orderly, lawful and quiet in his realm.

Not only would Jesus be born during this Pax Romana, but the Gospel would spread to many nations in Europe, Asia and Africa by the speed and security of Roman roads. In His amazing wisdom and goodness, He used even the imperfect governments of sinful men to accomplish the best:

> *"As for God, His way is perfect; the word of the Lord is proven;*
> *He is a shield to all who trust in Him." Psalm 18:30*

2) Read the article

Begins on Page 251 of Student Manual

> The article for Unit Eight is designed to help students think about the rise of Rome and its implication for people today. The materials covered in the audio recordings offer another look at this time period, covering slightly different information. In the article and recordings, along with introducing the basic understanding of history, we are also bringing in the biblical worldview.

SPIRITUAL

> You may choose to have your students read the article first and then listen to the audio recordings, or vice versa.

TEACHER TIP

3) Listen to the audio recording(s)

Listed on Page 262 of the Student Manual.

• The main concepts and chronological flow are contained in **What in the World's Going On Here?**

INTRO - PG 18

4) Read the Scripture listed in Read For Your Life

Listed on Page 262 of the Student Manual. You might choose to have the students read the Main Story verses either corporately or privately.

The Scriptures are central to our understanding, our character, and our decisions. Therefore, we must give the greatest weight possible to them. Help your students gain this perspective as they watch you handle the Scriptures with reverence and awe.

5) Recap (process & review) Activity

In different parts of the room, set up stations for the Eight Intelligences Recap Activities. Then allow students to work alone or together in small groups to accomplish the following suggestions. At the start of the next class, ask for 3-4 groups of volunteers to share. <u>For homeschoolers, rather than set up all eight stations, allow the student(s) to choose which of these activities they would most enjoy, and do that.</u>

INTRO-PG 19

Recap Suggestions:

SPATIAL: Create a series of three simple pictures to help you remember the three Punic Wars. (For example: boat, elephant, salt.)

BODILY-KINESTHETIC: In groups of three, choose one to be Rome, one to be Carthage and one to be Greece. The object of this process and review is to conduct an historical wrestling match. Rome will eventually be the winner, but it is hotly contested at times. (You might set some appropriate ground rules for the contestants!)

INTERPERSONAL: In groups of two, consider the ugly situation between Maurius and Sulla. Each one take a turn describing what steps a mediator would have attempted to try to bring peace between these two leaders.

MUSICAL: In groups of two or more, choose one to be the musical conductor, with everyone else choosing at least one appropriate sound for building and/or using a Roman road. Have the conductor start everyone together, and then conduct the sounds of a noisy Roman road. (Suggested sounds: digging, scraping, pouring gravel, pounding rock, clip-clop of mules' feet, people walking, soldiers marching, etc.)

LINGUISTIC: Write a three minute speech for Mark Antony in which he defends himself from the accusation that he has lost his Roman mind and gone crazy over that Cleopatra hussy. Make it good, since the Senate will judge afterwards whether he should live or die.

MATH-LOGICAL: Analyze the differences between the Roman Republic and Roman Empire. Make a simple chart to show the information.

INTRAPERSONAL: Imagine you are Scipio. Your good friend from the Senate wishes to debrief you after your victory over Hannibal. Either in a small group or on paper, share your thoughts about defeating Rome's greatest enemy, and about the way it has affected you.

NATURALIST: Go outside with a group of family or friends and designate a small creek or other natural boundary to be the Rubicon River. Each of you take turns as Julius Caesar. Will you try to convince your followers to cross the Rubicon with you? Or will you lay down your weapons, considering the ramifications of this fateful step? Share with each other what it was like to have to take a physical step which would result in a complete break with your government.

OR…Activity of Your Choice: What would you like to have your students do for a review activity concerning this week's introduction to the rise of Rome?

6) *Opinion Column and Critical Puzzling answers on their own*

Listed on Pages 262-263 of the Student Manual. Students may begin these questions after completing their Recap Activities listed above.

7) *Class Discussion*

Using the questions listed on Pages 262-263 of the Student Manual to get the students primed, create a discussion environment in the classroom. You may also want to draw from the open-ended questions listed below.

PHASE 1

KEY PEOPLE:

Romulus & Remus
— Legendary founders of Rome

218-146BC

Hannibal
— Carthaginian general in Punic Wars

Scipio
— Roman general who defeated Hannibal

100-44BC

Julius Caesar
— Greatest of all the Caesars

Mark Antony
— Julius Caesar's greatest general

Octavius
— Julius Caesar's heir

69-30 BC

Cleopatra
— Last reigning Ptolemy

➤ Listen to this!

• What in the World's Going on Here? Volume One

— The Rise of Rome

➤ Read For Your Life

• The Holy Bible

— The Main Story: Daniel 2:33-35,40-45; Luke 2:1-3

➤ Talk Together

• Opinion Column:

— What did you find to be the most interesting aspect, or the most fascinating person, you encountered in your introduction to the rise of Rome?

— Imagine you were with Hannibal as he crossed the Alps with his army and elephants. What would the trip through the mountains have been like? What would be your anticipation for the effectiveness of the elephants against the Romans?

— If you were a Roman soldier traveling to Gaul with Julius Caesar, what are some terms you could use to describe life in the army?

Can you see any Greek influence in the Roman civilization? (Consider: Look at their religion.) Why do you think the Romans were impressed with Greek culture? What was the impact of this Greco-Roman culture on the Jews in Palestine?

Cleopatra had an important role in this time period. Some biographers describe her as a shrewd political leader trying to hold onto her power in a tumultuous time, doing only what was necessary to save her throne. Others describe her as a bewitching woman with almost magical powers over men. Read Proverbs 14:12. How does this proverb help you interpret the life and death of Cleopatra?

Key People:

The people listed in this column are the main characters, if you will, of this unit. They are listed in the Student Manual, along with a brief identifier, so that the students can familiarize themselves with these people.

QUESTION

If you were a citizen of Rome living during the Empire, how would you describe the changes that have occurred since the end of the Republic?

Phase 1

• **Critical Puzzling:**

— What importance do you think the Punic Wars had in the history of Rome?

— Julius Caesar was assassinated on the Ides of March. How do you think history might have been different if this event had not occurred?

— The Romans created amazing bridges, aqueducts and roads which still exist in many places. Why do you suppose they put so much effort into building them?

— Jesus came and began His Church during the Roman Empire, and the Bible describes His advent in the world as being "in the fulness of time." What do you think the Roman Empire brought to the world that may have enhanced the spread of Christianity?

Remember:

Beware of Arrogance, Embrace Humility!

INTRO - PG 20

8) Choose books of interest/Internet search

A list of possible books for further reading is listed in the Student Manual beginning on Pages 264-267 Encourage your students to look for general information from this list and from other sources on ancient Rome. You may want to gather a selection of further resources prior to beginning Unit Eight, or you may encourage the students to be treasure hunters and find them on their own.

The Internet has a wealth of information concerning the rise of Rome, though the articles available vary widely in dependability, worldview and attitude. Help your students learn to recognize the differences.

EVALUATION **Review & Evaluation**

In this Phase of Unit Eight, your students should have had the opportunity to explore the rise of ancient Rome and its place in Scripture, through reading, listening, thinking and discussing. They will have:

1) informally discussed the Key Concepts;
2) read the article;
3) listened to the audio recording(s);
4) read the Scripture listed in Read for Your Life;
5) explored the Recap Activities;
6) completed the Opinion Column and Critical Puzzling answers on their own;
7) participated in Class Discussion;
8) chosen books of interest or searched the Internet.

You may wish to evaluate your students based on their *participation* in the **Class Discussion** and on their *participation* in the **Recap Activity**.

Phase 1

➢ *Reviewed Resources for Digging Deeper:*

Choose a few books that look interesting, or find your own.

Biographies:

Plutarch—Lives of Noble Romans
edited by Fuller

Plutarch was one of the earliest biographers in history! All the plays William Shakespeare wrote about the Romans were derived from Plutarch's biographies. Difficult reading, but some might enjoy it. Plutarch compared Roman leaders with Greek leaders. **HS+**

Famous Men of Rome
edited by Rob Shearer

A much gentler version of the following book, it gives a good introduction to the most important men of this empire. **E+**

Lives of Famous Romans
by Olivia Coolidge

Any set of biographies on the Romans is bound to be distasteful to some extent, since so many of the ruling Romans (especially of the Empire) were given over to utter immorality. My suggestion is to read these biographies in light of Daniel 2, and the perspective given in the gospels and Acts. **HS+**

World Leaders Past and Present: Cleopatra by Hoobler and Hoobler

This book takes a sympathetic look at the last reigning Ptolemy in Egypt. Cleopatra was revered by the Egyptians, loved by Caesar and Antony, and hated by the Romans. Learn why in this intriguing book. **MS+**

Cleopatra by Robert Green

This is a good, short biography of the last reigning Ptolemy, the woman who conquered both Julius Caesar and Mark Antony. **UE+**

Hannibal by Robert Green

Another short biography, this is an excellent introduction to Carthage's greatest general and Rome's greatest fear. **UE+**

Architecture:

City by David Macauley

Mr. Macauley helps us to see the incredible cultural dynamic of architecture. Learn how a Roman city was designed and built, in this fascinating book. **UE+**

PHASE 2

The Exploration and Discovery Week

Learning Style Emphasis: THINKER

Students will explore topics of interest through research and reporting, learn new vocabulary, and construct a timeline relating to the rise of Rome and its place in Scripture.

Monday-Tuesday:

1) Choose topic and begin research

Wednesday:

2) Vocabulary Practice

Thursday:

3) Construct the Timeline.

Friday:

4) Research projects completed; share in class or hand in.

Teachers can choose to have students do one or two activities, rather than the entire week's schedule. Please use what works for you in your unique setting.

INTRO-PG 21

1) Choose topic and begin research

Allow the students the freedom to choose one of the topics listed listed on Pages 268-269, or to suggest their own area which they would like to research.

Motivating Suggestions:

Especially for Non-Linguistic students, and those who are not motivated by written or oral reports, here are suggestions for alternative ways of reporting what has been researched.

MOTIVATE

Punic Wars

1) Paint or draw a scene from Hannibal's journey across the Alps which depicts some aspect of what you've learned from your research.

2) Create a chart or a series of three charts (one for each of the Punic Wars) which shows the major events of the Punic Wars, and the short term and long term results of these wars.

Roman Republic and Empire

1) Interview two senators - one from the Roman Republic and one from the Roman Empire. Through your questioning (which can be live, videotaped, or written), clarify the major differences between the Republic and the Empire. At the end, poll your audience to see which governmental structure they would prefer to live under.

---

2) Create an advertisement for real estate in Rome at the beginning of the Republic. Be sure to include the major selling features that might induce a family to locate in this new nation. Then, create another advertisement for a relocation company, in business at the close of the Republic. List the major reasons people are giving for moving away from Rome.

3) Do a first person presentation of life as a slave in Rome. Include such areas of interest as where you originally come from, how you were captured, your job description, work conditions, and your overall attitude towards slavery.

Calendar

1) Create a yearlong calendar based on the system used prior to Caesar's reformation of the calendar. If you would like, create a second calendar which uses Caesar's plan. See if others can find the differences between the two.

2) Write a song entitled, "Does Anybody Really Know What Day It Is?" which highlights the pre-Caesar need for a new calendar.

Julius Caesar

1) Some people saw Caesar as a hero, while others saw him as a villain. Analyze your research and decide what your personal perspective is concerning Caesar. Write a defense of your position with examples from his life, Scriptures, etc.

Compare and Contrast:

1) Make a flip-chart showing the major people and events of the first triumvirate (one person per chart), and the second triumvirate (one person per chart). Conclude your presentation with an overall look at the effect of these two political partnerships.

2) Create a series of analogies of Rome to Assyria, Rome to Babylon, Rome to Persia, and Rome to Greece. It might begin like this: Rome is to Assyria as a lava flow is to a flash flood.

PHASE 2

Exploration & Discovery Week

➢ *Research & Reporting*

Your mission, if you choose to accept it, is to explore one of these areas, and to discover something significant!

• **Punic Wars:**

— Research and write a detailed description of Hannibal's surprise route from Carthage to Rome.

— Discover and report on the Punic Wars, including such questions as: What was the short term result of the Punic Wars? What was the long term result for Carthage? Rome?

• **Roman Republic and Empire:**

— Find one of the books listed, or a book of your choice, for basic information on Rome—first, the Republic and then, the Empire. Report your findings.

— Research and report on the "Rise and Fall of the Roman Republic."

— Who were the slaves in Rome? How did the Romans acquire their slaves? What work did the slaves do? Share your findings.

• **Calendar:**

Discover and report on the changes made in the calendar by Julius Caesar.

• **Julius Caesar:**

Look up Julius Caesar in your history resources. How significant was this leader in Roman history? What is the significance of the Rubicon River in his life? How was the Republic affected by his death?

• **Compare and Contrast:**

— Towards the end of the Roman Republic there was the first triumvirate, or council of three men, who led Rome. Who were the three leaders and what was the result of that triumvirate? After Julius Caesar's death there was another triumvirate. Who were the three leaders, and what resulted from their union? Compare and contrast the first Triumvirate with the second Triumvirate.

— What can you discover about this culture in regard to their treatment of other peoples? Were they similar to the Assyrians, Babylonians, Persians or Greeks? In what ways? How were they different?

MOTIVATE

Then to Now

1) Make a collage showing elements of Italy's history from the Republic to the present. You might want to use magazines, photos, drawings, pictures from the Internet, etc. Since there are many pictures you will want to include, use a poster board for mounting the collage. (Labeling some of the pictures will be helpful for those who view your work.)

2) As a small group, decide what is the single most important fact of each epoch in Italy's history, and then as a group determine how best to teach others these facts in chronological order.

Builders

1) Using materials found outdoors, create the beginning of a Roman road. If you have the opportunity to create a permanent display of a completed section of Roman road outdoors, by all means do so. If that is not feasible, create a miniature display which demonstrates the methods used by the Romans.

Provisioning

1) Set up a Roman grocery store, with samples of all the items available for sale in Rome. Then, as the genial shopkeeper, sell your wares to your audience, telling them where the various items come from, why they are superior, and how you get your prices so low.

2) Make a list of all the types of supplies needed by the Roman soldiers, noting how they might be obtained in three separate locations—the city of Rome, the Italian countryside, and Palestine.

- **Then to Now:**

  In the library, or on the Internet, investigate the history of Rome (Italy) from the time of the Republic to the present. Report your findings.

- **Builders:**

  Discover the methods used by the Romans to build roads. Draw a diagram showing the different steps involved. Arches had been used in architectural design for centuries, but the Romans found a better design and use for the arch. Discover what made the Roman arched bridges and aqueducts so strong that many remain even two thousand years later.

- **Provisioning:**

  Discover and describe the climate and terrain of Rome. What kind of crops were grown? What kind of animals were raised? How were the large cities (like Rome) supplied with food, clothing and other goods? What impact did the conquests have on the people back in Rome?

➢ *Brain Stretchers*

- **A Scriptural View:**

  The Romans had been described in the book of Daniel hundreds of years before they emerged as world leaders. Using a study Bible, Bible handbook, Bible dictionary, commentary, etc., research the possible reasons God intended Jesus to come during this empire. What set this empire apart from earlier ones?

- **Naval Battles:**

  Find out about the use of navies in warfare during this time period. Research and report on the Battle of Actium, and why it is still studied by military strategists.

Create Your Own Research Topic:

_____

_____

_____

Brain Stretchers:

Brain Stretchers, listed on page 269, are intended for advanced students. Those who attempt the Brain Stretchers for their Research and Reporting can use the above list for ideas on how to report their findings.

2) *Words To Watch - Vocabulary Practice*

Listed on Page 270. You may find other words in this unit that are especially appropriate for younger children. Feel free to substitute another vocabulary list for the one provided.

Here is one idea for making vocabulary study interesting and fun: *Have the students choose appropriate background music for studying vocabulary lists.*

TEACHER TIP

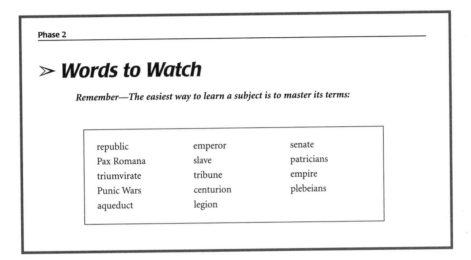

Phase 2

≫ *Words to Watch*

Remember—The easiest way to learn a subject is to master its terms:

republic	emperor	senate
Pax Romana	slave	patricians
triumvirate	tribune	empire
Punic Wars	centurion	plebeians
aqueduct	legion	

3) *Construct the Timeline*

Read the information listed with the "Key Dates" on Pages 272-273. Dialogue with your students about the issues involved. For ease of reference, the timeline is included in the Appendix on Page 363.

Find the dates for the key people and events listed.

At times of war and tremendous uncertainty we can lose sight of God's continuing presence with us, that He is, even at the darkest moments, working His purposes into the fabric of human history. Pray for your students that they will not be gripped with fear in periods of national and international turmoil, but rather that they will know it is right and appropriate to trust in His goodness and faithfulness, and that they would earnestly seek the Lord for what He would have them do at that moment of time.

SPIRITUAL

4) *Research projects shared in class and/or turned in.*

Create a safe environment for the presentations. Set ground rules prior to the presentations for all the students, so that they know each one will be honored and respected in their work by all those observing.

EVALUATION | Review & Evaluation

In this second Phase of Unit Eight, your students should have had the opportunity to explore the rise of Rome and its place in Scripture through researching, thinking, and reporting. They will have:

1) done a research project;
2) learned the vocabulary;
3) constructed a Timeline;
4) created a project report on what was researched.

You may wish to evaluate your students based on their *efforts* in the **Research and Reporting** projects and their active *participation* in the **Vocabulary** and **Timeline** exercises.

Learning Style Emphasis: Sensor

Students will gain cultural understanding through sensory activities as they explore interrelated subject areas relating to the rise of Rome and its place in Scripture.

Monday:

1) Create a map and discuss the issues in teams.

Tuesday:

2) Examine and discuss art masterpieces & architectural structures.

Wednesday:

3) Arts in Action—Do an art project.*

Thursday:

4) Do one science project or field trip.**

Friday:

5) Listen to and discuss the music.

6) Cook the food listed in the recipe, if desired.

*Art project will need to be planned ahead of time to acquire materials.
**Field trip will require extra planning time.

Teachers can choose to have students do one or two activities, rather than the entire week's schedule. Please use what works for you in your unique setting.

1) Create a map and discuss the issues in teams

INTRO · PG 23

The students each have an outline map on Page 275. They will be given assignments for drawing in rivers, mountains, cities, and regional boundaries, which are listed on Page 274. For details on where these things are, please consult a historical atlas, an encyclopedia, a study Bible, or any other source for geographic information. For ease of reference, the map is included in the Appendix on Page 364.

Upper elementary students might be satisfied to accomplish only this portion:

• *Physical terrain:* This part of the mapping exercise will help students locate and mark the geological dynamics of a region.

Middle school students might be satisfied to complete both the previous mapping exercise and this exercise:

• *Geo-Political:* This section of the mapping exercise will provide the students an opportunity to locate and mark the cities, nations and empires of history. It will require more digging.

High school students might be satisfied to complete both the previous mapping exercises and at least one exploration topic of this exercise:

• *Explore:* Discuss some selection from this portion of the mapping exercise in teams.

Encourage them to think for themselves, rather than parroting back information.

QUESTION

Christian Outreach

Students may wish to locate information about Christian missions work in Italy or other areas of the former Roman Empire. If it is possible to interview someone who has worked in that field, it will be even more helpful and insightful.

SPIRITUAL

The same perspective could be in effect here as was discussed in the last unit: many people in Italy are Roman Catholic. They have a difficult time reconciling to the idea of missionaries coming to share the Gospel with them in their "Christianized" nation. Discuss with your students the need to walk in humility and wisdom before others, not arrogantly as ones who have

---

PHASE 3

The Hands-On Week

➢ *Maps and mapping*

• **Physical Terrain:**

— Label and color the "boot" of Italy, which was the center of the Roman Republic and Empire.

— Label and color the island of Britain, which Julius Caesar attempted to conquer.

— Draw the Tiber river.

— Mark and color the Alps mountain range and the Alpennines mountain range.

— Color the Mediterranean Sea.

• **Geo-Political:**

— Draw the boundaries of the Roman Republic.

— Now, using a different color marker, draw the boundaries of the Roman Empire under Emperor Hadrian.

— Label and color the countries of France and Spain, which Julius Caesar conquered.

— Label the location of Carthage and Rome. Locate the sites where Roman governors commanded. What modern day cities are close to these ancient cities?

• **Explore:**

— *Christian Outreach:* What is the status of evangelical outreach today to Italy and the lands of the former Roman Empire? What opportunities and what difficulties face those who share the Gospel in these nations?

— *The Growth of an Empire:* After looking at a map of the Roman Empire, consider its natural boundaries and how they were enlarged significantly by conquering other lands. What words would you use to describe this empire?

---

come to teach the superiority of their own ways. Remember, it's not about outward traditions, its about a vibrant, living relationship with Jesus Christ.

As an American, I welcome missionaries of the Gospel of Jesus Christ who have come from other nations to evangelize in my nation. I recognize that they bring a much-needed word and that it may open more doors to the people of my country when it comes with a foreign accent from a non-American. (That was my experience in Belgium on a short-term missions trip—people couldn't believe Christianity was so important to me that I would come all the way to their nation to share the good news. It made an impact.)

"And a servant of the Lord must not quarrel but be gentle to all, able to teach, patient, in humility correcting those who are in opposition…" 2 Timothy 2:24-25

The Growth of an Empire

Daniel accurately described this devouring empire. It devoured more territory than any nation before it. When students actually examine the size of the Roman Empire in comparison to previous empires, they will begin to grasp the magnitude of this fourth empire in Daniel's vision. It also helps us to better understand why the Jews longed so desperately for a Messiah to overthrow the Romans—it was obvious to them that getting rid of such a powerful overlord would take a supernatural act of God!

2) Examine and discuss art masterpieces & architectural structures

Locate either a copy of these art forms, or Internet sites for each of the items listed on Page 276. Allow the students time to observe the art without any conversation, and then, when they are ready, engage them in some or all of the questions listed in the Student Manual or below.

Roman Portrait Heads

It is interesting to consider that, although the Romans imitated the Greeks in many areas, they chose to represent individual heads in an honest fashion, rather than granting each head a classic beauty. At least in the early stages of Rome, individuality was honored more than beauty.

• Ask your students what they think might have been some results of this honoring of individuality in Rome.

Consider:

From early in the Republic, the Romans showed great devotion to the concept of the family. This helps to explain their development of the individualized portrait bust. The Romans had a tradition of creating a wax, terra-cotta, or marble portrait head of the father in the family. Interestingly enough, these busts include the unique aspects of the particular person, such as wrinkles, large ears, etc., which shows an unusual respect for the individuality of the man represented.

➤ Art Appreciation

• **Look for examples of Roman portrait heads.**

— How would you describe these faces?

— Do they seem realistic to you?

➤ Architecture

One of the achievements of Rome was providing clean drinking water for the inhabitants of its cities. Aqueducts (from the latin aqua for water, and ductus for channel) were constructed to carry water from the springs in the high hills down to the towns and cities. One of the most famous of the Roman aqueducts is the one in Nimes, France. It was constructed of huge stone blocks, weighing as much as six tons! This aqueduct is one hundred sixty feet tall, and consists of three tiers of arches with the top tier containing the channel for the water. Enough water traveled through this aqueduct to provide for 50,000 people. The Romans were such good engineers that this structure was able to endure high winds and flash floods. It has stood for two thousand years.

— Find a photograph of the aqueduct at Nimes. It is one of the most popular scenic attractions in France, with more than two million visitors per year. What words would you use to describe this structure?

The Aqueduct at Nimes

Talk with your students about the effect of having clean water. Many parts of the world today have no source for clean water, and the results are disastrous. One reason that the cities of the Roman Empire could grow as large as they did was because they made provision for clean water—at great expense, using tremendous feats of engineering. Isn't it amazing that such a graceful architectural art form as the Aqueduct at Nimes could also be such an important, practical means of provisioning.

Ask the students, "What are some other artistic architectural structures that function as a help to humanity?"

INTRO - PG 23

3) Arts in Action

Listed on Page 277.

TEACHER TIP

Imitation

Have the students look again at the Roman portrait heads. Then, with art supplies of colored pencils, pastels, or paint, try to recreate on paper what is seen. Or, for students wishing to try sculpting in the Roman style, you will find helpful suggestions under "sculpting" in Phase Four of this unit in the Teacher's Guide.

Costuming

The toga is one of the most recognized styles of ancient Rome. Sheets and braided cords will transform students into Romans with very little expense. Depending on the ages of the students, they might want to go into greater detail for a truly historic creation.

Mosaic

Mosaics can range from actual tile pieces on wood to construction paper on poster board. Encourage the students to make outlines of the patterns they wish to create in mosaic, to decide on the color scheme,

and then to fill in the pattern with whatever mosaic material they have chosen to use. The first picture in Unit Nine (Page 285) is an early Christian mosaic which may give students some ideas about possible subject matter.

War Elephants

War elephants were well trained, well cared for, and well outfitted. Just as the knights of the Middle Ages had ornate decorations for their horses, so the war elephants were given elaborate and ornate decorations. Encourage students to find some descriptions or illustrations. Perhaps some of these outfits could be imitated using fabric.

Diorama

Dioramas can provide a vivid depiction of an historic event. Encourage your students to create as much three-dimensional reality as possible with their choices of features and pieces in this cardboard box.

➢ Arts in Action

Select one, and let your artistic juices flow!

- **Imitation:**

  Try creating or drawing a portrait bust in the style of the Romans

- **Costuming**

  Fashion historic Roman costumes with sheets or fabric. There are many books in the library which will give you ideas and suggestions.

- **Mosaic**

  Try making an artistic mosaic. There are many ways to do this, from very simple to very complicated. One wonderful idea is to create a papier maché bowl, paint it a base color, then create a pattern inside the bowl with colored bits of paper. Complete your masterpiece by giving a coat of varnish, inside and out.

- **War Elephants:**

  Trace a picture of a war elephant. Glue on beads, rice or glitter to show their armor. They were considered to be a vital part of the military maneuvers of that time period. If available in your area, you should ride an elephant. It is a moving experience.

- **Diorama**

  Get a big cardboard box. Paint the Swiss Alps on the inside back and sides. Using miniature figures, create a diorama of Hannibal crossing the Alps with his army, horses and elephants.

➢ Science

- **Roman Arched Bridge**

  — Make an arched bridge. We found books in the library (listed at the beginning of the unit) which gave detailed descriptions of how to do this. Be sure and learn what a keystone is, how it functions and why it is important.

- **Aqueduct**

  — Make an aqueduct. An incredible "build-it-together" example is found in **Make it Work! Buildings**.

---

4) Do a science project

Listed on Page 277. Feel free to choose one of these projects. If students love science, they might want to consider doing all of them!

Roman Arched Bridge

There are several books in the library which suggest ways of creating a Roman arched bridge out of readily available (and lightweight) materials. This would be a great team project! Depending on the number of students available, you might suggest that different teams build Roman arched bridges out of different materials so they can compare the results.

Aqueduct

Aqueducts had to support tremendous amounts of flowing water. If your students can build a channel and support it from below, they will have a great start on understanding how the Romans created these massive structures. Again, there are books in the library which will suggest materials and ideas to accomplish this. You might consider canvassing the students to see if, by looking at photos of Roman aqueducts, they can recreate on a small scale what they have seen.

➤ Music

The Romans developed many brass instruments used in military music. For example, the Roman straight trumpet (they called it a tuba) was like the herald trumpet used today at horse races. Another was the buccina, which had a wooden crossbar to allow soldiers to carry it on the march. These instruments were very simple in structure and so they had very limited range of pitches. Their purpose was not to entertain people, but for signaling. They could call the soldiers to assemble, or they could signal the soldiers to move.

It wasn't until centuries later that further developments allowed these instruments to have more melodic ability, thereby allowing them to come inside! Now, of course, it is very common to see trumpets and tubas, etc., in orchestras and bands. But there is still a certain thrill in hearing them played outdoors at concerts and celebrations.

• **Listen:**

— Play some of John Philip Sousa's march music, such as *Stars and Stripes Forever* or the *Washington Post March*.

• **Try this:**

— Cut the bottoms off plastic pop (soda) bottles. A 2-liter bottle gives a lower sound, while a 16 oz. bottle gives a higher sound. Now, play it like a trumpet: tighten your lips, center the mouth of the bottle over both lips, blow air through a small opening between your lips very fast—fast enough so your lips will buzz. This buzzing will make sound come out of the bottle. If you tighten your lips more and blow faster air, the pitch will go up. If you loosen your lips and blow slower, the pitch will go down. Try placing your fist in the bottom of the "tuba"—it will give a nice variation. Your pop bottle "tuba" will sound somewhat like those early instruments in that they weren't very pretty either!

5) Listen to and discuss the music

Listed on Page 278.

The music of John Philip Sousa is rousing and rhythmical. Even if you listen to only a short selection, it will convey to the students the sense of march music.

Try This

Prepare for this assignment by collecting plastic soda bottles of various sizes. Some students may have difficulty getting their "trumpet" to make a sound, especially if their lips react to the vibration! That's ok. Give everyone a chance to try, and through the hilarity, some of the previously unsuccessful students may be encouraged to try it again.

TEACHER TIP

INTRO · PG 24

6) Cook the food

Listed on Page 279.

TEACHER TIP

Even if students don't appreciate the taste of licorice, they will have an unforgettable experience embedded in their memory about the odd tastes of Roman emperors!

➤ Cooking

The Romans were extremely fond of an herb we usually use in licorice—anise. It was considered to be so delightful that kings perfumed their linen with it. (Imagine sleeping on a pillow that smelled like licorice!) This recipe is not from Roman times, but it is a delicious way to sample this favored herb.

• Anise Cookies

4 eggs	2 tbsp anise seed
1 cup sugar	3 cups flour
1 tsp vanilla	4 tsp baking powder
1/3 cup milk	1 cup butter, softened

Preheat oven to 375 degrees. Beat eggs well in large bowl. Add sugar, vanilla, milk, and anise. Stir well. In another bowl, mix flour and baking powder. Cut in butter. Combine 2 mixtures. Roll dough out onto floured board. Cut into shapes.

Bake on greased baking sheet 12 minutes, or until lightly browned.

Makes about 4 dozen.

EVALUATION ## Review & Evaluation

In this third Phase of Unit Eight, your students should have had the opportunity to explore the rise of Rome and its place in Scripture through various hands-on and creative sessions. They will have:

1) completed a Mapping section;
2) observed and discussed Art & Architecture;
3) worked on an art project;
4) experimented with a Science Project or taken a field trip;
5) listened to music;
6) tasted a food related to this unit.

You may wish to evaluate your students based on their *class participation* in these **Hands-on** activities.

Learning Style Emphasis: *Intuitor*

Students, through creative self-expression, using one or more creative activities, will present some aspect of what they have learned in the past three weeks relating to the rise of Rome and its place in Scripture. Areas of expression include linguistics, art, music, drama, movement and conceptual design.

Monday - Thursday

1) Choose area of expression and begin work either individually or in teams.

Friday

2) Share creative expressions in class.

> *Teachers can choose to have students do one or two activities, rather than the entire week's schedule. Please use what works for you in your unique setting.*

1) Choose area of expression and begin work either individually or in teams

INTRO·PG 25

Linguistics:

Located on page 280.

Journalism

- For students interested in writing a journalistic piece about Octavius' triumphal homecoming, to get a flavor of the way victory has been portrayed in newspapers and magazines, have them read some of the articles written after V-E day at the end of WW II.
- Sensationalism in journalism sells magazines and papers, though it is not a good source of truth! Students wishing to write a sensationalist piece about Romulus and Remus can either stretch the legendary truth of these two brothers or make up tabloid-style headlines. (Example: "Female charged with supplying wild drink to abandoned boys.")

Prose

- Rhodus, the Roman road builder, might lament his life—which would require one style of prose—or he might delight to do his duty, for which one would use an entirely different emphasis. Encourage the student interested in this suggestion to consider both angles to see which would be more interesting to write.
- Many children's books have been written from the perspective of an animal, such as *Bambi*. Have students look through several of these books to gain a more thorough grounding in this style of writing, then extend that style to an alpine elephant.

TEACHER TIP

Playing with Words

TEACHER TIP

Encourage students to examine the way crossword puzzles are formed before attempting this project. Perhaps a good preparation for creating the crossword would be to write out each word in block letters, trying various horizontal and vertical presentations. This will allow them to move the words around until the crossword looks good. Another suggestion: build the puzzle on a Scrabble board.

Timetable

Have students look at a copy of Simon and Schuster's *Timetables of History* to better understand the assignment. Students strong in math/logical intelligence will enjoy this one, as it allows them to thoroughly categorize and organize all of the material in a sequential manner.

PHASE 4

The Expression Week

➤ *In Your Own Way...*

We have seen the rise of Rome through the Punic Wars and onto center stage as a vast empire. In the midst of this final empire Daniel saw in the vision, Jesus, the Redeemer promised in Genesis 3, was born.

Now, choose a selection of these activities, or create your own, which will best express what you have learned from this unit.

Linguistics:

• Journalism:

— Be the newspaper reporter assigned to cover Octavius' triumphal entry into Rome after defeating Mark Antony and Cleopatra. Be sure to include the background information about Julius Caesar's will which promoted Octavius to power.

— You are the on-the-spot reporter for the news rag, "It's What's Happening!" Your current assignment is to discover whether the two brothers, Romulus and Remus, are newsworthy. If so, write a piece on how they're contributing to what's happening.

• Prose

— Write a fictional account of Rhodus, the Roman road builder. Of the 53,000 miles of road built by Rome, Rhodus has been told to build from Rome to Rhegium.

— Write a short story about a reluctant elephant on the march with Hannibal. Call it "The Bashful Behemoth."

• Playing with Words

Create a crossword puzzle. Choose words from this unit for the horizontal and vertical answers. Next, supply the clues which will enable your family to solve the puzzle.

• Timetable

Create your own version of Timetables of History showing what is taking place in the arts, in science, in math, in family life, and in government during the rise of Rome.

Art:

Located on page 281.

TEACHER TIP

Illustration

Encourage students to examine children's books, such as *Bambi*, to discover what options exist for illustrating this type of literature. They may enjoy working in watercolor, colored pencil, or pastels; realistic perspective, abstract, or stickman style; with lots of background detail or very simple; use a very developed or a quite unfinished appearance. Lots of possibilities!

Graphic Design

If students can think of a catchy slogan for the T-shirt, the design will probably be easier to create. It might be a one-sided T-shirt design, or a student could put the first part of the slogan on the front and the second part on the back. (Such as: "One if by land, two if by sea…" "Yep, Mark & Cleo, two by sea flee!")

Sculpting

If a student chooses to try sculpting a head, encourage observing a sculptor or reading descriptions of larger-scale sculpting. One suggestion that may make things easier is to create a form using wire mesh, in the approximate size desired, on which to form the clay head, and then mount the wire mesh on a stand.

Phase 4

Art:

- **Illustration:**

  Create illustrations that could be used in the short story, "The Bashful Behemoth" listed above.

- **Graphic Design:**

  Design a T-shirt for Octavius' troops after the Battle of Actium. Remember, they so intimidated Cleopatra, she fled from the battle!

- **Sculpting:**

  Sculpt a head of clay, in the Roman style.

- **Cartooning:**

  As a political cartoonist, show the attitude of the Roman women toward Cleopatra.

Music:

- **Compose:**

  Write a marching song for Caesar's troops, entitled "We're Seeing the World One Step at a Time." Use a military-style, marching rhythm, and words which would inspire soldiers to march for hundreds of miles.

- **Performance Practice:**

  With your teacher's help, select an appropriate piece of music which expresses some element from the Roman Empire, such as a military march. Prepare and perform the piece for an audience. Communicate with your audience the reason for your selection either in the program notes or in a short speech.

Cartooning

Cleopatra, who had lived for a time in Rome with Julius Caesar, was utterly despised by the Roman women. Caricature might be an appropriate form of political cartoon for this exercise. If students choose caricature, have them study several examples to learn the basis of this art form.

Music:

Located on page 281.

Compose

Marching songs are usually written in 2/4 time, which means each measure has two pulses. This creates a simple rhythmic beat for two feet (per person) to march to. Students might want to listen to some of the common marching chants to get the idea of the pulse, such as, "Left, left, left-right, left"; "I don't know but I been told, Streets of heav'n are paved with gold."

Performance Practice

For musical students, this selection may be a wonderful opportunity to express what they have learned. Make sure they have selected a piece that they have adequate time to prepare.

Drama:

Located on page 282.

Comedy

A familiar theme in fiction and film is that of a child suddenly being in charge. Encourage your students to think about as many ramifications of this change of status as possible, and then to incorporate the best ones into the comedy. For instance, a child in charge of the world might not ever have to make his bed again!

Tragedy

Julius Caesar fought his attackers with his stylus (a pen for writing) until he saw Brutus, his trusted friend. At that point, he put his cloak over his head, so that no one would see his face as he died, and gave up his struggle. Set the tragedy with a narration or explanation describing that the Senate felt the Republic was threatened by this would-be king.

Puppetry

Two very different stories are possible within this context: the struggle to survive across the Alps, and the continued successes gained by Hannibal's army over a period of years.

Phase 4

Drama:

- **Comedy:**

  Create a skit of Octavius, a schoolboy, receiving the news that he's now in charge of the entire Roman world!

- **Tragedy:**

  Produce the assassination of Julius Caesar on the Ides of March. Include Brutus, his close friend, whose participation in the assassination caused Caesar to give up his struggle against his attackers.

- **Puppetry:**

  Put on a puppet show of Hannibal's march across the Alps into Rome. You may choose to focus on the actual crossing, or, instead, on the triumphal march across Italy.

Movement:

Located on page 283.

Pantomime

In order to pantomime Caesar, a student needs to gain an understanding of his pride in his accomplishments, his plans to right the wrongs in Rome and the Republic, and his supreme confidence that he is the man for the job.

Dance

Horses and elephants have entirely different levels of grace and movement. Horses are agile, beauty in motion, and fleet of foot. Elephants are unbelievably strong and stable, and seemingly tireless. Encourage dance students to study video footage of both horses and elephants in motion.

Action

There are several stages involved in building a Roman road: digging the trenches, laying the foundations, cutting the stone, setting the stone in place. Encourage "Action" students to thoroughly consider and rehearse the various repetitive motions, so that the audience will be able to "see" the road constructed.

Phase 4

Movement:

• Pantomime:

Pantomime Julius Caesar crossing the Rubicon River in an arrogant manner. He does not lay down his arms, he does not dismiss his armies, and he does not enter Rome as a humble citizen.

• Dance:

Choreograph a piece showing the artistry and agility of horses on the march with Hannibal. Contrast them with the pondering and powerful elephants.

• Action:

Show through movement the actions of building a Roman road. Stylize the repetitive movements.

Conceptual Design:

• Design-A-City:

In the Roman style, design a city which includes straight, well-built roads, bridges, aqueducts, palaces, slave quarters, hippodrome, and whatever else would be appropriate in a Roman city.

Create Your Own Expression:

Conceptual Design:

Located on page 283.

Design A City

A student might wish to draw at least two perspectives of the city. For instance, a front view would show the various height of buildings rising above the city wall and the elevation of the aqueduct; and a top view which would present sizes of buildings, location of public sites, and roadways.

2) Share creative expressions in class.

The same rules apply as suggested in the reporting section of Phase Two.

Review & Evaluation

In this final Phase of Unit Eight, your students should have had the opportunity to express what they have learned about the rise of Rome and its place in Scripture through one or more various creative selections of their own choosing. These include:

1) Linguistics;
2) Art;
3) Music;
4) Drama;
5) Movement;
6) Conceptual Design.

You may wish to evaluate your students based on their *effort* in the **Creative Expressions**, either as individuals or in teams.

Teacher's Guide
JESUS CHRIST, IMMANUEL

UNIT 9

Christian Mosaic in Israel

Enthusiasm and delight are the best way to capture a student's interest and jump-start motivation, so:

Pray with the students at the beginning of each unit.

1) ***For the Auditory Students:*** Consider playing Christian hymns or worship music, such as **All Glory, Laud & Honor**, to capture their attention at the very beginning of class;

2) ***For the Kinesthetic Students:*** Have the students warm up as class begins by doing some active movement that is fun (such as, walking around the room as the risen Lazarus still wrapped head to toe in his grave clothes);

3) ***For the Visual Students:*** Bring a visual object to stimulate their interest in the new unit, such as Jan van Eyck's **Adoration of the Lamb**;

4) ***For the hearts of all:*** Pray with them at the beginning of the unit, that God would help them discover what He has for each one to learn in that unit.

PHASE 1

The Introduction Week

Learning Style Emphasis: *Feeler*

Students will be introduced to an historic view of Jesus Christ in Scripture and apologetics in this phase. You may follow this suggested schedule or adapt it to meet your students' needs:

Monday:

1) Informally discuss the Key Concepts

Tuesday:

2) Read the article
3) Listen to the audio recording(s)
4) Read the Scripture listed in Read For Your Life (could be done on their own)

Wednesday:

5) Recap Activity
6) Opinion Column and Critical Puzzling answers on their own

Thursday:

7) Class Discussion

Friday:

8) Choose books of interest/Internet search

Teachers can choose to have students do one or two activities, rather than the entire week's schedule. Please use what works for you in your unique setting.

INTRO-PG 18

1) Informally Discuss the Key Concepts

Listed in the Student Manual on page 285.

KEY CONCEPTS BACKGROUND INFORMATION

These are the main objectives of the unit. As you proceed through the four weeks, your students will be given various ways of understanding each of these objectives.

The fulness of Time—EXPLANATION

TEACHER TIP

To get an informal discussion started on this key concept, ask a simple, leading question, such as, *"The Bible says in Galatians 4:4 that Jesus came in the 'fulness of time.' Does anyone have an idea what 'the fulness of time' might mean?"*

Though God had promised One who would crush the enemy in Genesis 3:15, and though He had told Abraham that through him "all the families of the earth shall be blessed" (Genesis 12:3), and though hundreds of prophecies had been given over hundreds of years about the coming Redeemer, yet it was not until the reign of Caesar Augustus that the fulness of time was reached.

As we have seen through the previous units, God had been carefully and precisely setting into place all the necessary preparations for the advent of the Messiah during the time of the four empires of Daniel's vision. And at the exact moment, in the fourth empire, at the precisely right time, God sent His son.

He tells us in Isaiah 46:9-10:

"...For I am God, and there is no other;
I am God, and there is none like Me,
Declaring the end from the beginning,
And from ancient times things that are not yet done,
Saying, 'My counsel shall stand, and I will do all My pleasure.'"

In the coming of Jesus, the fulness of God's counsel—His unsearchable wisdom—was revealed from heaven, and His pleasure and purpose for the redemption of mankind was accomplished through the life, death and resurrection of our Lord and Savior.

The Historical Evidence—EXPLANATION

To get an informal discussion started on this key concept, ask a simple, leading question, such as, *"Have you heard about any evidences of Jesus' life, death and resurrection, apart from what you have read in the Bible?"*

For those in our culture who have no personal relationship to Jesus and no belief in the truth of Scripture, our communication of the historical evidences for His life, death and resurrection can be a powerful witness. The Church has used *apologetics* (a defense of truth) since its early years to defend the truths of Christianity before a critical world.

Apologetics provides people who have honest doubts—who have been steeped in the faulty reasoning of this age—the historical evidences that will help them see that Jesus Christ is who He says. However, since apologetics deals in the realm of the intellect (answering questions of the mind), it is important to realize that historical evidence will never be enough to bring someone to a personal relationship with Jesus. We are drawn to Him through faith by His love, which was shown on the cross:

"But God demonstrates His own love toward us, in that while we were still sinners, Christ died for us."
Romans 5:8

Apologetics also provides Christians the tools to think through the arguments of atheism, agnosticism, post-modernism, animism, Buddhism, Hinduism, Islam, the New Age, and liberal Christianity (those who think the Bible is not accurate but hold to some of its religious "teachings"). When we comprehend the literal, historical fact of Jesus—His life, death and resurrection—we will be able to love Him with our *mind*, as well as our heart, soul, and strength.

In my own life, knowing the historical evidences for the resurrection allowed my faith to expand from an emotional experience with no understanding to a faith of the mind as well as the heart. Pray for your students that they will be equipped to withstand the intellectual arguments of the age against Christianity, and that they will be filled with wisdom and compassion to share the truth of His life, death and resurrection with those who don't believe.

I highly recommend Josh McDowell's book, *The New Evidence That Demands A Verdict*, to delve into the area of apologetics. Every student should have their own copy of this powerful book before they leave home to attend university or work in a career!

Knowing Him - Philippians 3:10 - EXPLANATION

To get an informal discussion started on this key concept, ask a simple, leading question, such as, *"Paul wrote about Jesus in Philippians 3:10, 'that I may know Him and the power of His resurrection, and the fellowship of His sufferings, being conformed to His death.' What do you think he means?"*

There is a huge difference between these two statements:

"I know about the President."
"I know the President."

There is an even greater difference between someone who has met the President once in a receiving line for a one-second hand shake with an impersonal greeting versus someone who was born into the President's family. The first person could say, "Oh, yes, I know the President," but there would be no comparison to the child who says, "Yes, I know the President—he's my father!"

Knowing Jesus is not the same as knowing about Him. Believing there is a God is not the same as believing in Him.

"You believe that there is one God. You do well. Even the demons believe—and tremble!" James 2:19

It is a matter of relationship, just as in the example about the President. Remember what we learned in Unit One—that God designed us for Himself, to be in close, personal, family relationship to Him? That was the reason Jesus came to earth. He came to be Immanuel, God with us. His death brings us life, if we receive Him.

"But as many as received Him, to them He gave the right to become children of God, to those who believe in His name; who were born, not of blood, nor of the will of the flesh, nor of the will of man, but of God." John 1:12-13

All of history leads us to the startling revelation that it is all about relationship! Jesus came to restore us to the Father, to adopt us into His family.

"But when the fulness of the time had come, God sent forth His Son, born of a woman, born under the law, to redeem those who were under the law, that we might receive the adoption as sons. And because you are sons, God has sent forth the Spirit of His Son into your hearts, crying out, 'Abba, Father!' Therefore you are no longer a slave but a son, and if a son, then an heir of God through Christ." Galatians 4:4-7

Knowing Him is about relationship—close, personal, Family relationship.

Pray for your students, that this discussion would transcend the intellectual to touch their spirit. Pray that their relationship with God would deepen to the point that they would cry out, as Paul did, "that I may *know* Him," in all that that might include.

Sharing Him—EXPLANATION

Evangelism, or the sharing of our faith, has often been reduced to a method or formula. Though being prepared to share with others is biblical ("But sanctify the Lord God in your hearts, and always be ready to give a defense to everyone who asks you a reason for the hope that is in you, with meekness and fear." 1 Peter 3:15), yet, sharing about Jesus with others is a *relational* action. We share because of our compassion for others and because He is so wonderful that we can't keep the good news to ourselves!

If we see ourselves as starving beggars who just found a truckload of bread, we will begin to understand the motivation of sharing with other starving beggars where to find food. That is a beginning insight into the heart of evangelism, though this simplistic analogy quickly breaks down—some of the starving beggars we know don't know they are starving, nor beggars! But, there are many in the world, knowing their own desperate need, who truly hunger for the Bread of Life, and we can point them to Jesus.

So, we need first to pray, asking the Lord to give us a heart for evangelism. Then we can ask Him to give us wisdom and great compassion as He opens doors for us to share about Him.

UNIT 9

JESUS CHRIST, IMMANUEL

Christian Mosaic in Israel

KEY CONCEPTS:

- The Fullness of Time
- The Historical Evidence
- Knowing Him— Philippians 3:10
- Sharing Him

The Promised One has come...

"For unto us a Child is born, unto us a Son is given;
And the government shall be upon His shoulder.
And His name will be called Wonderful, Counselor,
Mighty God, Everlasting Father, Prince of Peace.
Of the increase of His government and peace there will
be no end.
Upon the throne of David and over His kingdom,
To order it and establish it with judgment and justice
From that time forward, even forever.
The zeal of the Lord of hosts will perform this." Isaiah 9:6-7

Unit Nine: *Jesus Christ, Immanuel* / 285

This article can be found in its entirety in the Appendix (see pg 365).

2) Read the article

Begins on Page 285 of Student Manual.

SPIRITUAL

The article for Unit Nine is designed to help students think about the reality of Jesus Christ, Immanuel, and the implication that His coming holds for people today. The materials covered in the audio recordings offer another look at this time period, covering slightly different information. In the article and recordings, along with introducing the basic understanding of history, we are also bringing in the biblical worldview.

TEACHER TIP

You may choose to have your students read the article first and then listen to the audio recordings, or vice versa.

Key People:

The people listed in this column are the main characters, if you will, of this unit. They are listed in the Student Manual, along with a brief identifier, so that the students can familiarize themselves with these people.

PHASE 1

KEY PEOPLE:

Jesus 4BC
—Messiah, Redeemer, Lord

John the Baptist 4BC-AD 26
—"Prepare the way of the Lord"

Peter
—the impetuous disciple

John
—the beloved disciple

Mary and Joseph
—the parents of Jesus

Caiphus
—the High Priest

Herod the Great 37 BC
—Idumean ruler who kills the infants

Herod Antipas
—Idumean ruler who murdered John the Baptist

➤ Listen to this!

• **What in the World's Going on Here? Volume One**

  — Jesus

• **More True Tales From the Times of…Ancient Civilizations & The Bible**

  — The Biblical Prophecies of Jesus Fulfilled

• **An In-Depth Look at…The First Christmas**

➤ Read For Your Life

• **The Holy Bible**

  — The Main Story: The book of Luke (or Matthew, Mark or John)

  — Other Helpful Verses: Isaiah 46:9-10; Romans 1:2-4

292 / Unit Nine: *Jesus Christ, Immanuel*

---

3) *Listen to the audio recording(s)*

Listed on Page 292 of the Student Manual.

- The main concepts and chronological flow are contained in **What in the World's Going On Here?**

- Examine many of the prophecies of Jesus fulfilled in His life, death, and resurrection in **More True Tales From the Times of…Ancient Civilizations & The Bible**

- A specific look at the events surrounding the birth of Jesus, including background information on the Roman Empire, the political structure in Israel, and more are contained in **An In-Depth Study of…The First Christmas**

Phase 1

— Prophecies Fulfilled in Jesus' Life:

Genesis 3:15	*Malachi 3:1*
Isaiah 7:14	*Zechariah 9:9*
Psalm 2:7	*Psalm 118:22*
Genesis 22:18	*Isaiah 60:3*
Numbers 24:17	*Psalm 16:10*
Genesis 49:10	*Psalm 41:9*
Isaiah 11:1-5	*Zechariah 11:12-13*
Jeremiah 23:5-6	*Zechariah 13:7*
Micah 5:2	*Psalm 35:11*
Jeremiah 31:15	*Isaiah 53*
Psalm 110:1 & 4	*Isaiah 50:6*
Deuteronomy 18:18	*Psalm 22*
Isaiah 33:22	*Psalm 109:24-25*
Isaiah 61:1-3	*Psalm 69:4, 20, 21,*
Psalm 69:7-9	*Psalm 38:11*
Isaiah 40:3	*Psalm 31:5*
Isaiah 9:1-2	*Psalm 34:20*
Isaiah 35:5-6,	*Amos 8:9*
Psalm 78:2	*Zechariah 12:10*

➤ *Talk Together*

- **Opinion Column:**

— What did you find to be the most interesting aspect you encountered in this introduction to Jesus Christ?

— Imagine you are one of the shepherds who had heard the angelic announcement. Consider your surprise, your amazement and your awe at actually seeing the Christ child. How would you describe your experience?

— Read Matthew 11:28-30. What does Jesus tell us to do, and how do we obey Him? How do you think this will change your life?

Unit Nine: *Jesus Christ, Immanuel* / 293

---

4) Read the Scripture listed in Read For Your Life

Listed on Page 292 of the Student Manual. You might choose to have the students read the Main Story verses either corporately or privately.

The Scriptures are central to our understanding, our character, and our decisions. Therefore, we must give the greatest weight possible to them. Help your students gain this perspective as they watch you handle the Scriptures with reverence and awe.

SPIRITUAL

The Prophecies Fulfilled, listed in the Student Manual on Page 293, include some of the most profound and well known descriptions of Jesus' life, death and resurrection. You might want to spend some class time reading the Old Testament prophecies and finding their New Testament fulfillment.

5) Recap (process & review) Activity

In different parts of the room, set up stations for the Eight Intelligences Recap Activities. Then allow students to work alone or together in small groups to accomplish the following suggestions. At the start of the next class, ask for 3-4 groups of volunteers to share. <u>For homeschoolers, rather than set up all eight stations, allow the student(s) to choose which of these activities they would most enjoy, and do that.</u>

INTRO - PG 19

Recap Suggestions:

SPATIAL: From the descriptions of Jesus in Isaiah 9:6-7, create a poster with images which suggest these aspects of His names and His character.

BODILY-KINESTHETIC: Select a series of appropriate motions or actions to accompany the worship song, "Lord, I Lift Your Name on High," (or a similar type of song). Those who know sign language might want to incorporate that, as well. Be ready to teach others the motions.

INTERPERSONAL: In a small group, hold a discussion concerning why Jesus was not universally accepted by the people of His time. Why did some love Him while others despised Him?

MUSICAL: In a small group, choose your favorite Christmas carol, your favorite Easter hymn, and your favorite worship chorus which focus on Jesus. Then sing together!

LINGUISTIC: Choose your favorite story of Jesus from the Scriptures. Write it out in your own words.

MATH-LOGICAL: List ten reasons why people reject Jesus as Lord, and then ten biblical answers to their reasons.

INTRAPERSONAL: Consider, alone or with a partner, "What is for you the single most important point, or the greatest revelation you have had, in the introduction to this unit?"

NATURALIST: Read these verses from Psalm 8, "When I consider Your heavens, the work of Your fingers, the moon and stars, which You have ordained, what is man that You are mindful of him, and the son of man that You visit him? For You have made him a little lower than the angels, and You have crowned him with glory and honor." Then go outside, look up at the sky, and consider God's amazing grace in sending His Son—the "Son of Man"—to us.

OR…Activity of Your Choice: What would you like to have your students do for a review activity concerning this week's introduction to Jesus Christ, Immanuel?

6) Opinion Column and Critical Puzzling answers on their own

Listed on Pages 293-294 of the Student Manual. Students may begin these questions after completing their Recap Activities listed above.

7) Class Discussion

Using the questions listed on Pages 293-294 of the Student Manual to get the students primed, create a discussion environment in the classroom. You may also want to draw from the open-ended questions listed below.

Phase 1

• **Critical Puzzling:**

— Why do you think God sent Jesus to be born of peasants rather than kings?

> — Read the book of Mark. It clearly reveals the miraculous power of Jesus to heal the sick, calm the storm, cast out demons, feed the multitude, die a sacrificial death and rise from the dead unto eternal life. What do you think someone who believes in a "closed system"—one who does not believe in God and does not believe in the supernatural—would say about these miracles?

— There is a significant difference between a person who says, "I don't know, but let's do some research to find out" and the person who says, "I already know it isn't true"? Why will the second person not believe any historic evidence for the truth of Christianity? What do you think will help them believe?

— The amazing thing about studying Jesus is that He is ALIVE! When we studied Moses, King Nebuchadnezzar, Xerxes, Alexander the Great, and Julius Caesar, we studied about important men who had accomplished much during their lifetimes. But they are all dead. When we study Jesus, He is with us, revealing Himself, changing us, making us into His image. Take some time, either alone or with your family, to talk to Jesus about what you are studying. Ask Him your questions, bring Him your thoughts, allow Him to show you that He is faithful and trustworthy; that He is the same, yesterday, today and forever.

• **Personal Application:**

— Ask the Lord to draw you into a closer walk with Him every day, to reveal His infinite love in your life. Keep an ongoing journal to show how this prayer is answered.

294 / Unit Nine: *Jesus Christ, Immanuel*

How has our study of history led us to a Person rather than just to academic knowledge?

What are the implications of this understanding for each of our lives?

What do you think our motivation should be for obeying the Lord?

—For sharing Him with other people?

—For worshipping Him?

—For living our lives for Him?

INTRO·PG 20

8) Choose books of interest/Internet search

A list of possible books for further reading is listed in the Student Manual beginning on Pages 295-296. Encourage your students to look for general information from this list and from other sources on Jesus—particularly from sources that hold to a biblical view of Jesus, rather than a humanistic or non-biblical view. You may want to gather a selection of further resources prior to beginning Unit Nine, or you may encourage the students to be treasure hunters and find them on their own.

Remember:

Beware of Arrogance, Embrace Humility!

The Internet has a wealth of information concerning Jesus Christ, though the articles available vary widely in dependability, worldview and attitude. Help your students learn to recognize the differences.

For the complete list of books from the Student Manual, refer to the Appendix (pg 368).

Phase 1

➤ Reviewed Resources for Digging Deeper:

Choose a few books that look interesting, or find your own.

Apologetics:

Evidence that Demands a Verdict
by Josh McDowell

This is not a book to sit down and read, it is a book to study. It will teach you the historical evidences for the Christian faith. (A term often used for this is "apologetics.") Filled with historical, archaeological, medical, legal references, this book will give you a very firm foundation for the defense of Biblical Christianity. **MS+**

Mere Christianity by C.S. Lewis

One of the classics of Christian apologetics, this considers the issue of whether Jesus was a liar, a lunatic, or Lord, as well as many other concepts. **HS**

EVALUATION ## Review & Evaluation

In this Phase of Unit Nine, your students should have had the opportunity to explore an historic view of Jesus Christ in Scripture and apologetics through reading, listening, thinking and discussing. They will have:

1) informally discussed the Key Concepts;
2) read the article;
3) listened to the audio recording(s);
4) read the Scripture listed in Read for Your Life;
5) explored the Recap Activities;
6) completed the Opinion Column and Critical Puzzling answers on their own;
7) participated in Class Discussion;
8) chosen books of interest or searched the Internet.

You may wish to evaluate your students based on their *participation* in the **Class Discussion** and on their *participation* in the **Recap Activity**.

Learning Style Emphasis: THINKER

Students will explore topics of interest through research and reporting, learn new vocabulary, and construct a timeline relating to an historic view of Jesus Christ in Scripture and apologetics.

Monday-Tuesday:
1) Choose topic and begin research

Wednesday:
2) Vocabulary Practice

Thursday:
3) Construct the Timeline.

Friday:
4) Research projects completed; share in class or hand in.

> *Teachers can choose to have students do one or two activities, rather than the entire week's schedule. Please use what works for you in your unique setting.*

1) Choose topic and begin research

Allow the students the freedom to choose one of the topics listed on Page 297, or to suggest their own area which they would like to research.

INTRO-PG 21

Motivating Suggestions:

Especially for Non-Linguistic students, and those who are not motivated by written or oral reports, here are suggestions for alternative ways of reporting what has been researched.

Fulfilled Prophecies

1) Create a dramatic presentation for some of the fulfilled prophecies using as a narration the Old Testament scriptures, and reenacting (either through acting, pantomime, or dance) their fulfillment.
2) Make a visual presentation of the prophecies of Jesus fulfilled in His life, death and resurrection. You may use drawings, paintings, illustrations, magazine photos, or any other form of visual portrayal. To aid the viewer, please include a list of the selected prophecies, or label them next to the drawings, etc.

The Time of Jesus:

1) Create a chart showing some of the distinctives of each Gospel as it represents Jesus. For instance, the gospel of Luke is written to a Greek audience, so many Jewish customs and the geography of Palestine are explained in greater detail than would have been necessary for a Jewish audience. *A good study Bible or Bible handbook will help greatly in this project.*
2) Interview people from different parts of the Roman Empire to discover what was of importance during the time of Jesus. Be sure to include at least one person from Rome, one from Greece, and one from Palestine.

MOTIVATE

MOTIVATE

Apologetics

1) Hold a debate with one group arguing for the reliability of the Scriptures from an apologetics position and one group arguing against the reliability of the Scriptures from postmodernist position.

2) Create a flip chart showing historical evidences in several areas of apologetics:
- evidence for the reliability of the Bible, including archaeological evidences;
- evidence for the historical life of Jesus;
- evidence for the resurrection of Jesus;
- evidence that Jesus is God.

Miracles

1) Gather testimonies of modern-day miracles (within the last two hundred years). Then combine these testimonies with the testimonies of Jesus' miracles related in Scripture. Create a chart which demonstrates that miracles—supernatural acts outside of natural law—continue to happen.

2) Using music and movement, portray some of the miracles of Jesus. If possible, show some of the varied responses of the crowd who saw Him doing the miracle.

PHASE 2
Exploration & Discovery Week

➤ Research & Reporting

Your mission, if you choose to accept it, is to explore one of these areas, and to discover something significant!

- **Fulfilled Prophecies:**

  Using either a Bible handbook, study Bible, commentary or **Evidence that Demands a Verdict**, make a chart showing the Old Testament prophecies of the Messiah, the date they were written, and the fulfillment of these prophecies in Jesus.

- **The Time of Jesus:**

  — Read the Gospels in the New Testament. Report on these questions:

  - *To whom did Jesus come?*

  - *What was His message?*

  - *How did the people respond?*

  - *How did the Resurrection impact the rulers of Jerusalem; of Rome?*

  - *How did it impact the disciples?*

  — In reference books, research what was happening in the Roman Empire during the time of Jesus' life. Find the poem, **One Solitary Life**, and show how it is historically accurate.

- **Apologetics:**

  — *Apologetics* is basically the intellectual defense of Christianity. Research and report on one area of apologetics, such as, fulfilled prophecy, evidence for the resurrection, the uniqueness and reliability of the Bible, etc.

  — Research and write about the claims of Jesus Christ. Who did He say He was? What did He claim to be able to do? What evidence exists to validate His claims? (**Consider:** I highly recommend investing in a copy of **Evidence That Demands a Verdict** or something similar. It will open up a whole world in understanding the reasonableness of our faith.)

- **Miracles**

  Make a chart showing the supernatural—outside of natural law—acts of Jesus. What did He do? What were the results of his miracles, both in the lives of those receiving the miracles and in the attitude of those watching Jesus do the miracles? In what ways do you see the same attitudes in people today?

TEACHER TIP

Many stories of miraculous provision, healing, and protection are found in missionary stories. Any story of God's answer to desperate prayer that cannot be explained away by natural circumstances will satisfy this project. For instance, look up the miracle of Dunkirk during WW II.

Phase 2

➤ *Brain Stretchers*

• Prophecy

Research the mathematical probabilities that one man could fulfill all the prophecies of the Messiah.

• Apologetics

C.S. Lewis in Mere Christianity wrote: *"I am trying here to prevent anyone saying the really foolish thing that people often say about Him: 'I'm ready to accept Jesus as a great moral teacher, but I don't accept His claim to be God.' That is the one thing we must not say. A man who was merely a man and said the sort of things Jesus said would not be a great moral teacher. He would either be a lunatic—on a level with the man who says he is a poached egg—or else he would the Devil of Hell. You must make your choice. Either this man was, and is, the Son of God: or else a madman or something worse."*

Research and report on the current arguments against Jesus being God's Son and Redeemer. How would C.S. Lewis' words effectively counter these arguments?

• Fullness of Time

Research and write on the flow of history from Creation up to the time of Jesus. Show how Daniel's vision has been fulfilled through the four great empires. Galatians 4:4-5 indicates that God chose the perfect moment for the Messiah. In hind sight, how can we demonstrate that this was the case?

Create Your Own Research Topic:

_____

_____

_____

Brain Stretchers:

Brain Stretchers, listed on page 298, are intended for advanced students. Those who attempt the Brain Stretchers for their Research and Reporting can use the above list for ideas on how to report their findings.

---

2) *Words To Watch - Vocabulary Practice*

INTRO · PG 21

Listed on Page 299. You may find other words in this unit that are especially appropriate for younger children. Feel free to substitute another vocabulary list for the one provided.

Phase 2

➤ *Words to Watch*

Remember—The easiest way to learn a subject is to master its terms:

natural	myth	ascension
supernatural	Messiah	commission
miracle	Emmanuel	crucify
hoax	Christ	tomb
history	disciple	swoon
validate	apostle	proof/theory
Lord	resurrection	

TEACHER TIP

Here is one idea for making vocabulary study interesting and fun: *Interview as many people as possible to see what definitions they can give for the vocabulary words. How many different answers did you find?*

3) *Construct the Timeline*

Read the information listed with the "Key Dates" on Page 301. Dialogue with your students about the issues involved. For ease of reference, the timeline is included in the Appendix on Page 370.

Find the dates for the key people and events listed.

Everything prior to Jesus looks forward to His coming. Everything since the time of Jesus looks back to His advent on the earth, as well as looking to His second coming. His life is the most critical date we will ever mark on any timeline, and His second coming is the most critical date we will ever keep. May we be found watching and waiting for it.

4) *Research projects shared in class and/or turned in.*

Create a safe environment for the presentations. Set ground rules prior to the presentations for all the students, so that they know each one will be honored and respected in their work by all those observing.

EVALUATION | Review & Evaluation

In this second Phase of Unit Nine, your students should have had the opportunity to explore an historic view of Jesus Christ in Scripture and apologetics through researching, thinking, and reporting. They will have:

1) done a research project;
2) learned the vocabulary;
3) constructed a Timeline;
4) created a project report on what was researched.

You may wish to evaluate your students based on their *efforts* in the **Research and Reporting** projects and their active *participation* in the **Vocabulary** and **Timeline** exercises.

Learning Style Emphasis: Sensor

Students will gain cultural understanding through sensory activities as they explore interrelated subject areas relating to an historic view of Jesus Christ in Scripture and apologetics.

Monday:
1) Create a map and discuss the issues in teams.

Tuesday:
2) Examine and discuss art masterpieces & architectural structures.

Wednesday:
3) Arts in Action—Do an art project.*

Thursday:
4) Do one science project or field trip.**

Friday:
5) Listen to and discuss the music.
6) Cook the food listed in the recipe, if desired.

*Art project will need to be planned ahead of time to acquire materials.
**Field trip will require extra planning time.

> *Teachers can choose to have students do one or two activities, rather than the entire week's schedule. Please use what works for you in your unique setting.*

1) Create a map and discuss the issues in teams

The students each have an outline map on Page 303. They will be given assignments for drawing in rivers, mountains, cities, and regional boundaries, which are listed on Page 302. For details on where these things are, please consult a historical atlas, an encyclopedia, a study Bible, or any other source for geographic information. For ease of reference, the map is included in the Appendix on Page 371.

Upper elementary students might be satisfied to accomplish only this portion:
- *Physical terrain:* This part of the mapping exercise will help students locate and mark the geological dynamics of a region.

Middle school students might be satisfied to complete both the previous mapping exercise and this exercise:
- *Geo-Political:* This section of the mapping exercise will provide the students an opportunity to locate and mark the cities, nations and empires of history. It will require more digging.

High school students might be satisfied to complete both the previous mapping exercises and at least one exploration topic of this exercise:
- *Explore:* Discuss some selection from this portion of the mapping exercise in teams.

Encourage them to think for themselves, rather than parroting back information.

QUESTION

Geography of the Promised One

During Unit Four, we looked at Israel's prominent position as the thoroughfare between Europe and Africa, and between Europe and Asia. Consider at this point that the Roman Empire believes the whole world revolves around Rome—"all roads lead to Rome"—and talk together about God's perfect wisdom in bringing Jesus, not to Rome, but to Palestine.

PHASE 3

The Hands-On Week

➢ *Maps and mappping*

- **Physical Terrain:**

  — Label and color the Sea of Galilee and the Mediterranean.

  — Label and color the Jordan River.

  — Locate and indicate the mountain ranges, deserts, and green areas.

- **Geo-Political:**

  — Draw the boundaries of Israel in the time of Jesus. Where are the boundaries of Israel today?

  — Label the cities of Bethlehem, Nazareth, Jerusalem and the cities of the Decapolis. What modern day cities are close to these cities?

  — Locate and label the area known as Samaria. What is the modern name of this area today.

- **Explore:**

  — *Geography of the Promised One:* Though Israel was a backwater, out-of-the-way country of the Roman Empire, God chose to send His Son to that geographic location. Looking at a map, consider and discuss God's unfailing wisdom and perfect knowledge in bringing the promised Redeemer for all the families of the earth to that nation.

INTRO - PG 23

2) Examine and discuss art masterpieces & architectural structures

Locate either a copy of these art forms, or Internet sites for each of the items listed on Pages 304-305. Allow the students time to observe the art without any conversation, and then, when they are ready, engage them in some or all of the questions listed in the Student Manual or below.

QUESTION

The Annunciation - *by Jan van Eyck*

Jan van Eyck was actively painting between 1422 and 1441 A.D. in the Netherlands (Holland), long before the Reformation, yet his paintings portray a deep understanding and reverence for the Scriptures.

Ask your students what they think might be the reason for such understanding during a time when most people were ignorant of all but a cursory knowledge of the Bible.

➤ Art Appreciation

Consider:

Jan van Eyck was a fourteenth century Flemish painter with an amazing grasp of Biblical truth. He perfected the technique of painting with oil paints, which can be seen when studying his masterpiece, *The Adoration of the Lamb*. His painting, *The Annunciation*, is a stunning example of Biblical symbolism, which anticipates the restoration of Sola Scriptura in the Reformation by nearly a hundred years.

- **The Annunciation** *by Jan van Eyck*

  — Do you think this reflects what the Bible describes?

  — How does it differ from your own impression of this historic event?

  — How would you describe the **Annunciation**?

  — How many symbols can you find in this painting?

- **The Pieta—A Sculpture** *by Michelangelo*

  — Do you think this reflects what the Bible describes?

  — How does it differ from your own impression of this historic event?

  — How would you describe the **Pieta**? Why do you think it is considered to be one of the best sculptures ever created?

    - *Michelangelo was in his early twenties when he created this life-size sculpture of Mary holding the crucified Jesus in her arms. He created this in less than two years from a single slab of marble—one of the most magnificent sculptures ever created!*

➤ Architecture

Though Solomon's Temple was destroyed in 586 B.C., the repatriated Jews returned to Jerusalem, under the patronage of Cyrus, to rebuild it. In 20 B.C., King Herod began an ambitious undertaking to Hellenize the look of the Temple. It took eighteen months and 1000 specially trained priests (only priests could walk in the sacred area) to complete the main work, though craftsmen continued on sections until 64 A.D. The Temple platform was thirty-five acres in size, and the massive enclosure walls were up to fifteen feet thick! The western section of the wall is known today as the Wailing Wall.

— Look for an artist's rendition of The Second Temple (built by Zerubbabel, refashioned by Herod the Great, destroyed in 70 A.D.).

  - *In what way does this reflect the Greek style of architecture?*

  - *How would you describe this structure?*

— Find a photo of the Wailing Wall in Jerusalem.

  - *How would you describe the Wailing Wall?*

  - *What do people do at this sacred site?*

The Pieta - *A Sculpture by Michelangelo*

QUESTION

Michelangelo (1475-1564) was born in Italy during the Renaissance, and studied art in the city of Florence, known as a center for the arts. Eventually, he came to work for Lorenzo de' Medici, one of the most notable patrons of art in the Renaissance. After the death of his patron, Michelangelo worked mainly in Rome, under the patronage of the popes, rebuilding St. Peters. When we examine his amazing marble creations, we see that his artistry in sculpture was powerful and sublime.

Ask your students what emotions the **Pieta** evokes in them. Do they think that Michelangelo created this statue as an act of worship? Would they describe it more as a product of the Renaissance or the Reformation?

The Second Temple (built by Zerubbabel, refashioned by Herod the Great)

QUESTION

Ask your students what they think Herod's motivation might have been in pouring such time and money into the Jewish Temple, since he was not Jewish.

INTRO·PG 23

3) Arts in Action

Listed on Page 306.

TEACHER TIP

Animal Crafting

This could be a great project to give to younger siblings or other young friends! If the students are going to give the lamb to a child under three years old, make sure it doesn't have any tiny buttons that could accidentally be swallowed by a little child.

Batting is an ideal stuffing for sewn animals. A capped pen or crochet hook is very useful in pushing batting into small spaces such as legs and ears. Help the students to understand that the more batting used, the rounder the animal will be.

Crèche Making

The students who enjoy going outside might enjoy this project tremendously, as it affords them the chance to find and collect appropriate materials. Be sure to give them the time and opportunity.

Bread dough figures can be baked and then painted, which will greatly extend their usability.

Phase 3

➢ Arts in Action

Select one, and let your artistic juices flow!

• Animal Crafting:

Sew a Passover lamb out of fleecy acrylic. Check in the library for the how-to information. Remember, the Passover lamb had to be without spot or blemish.

• Crèche Making:

Build a crèche for a Nativity scene using twigs, wood, moss, bark, etc. This would be a great present to give your mother! To complete the crèche, try to find a craft book to show how to make bread dough figurines which can be painted. Or, it may be possible to buy greenware, clean it, paint it, and have it fired in a kiln. Ask a local ceramics or crafts expert how to do it.

• Imitation:

Try your hand at creating a Biblical scene in the style of van Eyck

• Diorama:

Create a miniature Resurrection Day scene with bread dough, clay, or papier maché. Form it, paint it, add figures. The most important element is the Empty Tomb!

➢ Science

• Leaven:

— Jesus said, "A little leaven leavens the whole lump." Leaven is another term for yeast. Learn the meaning of Jesus' words by making a loaf of bread from scratch. How much yeast do you use in comparison to flour? What happens if the water is too hot? What if the water is too cold? What is the application to our lives?

• Diffusion:

— 2 Corinthians 2:14 says "…and through us diffuses the fragrance of His knowledge in every place." Experiment with diffusion. Borrow a bottle of perfume from your mother. Set the closed bottle on a table. Does it smell? Now, hold your breath and spray the perfume in the air. Quickly step out of the room, and then return, breathing deeply. Can you smell the perfume? Try setting a bowl of potpourri in the kitchen. Can you smell it throughout the house? Now try heating the potpourri. Can you smell it throughout the house? Why? What can we learn about our life in Christ from this experiment?

306 / Unit Nine: *Jesus Christ, Immanuel*

Imitation

Van Eyck used a new kind of oil paint, that could be built up in translucent layers, allowing him to produce a natural lighting effect, as well as the amazingly fine detail he was known for. If your students wish to produce an imitation of his work, encourage them to create as much detail as possible without becoming frustrated!

Diorama

Students may wish to use purchased figures for the Roman soldiers. Be sure to emphasize that the huge stone covering the tomb has been rolled to the side so everyone can see that the tomb is empty.

4) Do a science project

Listed on Page 306. Feel free to choose one of these projects. If students love science, they might want to consider doing all of them!

Leaven

For those familiar with bread making, it will be simple to test the water for appropriate temperature so that the yeast is not killed. For others, test the water temperature by pouring it across your wrist—when you can feel neither warmth nor cold, the temperature is right. There are also different types of yeast—some prefer warmer water—so be sure to check the label on the yeast package.

Diffusion

Students may wish to experiment with different kinds of aroma-producing materials. Try popping popcorn (an old trick known by those who run concessions in movie theaters), or, for a less pleasant experience, wipe a counter with a cleaning solution. Ask the students the personal implications for a lingering aroma that is not pleasant.

Phase 3

➢ Music

"By faith we understand that the worlds were framed by the Word of God." Hebrews 11:3

Have you ever noticed the remarkable structure evident in the universe? Rain falls, the moisture waters the earth, the water evaporates, the evaporation forms clouds, and the clouds produce rain. Everything that God created has structure and form, even if it is invisible to us.

In music, there is also a structure, a form. Form is the fifth element of music, and it is what holds all of the rest together. Without form there would not be familiar songs. There would only be random high notes and short notes and loud notes and low notes and fast notes and slow notes without any order. Does this sound somewhat like an evolutionary worldview—meaningless, chance and chaos? Actually, there are 20th century composers whose music reflects this worldview.

To reflect the Biblical worldview, our music will have some form, some structure, some purpose. Handel's Messiah is a wonderful piece of musical literature about Jesus the Messiah. It incorporates many Old Testament prophecies in a rich setting of voices.

> ### Consider:
>
> *"For by Him all things were created that are in heaven and that are on earth, visible and invisible…All things were created through Him and for Him. And He is before all things, and in Him all things are held together."* Colossians 1:16-17
>
> And Paul wrote in I Corinthians 14:40 that *"all things should be done decently and in order."*

The Messiah is an **oratorio**, which means that it has a special form:

- a long text, usually religious—rapid dialogue between characters
- performed in a church or theater—scenery, costumes, and action
- emphasis on chorus, with solos—emphasis on solos, with chorus
- accompanied by orchestra—very long sections

The form of the oratorio is what distinguishes it from operas, symphonies, or choir concerts.

5) Listen to and discuss the music

Listed on Pages 307-308.

Listen

Feel free to listen to brief selections rather than entire oratorios, symphonies or operas. Students will be able to grasp some of the significant differences even with short sessions of listening.

Try This

Depending on the age of the students, it may be easier to try the variation listed in the Student Manual, though operas will probably be easily distinguished from other forms of classical music!

• **Listen:**

— Listen to these different pieces of music:

- Handel's *Messiah*

- an opera such as Mozart's *The Marriage of Figaro*

- a symphony such as Beethoven's *Fifth Symphony*.

— Notice the differences in form, or structure, between these types of music. Name the differences you hear.

• **Try this:**

— After the above listening exercise, play "drop the needle" (which is an old-fashioned name since the advent of CD's!) One person will be the maestro and will secretly choose a recording and select portions, which the others will listen to. Play the recording at some randomly chosen spot and see who can identify the form of music being played.

- *Variation: Select any three different kinds of music for the maestro to choose from, such as country, jazz, and gospel. Can anyone in your family or class identify the form of music being played?*

INTRO - PG 24

6) Cook the food

Listed on Page 309.

If you are not able to find whitefish, some other possibilities for this recipe are: cod, haddock, trout, flounder, or perch.

➢ Cooking

The fish was chosen to be one of the earliest Christian symbols. Taste & see!

• **Stuffed Baked Whitefish**

3 cups bread cubes	3 tbsp water
1/4 cup melted butter	1/2 tsp salt
3/4 cup chopped cucumber	1/8 tsp freshly ground pepper
1/4 cup chopped onion	3 pounds whitefish, cleaned and boned

Combine the first seven ingredients and toss to mix well. Place stuffing lightly in fish cavity. Place in a greased baking pan; brush with oil. Bake in 375 oven for 30 min. or until fish flakes easily. Baste occasionally with oil. Serves 6.

Review & Evaluation

In this third Phase of Unit Nine, your students should have had the opportunity to explore an historic view of Jesus Christ in Scripture and apologetics through various hands-on and creative sessions. They will have:

1) completed a Mapping section;
2) observed and discussed Art & Architecture;
3) worked on an art project;
4) experimented with a Science Project or taken a field trip;
5) listened to music;
6) tasted a food related to this unit.

You may wish to evaluate your students based on their *class participation* in these **Hands-on** activities.

PHASE 4

The Expression Week

Students, through creative self-expression, using one or more creative activities, will present some aspect of what they have learned in the past three weeks relating to an historic view of Jesus Christ in Scripture and apologetics. Areas of expression include linguistics, art, music, drama, movement and conceptual design.

Monday - Thursday

1) Choose area of expression and begin work either individually or in teams.

Friday

2) Share creative expressions in class.

Teachers can choose to have students do one or two activities, rather than the entire week's schedule. Please use what works for you in your unique setting.

1) Choose area of expression and begin work either individually or in teams

Linguistics:

Located on page 310.

TEACHER TIP

Journalism

• Many weekly news magazines (such as *Time* or *Newsweek*) use eyewitness style of reporting, including on-location interviews. Encourage students to look through some examples of this style in order to gain an understanding of what is involved.

• Have students look for examples of world-shaking events (such as 9/11) to see the way reporters write about things beyond their comprehension. Obviously, the Resurrection is a cause for jubilant worship among Christian believers, but, to those in authority at the Temple at the time of Jesus' death, it was not good news. Imagine their absolute shock!

Prose

Donkeys tend to plod. Students might wish to write the meditative reflections of a donkey who is not excitable about much beyond his next meal. The tone would be vastly different for this piece than for one written from the viewpoint of, for instance, a chihuahua.

TEACHER TIP

Poetry

A good place to start on this project is found in the Magnificat, Mary's praise to God, which is found in Luke 1:46-55.

PHASE 4

The Expression Week

➤ *In Your Own Way...*

We have seen the fulfillment of the promise made by God, that He would send a Redeemer to save His people from their sins at the perfect moment in time. We have observed the life, death, and resurrection of Jesus Christ, Immanuel. We have considered the historical evidences, and how we might share Him with others. Now, choose a selection of these activities, or create your own, which will best express what you have learned from this unit.

Linguistics:

• Journalism:

— The magazine, "Religion Today," has asked you to do an eyewitness report on the miraculous healings that are being reported throughout Judea and Galilee. Join the throng following Jesus and write what you see, including interviews with those who have been healed.

— Be a newspaper reporter for "The Temple Times" investigating the incredible story of the empty tomb! You should include the background information that leads to this event.

• Prose:

Write a short story of the birth of Jesus from the perspective of the donkey who carried His mother to Bethlehem.

• Poetry:

Mary, as she watched the unfolding of the events in Jesus' life, "pondered these things in her heart." Write a poem, from her perspective, on Jesus the Messiah.

Art:

Located on page 311.

TEACHER TIP

Painting/Drawing

Encourage the students to observe paintings of historic scenes to determine how different artists emphasize what is important to them. Some have an inclusive viewpoint while others focus on a small segment of the event. Will the students depict the masses of people and the landscape, or will they choose to show a cropped version emphasizing Jesus with the little boy?

Graphic Design

In creating a timeline for young children, help the students recognize that simplicity is best. Too much detail will overwhelm them.

This will actually help the students choose what they consider to be the most significant items from history to include. I would suggest limiting the B.C. portion to approximately ten to twenty items.

Sculpting

Pietas could be crafted from a number of materials, from clay to fabric to wood to metal. The range is almost unlimited.

Cartooning

Some students will likely focus on aspects of evil. Remind them to portray Jesus as the Victorious One and to think Christianly, even if the depiction is dark and terrifying.

Students who really enjoy cartooning might consider purchasing a book on cartooning, such as Vic Lockman's *The Big Book of Cartooning in Christian Perspective.*

Music:

Located on page 311.

Compose

There are hymns and worship choruses about Immanuel. Encourage students to find some of these in order to understand how various composers have written about Him. Then, as they worshipfully contemplate what it means to have God with us, composing a song will flow out of worship and adoration.

Worship

2nd Chapter of Acts recorded a song entitled *The Easter Song* to which Keith Green later added a second verse. If it is possible, find one of these recordings for a joyful addition to your celebration of the Resurrection.

Performance Practice

For musical students, this selection may be a wonderful opportunity to express what they have learned. Make sure they have selected a piece that they have adequate time to prepare.

Phase 4

Art:

• **Painting/Drawing:**

Paint or draw the scene from the Gospels where the little boy gives Jesus his loaves and fishes.

• **Graphic Design:**

Design a timeline for young children showing Jesus Christ as the Centerpiece of all of human history. You will be able to add to this as you study further in history.

• **Sculpting:**

Sculpt a "pieta" (like Michelangelo's Pieta) in the material that seems best to you. It can be anything from realistic to abstract, as long as there is reverence shown.

• **Cartooning:**

Create a political cartoon showing how Satan's plan for killing Jesus backfired in an unexpected way!

Music:

• **Compose:**

Compose a song about Immanuel, God with us.

• **Worship:**

Choose your favorite hymns, worship choruses, and/or songs about the resurrection of Jesus, and then prepare to share a time of worship, scripture, and praise to our God for what He has done through our Lord Jesus Christ.

• **Performance Practice:**

With your teacher's help, select an appropriate piece of music which expresses some element from this unit, such as the wonder of His birth, the sorrow of His death, or the joy of His resurrection. Prepare and perform the piece for an audience. Communicate with your audience the reason for your selection either in the program notes or in a short speech.

Drama:

Located on page 312.

Heavenly

There is much scope for imagination in the heavenly drama, as we do not have any idea how angels act when they are excited! However, as actors portraying angels, students could be encouraged to strive to show the absolute fever pitch of excitement in heaven as the moment for the advent of the Redeemer arrives.

Comedy

This could be a one-person presentation, especially if the farmer mumbles to himself about the different kinds of soil, the birds, the hot sun, etc. It also makes an excellent skit for several actors, with one portraying the farmer and the rest representing the different kinds of seeds with their unique experiences.

Phase 4

Drama:

- **Heavenly:**

Act out the angels listening to Augustus Caesar's proclamation to register all the people in the Empire. Caesar is trying to make up his mind how and when he wants this done. The angels know the prophecies, so they are very excited when he finally makes a decision. They all get in line to volunteer for messenger duty to the shepherds! Use your imagination to create props, sets and costumes.

- **Comedy:**

Do a humorous skit about the sower who went out to sow his seed. Be sure to include birds, hot sun, shallow roots, weeds, and fruitful plants.

- **Role Playing:**

Role play a conversation using apologetics to explain to a non-believing friend the historical foundation of Christianity.

Role-Playing

Role-playing can be a powerful teacher, so encourage the students to find realistic arguments on the part of the non-believing friend, and appropriate answers from what has been studied of apologetics.

Movement:

Located on page 313.

Pantomime

There are many miracles to choose from which would make excellent subjects for pantomime. Encourage students to think of what would create dramatic effect—such as the healing of the ten lepers, with only one returning to thank Jesus.

Dance

The raising of Lazarus from the dead is one of the most dramatic, most unexpected events in Jesus' ministry. Encourage your students to use appropriately dramatic music to set the choreography, perhaps changing to music with a sense of wonder or celebration.

Action

One way of creating the action project is to use "living statues." As the narrator describes an event, the statues change poses, then freeze. The more statues, the greater the effect.

TEACHER TIP

Conceptual Design:
Located on page 313.

Multimedia

This could actually be a powerful presentation to share at churches, schools, nursing homes, and other appropriate settings. Pray with your students that they would find the right materials to include, and that the Lord would give them a heart of understanding to best know how to communicate the Gospel through this unique means.

INTRO · PG 26

2) Share creative expressions in class.

The same rules apply as suggested in the reporting section of Phase Two.

Phase 4

Movement:

• **Pantomime:**

Choose some scenes from the miracles of Jesus to pantomime. Find some appropriate recorded music (or have another student or someone in your family perform) while these miracles are acted out.

• **Dance:**

Choreograph a dance of Lazarus being raised from the dead. If there is more than one involved, you could each dance a different character.

• **Action**

Create a stylized movement showing the betrayal, trial and crucifixion of Jesus. If this ends at the death of Jesus, be sure to have someone read the scriptures or tell the story of His resurrection—on which our living faith depends.

Conceptual Design:

• **Multimedia**

Plan, and if possible, create a multimedia presentation for nonbelievers, showing who Jesus is and what He has done. As you create this, use only the most compelling music, video, artwork, photos, etc., so as to best represent both His humility in dying for us and the majesty of His resurrection.

Create Your Own Expression:

_____
_____

EVALUATION ## Review & Evaluation

In this final Phase of Unit Nine, your students should have had the opportunity to express what they have learned about an historic view of Jesus Christ in Scripture and apologetics through one or more various creative selections of their own choosing. These include:

1) Linguistics;
2) Art;
3) Music;
4) Drama;
5) Movement;
6) Conceptual Design.

You may wish to evaluate your students based on their *effort* in the **Creative Expressions**, either as individuals or in teams.

APPENDICES

APPENDICES

Descriptions of Learning Styles, Modalities, and Intelligences

There are three foundational building blocks undergirding this curriculum, three approaches to learning which help explain some of the differences in the ways people learn:

- **Four Learning Styles**

- **Three Learning Modalities**

- **Eight Intelligences**

These three foundational building blocks are integrally woven into the curriculum—they are already written into the lessons for you. This means that you do not have to figure out what learning style, modality or intelligences your students have, you can simply allow them to learn in ways that are interesting and enjoyable.

Four Learning Styles

Learning Styles refers to the categorization of how a particular personality style best learns. The method we refer to was developed by Myers-Briggs. Here is a brief description of each of the four learning styles:

The Feeler

This is the "people person" learning style. A Feeler wants to know the people perspective, i.e. how this subject affects people; how does this impact our lives now; who were the people of history, as opposed to the events or things. This learner needs to be in good relationship with the people around him—his teacher, siblings, friends, etc. They love to be with other people in one-on-one conversations and in group activities, especially when they are part of a "team effort."

The Thinker

"Give me the facts, ma'am, just the facts." The Thinker has an objective, black & white approach to knowledge, wanting authoritative input, not just someone's opinions. This learner truly enjoys using textbooks, encyclopedias, charts, diagrams. There is a need to know exactly what the rules are in the class, when assignments or projects are due, what is required for good grades. They are organized and expect organization.

The Sensor

The "hands-on," get-it-done-now person. The Sensor is the one who can make projects happen—taking them beyond the blueprint stage and into production. This learner does NOT enjoy sitting for long periods of time, looking through books for information, or discussing things for hours on end. Instead, the Sensor prefers to be involved with things that can be efficiently accomplished with physical effort.

The Intuitor

"Wait! I have an idea!" The Intuitor is the one brimming over with ideas about how this might have happened, or about how you might put on a play for the whole city portraying an historic event, or about what it must have been like to live in ancient times, and on and on. This learner is very good at coming up with suggestions, but is not as strong at seeing things through to completion. The Intuitor needs a lot of flexibility in schedule, and a "safe haven" for suggesting and trying out ideas.

Three Learning Modalities

Learning Modalities refers to the approach learners use to receive new information, how they best concentrate, process, and retain. Here is a brief description of each of the three modalities:

Visual: learn best by seeing, whether through reading, looking at pictures, watching a documentary, observing.

Auditory: learn best by hearing, whether through audio recordings, conversations, lectures, or reading out loud.

Tactile/Kinesthetic: learn best by touching objects or moving, whether through hands-on projects or physical action: jumping, running, dancing, even wiggling.

Eight Intelligences

Eight Intelligences refers to natural potential and areas of talent. Howard Gardner of Harvard University theorized that intelligence is made up of more than verbal and mathematical skills, and that people can strengthen their natural giftings and improve their weaknesses. Here is a brief description of each of the eight intelligences:

Intrapersonal

This could be described as Self-Smart. It is the ability to enjoy being alone, working independently, and relying on self-motivation. This person needs solitary time in order to think.

Naturalist

This could be described as Nature Smart. It is the ability to observe, investigate, experiment, and discover the natural world, including weather, animals, plants, and geologic structures. This person needs to go outside!

Musical

This could be described as Music Smart. It is the ability to learn through rhythm and melody, sing or play musical instruments, enjoy listening to music, remember songs, and study more effectively when music is played. This person needs music, whether it is music lessons or musical recordings.

Math/Logical

This could be described as Number Smart. It is the ability to reason mathematically, discover abstract patterns, classify and organize, enjoy mathematical computations, and think logically. This person needs to see the logic and organization in what is being learned.

Bodily-Kinesthetic

This could be described as Body Smart. It is the ability to use one's body through touch and movement to accomplish what is desired. It includes being able to process knowledge through bodily movement or through sensation, enjoying physical activity, and being constantly in motion even while sitting down. This person needs to move!

Interpersonal

This could be described as People Smart. It is the ability to understand and enjoy people. A person who is interpersonal learns best when other people are involved, whether through games, team work, or cooperative learning sessions. This person needs people.

Linguistic

This could be described as Word Smart. It is the ability to enjoy and use language through word games, books, recordings, trivia, poetry, papers, discussion, and other forms of using words. This person needs words in order to communicate.

Spatial

This could be described as Picture Smart. It is the ability to see in pictures rather than words, and includes drawing and design, three-dimensional constructing (such as Legos), and other visual arts (photography, sculpting, painting). This person needs pictures, maps, diagrams, charts, photos, and other visual/spatial material.

APPENDIX B

Worldviews in the Study of History: Our Approach to History

While attending a secular university, I took some anthropology courses. Anthropology is the scientific study of mankind, especially its origins, development, customs, and beliefs. At the very introduction to General Anthropology, I was alarmed and put on guard because it was announced that Christian missionaries were **always destructive** to the cultures they went to convert; that by changing the primitive peoples' belief systems and destroying their uniqueness with a western religion, the missionaries had ruined them. In sharp contrast, the anthropologists were engaged in the "scientific" study of these people groups and wouldn't think of changing anything about them (much like a "nature" photographer will take pictures of predators killing a baby elephant without doing anything to help preserve the life of the baby.)

One particular people group that we studied extensively in this class made a deep and lasting impression on me. They were the Dani of Irian Jaya (Papau New Guinea shares the same South Pacific island). The anthropologists studying the Dani had filmed them during the time that a small argument between a few escalated into a violent battle with many men killed. Throughout the film and the documents prepared on the Dani, we were "treated" to a look at a Stone Age tribe that was brutal, violent, aggressive, and dominated by a religion of evil spirits. This "scientific study" of the Dani left me with the sense of darkness and hopelessness because of the despair and depravity in this people group.

Twenty years later, I picked up the book, **Torches of Joy** by John Dekker (YWAM Publishing). Can you imagine the astonishment and delight when I discovered that this book was about a Christian missionary family that devoted themselves to the Dani people?! It described a complete, miraculous turnaround for these precious "Stone Age" people. The Dani burned their fetishes, forsook tribal warfare, and began to walk in the joy and freedom of their deliverer, Jesus Christ. The missionaries taught them basic medical knowledge, hygiene, nutrition; built fish ponds and imported fish so the Dani could increase the protein in their meager diets; helped set up trade stores which the Dani owned and operated; taught them how to read, so they could read the Bible in the newly written form of their oral language; discipled them in Biblical principles so the Dani men began to truly love their wives (rather than treating them as slaves), as well as loving their neighbors as themselves; appointed native leadership for the young church, which resulted in Dani missionaries actually going out to other tribal peoples in Irian Jaya!

The difference between these two approaches, between the "scientific study" of a Stone Age tribe by the anthropologists, and the compassionate, life giving ministry of the Christian missionaries, is the difference between darkness and light; the difference between secular humanism and biblical Christianity; it reveals how godless man looks at cultures and how God looks at people. Seeing with God's heart will prevent bigotry and hate, replacing it with outreach and compassion.

As we study ancient civilizations together, please remember this illustration because it will be the difference between

- learning merely the facts and figures of a people group,

OR...

- seeing fully the loving heart of God towards those people.

The first will give head knowledge of important data that may impress our audience and make us think that we really know a lot. However, the second will give heart understanding of God's involvement in human history, so that we might be effective ministers in obedience to the Lord of all.

As we learn the details of history, of ancient civilizations, of kingdoms and empires, scientific discoveries, explorations, and more, we will begin to see God's fingerprint on the lives of people and cultures. History will become a window of adventure as we observe His faithfulness and provision for those who seek Him, His timing in raising up one nation and bringing down another, His perfect ability to work through imperfect people, and His wonderful plan revealed in Jesus—to bring us to Himself—all of which is revealed in the Bible.

APPENDIX C

Teachers As Followers of the Lord

My journey in teaching history has taught me far more than the date Julius Caesar was assassinated. As the Lord has taken me on an amazing adventure of discovery, I have encountered the most unexpected sources in the most unusual places:

- *While visiting the British Museum, I noticed a small untitled sculpture. On my return to the U.S., during a Bible study on Abraham, Genesis 22:13 stood out: "Then Abraham lifted his eyes and looked, and there behind him was a ram caught in a thicket by its horns." My thoughts exploded as the small sculpture in London jumped back into my memory. Though unmarked in the exhibit, it was titled by the archaeologist who discovered it in a burial pit of ancient Ur, "The Ram Caught In The Thicket." Realizing that God might have placed a prophetic witness of His provision for Abraham in the pagan culture of Ur, I rushed home to research the dating of the sculpture, to see if Abraham had lived prior to its creation. Amazingly, it was made at least 200 hundred years before Abraham walked the earth!*

- *At a small country museum in Maine, a book title grabbed my attention:* Ninevah and Its Remains, *by Austen Layard. I had only a brief glance to see if it was useful in my studies. Opening the book at random, I began to read the author's description of how nineteenth century intellectuals had discounted the truth of Scripture, in part because of its description of the ancient Assyrians—who were totally unknown through any other source. With Layard's discovery and excavation of Ninevah, the Bible stories leaped squarely onto the pages of history AND shut the mouths of the critics! This opened my eyes to the amazing place Assyria has held in both world history and biblical apologetics.*

- *During a discussion concerning the Exodus, a friend casually handed me a book written by a man who had ascended Jebel El Lawz in Saudi Arabia. Larry Williams' experience, along with his co-adventurer, Bob Cornuke, presented a first-hand description of the Mountain of Moses, which, differing from traditional views, corresponds to the book of Exodus and Galatians 4:23. As I began to read, the realization that God had taken His people through the Red Sea and into Arabia brought a growing respect for how intricately accurate is the Word of God.*

Through these experiences, as well as many others, my eyes were opened to the fact that, though I was limited in my knowledge, God was actively leading me to keys of understanding—all I needed to do was follow Him. What an amazing discovery! He wants to lead us—you as much as me—to teach us, show us, and open doors of knowledge for us. If we ask, we will receive. If we seek, we will find. If we knock, the door will be opened.

You see, I find that God did not relegate the subject of education to a closed academic system (which would be similar to the evolutionists' view that we live in a "closed system"—one without God). Learning was intended by God to be **revelational**—because He, the source of all wisdom and knowledge, is intently involved in it:

> *"However, when He, the Spirit of truth, has come, He will guide you into **all** truth..." John 16:13*

As dearly beloved followers of Jesus Christ, we who are teachers need to understand this: the essential truth at the very foundation of education is that God is the True Teacher, the Master Teacher, the Actively-Changing-Lives Teacher. To teach as a "student teacher" under His authority and His leading will transform our hearts and attitudes, it will dramatically affect our students' experience, and, in the final analysis, it will reflect the heart of God.

Instead of a mere dispenser of facts, requiring our students to regurgitate the same facts back to us, we can teach with anticipation and a sense of wonder, expecting God to show us new insights, new connections, new understandings we never had before. We can enthusiastically and humbly share with our students what and how God has taught us, eagerly encouraging them to watch for His involvement in their own lives.

Practically, here are some points we need to consider as we follow God in teaching:

#1) Education that conforms to God's ways will first of all be **relational**, because He has called us to be His children (a profoundly intimate relationship with our Father), and He has set us in one Body (a necessarily cooperative, healthy, and interdependent relationship with each other).

> *"...whatever things are true, whatever things are noble, whatever things are just, whatever things are pure, whatever things are lovely, whatever things are of good report, if there is any virtue and if there is anything praiseworthy..."*

We learn about all subjects in relationship to Him. We see all fields of knowledge (biology, mathematics, physics, music, literature, history, architecture, etc.) as having their beginnings in God:

- He created all things (the sciences);

- He set order into the universe (mathematics);

- He created ears to hear the sounds of birds singing, leaves rustling, water swishing, AND He created voices for singing (music);

- He spoke the universe into existence AND gave us His Word (literature);

- He created man in His own image and likeness (the start of our history);

- He designed the world (architecture);

- ...and on and on and on.

We teach our students relationally, not as mechanical computers intent solely on transmitting facts—with no heart, no artistry, no intuition, no comprehension of others, no lively debates, no symbiotic learning, no creativity, no opportunity to defend oneself—but as brothers and sisters in the Body of Christ:

We honor them;
We allow individuality to them;
We listen to them;
We ask them;
We learn from them;
We respect them;
We humble ourselves before them;
. . . and on and on and on

#2) Education that conforms to God's ways will also be **revelational** because God actively leads us and guides us into all truth. We facilitate the students' learning, but He is the One who can communicate and bring illumination to the students in ways that will change their lives. God's revelation as the foundation of Christian education is dramatically opposed to the common system of education which looks no higher than human reason, and sets teachers as the authoritative experts in charge of distributing knowledge. This has its foundation in the Greco-Roman worldview:

> *"The ancient Greeks believed that humans could, by using their ability to think rationally, discover and understand the fundamental order of the universe and everything in it.... They developed the belief that humans could equal (and even exceed) the gods in understanding..." Dr. Perry Seymour, astrophysicist*

In other words, the ancient Greeks (and later, the Romans) depended solely on human reasoning rather than on God's revelation. This viewpoint is diametrically opposed by Scripture:

> *"For Jews request a sign, and Greeks seek after wisdom; but we preach Christ crucified, to the Jews a stumbling block and to the Greeks foolishness, but to those who are called, both Jews and Greeks, Christ the power of God and the wisdom of God." 1 Corinthians 1:22-24*

The Greeks enthroned human reason, educating and indoctrinating their students in this point of view. As Christians, we must choose a different path.

"Beware lest anyone cheat you through philosophy {such as, ancient Greek philosophy} and empty deceit, according to the tradition of men, according to the basic principles of the world, and not according to Christ." Colossians 2:8

We must enthrone Jesus Christ—the power of God and the wisdom of God—educating and discipling children in a biblical worldview. We can open doors for the students into their own personal adventure of discovery with the Lord. We can be their enthusiastic audience and wise advisors, encouraging them to learn in light of God's active and intimate revelation.

Teachers who follow the Lord, who teach under His Lordship, need to consider that biblical education:

• is both relational and revelational;

• leads us beyond mental comprehension to life application;

• has its beginning and ending in the character and nature of God;

• finds its true test, not in a graded essay question, but in a life lived in obedience—a life well-lived.

"Happy is the man who finds wisdom,
And the man who gains understanding;
For her proceeds are better than the profits of silver,
And her gain than fine gold.
She is more precious than rubies,
And all the things you may desire cannot compare with her.
Length of days is in her right hand,
In her left hand riches and honor.
Her ways are ways of pleasantness,
And all her paths are peace.
She is a tree of life to those who take hold of her,
And happy are all who retain her."

Proverbs 3:13-18

APPENDIX D

Supplemental Materials from the Student Manual

On the following pages you will find these items from the Student Manual:

- Introductory Articles

- Reviewed Resources

- Maps & Timelines

The pages are organized by Unit and can be used as a quick-reference guide instead of referring to the actual Student Manual.

UNIT 1 MATERIAL

Creation and the Flood

"In the beginning God..."

Article from Student Manual pages 21-28

Our study of human history begins at the very beginning of all things—Page One, if you will—with the focus and emphasis on the Creator. Many people who study history in our day do not start on that page. They begin with pre-historic man, just after he "evolved" from the ape—our supposed evolutionary predecessor! They have drawings of Neanderthal, photos of cave paintings, imaginative descriptions of the earliest humanoids. However, to those who recognize the reliability of Scripture for true knowledge and understanding—to those who accept the historic, scientific, and revelational truth of God's Word—the Bible becomes an insiders' look at the actual events of the beginning of history. You might consider it an absolutely accurate journalistic report of the "Lifestyles of the Perfect and Fallen." It is crucial to our understanding of history to start with the book of Genesis, which is an eyewitness account (with God being, obviously, the first and most reliable Eyewitness) of the earliest history of man. Armed with this insight and understanding, we will be well-equipped to take our journey together through the history of ancient times.

In the first chapter of Genesis, we discover the amazing story of how God created the planets, the sun and moon, the stars, the plants and animals, and how He saw that they were good. Then, as the crowning act of the Creation drama, God made man in His own image and likeness—male and female He created them. What does that mean? What does it mean to be created in the image and likeness of God Himself? The innumerable facets of this truth have occupied scholars and theologians for centuries. Interestingly enough, however, this is not merely an academic exercise for philosophers and ministers. It answers one of the deeply-felt needs common to all people in all time periods—"Who am I, and what value does my life possess?" This question is vitally important to each one of us, and when we discover in God's Word the answer (that I am a handmade creation of God, made in His very image), it provides what we need for living life with a purpose. I encourage you to spend some time considering this foundational question—"Who am I, and what value does my life possess?"—perhaps journalling or sharing with your family or another student.

When we read in Genesis 1 and 2 about the way God created everything to be good, even VERY good, and as we see Adam and Eve living in a perfect place (can you imagine?), questions may begin to arise concerning what it would be like today in the world if things had continued in this state of perfection. Take a minute to suspend the everyday reality around you and consider our world without the effect of sin: What would nations look like? How would marriages and family function? What would technology and the economy be like if they were being run by people without sin? How would the artists and musicians and writers and dancers in a perfect world perform, and what kind of masterpieces in art would we be seeing? What would be the impact on the animal kingdom—would the lion lie down with the lamb? It is important for us to remember that God created a perfect world, and that His plan for mankind was to live in that perfect world. So, what happened? What went wrong? Why is there evil and suffering in the world today? That question is another one of the most significant to all people throughout history, and the Bible holds for us a true and reliable answer.

Have you recognized that sometimes we hear a story so often that it becomes almost meaningless? It is kind of like repeating a nursery rhyme over and over and over again:

Pease porridge hot, pease porridge cold,
Pease porridge in the pot nine days old...

What on earth does that mean? Our answer would probably be, "Nothing," because it makes no sense to us today. In the very same way, we often relegate Scripture—especially the early chapters of Genesis—to a mindless storybook nonsense.

With that in mind, I'd like you to do something fresh and new. Please read these verses from Genesis 3 (on the next page) as if they were in vibrant technicolor with camera lighting and surround sound.

Much of the drama and tragedy in history has occurred because of the actual, historic event we term the Fall! Wars, enslavement, genocide, sickness and suffering of every kind can be directly traced back to the Fall of mankind in the Garden of Eden from relationship with God.

Remember my statement about our being made in the image and likeness of God? Consider that one vital aspect of our being made in the image and likeness of God is found in our capacity for relationship. Relationship. God, the holy Trinity—God the Father, God the Son, God the Holy Spirit—was in divine relationship, each with the other, from eternity. How do we know?

> *"Then God said, "Let US make man in OUR image, according to OUR likeness…"* Genesis 1:26

From the very beginning of time, human beings created in the image and likeness of God were made to be in relationship: relationship with God, relationship with one another, and relationship with the created world. It was to be a deep, intimate relationship, a day by day walking with God in the Garden, sharing all of the delights and discoveries of what He had created. The man's and woman's relationship was to be a human expression of this same kind of fellowship. He made us for relationship, deeper and more satisfying than anything we have ever imagined.

But, as we have discovered in Genesis 3, relationships were broken at the Fall of Man: the open and deep relationship between God and man, the fellowship and relationship between all people, and the relationship between people and the created world. As we'll see over the course of our study, the continuing effects of the Fall—evil and suffering of all kinds—are clearly visible throughout the pages of history.

However, along with this devastating thread of sorrows and suffering is woven the scarlet thread of Redemption. God, the Creator who made us in His image, did not leave us alone in our sufferings, but set in motion an unfolding drama beyond the wildest imaginings of Hollywood. He made a promise to the serpent which gave Adam and Eve hope of His infinite mercy and grace, which would impact all peoples throughout time.

> *"And I will put enmity between you and the woman, and between your seed and her Seed; He*

shall bruise your head and you shall bruise His heel." Genesis 3:15 (This is generally considered the first prophecy of Jesus.)

As we look at history, we will examine and consider these two threads woven into the pages of mankind: the sinful effects of the Fall and the powerful, redeeming grace of God. Another one of those significant questions people ask is, "What does history mean?" Keep your eyes open, looking for these threads of sin and Redemption, and you will have the answer to that question.

One of the first human tragedies after the Fall was the brokenness of relationship between Cain and Abel. Genesis 4 tells us Cain killed his brother because he was angry that the Lord had accepted Abel's sacrifice and not his own. Jealousy, anger, murder, lying are all visible at this very early moment in history. We also see the impact on the very ground that Cain had tilled—God told him that the ground would no longer yield its strength to him. What happens to a farmer when the ground produces nothing? It is devastating physically, emotionally, mentally, financially. The devastation surrounding Cain goes much further even than that. His relationship with his parents and other siblings is so broken that he is terrified one of them will kill him for his sin against Abel. Finally, as he cries out his anguish before God, we see the greatest devastation of all. He says, "Surely You have driven me out this day from the face of the ground; I shall be hidden from Your face…" His relationship with God is severed, at least from his perspective. This is an amazingly accurate picture of what happens to individuals, families, and nations when sin reigns unrestrained.

After this destruction, God made provision for His promise in Genesis 3:15 by giving another son, a godly son, to Adam and Eve. This son they named Seth, which means, "appointed," because Eve knew, "God has appointed another seed for me instead of Abel, whom Cain killed." It was from this line that Noah would eventually come.

As we wait for the days to unfold before the Flood, let us discover some of the amazing historical information contained in Scripture. Genesis 4:20-22 describes the offspring of the great, great, great grandson of Cain. We find the "father" of those who live in tents and have domesticated livestock (nomadic ranchers), the "father" of all those who play the harp and flute (concert musicians), and the "instructor" of every craftsman in bronze and iron (the local Tech School professor). These three areas of knowledge and skill are all considered to be aspects of high civilization. When you read a secular history book, you will be told that the domestication of animals was a huge step for evolutionary man, as it allowed a more dependable source of food. Music is one of the most advanced technologies of an advanced civilization, according to musicologists. And iron and bronze both require high levels of technology to obtain, which is not supposed to appear for several thousand years more.

So, why does the Bible describe this technology and advancement as present in the very early days of mankind while secularists today teach an opposite view? Is it because most history books today begin with evolution rather than Creation? If man has just recently evolved from pond scum, it will take him a while to evolve enough to be able to have "higher level" thinking skills. (For your consideration, the paleontological and archaeological data do not clearly support this theory). On the other hand, if Adam and Eve were handmade by the Creator God, in His very image, it would be perfectly reasonable to believe that they and their offspring were quite capable of thinking and creating. It is probable that they were actually more intelligent and able to create than people today, since they were so close to Creation and the Garden of Eden, and we, in all of our doings and all of our technology are but a poor representation of what early man was able to accomplish. Isn't that a wild thought! In fact, "OOP Arts" (out-of-place artifacts) display this very idea.

After more than fifteen hundred years (there is some debate about whether the genealogies of Genesis 5 give a definitive timeframe for the Flood), the Bible records this horrific truth:

> *"Then the Lord saw that the wickedness of man was great in the earth, and that every intent of the thoughts of his heart was only evil continually."* Genesis 6:5

Can you imagine a time when all but the family of Noah thought only evil thoughts every second of every day? With the long lives of men in the days before the Flood, evil men and women would have time to really develop their strategies of evil, and to train their offspring in all kinds of wickedness. If you have ever read the book, "Oliver Twist," you can imagine Fagin as a nine-hundred year old trainer of pickpockets. On how many generations would one man such as that have influence? It boggles the imagination! And the evil being committed was far more

deadly than mere pick pocketing. There was no reverence or honoring of God left in the earth, apart from Noah and his family.

The Scripture tells us that God was sorry that He had made man on the earth, and He was grieved in His heart (Genesis 6:6). God had intended such incredible blessings for mankind. He had created a world where people could walk in deep fellowship with God Himself, and in deep fellowship with the people and the creation around them. He had established a place of beauty and creativity, filled with every joy and delight imaginable, all at their disposal. But each of these amazingly good things was thrown away by mankind at this point, like so much rotting garbage. Evil was what they wanted, evil was what they craved, evil was the only thing that brought satisfaction—but that in the same way that heroin satisfies the addict, only for a moment, and then the craving returns.

God made His plans for destroying the earth, but He did not carry them out immediately. He told Noah, a man who walked in relationship with Him (Genesis 6:9), about these plans for destruction, and instructed him to build an ark. It is fascinating to consider that the God who had spoken the worlds into existence, and who could certainly have miraculously provided an ark at the moment He decided to destroy the earth, instead gave the hundred-twenty year task to a "preacher of righteousness" (2 Peter 2:5). Why the delay? Why give evil men another hundred plus years to commit heinous acts? What does Scripture say?

> *"The Lord is not slack concerning His promise, as some count slackness, but is longsuffering toward us, not willing that any should perish but that all should come to repentance."* 2 Peter 3:9

We see at this moment the twin threads of man's sin and God's mercy. Through the very visible building of the Ark, and through the preaching of Noah, God was giving men a chance to repent and escape the deluge. Tragically, only Noah's wife, three sons and their three wives listened to Noah's warnings. They, along with a God-ordained selection of each kind of animal in the animal kingdom, escaped the worldwide flood which not only destroyed the rest of mankind but dramatically changed the world itself. No longer would men live seven, eight or nine hundred years. Instead, lives would be shortened considerably, to the point where seventy years was considered normal. The original atmosphere, designed by God to gently water and nourish the earth, was changed to what we know today—capable of floods, droughts, storms, cyclones, hurricanes, tornados, and other weather-induced tragedies. The Bible also records a dramatic change between mankind and the animal kingdom,

"And the fear of you and the dread of you shall be on every beast of the earth, on every bird of the

air, on all that move on the earth, and on all the fish of the sea..." Genesis 9:2

From this point on, the world will look much like we see it today. Civilizations will rise and fall, discoveries will be made and forgotten, people will live and die, and throughout time, we will encounter the two threads woven in and out of our story, HisStory.

Reviewed Resources for Digging Deeper:
From Student Manual pages 32-35

Creation

Unlocking the Mysteries of Creation by Dennis Peterson

This is an eye-opening book about Creation! Divided into three sections, it deals with evidences for a young earth, the questions about fossils and dinosaurs, and fascinating discoveries showing the astonishing accomplishments of early man (early civilizations). **AA**

Adam & His Kin by Ruth Beechick

A speculative, but fascinating look at what life might have been like during the first several chapters of Genesis. **RA UE+**

The Great Dinosaur Mystery and the Bible by Paul S. Taylor

Children often want to know, "What about the dinosaurs?" when we talk about Creation. This is a great picture book to introduce the answers on a child's level (though I learned a lot too!). **E+**

Understanding The Times (abridged edition) by David Noebel

This book (especially Ch. 15 through 18) will greatly help to clarify the worldview positions of evolutionists and creationists. We think it is absolutely critical to understand the issue of worldview, and of its impact on every branch of learning. Dr. Noebel has written an excellent resource. **HS**

Darwin on Trial by Phillip E. Johnson

"The controversial book that rocked the scientific establishment! Why? It shows that the theory of evolution is based not on fact but on faith—faith in philosophical naturalism." This fascinating book was written by a professor of law, and is laid out so simply that the nonscientist can follow the arguments. It is very helpful for understanding the fallacies in the evolutionist argument. **HS**

Darwin's Black Box—The Biochemical Challenge to Evolution by Michael L. Behe

Don't let the subtitle scare you. This is a very readable book about a very complex subject. The result is that the reader will have an entirely new arsenal of defenses against evolution. Fascinating! **HS**

Reasonable Faith—The Scientific Case for Christianity by Dr. Jay Wile

Dr. Wile's book is a well-written, well-researched apologetic (defense) of Christianity. It describes the scientific evidences for God's intelligent design in creation, along with amazing descriptions of God's scientific reasons for some of the commands He gave (i.e. circumcision on the 8th day). **MS+**

The Creation Interpretation—A Basic Biblical View of Science and Natural History by Catie Frates

An excellent introduction to Creation science for younger students. Highly recommended! **UE+**

Fearfully & Wonderfully Made by Dr. Paul Brand & Philip Yancey

Discover the amazing ways God has designed people in this story-filled book. It would make a great book for short read alouds and discussions. **MS+**

In Six Days—Why 50 Scientists Choose to Believe in Creation edited by John Ashton, Ph.D.

There is a general view in the media and Hollywood that only ignorant buffoons believe in Creation. This book debunks that myth quite handily with essays by 50 scientists who hold doctorates from State-recognized universities. **HS**

Buried Alive—The Startling Truth About Neanderthal Man by Jack Cuozzo

A Creation scientist recommended this book to us, and we found it an incredible read! It is more like a spy thriller than a science book, but one discovers through the real life adventure of an orthodontist, the amazing fraud perpetrated on the public concerning ancient man. Worth the search! **MS+**

The Flood

Dry Bones and Other Fossils by Dr. Gary Parker

Written in an engaging style for children, this is a captivating, information-filled book that will give a basic understanding of the Flood and its impact on the earth. **E+**

Noah's Ark by Rien Poortvliet

This is an oversize beautiful book of paintings and sketches about Noah's Ark. It is quite expensive, so check to see if your library can get it. **AA**

The True Story of Noah's Ark: It's Not Just For Kids Anymore by Tom Dooley

With beautiful illustrations, this book will appeal to adults as well as children. **AA**

The Genesis Flood by Whitcomb and Morris

This is an excellent resource for understanding the scientific evidences for the biblical Flood, as well as the inadequacies of evolution to explain what is seen in the geologic, archaeological, and fossil record. **HS**

General

History of the World by Josephus; Edited by Paul Maier

Josephus was a Jewish historian who survived the destruction of Jerusalem in 70 A.D. He was taken to Rome and befriended by Emperor Titus, who asked Josephus to write an account of the history of the Jews. An original source document and one of the few histories written in antiquity, this book is a veritable gold mine of information. **MS+**

Genesis—Finding Our Roots by Ruth Beechick

Believing that Genesis forms the foundation of our understanding of all of life's major questions, Dr. Beechick has created this fascinating, insightful book which provides students the opportunity to study in depth the first eleven chapters of Genesis. **UE+**

The Discovery of Genesis by C.H. Kang and Ethel R. Nelson

This incredible book shows the book of Genesis, in tremendous detail, as depicted in ancient Chinese pictographs (or ideograms). The authors' contention is that the founding of China in circa 2500 B.C. was close enough to the time of the Tower of Babel that the memory of what had occurred prior was still fresh in the minds of the Chinese people. Highly recommended! **MS+**

The Puzzle of Ancient Man by Dr. Donald Chittick

Dr. Chittick has compiled an astonishing selection of OOP Arts (Out Of Place Artifacts) with a thoroughly biblical explanation. Worth searching for! **MS+**

The Answers Book—The 20 Most-Asked Questions About Creation, Evolution, and the Book of Genesis, Answered! by Ken Ham, Jonathan Sarfati, Carl Wieland

This book is worth purchasing, as it will be referred to over and over again. The questions are pertinent questions students ask and the answers are well-researched and very understandable. **UE+**

Ancient History from Primary Sources by Harvey & Laurie Bluedorn

Including the literature of Egypt, Mesopotamia, Greece and Rome, this compilation is an excellent resource. **MS+**

For more books, use these Dewey Decimal numbers in your library:

Bible: #220

Genealogy: #929

Creation: #213

Evolution: #575

Fossils & Prehistoric Life: #560

Ancient History: #930

Ancient Middle & Near Eastern: #930

Ancient Mesopotamia & Iranian Plateau: #935

Phase 2

➤ *Timeline*

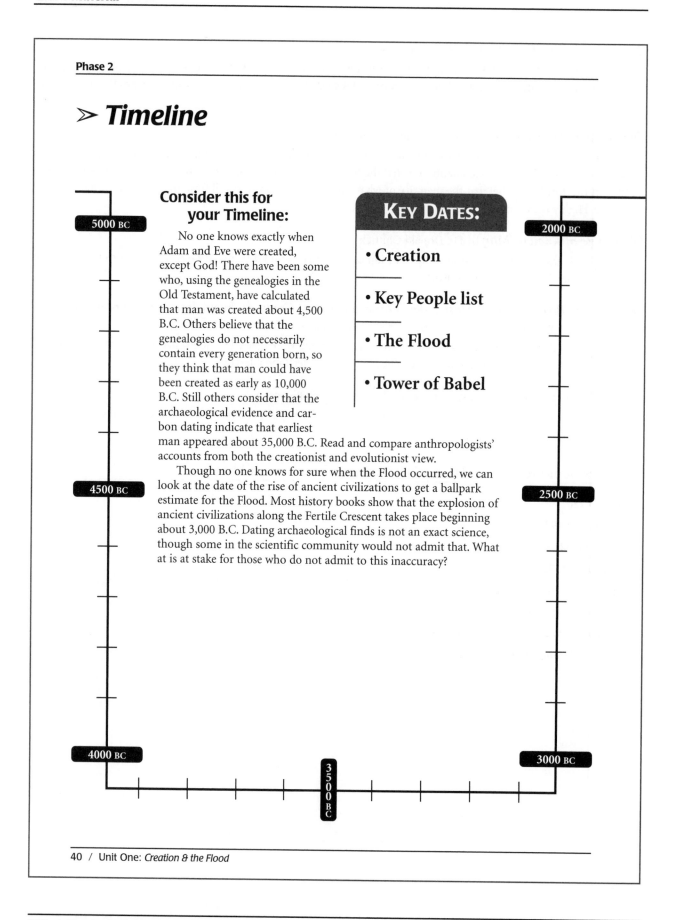

5000 BC

Consider this for your Timeline:

No one knows exactly when Adam and Eve were created, except God! There have been some who, using the genealogies in the Old Testament, have calculated that man was created about 4,500 B.C. Others believe that the genealogies do not necessarily contain every generation born, so they think that man could have been created as early as 10,000 B.C. Still others consider that the archaeological evidence and carbon dating indicate that earliest man appeared about 35,000 B.C. Read and compare anthropologists' accounts from both the creationist and evolutionist view.

Though no one knows for sure when the Flood occurred, we can look at the date of the rise of ancient civilizations to get a ballpark estimate for the Flood. Most history books show that the explosion of ancient civilizations along the Fertile Crescent takes place beginning about 3,000 B.C. Dating archaeological finds is not an exact science, though some in the scientific community would not admit that. What at is at stake for those who do not admit to this inaccuracy?

KEY DATES:

• Creation

• Key People list

• The Flood

• Tower of Babel

2000 BC

4500 BC

2500 BC

4000 BC

3000 BC

3500 BC

ad maiorem Dei gloriam!

© 2004 Geography Matters

Unit One: *Creation & the Flood* / 43

UNIT 2 MATERIAL

The Rise of Civilizations

The adventures of early mankind continue...

Article from Student Manual pages 53-59

As Noah and his family came out of the Ark and began a new life in a vastly changed world, we see described in the Bible the foundations of nations, the emergence of many languages, and the first of the world empires. There is contained within those first post-Flood people the latent effect of pre-Flood problems: active rebellion, willful disobedience, and separation from God. But with these problems also comes the second thread of God's provision and promise of redemption, as we shall soon discover in the life of Abraham.

> *"Now the sons of Noah who went out of the ark were Shem, Ham and Japheth. And Ham was the father of Canaan. These three were the sons of Noah, and from these the whole earth was populated."* Genesis 9:18-19

Isn't it amazing to consider that everyone who lives on the face of the earth today is a descendant of Ham, Shem or Japheth, which, of course, means that we are all descendants of their father, Noah! The Bible gives in great detail the geographic locations and specific family names of the early descendants of the three sons of Noah in Genesis 10, which is often called the "Table of Nations." Simply put, the descendants of Japheth were the northern people (who inhabited the northern coastal regions of the Mediterranean), the descendants of Ham were the southern people (who migrated to the southern part of Mesopotamia, as well as Egypt), while the descendants of Shem were the people of the central area in the Middle East (as far north as Syria and as far south as Arabia). From these early days, and for various reasons including the Ice Age, drought, warfare, "greener pastures," and exploration, tribes of people began to colonize the entire earth—from the continents to the islands, from North to South, and from East to West.

The Bible tells us that God used this movement of people across the face of the earth for His redemptive purpose, to give each people group the hunger and opportunity to seek the Lord in their unique settings and circumstances:

> *"And He has made from one blood every nation of men to dwell on all the face of the earth; and has determined their preappointed times and the boundaries of their habitation, so that they should seek the Lord..."* Acts 17:26-27a

Genesis 11 gives us a very descriptive account of the attitudes and plans of the people of earth at this post-Flood moment. As they came to the plains of Shinar (the very fertile area between the Euphrates and the Tigris rivers in the area of Babylon), they said,

> *"Come, let us build ourselves a city, and a tower whose top is in the heavens; let us make a name for ourselves, lest we be scattered abroad over the face of the whole earth."* Genesis 11:4

Notice whose name they were intent on glorifying! Do you see in their words an attitude of trust in God? How instead would you describe their attitude? These descendants of Noah were evidently not concerned with walking in obedience to the Lord who had told their ancestors to "be fruitful and multiply, and fill the earth." You can almost see mankind thumbing its nose at the God in whose image they were made. It is sobering to consider how quickly we, as the race of mankind, forget His goodness and mercy, even His miraculous provision to us, and turn our face towards rebellion.

The Scriptures describe the phenomenal power that was available when they had one mind and one language among all the people. The fact that they were of one mind and their hearts were set to do evil, combined with this ability to communicate freely, without the misunderstandings common when two or more languages are present, unleashed an unstoppable ability to accomplish whatever post-Flood mankind wanted to do, as they worked together in their rebellion.

> *"Indeed the people are one and they all have one language, and this is what they begin to do; now nothing that they propose to do will be withheld from them."* Genesis 11:6

In His mercy and long-suffering, God chose not to destroy mankind again, but to supernaturally and permanently confuse their language, so that they would no longer be able to plot and plan rebellion unimpeded. Can you imagine these people suddenly unable to understand what their neighbor was so emphatically trying to tell them? Picture for a moment the terror and fear that must have accompanied this dramatic change, as they struggled to find anyone with whom they could converse. Breathlessly they would run from place to place trying to find their husbands, wives, mothers, fathers, children. We could assume that nuclear families spoke the same tongue—be it an early form of Chinese, Arabic, French, German, Japanese, English, Latin, Hebrew, Spanish, Greek, Babylonian, Celtic, or any of thousands more. Perhaps a few close relatives would have at least a related language and could join them as they began to make plans to flee from the center of such confusion. Whether or not we can accurately reconstruct the scenario, God used this moment to scatter our ancestors over the face of the earth. His plan for the boundaries of their habitation and their preappointed times would be fulfilled, whether they were willing or not.

(Those who study languages and their history have proposed that at one point in the misty past there was a "protolanguage," the mother language for us all. Interesting how the Bible told how this happened to those of us who would listen!)

Genesis 10:8-10 describes one of the great grandsons of Noah as a builder of cities and as a mighty hunter before the Lord. This one man, Nimrod, received such prominence in Scripture because he was a "mover and shaker" in the earth, building such notable cities as Babel (or Babylon, capitol city of the Babylonian civilization), Erek (ancient Uruk, a city close to Ur), Akkad (the Akkadian empire was an early power in Mesopotamia), Nineveh (one of the capitol cities of the Assyrian civilization), and Calah (later called Nimrud, after its builder). Though we have limited information in Scripture concerning this man, it is obvious just from this list of foun-

dational cities that he was a power to be reckoned with (notice that three of the cities that Nimrod built were centers of mighty pagan empires), and that as a "mighty hunter before the Lord," he was held in awe by the people who followed him. There have been scholars who, based on Scripture and the writings of antiquity, believe that Nimrod actually headed the rebellion at the Tower of Babel, and was the world's first dictator. Unger's Bible Handbook points out that there is a tremendous difference in the character of a godly leader—a "shepherd" of the people—and a godless leader—a "hunter." Consider that carefully. Would you prefer to be ruled over by one known as a "shepherd" (like David) or by one known as a "hunter" (like Nimrod)? That should give a comparative taste of what it may have been like to live in the time of Nimrod.

From this moment of man's rebellion and God's scattering, we see the evidence of civilizations in the archaeological record. From the ancient Chinese to the Indus Valley, from Ur to Egypt, from the Minoans to the Olmecs, mankind continues to build with the technology and knowledge gained before the Flood and retained in their memory. Ancient Ziggurats and even more venerable pyramids dot the landscape of antiquity with puzzling regularity. Discoveries in archaeology show that ancient music had many common characteristics in civilizations widely separated across the globe. Gigantic, carved stone heads were found in Central America showing the distinctive looks of two different people groups—European and African—neither of which were native to the region! These discoveries, along with ancient maps, such as the Piri Reis Map containing the actual coastline of Antarctica (which was not known by modern geographers until the 1900's!), show that there was a tremendous amount of travel in antiquity with the accompanying technologies of boat building, surveying, navigating, and economics. (There is evidence of trade between widely divergent ancient cultures across the earth.)

Rather than a glimpse of primitive man barely able to outrun the saber tooth tigers, slowly banding together into small communities, and eventually into larger cities, resulting, after many thousands of years, in what we call "civilization", we see rather a highly technical, fully developed group of civilizations which seem to pop up in the archaeological record without warning. It is disconcerting to secular historians and archaeologists, to say the least. Remember, they have even given an acronym to describe this "phenomena" in the archaeological record—OOP Arts!

It might be helpful at this point to discuss the functions and limitations of archaeology. Archaeology comes from two root words which mean "ancient" and "study." So it is the study of antiquity through the material remains (such as fossils, relics, artifacts, and monuments). This is a recent branch of science, dating from the 1800's, and is different from the other pure sciences, like physics or chemistry, since it does not provide an opportunity to test one's hypothesis in the lab over and over again. Instead, it is a matter of searching for the proverbial needle in a haystack of stone, dirt and rubble. There have been some absolutely spectacular finds in archaeology that have illuminated the historic past in fascinating and incredible ways, which we will examine in later chapters. However, archaeology is also significantly **limited** in that the discoveries are partial, fragmentary, perhaps even misleading at times.

To explain what I mean, imagine you and your family went through a holiday time where you ate box after box after box of chocolate-covered cherries. All the empty boxes filled a metal trash can, and before the garbage truck could remove the debris, the garbage can was swept away by a minor flood into a mud pit. Hundreds of years later, archaeologists suddenly discover your garbage can. If they don't find anyone else's garbage from your neighborhood, they may erroneously conclude that people of your region in your time period lived solely on chocolate-covered cherries! Though that seems silly to us, it is the kind of struggle archaeologists deal with since they simply don't know what they have not yet found. They are left to make assumptions with the collection of material they *have* found.

Archaeology is a wonderful tool for the historian, but it is not nearly as reliable as the Bible itself. So, as you read about discoveries in archaeology, always remember that it does not hold the whole story nor the eternal perspective. If archaeologists, or historians interpreting archaeological finds, say that their discovery disproves the Bible, recognize that their tools are falling apart and need to be replaced!

One of the earliest cities found in the archaeological record is the city of Ur, with its ziggurat, its worship of the moon goddess, and its royal tombs with ornate harps and perfectly coiffured dead servants. The Bible tells us a fascinating truth about Ur: it was a place for a *friend of God* to get out of!

> *"Now the Lord had said to Abram: 'Get out of your country, from your kindred and from your father's house, to a land that I will show you. I will make you a great nation; I will bless you and make your name great; and you shall be a blessing. I will bless those who bless you, and I will curse him who curses you; and in you all the families of the earth shall be blessed."*
> Genesis 12:1-3

As Abram obeyed, he journeyed from the very southern end of Mesopotamia (close to the Persian Gulf) all the way to Canaan (by the Mediterranean), and then on to Egypt. We see in the Biblical account a description of pharaohs, kings, armies, cities, battles, and amazing deliverances out of dangerous situations! Even from this early time in human history, we have all the intrigues, all the greed, all the lust, all the evil that whirl through our cultures today. The names and dates have changed, but the basic ways we deal with one another have not changed at all. Mercifully, God has continued throughout the ages to work in us and through us, and often in spite of us. He never wound the earth up and walked away.

From the rebellion of the Tower of Babel to the blessing God intended through Abraham, we see the two threads continuing to weave through the pages of HisStory. From here, the Bible begins to follow the specific steps of Abraham and his descendants. Though there are many other stories of antiquity, even stories of God's amazing work in preserving the knowledge of Himself in ancient cultures (a fascinating study!), we will pursue the story of Abraham's seed and the various civilizations and cultures which the Bible describes. Through this we will watch the unfolding of God's marvelous plan to bless "**all** the families of the earth."

Reviewed Resources for Digging Deeper:

From Student Manual pages 62-65

Biblical Perspective

After the Flood by Bill Cooper

This is one of the MOST amazing books concerning the truth of the Scriptures! Mr. Cooper spent more than twenty years examining the accuracy of the Table of Nations in Genesis 10, and found the descendants of Ham, Shem and Japheth throughout the pagan king lists—which are the best chroniclers of families and chronologies in the ancient world. One of the watershed books of our time. Highly Recommended! **HS**

The Puzzle of Ancient Man by Donald E. Chittick

Dr. Chittick has compiled an astonishing selection of OOP Arts (Out Of Place Artifacts) with a thoroughly biblical explanation. Worth searching for! **MS+**

The NewUnger's Bible Handbook by Merrill F. Unger, Revised by Gary N. Larson

This book is one of my most-used reference books in the study of ancient history and the Bible. Highly recommended! **MS+**

Asia: A Christian Perspective by Mary Ann Lind

Published by YWAM Publishing, this book is filled with information about Asia. Though our main focus in this study guide is the rise of civilization in the Fertile Crescent, Egypt and Greece, there are many other early civilizations found in the archaeological record. What I found particularly helpful about this book was the historical background of some of these civilizations such as India and China. This book tells about the rise of Confucianism, Hinduism, and Buddhism—a significant part of understanding Asian cultures and early Asian civilizations. **MS+**

Strongholds of the 10-40 Window edited by George Otis, Jr.

Published by YWAM Publishing, this is an intercessor's guide to the world's least evangelized nations. It includes basic facts, historical background, Christian outreach and specific prayer requests from resident Christians. This book will help you turn *head knowledge* to *heart compassion* as you pray for the nations. **MS+**

Archaeology

Then & Now by Perring & Perring

A fascinating look at the archaeological ruins of antiquity by two British archaeologists. This was the book that shows the ruins of Nimrud (in ancient Assyria), which was built originally by Nimrod! Includes several civilizations that we will be studying in this study guide. Each picture of an ancient site is accompanied by a full color overlay depicting how that place would have looked in its prime. **AA**

Treasures from Bible Times by Alan Millard

If you can find this book, you will have found a treasure indeed. Beautiful pictures, archaeological data and helpful maps make this a tremendous resource. **MS+**

Old Testament Archaeology and the Bible by Dr. Alfred Hoerth

Not a book, this is actually a full-color chart from Rose Publishing, which lists archaeological finds, a description of them, and their importance to Bible students. A great tool! **UE+**

Mesopotamia by Julian Reade

For those with access to books from the British Museum, this book will prove a fascinating look at early Mesopotamia, including Ur. This is the book where I learned that there was a mass-produced, bevelled-rim bowl which was probably used the way we use throw away wrappers on fast food! **HS+**

The Bible in the British Museum by T. C. Mitchell

Another incredible resource from the British Museum, this book lists all of the artifacts in the museum that reference Bible events, times or people. **HS+**

The Usborne Young Scientist: Archaeology by Barbara Cork & Struan Reid

A brief, concise overview of what archaeologists do and some of what they have found. Excellent pictures help to tell the story. **UE+**

Archaeology for Kids by Richard Panchyk

For students truly interested in understanding archaeology, this is a hands-on, activity based approach. You may want to skip the sections on early man. **UE+**

Dig This! How Archaeologists Uncover Our Past by Michael Avi-Yonah

This a great introduction to the ways and means of archaeologists. It has lots of pictures of archaeological digs, which is tremendously helpful in trying to understand what a dig is really like. **E+**

Digging to the Past: Excavations in Ancient Lands by W. John Hackwell

This children's book has wonderful descriptions of excavating archaeological sites. Even if you can't find this book or the one listed above, try to find an elementary book on archaeology so your students will be able to comprehend the incredible "detective work" that is necessary to decipher ruins. **E+**

Treasures Under the Sand—Wooley's Finds at Ur by Alan Honour

This is an incredible book if you can find it! It is a children's biography of Leonard Wooley, the man who began excavating Ur in 1922. (*Unfortunately, the author's worldview doesn't see the Bible as literal history, and so the chronologies and explanations of the Old Testament events in this book are mistaken.*) Even with this problem, I still recommend it. This is the book that describes, among other things, Wooley's work with T.E. Lawrence—Lawrence of Arabia—prior to WWI. **UE+**

Gods, Graves and Scholars by C. W. Ceram

Often listed as required reading for college-level archaeology, this is an absolutely riveting book describing the real-life adventures of archaeologists from the 1800's to the early 1900's. The author's worldview is not a Biblical worldview, but he unwittingly continues to relate astonishing evidences pointing to the inerrancy of the Bible! Wondering if this book was really interesting, I asked my junior and senior high boys to read it. They couldn't put it down! **MS+**

Cities

City Planning in Ancient Times by Richard Currier

This book shows the high level of city planning found in even the earliest civilizations. It is a very good introduction to what goes into planning cities. **UE+**

Street Smart! Cities of the Ancient World

Another book showing how well planned many of the cities of antiquity were. Fascinating reading! **E+**

Antiquity

Ancient Crete by Frances Wilkins

A fascinating look at an ancient civilization that was not known until the early 1900's. The Minoans were a highly advanced people whose civilization flourished around 2900 B.C. **UE+**

The Sumerians by Elaine Landau

It is difficult to find books which are both appropriate and understandable for younger students about this time period. This book, however, is worth the search. **E+**

Dazzling! Jewelry of the Ancient World

Jewelry is an art form, it involves advanced technology, is a form of economics and was seen to be valuable in the afterlife. For example, the ancient royal tombs in Ur, excavated by Leonard Wooley, were found to contain vast quantities of jewelry. **E+**

General

Kingfisher Illustrated History of the World

This is the best resource book for world history that we've seen. Though offered by a secular publisher, it is an excellent tool for seeing the "big picture" in history. **UE+**

Ancient Times—A Watts Guide for Children by Guy I. Austrian

Set in alphabetical order, this book is a series of short articles about people, ancient nations, early developments such as the alphabet, and concepts such as democracy. This would make a good resource. **UE+**

Usborne World History—Ancient World by Fiona Chandler

If you are familiar with Usborne books, you know that they are filled with short descriptions and great pictures. This is a wonderful, concise, fact-filled book about ancient nations and people. **E+**

For more books, use these Dewey Decimal numbers in your library:

Bible: #220

Ancient History: #930

Ancient Middle & Near Eastern: #930

Ancient Mesopotamia & Iranian Plateau: #935

Archaeology: #930.1

Also, look for biographies on the archaeologists listed.

Phase 2

➤ *Timeline*

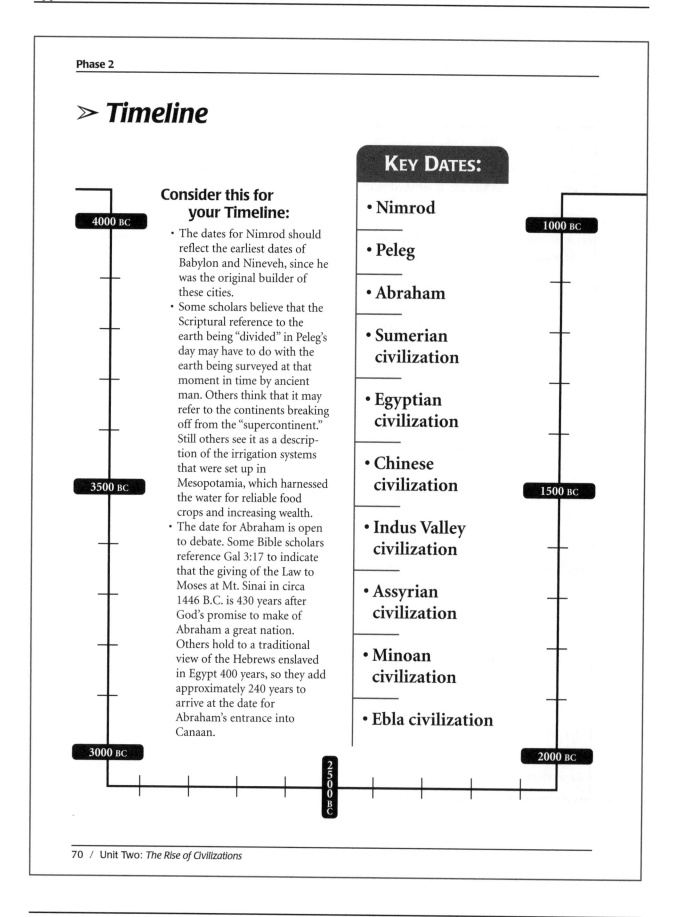

4000 BC

3500 BC

3000 BC

Consider this for your Timeline:

- The dates for Nimrod should reflect the earliest dates of Babylon and Nineveh, since he was the original builder of these cities.
- Some scholars believe that the Scriptural reference to the earth being "divided" in Peleg's day may have to do with the earth being surveyed at that moment in time by ancient man. Others think that it may refer to the continents breaking off from the "supercontinent." Still others see it as a description of the irrigation systems that were set up in Mesopotamia, which harnessed the water for reliable food crops and increasing wealth.
- The date for Abraham is open to debate. Some Bible scholars reference Gal 3:17 to indicate that the giving of the Law to Moses at Mt. Sinai in circa 1446 B.C. is 430 years after God's promise to make of Abraham a great nation. Others hold to a traditional view of the Hebrews enslaved in Egypt 400 years, so they add approximately 240 years to arrive at the date for Abraham's entrance into Canaan.

KEY DATES:

- Nimrod
- Peleg
- Abraham
- Sumerian civilization
- Egyptian civilization
- Chinese civilization
- Indus Valley civilization
- Assyrian civilization
- Minoan civilization
- Ebla civilization

1000 BC

1500 BC

2000 BC

2500 BC

70 / Unit Two: *The Rise of Civilizations*

© 2004 Geography Matters

ad maiorem Dei gloriam!

Unit Two: *The Rise of Civilizations* / 73

UNIT 3 MATERIAL

Egypt & the Exodus

Let my people go...

Article from Student Manual pages 83-93

"Go and gather the elders of Israel together, and say to them, 'The Lord God of your fathers, the God of Abraham, of Isaac, and of Jacob, appeared to me, saying, "I have surely visited you and seen what is done to you in Egypt; and I have said I will bring you up out of the affliction of Egypt to the land of the Canaanites and the Hittites and the Amorites and the Perizzites and the Hivites and the Jebusites, to a land flowing with milk and honey." Exodus 3:16-17

Egypt. Land of mystery and antiquity, the scene of biblical refuge and tyrannical slavery, home of the pharaohs and the pyramids, a place where the complex process of mummification was extended even to crocodiles... one of the most fascinating places on earth. Geographically unusual, Egypt is a long, narrow strip of rich, dark earth in northeastern Africa bordered by the unrelenting dryness of the desert, drawing its life from the annual flooding of the Nile River. At the time Abraham journeyed there to escape famine in Canaan, the Great Pyramid had already been standing more than three hundred years, mute testimony to the technology and drive of an earlier pharaoh. Beauty, wealth, medicine, mathematics, technology, military might, vast trade networks—this was the culture of ancient Egypt. But, along with all of its wonders, Egypt at this time embraced a polytheistic (many gods) religion, in which even the lowly cat was seen as divine. This brought a terrible bondage and darkness to the Egyptian people, and eventually, as we shall see, it brought a catastrophic confrontation between the Creator of the Egyptians and the gods of the Egyptians.

But that's jumping ahead! Let's return to the journey of Abraham and bring the story up to speed. God had promised that He would make of him a great nation and through him "all the families of the earth would be blessed." (Genesis 12:1-3) So Abraham and his wife, Sarah (called Abram and Sarai until God changed their names at the time of His covenant with them—Genesis 17), moved

lock, stock, and barrel to the area of Canaan, located between the Jordan River and the Mediterranean Sea. During a local famine, Abram and Sarai traveled to the bountiful land of Egypt. Genesis 12 gives a fascinating description of Abram's unusual encounter with the reigning Pharaoh. Using the new Egyptian chronology suggested by David Rohl (see the end of this article for more information), it is possible to theorize that Abram's brief sojourn in Egypt was toward the end of the time period known to historians as the "Old Kingdom."

The Old Kingdom is also known as the Pyramid Age, since it was the time that the most magnificent pyramids were built. When the Nile was in flood and the farmers could not work the land, the pharaohs had them work alongside craftsmen to build these gigantic tombs. It has been estimated that perhaps as many as 100,000 men labored for twenty years (four months at a time) to build each one of the pyramids. That's a LOT of manpower! The Old Kingdom was also known for it's intellectual achievements in medicine, engineering, mathematics, and astronomy. Towards the end of this kingdom, the pharaohs lost increasing amounts of tax revenue and governmental power over the outlying "nomes," or districts. After several years of insufficient flooding of the Nile, many nomarchs (or governors of nomes), declared themselves kings, and Egypt slid into the chaos of the First Intermediate Period.

When Abram and Sarai returned to Canaan, they took matters into their own hands concerning what God had told Abram about becoming the father of descendants more numerous than the stars of heaven. After a sticky relational mess between Abraham, Sarah and Sarah's maid resulted in a son named Ishmael (the beginning of the Arab nation), God told Abraham that, despite his and Sarah's advanced age, they would, indeed, bear a son to fulfill the promise God had given. When Sarah heard this, she laughed. Thus her son, born the following year, was given the name "Isaac" which means laughter! From this son and his son, Jacob, the nation known as Israel was born. Isn't it amazing that from Abraham came two mighty nations, and the source of three world religions—Judaism, Christianity, and Islam! What do you think would be the impact on the world today if Abraham and Sarah had trusted God's timing for a son, rather than trying to help bring about the promise of an heir through Hagar, Sarah's maidservant?

Fast forwarding through the next several chapters of Genesis, we meet Joseph, Jacob's favored son. Joseph—the dreamer of dreams, the wearer of a many-colored coat, the hated of his brothers—was secretly sold as a slave to traders heading to Egypt (Genesis 37). Using the new Egyptian chronology, we may theorize that Joseph was taken to Egypt during the Twelfth Dynasty in the years of the Middle Kingdom.

Egypt began to recover from the confusion of the First Intermediate Period when Mentuhotpe reunited the country in the Eleventh Dynasty. By far the most important dynasty of the Middle Kingdom, however, was the Twelfth. It began when the vizier Amenemhet took the reigns of power and made himself Pharaoh. He moved the capital from Memphis to Itjawy (whose site is not certain, but may be in the Nile Delta). There is not agreement between Bible scholars concerning which Pharaoh was the Pharaoh who elevated Joseph to the position of vizier (second in command of the kingdom). However, it seems most likely, with the information that is currently available to Bible-believing scholars, that this was either Senwosret I or Amenemhet III.

In Genesis 41, we are told that one night this Pharaoh had a disturbing dream about cows. No one in his retinue of magicians and wise men could interpret the dream, which made him very angry. Suddenly, his chief butler remembered his fellow prisoner who had correctly interpreted a dream.

> *"Then Pharaoh sent and called Joseph, and they brought him hastily out of the dungeon; and he shaved, changed his clothing, and came to Pharaoh."* Genesis 41:14

Isn't the Bible great in its details? Not only are we told that Pharaoh called for him, but we get a glimpse of the great commotion this caused the jailers. You can almost see them falling all over themselves, trying to find Joseph a razor (the Egyptians liked to be clean-shaven!) and some decently fitting clothes appropriate for an audience with an angry Pharaoh.

When Joseph appears, Pharaoh tells him that he has a reputation of being able to interpret dreams. Listen to Joseph's reply:

> *"It is not in me; God will give Pharaoh an answer of peace."* Genesis 41:16

Who receives the glory from that statement? How is that attitude different from the builders of the tower of Babel (Genesis 4:11)? How is it different from those today who want to get close to someone who is powerful or famous? Joseph was not into promoting Joseph, he was into glorifying God. And that was so amazingly refreshing to the Pharaoh, that when he heard Joseph's interpretation of the dream and his recommendation to prepare for the famine during the time of plenty, he decided to make Joseph, a thirty-year old Hebrew foreigner and former slave/prisoner, his vizier—second-in-command throughout the land of Egypt!

> *"You shall be over my house, and all my people shall be ruled according to your word; only in regard to the throne will I be greater than you... See, I have set you over all the land of Egypt."* Genesis 41:40-41

During the time of tremendous plenty, Joseph oversaw the gathering of grain which was stored in the cities. There was such an overabundance that, according to the Bible, they finally stopped counting the grain since it was as the sand of the sea—without number! It is interesting to note that discoveries have been made of Egyptian art showing government officials overseeing the gathering of a huge grain harvest into storehouses.

As the time of famine came, and the people began to cry out, Joseph opened the storehouses of grain and sold it to the Egyptians. As the famine worsened, people from the surrounding nations also came to Egypt to buy grain. That was the motivation for Joseph's brothers to come from Canaan to Egypt, but it brought about a far greater result than a few loaves of bread! You can read one of the most amazing stories ever recorded, about the reunion of these brothers with one they thought lost forever, in Genesis 42-45. Only God Himself could have worked such good from such evil: the dramatic salvation of a family through the vicious enslaving of a hated brother.

The seven years of famine resulted in Pharaoh owning all of the money, livestock, land, and people of Egypt (except for the priests and their land). Normally, famines do not create great wealth, but, due to Joseph's administration, this was a significant exception. The famine also resulted in Joseph's entire family moving to Egypt, into an area known as Goshen, which the Bible describes as being the "best of the land." Most biblical archaeologists would agree that Goshen is located in the Wadi Tumilat, in the northeastern part of the Delta (in Lower or northern Egypt). They remained there until the Exodus out of Egypt.

A fascinating clue to Joseph's presence in Egypt can be seen in an ancient canal known as the "Bahr Yusef" (or The Joseph Canal), which was built during the time of the Twelfth Dynasty, connecting the Nile River to Lake Moeris through 200 miles of canal. It is still used today in irrigation, as it has been for centuries. Doesn't it amaze you to discover a still-existing proof of Joseph's presence and prestige in Egypt?

After Joseph's death, the Bible tells us a chilling truth:

> *"Now there arose a new king over Egypt, who did not know Joseph. And he said to his people, "Look, the people of the children of Israel are more and mightier than we; come, let us deal wisely with them, lest they multiply, and it happen, in the event of war, that they also join our enemies and fight against us, and so go up out of the land." Therefore they set taskmasters over them to afflict them them with their burdens. And they built for Pharaoh supply cities, Pithom and Rameses.*" Exodus 1:8-11

The Hebrews, the descendants of Abraham, Isaac and Jacob, were enslaved at this point by the ruling Pharaoh. The Egyptians feared these descendants of Jacob (the "children of Israel"), and so not only increased their workload, but also commanded the Hebrew midwives to kill all of the baby boys born to the Hebrew women. In the midst of this oppression and suffering, Moses was born. Rather than obeying Pharaoh and throwing him to the crocodiles in the Nile, his mother fashioned an "ark of bulrushes" for him, and gently placed his basket in the reeds of the Nile. Pharaoh's daughter found the baby, recognized him as a Hebrew, and rather than obeying her father's command (Exodus 1:22), took him home to the palace to raise as her own son. Hebrews 11:24-26 tell us:

> *"By faith Moses, when he became of age, refused to be called the son of Pharaoh's daughter, choosing rather to suffer affliction with the people of God than to enjoy the passing pleasures of sin, esteeming the reproach of Christ greater riches than the treasures in Egypt; for he looked to the reward."*

Amazing as it may seem, this man who "had it all," who was raised in the very lap of Pharaonic luxury, who, according to Josephus (a first-century Jewish historian), successfully led an Egyptian army to war with Kush (Ethiopia), who was adopted kin of the most powerful ruler of that time, this man gave it all up to be identified with and suffer alongside the children of Israel. At age 40, after the murder of an Egyptian who was beating a Hebrew, Moses was forced to flee for his life from the wrath of Pharaoh and go to the land of Midian (in western Arabia). For the next forty years, he tended sheep as God prepared him for his next role. Beginning in Exodus 3, we see how God takes this reluctant prince turned shepherd and turns him into a powerful leader, able to confront the might of Egypt with the power of the Lord.

Thus begins one of the most dramatic confrontations in human history. As Moses with his brother Aaron bring the word of the Lord to Pharaoh—"Let My people go"—Pharaoh hardens his heart, which brings, plague by plague, destruction and devastation to his nation. After the tenth and final plague, the death of the firstborn of both man and beast, the children of Israel were released from their enslavement, with their wages given in silver and gold by their Egyptian neighbors.

However, when Pharaoh realized that he had just lost a whole nation of slaves (estimates run up to three million people!), he changed his mind. Gathering his entire army, he chased after the fleeing Hebrews all the way to the Red Sea, which you might call his "Waterloo." It was there that the Hebrews crossed safely to freedom and Pharaoh with his army drowned, decisively ending the contest between the finite gods of the Egyptians and the infinite Creator of all. It was the final sign to the Egyptian people indicating who was really Lord. They had seen their Pharaoh as divine, as a god, but now they understood who was truly reigning in heaven.

Again, there is not a consensus among scholars concerning which Pharaoh drowned in the Red Sea with his army. The two most likely candidates, based on the new

Egyptian chronology, are Amenemhet IV of the Twelfth Dynasty and Dudimose I of the Thirteenth Dynasty. It is interesting to note that, in favor of the first candidate, Amenemhet's tomb was never found, and his widow reigned only a short time after his demise. From that point, Egypt enters into the Second Intermediate Period (13th to 17th Dynasties) under weak pharaohs and conquering foreigners known as the Hyksos.

After the Hyksos were driven out of Egypt, a new period, known as the New Kingdom, began. This was the time that the greatest expansion of Egypt beyond its borders occurred, and it lasted for approximately five hundred years. One of the most interesting pharaohs of this period was Akhenaton, who declared that there was only one god, the god of the sun. He built a new capital city, whose ruins today lie near Tell el Amarna. When he died, his beliefs were declared heretical by the priests, and everything went back to the old ways. His successor was Tutankhamon, the boy pharaoh who was mysteriously murdered at about age eighteen. With the Twentieth Dynasty, the power of Egypt dramatically waned, and it was soon under the control of foreign rulers.

When we look at the contest of power between the gods of the Egyptians and the Creator of the Egyptians during the Exodus, we need to discover God's heart from the scriptures, lest we think wrongly of Him:

> *"And the Lord will strike Egypt, He will strike and heal it; they will return to the Lord, and He will be entreated by them and heal them. In that day there will be a highway from Egypt to Assyria, and the Assyrian will come into Egypt and the Egyptian into Assyria, and the Egyptians will serve with the Assyrians. In that day Israel will be one of three with Egypt and Assyria, even a blessing in the midst of the land, whom the Lord of hosts shall bless, saying, "Blessed is Egypt My people, and Assyria the work of My hands, and Israel My inheritance."* Isaiah 19:22-25

The Egyptians were not the bad guys in the Exodus scenario. That role belonged to Pharaoh. But God did use the plagues and the Exodus to demonstrate to the people of Egypt who was worthy of their worship. This nation, which many centuries later would be a haven to Joseph, Mary and Jesus at the time of Herod's rampage, was intended by God to be a blessing and a safe place of refuge, not a place of enslaving others or being enslaved

by false religions. As we know, however, pride goes before destruction and a haughty spirit comes before a fall (Proverbs 16:18), and the Pharaohs of ancient Egypt had a tremendous amount of pride. In fact, the book of Ezekiel describes the pride of a later Pharaoh:

> *"Behold I am against you, O Pharaoh king of Egypt, O great monster who lies in the midst of his rivers, Who has said, 'My River is my own; I have made it for myself.' "* Ezekiel 29:9

He thought he had made the Nile River? By himself? What a foolish delusion. That is what happens when you think you are a god.

With all of the specific Biblical information about the Hebrews' time in Egypt (Goshen, Joseph's viziership, Hebrew enslavement, supply cities built of mud and straw bricks, the destruction of Pharaoh in the Red Sea, etc.), you would think the Egyptologists, archaeologists and historians would be shouting to the world, "Here!" "Here!" "Over here!" as they found verification of the biblical events in Egyptian relics and digs. Perhaps you may have noticed the silence instead? Perhaps you may have wondered about the silence, or even, the vocal dissent which dismisses the biblical record, all the way from Creation through the time of David and Solomon, as myth and legend. Let's consider the problems and the possible solutions.

In the third century B.C., Manetho, an Egyptian priest, compiled a history of Egypt, including a list of the Pharaohs, divided into thirty-one dynasties. That seems fairly simple and straightforward, doesn't it? A list of kings, grouped into families—everything made nice and tidy. This was more or less accepted for many years as the standard by which to date the various Pharaohs and their reigns. The problem for Bible believers is that, as the Pharaohs march through time, one by one, the years and events of their reigns do not correspond with Biblical events and people—not in recovered documents of the time nor in the dating of archaeological debris. In the *traditional* chronology, the Exodus (1446 B.C.) falls during the New Kingdom. However, since there are some **serious** difficulties with this time period, including the capital city of the 18th Dynasty being located 475 miles from Goshen (a long daily walk for Moses as he confronts Pharaoh), another suggestion was made to date the Exodus to the 19th Dynasty under Rameses II since his capital city was in Goshen. The problem with this choice is that, under the traditional chronology, Rameses II ruled Egypt from 1290—1224 B.C., which does not agree with the Biblical date for the Exodus. So, neither of these choices is a good one for those who believe the Bible describes accurately the events of its time.

A new wave of archaeologists and Bible believers have begun to question the accepted chronology of Manetho. You see, it is not clear from the archaeological record whether the Pharaohs lived one at a time, shared their reign, or reigned over only a portion of Egypt while another dynasty (or two, or three) ruled over other parts of Egypt. And, to make it more difficult, when archaeologists uncover a monument with a list of Pharaohs, the years of their reign are often not included or obliterated through the aging, so, along with pottery fragments, isolated hieroglyphic inscriptions, and surviving documents, the information needed for creating an accurate timeline is scanty at best. Even though this forms—along with wrong assumptions made by early Egyptologists—the shaky foundation of Egyptian chronology, decisions have been made in the last sixty years in academic circles, in museums, universities and scholarly journals, to throw out the veracity and historicity of Scripture because the Egyptian artifacts have not lined up with the names, dates, and events of the Bible.

That is, until the mid-1990's. In 1995, David Rohl, working on his doctoral thesis at University College in London, released his book, *A Test of Time: The Bible From Myth to History,* which has brought about a flurry of new ideas. Basically, through the research Rohl has done with existing documentation, he has shown that the Third Intermediate Period of Egyptian history is 200 years shorter than previously thought, due to parallel dynasties. That, along with other adjustments in the chronologies, results in a reduction of 345 years in the ancient Egyptian timeline.

This makes Rameses II no longer the Pharaoh of the Exodus, but, rather, the Pharaoh who ransacked the temple in Jerusalem in 925 B.C.—and, not surprisingly, there is good archaeological evidence for this event! It also makes the Twelfth and, possibly the Thirteenth Dynasty(ies), the Pharaohs of Joseph and the events through the Exodus. Amazingly, in 1987, a statue was discovered in a palace in Goshen which had a most un-Egyptian face, with red hair and a coat of many colors. Could it be a statue of Joseph? Rohl thinks the answer to that question would be, "Yes!"

Tremendous research is taking place, since the Egyptian chronology has been adjusted, to discover whether there is now, in the right places, all the evidence for the Hebrews that was previously missed. We will consider some of the new evidence from old discoveries in the next chapter. With all that's happening, with all the discoveries opening up the evidence of the Bible's accuracy for all to see, it is an exciting moment to be a student!

Reviewed Resources for Digging Deeper:
From Student Manual pages 96-98

Egypt

Cultural Atlas for Young People—Ancient Egypt by Geraldine Harris

The Cultural Atlas books are among the most informative, best laid-out history books for young people. Highly recommended! **MS+**

Pyramid by David Macauley

An incredible look at the construction of a pyramid—you actually get the sense that you are inside a pyramid with the workers! **AA**

Growing Up in Ancient Egypt by Rosalie David

This is an excellent introduction to the many facets of living in ancient Egypt. Though it is written for children, the information and layout makes it valuable to all ages. **E+**

The Pharaohs of Ancient Egypt by Elizabeth Payne

Landmark books are always good value, and this is no exception. Excellent for younger students. **UE+**

Tut's Mummy Lost and Found by Judy Donnelly

For elementary students, this book shows the fascinating adventure of Howard Carter who found King Tut in 1922. **E+**

Look What Came From Egypt by Miles Harvey

What a wonderful picture book of Egypt! Filled with photos and simple descriptions, this will be a great introduction for elementary students. **E+**

Make it Work! Ancient Egypt by Andrew Haslam & Alexandra Parsons

This is one of a series of the most incredible hands-on books of projects I've ever seen! It shows how to construct clothing, make jewelry, create instruments, even make a chariot! **UE+**

The Riddle of the Rosetta Stone: Key to Ancient Egypt by James Cross Giblin

An absolutely fascinating book about the man who deciphered the Rosetta Stone. **AA**

Seeker of Knowledge—The Man Who Deciphered Egyptian Hieroglyphs by James Rumford

If you collect excellent children's books, this is one for your shelves. It is the story of Jean- François Champollion, told with exquisite style and illustrations. **E+**

Hatshepsut—His Majesty, Herself by Catherine Andronik

Another excellent children's book, this one is concerned with one of the most interesting and unusual pharaohs of ancient Egypt. **E+**

Pharaohs and Kings by David Rohl

Discover for yourself the compelling reasons for revising the traditional Egyptian chronology, and see how this affects the archaeological evidences for Joseph and Moses in Egypt. Fascinating! **MS+**

Ancient Egypt—A Cambridge Junior History by Philip Cummins

Cambridge University Press has published some of my favorite history books. This is an excellent introduction to ancient Egypt for pre-high school students. **UE+**

Historical Fiction

The Golden Goblet by Eloise McGraw

We really like this author! This book focuses on the intrigue and mystery of one orphaned boy's life. Another exciting means of making ancient Egypt come alive! **UE+**

Mara, daughter of the Nile by Eloise McGraw

Riveting historical fiction! This is a wonderful way to make the ancient Egyptians, the political intrigues, and the places of power come to life. **UE+**

The Cat of the Bubastes by G. A. Henty

A fascinating look at the religious life of the Egyptians, with a Judeo-Christian insight. Historical fiction at its best: includes Moses! **MS+**

The Exodus

Celebrate the Feasts by Martha Zimmerman

This book is filled with the why's and how-to's of celebrating the feasts of Israel. We learned so much about the meaning of the Last Supper, and the incredible picture of the Messiah depicted in the feast of Passover from this book—which also shows how to celebrate this and the other feasts. **AA**

The Story of Passover by Norma Simon

A beautiful children's picture book about Passover. Learn not only the historic passover, but how it has been celebrated both in history and currently. **E+**

Exodus by Brian Wildsmith

Filled with wonderful illustrations, this hardbound children's book brings the story of the Exodus to life. **E+**

The Gold of Exodus—The Discovery of the True Mount Sinai by Howard Blum

The author of this book is an award-winning journalist for the New York Times. After interviewing several people involved in the search for Mount Sinai just prior to the Gulf War, he concludes that what Larry Williams and Bob Cornuke believe about Mt. Sinai is true. Absolutely riveting. **MS+**

The Mountain of Moses: The Discovery of Mount Sinai by Larry Williams

Out-of-print. If you can find a copy, this is a fascinating book detailing the problems associated with the traditional site of Mt. Sinai, the problem of where the Israelites crossed over the Red Sea, and more. It not only details the problems, it offers a solution. **MS+**

In Search of the Mountain of God by Robert Cornuke & David Halbrook

This is Bob Cornuke's version of his trip into Saudi Arabia with Larry Williams. It is a fascinating account of what may, in fact, be the true Mt. Sinai. **MS+**

Solving the Exodus Mystery by Ted Stewart

Ruth Beechick recommended this book to me as the best solution for the question about which pharaohs were the pharaohs of the Bible events. It is wordy and filled with lots of specific information, but if you can persevere, Mr. Stewart has incredible conclusions. **HS+**

Video: *The Ten Commandments* **AA**

Video: *Prince Of Egypt* **AA**

For more books, use these Dewey Decimal numbers in your library:

Bible: #220

Ancient Egypt: #932

Ancient Palestine: #933

Anthropology: #300

Also, look for biographies on the key people listed.

Phase 2

➢ *Timeline*

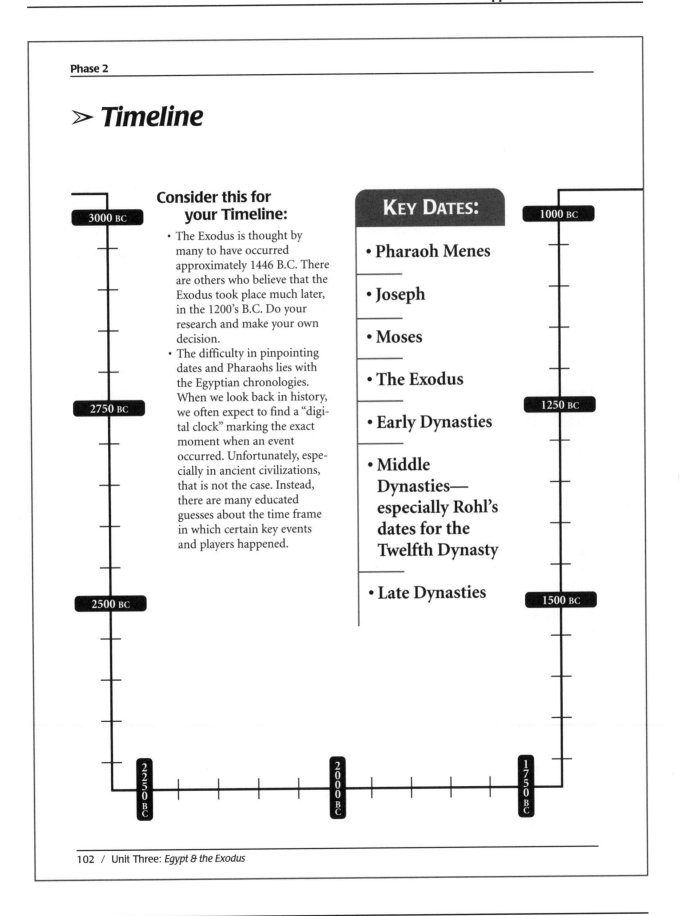

3000 BC

Consider this for your Timeline:

- The Exodus is thought by many to have occurred approximately 1446 B.C. There are others who believe that the Exodus took place much later, in the 1200's B.C. Do your research and make your own decision.
- The difficulty in pinpointing dates and Pharaohs lies with the Egyptian chronologies. When we look back in history, we often expect to find a "digital clock" marking the exact moment when an event occurred. Unfortunately, especially in ancient civilizations, that is not the case. Instead, there are many educated guesses about the time frame in which certain key events and players happened.

2750 BC

2500 BC

KEY DATES:

- **Pharaoh Menes**

- **Joseph**

- **Moses**

- **The Exodus**

- **Early Dynasties**

- **Middle Dynasties— especially Rohl's dates for the Twelfth Dynasty**

- **Late Dynasties**

1000 BC

1250 BC

1500 BC

2250 BC

2000 BC

1750 BC

102 / Unit Three: *Egypt & the Exodus*

© 2004 Geography Matters

ad maiorem Dei gloriam!

Into the Promised Land...

Article from Student Manual pages 115-122

"So the Lord saved Israel that day out of the hand of the Egyptians, and Israel saw the Egyptians dead on the seashore. Thus Israel saw the great work which the Lord had done in Egypt; so the people feared the Lord, and believed the Lord and His servant Moses." Exodus 14:30-31

Out of Egypt! Deliverance and freedom! A new hope and a new future! Standing on the other side of the Red Sea, watching with incredulity the towering waters collapse on Pharaoh and his army, must have unleashed a torrent of emotions and thoughts in the escapees. Consider: first, the thrill of being alive and free when they expected to be either dead or re-enslaved, and secondly the very present and human concern, "What do we do now?"

Moses, their God-appointed leader, faced a number of obstacles in leading this massive group of people (estimated between one and three million!) and their livestock, not least of which was finding food and water for them in a dry and thirsty land. As they journeyed into the wilderness, God both led them and provided for them— but not without testing. As someone once observed, "You can deliver the man out of Egypt, but you can't deliver Egypt out of the man!" There was an ongoing process of actively putting their trust in the God who had proved His trustworthiness. These things take time and experience, however. So, God very wisely gave them opportunities: like having the chance to look around the desert, noticing a lack of water, that they might cry out to Him and see His miraculous provision of water; or wondering where the bakeries were, crying out to Him and seeing God give them heavenly bread—manna—day by day for forty years; or considering the lack of shoe stores in the wilderness and experiencing the miracle of shoes that didn't wear out in the hot desert sun or on the baked rocks and sand! On and on the list goes, as the fledgling nation learned of the amazing ability God had to provide all they needed—an important lesson for the nation designated to show God's goodness to all the world.

This was not a one-sided, vending machine, grumpy-request-automatic-answer sort of provision, however. We see in the book of Exodus an ongoing issue of relationship between the people and God. The people, who had just seen their miraculous deliverance from slavery, when confronted by a problem, began to whine and complain to Moses about how he had brought them into the wilderness to die. The Bible tells us that their complaints were not really against Moses but against God. Yet, despite the people's ungratefulness, He continued in His mercy and kindness to take care of them, while at the same time teaching them that He was not a "tame lion" (in the words of C.S. Lewis) that could be pushed and pulled at whim. Read the book of Numbers to discover some of the wild occurrences that happened in the wilderness, including the day that the earth "opened its mouth" and swallowed the leaders of a rebellion against Moses (Numbers 16). The people learned, experience by experience, that God was not mocked—*"for whatever a man sows, that he will also reap."* (Gal 6:7)

As part of His discipleship of the children of Israel, God led them to a place called the Wilderness of Sinai in the third month of their wanderings to make a formal, binding agreement, or *covenant,* with them.

"You have seen what I did to the Egyptians, and how I bore you on eagles' wings and brought you to Myself. Now therefore, if you will indeed obey My voice and keep My covenant, then you shall be a special treasure to Me above all people; for all the earth is Mine. And you shall be to Me a kingdom of priests and a holy nation." Exodus 19:4-6

The people listened to these words, which Moses gave them, and readily agreed to obey the Lord. In that desert setting, with Egypt behind them and the unknown before them, the children of Israel gave themselves willingly, albeit imperfectly, to this Delivering God. At that moment He gave them, written on stone by His own hand, an understanding of His ways and His design for all people that has impacted the world ever since. We call it the Ten Commandments.

Think about it. These commandments were not given in anger, as punishment for a disobedient people. They were not given by a killjoy God who only wanted the worst for His children. No! Stop for a moment and consider the setting, and contemplate the motivation... God offered to make them a special treasure, and they willingly said that was what they wanted. In that atmosphere of relationship, when One offered and the other responded, God gave the people a depth of understanding that no one before that time had ever known. He told them aspects of how they were designed to live in relationship to Him (the first four commandments) and how they were designed to live in relationship with one another (the last six commandments). It was a gift, it was a communication of loving truth that would, if obeyed, give tremendous blessing to the people who lived it out. It would not make them righteous (Isaiah 64:6)—that belongs to God alone (Phil 3:9)—but it would immeasurably bless them and teach them about how to live out their relationships.

After the giving of the Ten Commandments (Exodus 20), the people were so afraid of the awesome power and presence of God that they begged Moses to be the one who spoke directly to and heard directly from God. It was at that point that the precise details of how to live and how to worship were given to Moses to convey to the people. In the book of Hebrews, we are told that the Tabernacle, the priesthood and the daily sacrifices were earthly symbols of the heavenly reality of what Jesus would later accomplish as the Savior.

> *"For if He were on earth, He would not be a priest, since there are priests who offer the gifts according to the law; who serve the **copy and shadow** of the heavenly things, as Moses was divinely instructed when he was about to make the tabernacle. For He said, "See that you make all things according to the pattern shown you on the mountain." But now He has obtained a more excellent ministry, inasmuch as He is also Mediator of a better covenant, which was established on better promises."* Hebrews 8:4-6

Moses spent forty days and nights on the mountain receiving specific instruction from God, while the people waited impatiently below. They reached a point where they assumed Moses had been consumed, or had forgotten about them, or had lost his mind and was wandering somewhere in the wilderness, or had somehow been incapacitated as their leader. This conclusion made them very insecure and very forgetful about the God who had delivered them out of Egypt. How do we know this?

> *"Now when the people saw that Moses delayed coming down from the mountain, the people gathered together to Aaron, and said to him, "Come, make us gods that shall go before us; for as for this Moses, the man who brought us up out of the land of Egypt, we do not know what has become of him."* Exodus 32:1

This is just a few short weeks after telling God that they would obey Him! How quickly people seem to forget God's faithfulness, His goodness, His wisdom and His provision. In my own life, I can think of many instances where, shortly after seeing God's mighty work in my life, I begin to worry about the future. How foolish! The Bible tells us that God is the same yesterday, today and forever. His character never changes. He never forsakes us. Never.

These fearful, complaining ones, whom God graciously forgave, made what possibly might have been their greatest failure at the border of the Promised Land. When Moses sent out leaders from each tribe of Israel to spy out Canaan and to bring back some of the fruit of the land, the men returned after forty days with tales of well fortified cities and fearsome giants. Though the land was "flowing with milk and honey," it was certainly too dangerous a place to think about calling home. When the people heard this, they began to weep and wail through the night. In addition to tearfully wishing that they had died before getting to this scary place, they determined to choose a leader to take them back to Egypt!

> *"Then Moses and Aaron fell on their faces before all the assembly of the congregation of the children of Israel. And Joshua the son of Nun and Caleb the son of Jephunneh, who were among those who had spied out the land, tore their clothes; and they spoke to all the congregation of the children of Israel, saying: "The land we passed through to spy out is an exceedingly good land. If the Lord delights in us, then He will bring us into this land and give it to us, 'a land which flows with milk and honey.' Only do not rebel against*

the Lord, nor fear the people of the land, for they are our bread; their protection has departed from them, and the Lord is with us. Do not fear them." And all the congregation said to stone them with stones…" Numbers 14:5-10

This was not a pretty picture, was it? It seems somewhat reminiscent of man's rebellion after the Fall (with God's provision of mercy) and man's rebellion after the Flood (with, again, God's provision of mercy). Now, in the same way, we see man's rebellion after the Exodus. It is the same thread of the sinfulness of man which we saw in the first chapter, intertwined with the thread of God's purpose for redemption, woven throughout each page of history. Though the children of Israel were ready to throw away obedience and pursue rebellion, this Scripture shows again a marvelous depiction of God's mercy and patience. He did not destroy them (which would have been a reasonable, human reaction at that point!), but continued to call them His own and to lead them faithfully. Pay attention, though, to the fact that He did not let them go into the Promised Land at that moment in time, even though that had been His original intention. In fact, after Moses communicated God's displeasure with the people, they said they were now sorry and were ready to take the Promised Land after all. Too late. The die had been cast. God told them that all of the people who were twenty years old and above would eventually die in the wilderness (except for Joshua and Caleb who believed Him). Because of their unbelief and murmuring, they would wander in the wilderness one year for every day that the spies had been in Canaan—forty years in all.

Exodus, Leviticus, Numbers and Deuteronomy contain the account of the wanderings in the Wilderness, as well as the Law of the Old Testament. It is a fascinating read, filled with the wildest things you've ever heard. Can you imagine following a huge cloud by day and a towering pillar of flame by night? What would it have been like to travel for forty years with such a massive bunch of whiners and complainers? Do you suppose it gradually got better as far as attitudes were concerned? Or, perhaps things improved as the older ones who didn't believe God died off! One way or another, they managed to muddle along through the barren wastelands, eating daily from God's own hand.

Finally, after forty years of camping out in the desert, we read these words:

"Moses My servant is dead. Now therefore, arise, go over this Jordan, you and all this people, to the land which I am giving to them—the children of Israel. Every place that the sole of your foot will tread upon I have given you, as I said to Moses… Be strong and of good courage, for to this people you shall divide as an inheritance the land which I swore to their fathers to give them." Joshua 1:2-3,6

Yahoo! School's over! Passing grades for all! Out of the desert and into real living!!

Crossing the Jordan River and entering the Promised Land must have been one of the most amazing sensations of having "arrived" that any traveler has ever known. The only cloud on the horizon was the necessity of convincing all of the inhabitants that God had given the land of Canaan to the Israelites. And it took one of the most amazing miracles of God recorded in the Bible to accomplish that.

The city of Jericho was situated at a strategic location, acting as a fortified guard post into Canaan. Archaeological discoveries show that, though the city never got larger than twelve acres in size, it's position and fortifications made it a formidable defensive weapon against intruders. So, what plan of attack did God give the children of Israel? Catapults and sieges? Ramming poles and ladders? Snipers and decoys? No, none of the above. In His painstaking method of teaching them that the battle belongs to the Lord (1 Sam 17:47), God told them that their battle plan was to march around the city once a day for six days, with seven priests blowing ram's horn trumpets as they marched. On the seventh day, they were to march around the city seven times, and at the end of it, to shout. This unorthodox strategy would result, so they were told, in the city's walls falling down. Fortunately, Joshua and the children of Israel believed God could do what He promised, so they did just what they were told. The results, as they say, are history!

From that very promising beginning, the Israelites gradually occupied the land of Canaan. During the life of Joshua and the elders who served with him, the people obeyed the Lord and followed Him. However, shortly after that generation had died out, the children of Israel began to revert to old tricks—worshipping other gods and forsaking the One who had chosen them. You can read about this three hundred-plus years in the book of Judges, which has some fascinating stories including ones about Gideon and Samson.

Eventually, though, the people had had enough of depending on God to lead them and take care of them. They looked around at the other nations surrounding them and saw that those nations had something more enviable than an invisible God—they had a human king! And the Israelites began to beg God, through the prophet Samuel, for a king of their very own.

Thus began the Kingdom Years, the time of King Saul, King David and King Solomon. Their stories range from giant killing to Temple building, from godly wisdom to raving insanity, from careful obedience to flaunting disobedience. During the time of Solomon, though other nations were powerful in their own right, Israel became distinguished among the nations as a place of wealth, grandeur and unsearchable wisdom. From this rags-to-riches pinnacle of success, Israel soon plummeted to the depths of captivity and enslavement. That story, however, belongs to the next chapter.

Reviewed Resources for Digging Deeper:

From Student Manual page 125-126

Israel

Halley's Bible Handbook

This book contains wonderful study helps and insights related to the Old and New Testaments. It includes archaeological explanations from a Biblical perspective. (However, the archaeologists' findings in the Fertile Crescent are interpreted to mean that the Flood was a localized event.) **UE+**

The New Unger's Bible Handbook revised by Gary Larson

This is my preferred source for information and insight on the archaeological record from a Biblical perspective. It is filled with color pictures, timelines, notes, helps, and exciting tidbits! **UE+**

Victor Journey Through the Bible by V. Gilbert Beers

With photos, maps, and charts and brief articles, this book gives an excellent enhancement to the reading of the Bible. **UE+**

Daily Chronological Bible

Reading this Bible was our basic introduction to the concept of studying ancient civilizations and the Bible. It is set up chronologically with wonderful insights into the history of the Scriptures. **UE+**

Josephus

Since one of Josephus' purposes was to explain the history of Israel, this is an excellent (although difficult) resource for studying this subject. **HS+**

A Family Guide to the Biblical Holidays by Robin Scarlata and Linda Pierce

A wonderful resource for celebrating the feasts of Israel in your family. Many helpful ideas and suggestions—an excellent addition to this study. **AA**

Dance, Sing, Remember—A Celebration of Jewish Holidays by Leslie Kimmelman

Written and illustrated for children, this is a delightful book. Discover recipes, games, history and more. **E+**

Student Bible Atlas

A Bible atlas is an indispensable tool in understanding the history of the children of Israel. This particular one is excellent for students. **AA**

Then and Now by Perring and Perring

The ruins of ancient civilizations, including Israel, will come to life for your family as you see the artist's rendition of what it once looked like superimposed over the ruin that now exists. See Masada, Jerusalem and more! **UP+**

Video Series: **That the World May Know** from Focus on the Family

Both an incredible introduction to the Holy Land and also valuable "faith lessons" from the history of this people. **AA**

Trade

Sold!—The Origins of Money & Trade

Economics and trade routes had a mighty impact on cultures from earliest times. Learn more about how this worked, and then apply it to the country of Israel. **UE+**

For more books, use these Dewey Decimal numbers in your library:

Bible: #220

Ancient Palestine: #933

Judaism: #296

Also, look for biographies on the key people listed.

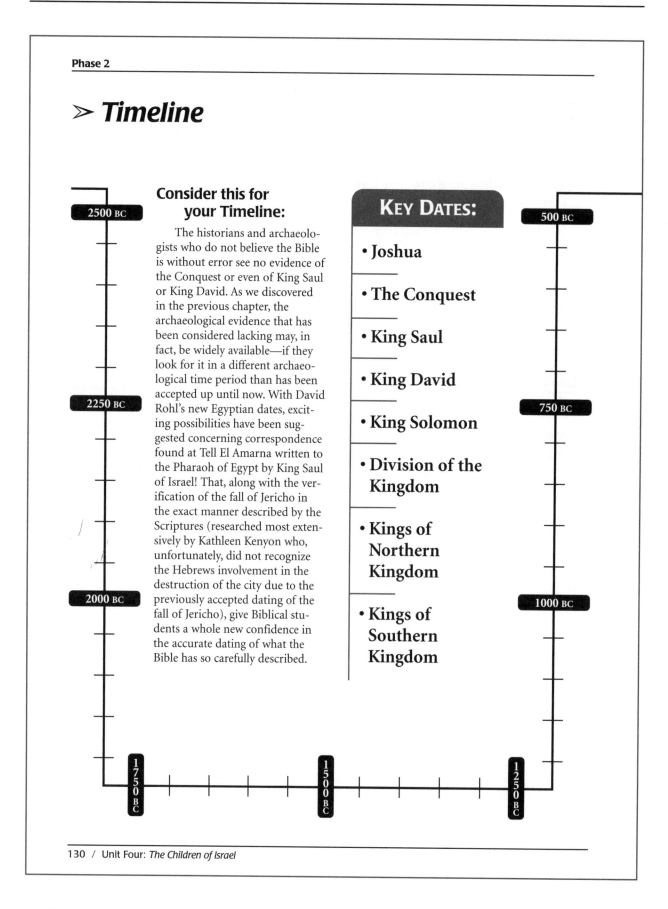

Phase 2

➤ *Timeline*

2500 BC

2250 BC

2000 BC

Consider this for your Timeline:

The historians and archaeologists who do not believe the Bible is without error see no evidence of the Conquest or even of King Saul or King David. As we discovered in the previous chapter, the archaeological evidence that has been considered lacking may, in fact, be widely available—if they look for it in a different archaeological time period than has been accepted up until now. With David Rohl's new Egyptian dates, exciting possibilities have been suggested concerning correspondence found at Tell El Amarna written to the Pharaoh of Egypt by King Saul of Israel! That, along with the verification of the fall of Jericho in the exact manner described by the Scriptures (researched most extensively by Kathleen Kenyon who, unfortunately, did not recognize the Hebrews involvement in the destruction of the city due to the previously accepted dating of the fall of Jericho), give Biblical students a whole new confidence in the accurate dating of what the Bible has so carefully described.

KEY DATES:

• Joshua

• The Conquest

• King Saul

• King David

• King Solomon

• Division of the Kingdom

• Kings of Northern Kingdom

• Kings of Southern Kingdom

500 BC

750 BC

1000 BC

1750 BC

1500 BC

1250 BC

130 / Unit Four: *The Children of Israel*

Phase 3

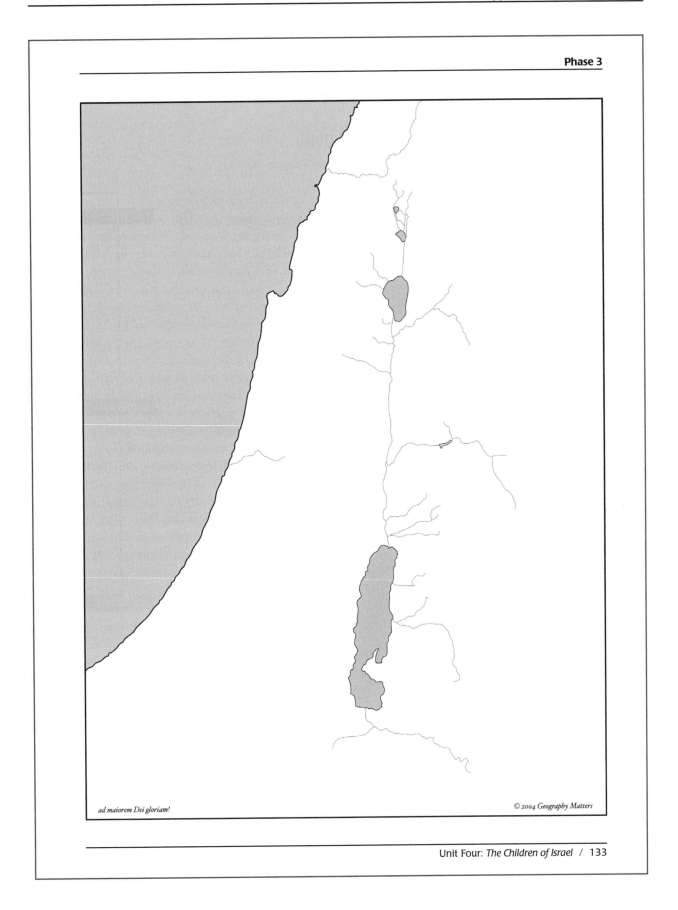

ad maiorem Dei gloriam!

© 2004 *Geography Matters*

Unit Four: *The Children of Israel* / 133

UNIT 5 MATERIAL

Assyria & Babylon: The Mesopotamian Conquerors

Into captivity...

Article from Student Manual pages 143-153

From the northeast part of Mesopotamia, on the banks of the Tigris River, arose a mighty nation of conquering warriors who would eventually become both a watchword among the nations for cruelty, as well as participants in the greatest revival ever witnessed.

In the southeast part of Mesopotamia, on the banks of the Euphrates River, came a king from a powerful empire both to triumphantly destroy Jerusalem and to discover God's power humbling the greatest of kings.

Two gentile nations, two conquering empires, both from the cradle of Mesopotamia: Assyria and Babylon take their place now on the stage of world history. Each find, in their own specific situation and moment of time, that the Hebrew God is more powerful than any god they have worshipped, and some willingly choose to worship Him.

Beginning in 2 Kings 15, we see the convergence of Israel with the Assyrians, and it is not a pretty picture, at least, not for the Israelites. How did they end up in such dire circumstances after having experienced the magnificence of Solomon's reign? What brought about such a complete reversal?

The answer lies in 1 Kings 11:9-13:

"So the Lord became angry with Solomon, because his heart had turned from the Lord God of Israel, who had appeared to him twice, and had commanded him concerning this thing, that he should not go after other gods; but he did not keep what the Lord had commanded. Therefore the Lord said to Solomon, 'Because you have done this, and have not kept My covenant and My statutes,which I have commanded you, I will surely tear the kingdom away from you and give it to your servant. Nevertheless I will not do it in your days, for the sake of your father David; but I will tear it out of the hand of your son. However I will not tear away the whole kingdom, but I will give one tribe to your son for the sake of my servant David, and for the sake of Jerusalem which I have chosen.'"

After the death of Solomon, his son Rehoboam very foolishly decided to ignore the counsel of his father's wise men, choosing to take the advice of his peers and show the people who was boss. Most of them responded by leaving him and following Solomon's former servant, Jereboam. Jereboam went north into the region of Galilee, while Rehoboam stayed with Jerusalem and the Temple. From this point, the nation was divided into Israel in the north and Judah in the south. Jereboam, fearing that his fickle followers would switch sides if they returned to offer sacrifices in the Temple, made two calves of gold and told the people they no longer needed to go to Jerusalem. They could stay in the north to worship because these calves were the ones that had brought them out of Egypt! Things went downhill for Israel from that point.

Though the people had turned away from God, He kept calling them back to Himself. Elijah and Elisha kept confronting the people with the preeminence of the Lord, in such momentous events as when Elijah called for a showdown between the prophets of Baal and the Lord. But even with that vivid demonstration of God's reality, the people would not permanently abandon their rebellion. The prophets Amos and Hosea brought the word of the Lord to the northern kingdom by warning them that impending judgment for sin was imminent. Along with the warning came the promise that God would turn from His wrath if they would quit offering themselves in worship to other gods.

"I will heal their backsliding, I will love them freely, for My anger has turned away from him... Ephraim shall say, 'What have I to do anymore with idols?'..." Hosea 14:4,8

As we shall soon see, however, the people of Israel did not take the warning of the prophets to heart. They continued to walk in disobedience and disregard of the God who had rescued and redeemed them from slavery.

"I taught Ephraim to walk, taking them by their arms; but they did not know that I healed them. I drew them with gentle cords, with bands of love, and I was to them as those who take the yoke from their neck. I stooped and fed them. He shall not return to the land of Egypt; but the Assyrian shall be his king, because they refused to repent."
Hosea 11:3-5

Beginning in 2 Kings 24, the southern kingdom of Judah comes into catastrophic contact with the other Mesopotamian empire, Babylon, as God's judgment on their sin unfolds. How was it that they did not learn the lesson of listening to God and obeying Him when they saw what happened to Israel? Much of the answer lies in the character qualities of their kings. In Judah, there were bad kings interspersed with good kings. Some of the kings, including Hezekiah and Josiah, served the Lord with gladness and the people followed them. Other kings encouraged the worship of false gods, even to the point of sacrificing their own children in hideous religious ceremonies, and the people followed them as well. Since God's judgment is usually delayed, people begin to think they can do whatever they want without suffering consequences, especially when their leaders are leading the way.

As in the case of Israel, God sent the people of Judah warning after warning over a period of more than a hundred years. He spoke of impending judgment through the prophets Joel, Isaiah, Micah, Zephaniah, Jeremiah, and Habakkuk. However, the people of Judah did not return to the Lord to serve Him alone. Because of the increasing apostasy of the nation, Jeremiah prophesied that King Nebuchadnezzar would take them captive to the land of Babylon. Mercifully, it was not to be a permanent removal from the land of Palestine:

"For thus says the Lord: After seventy years are completed at Babylon, I will visit you and perform My good word toward you, and cause you to return to this place. For I know the thoughts that I think toward you, says the Lord, thoughts of peace and not of evil, to give you a future and a hope." Jeremiah 29:10-11

If you read any of these prophets, you will hear over and over again God's heart of yearning for His people. Though He can not let their rebellion and sin continue forever in the land, He longs for them to repent and be healed rather than face well-deserved judgment. Though they spit in His face by worshipping false and worthless gods, He still loves them and seeks their restoration. What an amazing God He is! The Scripture helps us understand this mystery a little better when it says,

"For My thoughts are not your thoughts, nor are your ways My ways," says the Lord. "For as the heavens are higher than the earth, so are My ways higher than your ways, and My thoughts than your thoughts." Isaiah 55:8-9

His lovingkindness and mercy, and His wisdom and justice go far beyond human ability or thought. At this particular moment in history, His mercy and His judgment allowed His people to be both warned and, eventually, punished. Even in punishment, though, there was hope for the future.

"I will bring back the captives of My people Israel; they shall build the waste cities and inhabit them; they shall plant vineyards and drink wine from them; they shall also make gardens and eat fruit from them. I will plant them in their land, and no longer shall they be pulled up from the land I have given them," says the Lord your God." Amos 9:14-15

So who were these Mesopotamian conquerors, these nations used by God to accomplish His judgment on Israel and Judah? How did they rise to prominence in the earth? And what were their distinguishing characteristics?

The Assyrian people were warriors, hardened by the constant threat of attack from the mountainous tribes of the north, and made wealthy by their great conquests. Their greatest capital city, Nineveh, was the place of Jonah's message and the resulting revival. The Babylonians, by contrast, were the commercial center of the Near East, facilitating trade with the Middle East, Asia and Africa through roads and the national "highway"— the Euphrates River. Great commerce brings great wealth, and Babylon—the most magnificent city of the ancient world—was visible proof of this.

Because both of these empires emerged out of Mesopotamia, birthplace to the earlier Sumerian and Akkadian nations, they share some characteristics, such as similarity in language and art. But, much as two brothers can struggle for the upper hand, so did Assyria and Babylon struggle for mastery over their lands and each other.

Here is a brief accounting of the most important Assyrian and Babylonian rulers and events, especially those who are mentioned in Scripture, or who connect archaeology to the Bible.

Old Babylonian Empire:

Hammurabi (reigned c. 1792-1750 B.C.): The most famous of Babylon's earliest rulers, this great king of the Old Babylonian Empire, produced a code of 285 laws which dealt with everything from real estate to trade, from the family to personal property. There are modern scholars who, because they do not recognize the veracity of the Biblical account, believe that Moses derived the Ten Commandments from Hammurabi's Code. This helps them explain away the profound wisdom of God's law. Hammurabi conquered the neighboring nations, forging an empire which lasted just a short time after his death.

Assyrian Empire:

Tiglath Pileser I (reigned c. 1115– c. 1077 BC): Assyria's rise to prominence began under this man. He was a fierce warrior and a terrifying enemy. He conquered not only Babylon but the Hittites, the Armenians and forty other nations. Egypt sent him gifts, including a crocodile, to pacify and keep this conqueror out of their territory. He built many temples and palaces with the wealth of his conquests, but at the end of his reign, the Babylonians revolted and took his man-made gods back to Babylon.

Assunasirpal II (884-859 B.C.): The Assyrians, after a few hundred years of decline, begin a new campaign of conquest under this king. He restored the lands which had been lost to the Assyrian Empire and encouraged trade all the way to the Mediterranean.

Shalmaneser III (858-824 B.C.): He continued to expand the Empire all the way to Damascus, killing 16,000 Syrians in one battle, and receiving tribute from lesser kings and nations. One of these was found to be a Jewish king of Israel by the name of Jehu. Though it is not described in Scripture, a carved pillar unearthed in the 1800's literally names Jehu and depicts him offering tribute to Shalmaneser III. The discovery of this black obelisk was revolutionary, as it was among the first extra-biblical sources showing Israel's connection to Assyria.

From 824 B.C. until 747 B.C., there was a series of weak kings in Assyria, who could not prevent the empire

from going into decline. It was during this time, in approximately 760 B.C., that **Jonah** reluctantly went to Nineveh to take the word of the Lord to the Ninevites. Their reputation for cruelty to enemies was known to Jonah, and he loathed the thought of God forgiving them if they repented. However, God's mercy continued to shine out of the pages of the Old Testament, as He relented from destroying their city when they cried out to Him.

Tiglath Pileser III (also known as *Pul*) (747-727 B.C.): The Assyrian king who brought the prophecies of Amos and Hosea to pass, he took most of the northern kingdom of Israel captive. The policy of the Assyrian kings was to remove the people of a land and replace them with foreigners from other conquered lands. This is described in 2 Kings 17:24:

> *"Then the king of Assyria brought people from Babylon, Cuthah, Ava, Hamath, and from Sepharvaim, and placed them in the cities of Samaria instead of the children of Israel; and they took possession of Samaria and dwelt in its cities."*

Shalmaneser V (726-722 B.C.): 2 Kings 17:3 says that Shalmaneser V, who has often been confused with an earlier king of the same name, came up against Hoshea, king of Israel in Samaria and Hoshea became his vassal, paying him tribute.

Sargon II (722-705 B.C.): This ruler took the reins of power and captured Samaria in 722 B.C. He had this inscribed at his royal palace in Khorsabad, "I besieged and captured Samaria, carrying of 27,290 of the people who dwelt therein…" He also reconquered Babylon and defeated Egypt, leading his troops personally.

Sennacherib (705-681 B.C.): The son of Sargon II, this was the Assyrian king who threatened Jerusalem and King Hezekiah in 2 Kings 18-19. Though he failed in that locality, he went on to completely destroy Babylon, burning it to the ground and killing nearly all of the inhabitants. In his conquests, he captured 80,000 oxen, 800,000 sheep and 208,000 prisoners. With this infusion of capital, he renovated the city of Nineveh, which remained the premiere city in the empire until its destruction at the hands of the Babylonians and Medes.

Esarhaddon (680-669 B.C.): One of the sons of Sennacherib, he invaded Egypt and made it a province of Assyria, and then went on to rebuild the city of Babylon, which made him popular with the inhabitants of that nation! Before his death, he made Assyria the master of the entire Near East.

Ashurbanipal (668-627 B.C.): The prosperity of Assyria continued and grew during the reign of this king. When Ashurbanipal's palace was excavated in the mid-1800's, a library of unprecedented proportions came to light with more than 30,000 clay tablets dealing with such subjects as medicine, religion, history, and literature. With the end of Ashurbanipal's reign, the Assyrian Empire declined, until it was completely overthrown by the Babylonians in 612 B.C. with the destruction of the great city of Nineveh.

New Babylonian Empire:

Nabopolassar (626-605 B.C.): This conquering leader founded the New Babylonian Empire, as well as leading the Babylonian army in the destruction of Nineveh.

Nebuchadnezzar II (605-562 B.C.): Son of Nabopolassar, this was the ruler who brought the Babylonian Empire and the city of Babylon to their greatest heights. Jeremiah prophesied about the role of Nebuchadnezzar in history:

> *"'And now I have given all these lands into the hand of Nebuchadnezzar the king of Babylon, My servant; and the beasts of the field I have also given him to serve him. So all nations shall serve him and his son and his son's son, until the time of his land comes; and then many nations and great kings shall make him serve them. And it shall be that the nation and kingdom which will not serve Nebuchadnezzar the king of Babylon, and which will not put its neck under the yoke of the king of Babylon, that nation I will punish,' says the Lord, 'with the sword, the famine, and the pestilence, until I have consumed them by his hand.'"* Jeremiah 27:6-8

Nebuchadnezzar started his conquests in 605 B.C. as he commanded the Babylonian army against the Egyptians in the battle of Carchemish. He also came to Jerusalem and made King Jehoiakim his vassal, taking some of the most promising young men of Judah, such as Daniel, back to Babylon. He ascended the throne later that year, and reigned for forty-three years. Though he preferred to stay in his capital city, he was not adverse to personally dealing with rebellious subjects. That is why he went back to Jerusalem in December 598 B.C. The teenage king, Jehoiachin, was captured along with his mom, his wives, his officers, his craftsmen, and the mighty men of the land, and taken back to Babylon. Nebuchadnezzar placed a new king, Zedekiah, on the throne. Zedekiah, neither listening to the wisdom of the Lord in the prophets, nor learning a lesson from the previous king's experience, formed an alliance against Babylon with Egypt. When Nebuchadnezzar learned of this treachery, he determined to destroy Jerusalem and remove her last king. This was accomplished with a severe finality by 587 B.C. Solomon's Temple was destroyed, the city walls were broken down, the houses of the rich and mighty were torched, and the rest of the inhabitants of Jerusalem were taken back to Babylon, leaving only a few of the poorest to farm the land.

This mighty ruler was a significant player in God's plan. In fact, it was Nebuchadnezzar who had the famous dream of a great statue, which Daniel then saw in prayer and interpreted. He told the troubled king that this image, with its "head of fine gold, its chest and arms of silver, its belly and thighs of bronze, its legs of iron, its feet partly of iron and partly of clay" described four kingdoms which would rule on the earth, with the first kingdom being his own:

> *"You, O king, are a king of kings. For the God of heaven has given you a kingdom, power, strength, and glory; and wherever the children of men dwell, or the beasts of the field and the birds of the heaven, He has given them into your hand, and has made you ruler over them all—you are this head of gold."* Daniel 2:37-38

Daniel went on to describe three more conquering kingdoms in this dream, which we learn later in the book of Daniel are the kingdoms of the Persians & Medes, the Greeks, and finally, the Romans. These kingdoms are described with such detailed accuracy, that modern critics say it could not have been written in the mid-500's B.C., but must have been written in 165 B.C. (after Antiochus Epiphanes desecrated the Temple in Jerusalem in 167 B.C.). In reality, however, He is able to give His servants wisdom and knowledge of the future. After all, God is the One, *"declaring the end from the beginning, and from* ancient times things that are not yet done, saying, 'My counsel shall stand, and I will do all My pleasure.'" Isaiah 46:10

These four kingdoms, which were represented by the great statue, were destroyed in the dream by a great stone which struck the image, "…became a great mountain and filled the whole earth." (Daniel 2:35) Daniel told the king: "And in the days of these kings the God of heaven will set up a kingdom which shall never be destroyed…" (Daniel 2:44). By the end of this book, we will discover how truly this prophetic dream came true.

Evidently, Nebuchadnezzar agreed with God's assessment of him being a king of kings and a ruler over all, as most of the bricks which have been recovered from Babylon are stamped with these words: "I am Nebuchadnezzar, king of Babylon, son of Nabopolassar, king of Babylon." He went on to boast, "Is not this great Babylon, that I have built for a royal dwelling by my mighty power and for the honor of my majesty?" (Daniel 4:30) Scripture describes that at the moment of his greatest glory and pride, he was humbled by going stark, raving mad for a period of seven years (most scholars agree that the time period mentioned was years.) When he came back to sanity, he began to praise and honor the God of the Jews. This experience has not been found in the official Babylonian records, but then, archaeologists have not recovered records for the last thirty-two years of Nebuchadnezzar's reign.

Beyond maintaining order in his empire and having dealings with the God of the Jews, Nebuchadnezzar finished the reconstruction of Babylon which his father had envisioned and planned. The city of Babylon was in two sections, divided by the palm-fringed Euphrates River. Herodotus, the Greek historian who saw Babylon a hundred and fifty years after Nebuchadnezzar, said that the city was surrounded by an outer wall sixty miles in length, fifteen miles wide, 300 feet high, and 85 feet thick! Between the outer walls and inner walls was a wide moat, and people were only able to enter the city through eight huge bronze gates. It seemed impregnable, impossible to successfully invade. However, after the seventy years of captivity for the Jews was completed, the Persians took mighty Babylon in one night. How were they able to accomplish such a task? Though you can read the story in Daniel 5, the true reason behind the military success is this:

"Blessed be the name of God forever and ever, for wisdom and might are His. And He changes the times and the seasons; **He removes kings and raises up kings;** He gives wisdom to the wise and knowledge to those who have understanding."
Daniel 2:20-21

We have seen God's incredible mercy towards those who knew Him and towards those who did not know Him, His long-suffering towards Israel and Judah (and even Nebuchadnezzar!) with prophetic warnings of impending judgment so that they might repent, and His on-time delivery of His promises. What an awesome God!

Reviewed Resources for Digging Deeper:
From Student Manual pages 157-159

Archaeological Finds of Assyria:

Secrets of the Royal Mounds by Cynthia Jameson
   This delightful book is the story of Austen Layard, a British adventurer in the mid-1800's, who was the first to discover the cities of Assyria. It's certainly worth the trouble to find, as it is written in a capture-your-interest style. **UE+**

Nineveh And Its Remains by Austen Layard
   Read a first hand account of the unbelievable discovery of Nineveh in the mid-1800's. It is an amazing read for older students, and has recently been reprinted! **HS+**

The Assyrians by Elaine Landau

It is difficult to find books on the Assyrian time period which are appropriate for younger students. This is the best we have seen! **UE+**

Discoveries Among the Ruins of Nineveh by Austen Layard

This is a fascinating first-person account of Layard's second dig at Nineveh. It was published in the mid-1800's, so may be difficult to locate, but again, it's certainly worth the trouble. **HS+**

The Assyrians Activity Book by Lorna Oakes

Published by the British Museum, this is a book with great suggested activities, interesting articles to read, and fascinating pictures to color. **UE+**

Then and Now by Perring and Perring

One chapter of this great archaeological resource deals with Nimrud (known as Calah in the Bible) which was once the capital city of Assyria. **UE+**

Poetry

The Destruction of Sennacherib by Lord Byron

A poem showing the power of the Lord over the Assyrians. **RA**

Babylon

Heroes & Warriors: Nebuchadnezzar by Mark Healy

This is a fairly detailed, fairly dry book about King Nebuchadnezzar of Babylon. However, it is the only book that we found about this important historical figure. **MS+**

Great Wonders of the World by Russell Ash

Dorling Kindersley books are filled with amazing full-color drawings and helpful information. This one is devoted to the Seven Wonders of the Ancient World. **UE+**

The Seven Wonders of the Ancient World by Robert Silverberg

The Hanging Garden of Babylon was one of the wonders of the ancient world, along with the Pyramid of Cheops (Egypt), the statue of Zeus (Greece), the temple of Artemis (Ephesus), the Mausoleum of Halicarnassus (Asia Minor), the Colossus of Rhodes (Rhodes) and the Pharos Lighthouse (Alexandria, Egypt). This is an excellent introduction containing fascinating stories about these man-made marvels. **UE+**

Scrawl! Writing in Ancient Times

One of the most amazing finds in the archaeological digs of Assyria was the library of Asshurbanipal, containing 30,000 books! Learn more about early writing and the steps involved in deciphering it, using this and the following book. **UE+**

Ancient Scrolls by Michael Avi-Yonah, retold by Richard Currier

This is a very interesting book about a fascinating subject. "The pen [including the stylus] is mightier than the sword," has held true from the very beginning! **MS+**

Pottery

Fired Up!—Making Pottery in Ancient Times

Pottery is the most basic "book" archaeologists read as they try to understand ancient civilizations. This book is filled with pictures and descriptions of the types of pottery found in archaeological digs. Fascinating! **UE+**

Videos

Gateway to the Gods: Babylon Anthony Roland Collection

Probably available from a university or state library, this film gives an excellent understanding of the ruins of Babylon, the archaeological treasures, and the history of this city. Not as exciting as the following video, this is still an informative, interesting resource on the history of Babylon. **AA**

Assurnasirpal, The Assyrian King The Anthony Roland Collection

Probably available through your state or university library, this is a fascinating video of the Assyrians. One section is told from the viewpoint of Assurnasirpal, an Assyrian king. It utilizes the sculptures and artistic carvings on the now excavated palace walls to tell the stories of the culture. The video may seem long to younger children, but the entire family will benefit from seeing the surrounding terrain and amazing art. **AA**

The Sevens Wonders of the Ancient World by Questar

Absolutely captivating! This video really makes these wonders come to life, and helps us to understand more about the geography, the history and the cultures of the seven locations. **AA**

For more books, use these Dewey Decimal numbers in your library:

Bible: #220

Ancient Middle & Near Eastern: #930

Ancient Mesopotamia & Iranian Plateau: #935

Ancient Palestine: #933

Also, look for biographies on the key people listed.

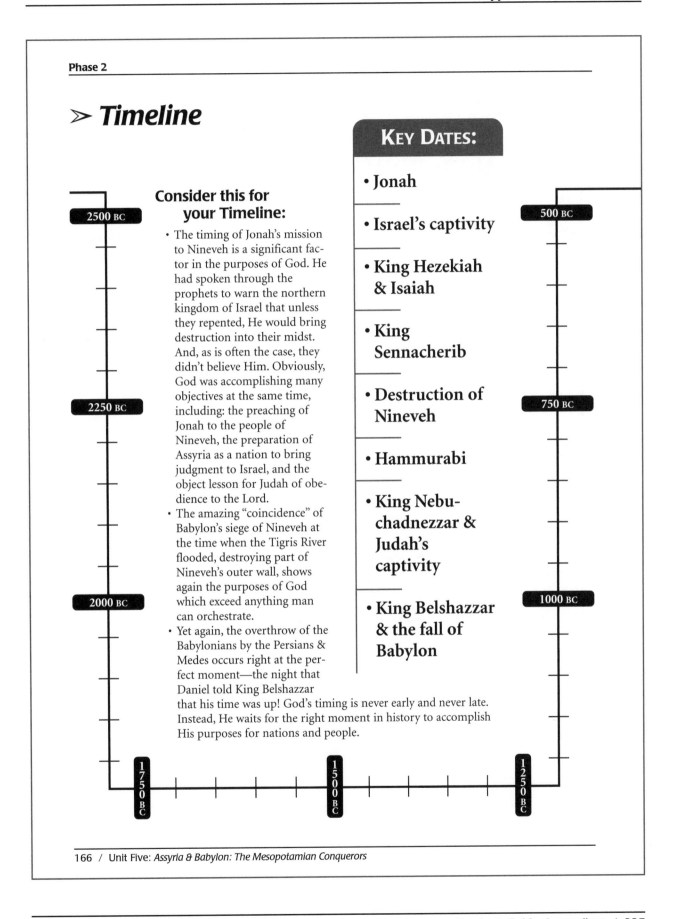

Phase 2

≫ *Timeline*

Consider this for your Timeline:

- The timing of Jonah's mission to Nineveh is a significant factor in the purposes of God. He had spoken through the prophets to warn the northern kingdom of Israel that unless they repented, He would bring destruction into their midst. And, as is often the case, they didn't believe Him. Obviously, God was accomplishing many objectives at the same time, including: the preaching of Jonah to the people of Nineveh, the preparation of Assyria as a nation to bring judgment to Israel, and the object lesson for Judah of obedience to the Lord.
- The amazing "coincidence" of Babylon's siege of Nineveh at the time when the Tigris River flooded, destroying part of Nineveh's outer wall, shows again the purposes of God which exceed anything man can orchestrate.
- Yet again, the overthrow of the Babylonians by the Persians & Medes occurs right at the perfect moment—the night that Daniel told King Belshazzar that his time was up! God's timing is never early and never late. Instead, He waits for the right moment in history to accomplish His purposes for nations and people.

KEY DATES:

- Jonah
- Israel's captivity
- **King Hezekiah & Isaiah**
- **King Sennacherib**
- **Destruction of Nineveh**
- **Hammurabi**
- **King Nebuchadnezzar & Judah's captivity**
- **King Belshazzar & the fall of Babylon**

2500 BC
2250 BC
2000 BC
1750 BC
1500 BC
1250 BC
1000 BC
750 BC
500 BC

166 / Unit Five: *Assyria & Babylon: The Mesopotamian Conquerors*

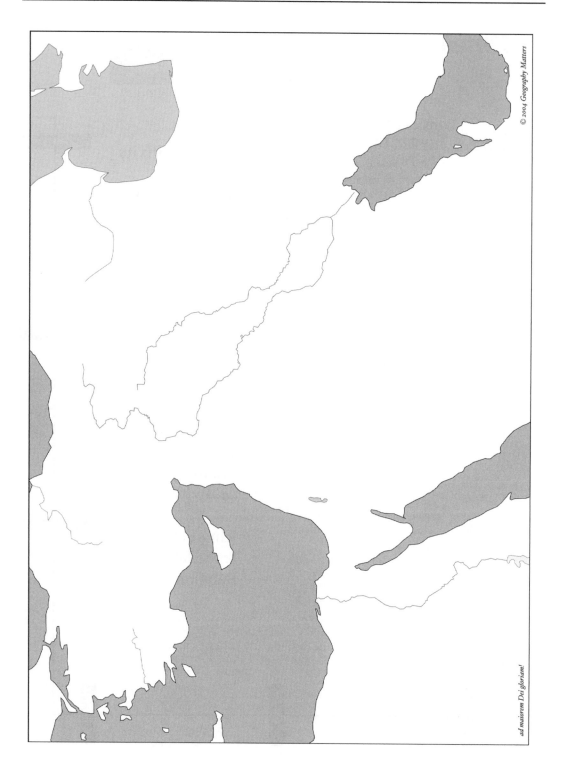

© 2004 Geography Matters

ad maiorem Dei gloriam!

Unit Five: *Assyria & Babylon: The Mesopotamian Conquerors* / 169

Repatriation to Jerusalem...

Article from Student Manual pages 181-191

"Thus says the Lord to His anointed, to Cyrus, whose right hand I have held, to subdue nations before him and loose the armor of kings, to open before him the double doors, so that the gates will not be shut; I will go before you and make the crooked places straight; I will break in pieces the gates of bronze and cut the bars of iron, I will give you the treasures of darkness and hidden riches of secret places, that you may know that I, the Lord, who call you by your name, am the God of Israel. For Jacob My servant's sake, and Israel My elect, I have even called you by your name; I have named you, though you have not known Me. I am the Lord, and there is no other, there is no god besides Me. I will gird you, though you have not known Me, that they may know from the rising of the sun to its setting that there is none besides Me. I am the Lord and there is no other; I form the light and create darkness, I make peace and create calamity; I, the Lord, do all these things." Isaiah 45:1-7

A king named Cyrus came to the throne of Persia in 558 B.C.—about eighty years after Isaiah's prophecy. He immediately made preparations to throw off the yoke of the neighboring Median Empire which had grown in size and power since the time of Ninevah's destruction. The Medes and Babylonians together had sacked Ninevah and had divided the Assyrian Empire between them. These two budding empires, along with Egypt and Lydia (who controlled most of Asia Minor), had maintained a balance of power until 589 B.C., when the Median king, Cyaxares, decided to enlarge his kingdom by attacking Lydia. Though the war had lasted five years, Cyaxares was not successful. When his successor came to the throne, the Median Empire began to wane, and was held together only by a fragile thread of power which was to soon come undone when Cyrus gave it a tug.

In 550 B.C., after waging war for three years, Cyrus triumphantly marched into the capital city of the Medes. We

see his great statesmanship and wisdom displayed in the way he honored the defeated Medes, giving many of their nobles a place in his own court, taking their capital city as his second capital, by referring to the Persian empire as that of the "Medes and Persians," and by allowing their king to live to the end of his natural life in the royal court of Cyrus.

With his formidable army, Cyrus next successfully attacked and conquered Lydia in 546 B.C. Two down, two to go. Before he left the area, Cyrus decided to complete the conquest of the area by capturing the Greek cities of Ionia (on the eastern edge of the Aegean Sea) and subjecting them to both tribute and service in his army. Having nearly doubled the size of his empire, Cyrus entered Babylonia in 540 B.C. and in October the following year, defeated Nabonidus, the Babylonian king. Nabonidus' son and co-regent, Belshazzar, was killed and the city of Babylon was taken a week later by Cyrus' general, Gobryas (probably the man named in Scripture as Darius the Mede). Cyrus actually entered the city in a triumphant procession on October 29, saying in his first official proclamation: *"I am Cyrus, king of the universe, Great King, mighty king, king of Babylon, king of Sumer and Akkad, king of the world quarters."*

This king was the ruler of the second kingdom in the great image Daniel had seen, the one with the chest and arms of silver. In Daniel 7:5, King Cyrus and the Medo-Persian Empire are described, not as a part of a statue, but as an animal:

"And suddenly another beast, a second, like a bear. It was raised up on one side, and had three ribs in its mouth between its teeth. And they said thus to it: 'Arise, devour much flesh!'"

Cyrus had just grabbed the third rib when he took Babylon and its empire. The first rib had been the empire of the Medes; the second, the Lydians. And from this beginning, the Medo-Persian Empire would go on to conquer many people and many lands—"much flesh." Isn't it incredible to know the One who knows it all?

2 Chronicles 36:22-23 tell us that in 538 B.C., the first year of his conquering Babylon, Cyrus changed the prevailing custom followed by conquering empires, which had been to rip people away from their land and forcibly resettle them elsewhere. Instead, he began a new and humane policy of repatriation for the displaced peoples of his empire, specifically the Jews, when he made this proclamation:

> *"All the kingdoms of the earth the Lord God of heaven has given me. And He has commanded me to build Him a house at Jerusalem which is in Judah. Who is there among you of all His people? May the Lord his God be with him, and let him go up!"*

Among the Jews in Babylon, there was a group of courageous and visionary people who responded to Cyrus' words and, with Zerubbabel as their leader, returned to the ruins of Jerusalem. They first erected an altar of sacrifice in 536 B.C., and then began to build the Temple in 535 B.C., seventy years after the initial conquering of Jerusalem by Nebuchadnezzar.

However, as they began the work, their neighboring enemies did everything possible to threaten and demoralize them:

> *"Then the people of the land tried to discourage the people of Judah. They troubled them in building, and hired counselors against them to frustrate their purpose all the days of Cyrus king of Persia, even until the reign of Darius king of Persia."* Ezra 4:4-5

Not only did they deal with nasty neighbors, the Jews also dealt with a desolated land, hard work, crop failure, and a sense of the paltriness of this Temple in comparison to Solomon's Temple.

> *But many of the priests and Levites and heads of the fathers' houses, who were old men, who had seen the first temple, wept with a loud voice when the foundation of this temple was laid before their eyes; yet many shouted aloud for joy, so that the people could not discern the noise of the shout of joy from the noise of the weeping of the people..."*
> Ezra 3:12-13

Can you imagine? From the luxuries of Babylon to the ruins of Jerusalem…from the blessing of the king to the taunts of their enemies…from the magnificence of Solomon's Temple to the seemingly insignificant foundations of a new temple, all worked insidiously on the hearts and minds of these repatriated Jews. Within two years, work on the Temple ceased. The people lost their focus and began to worry about their own needs, building luxurious, paneled dwellings for themselves. As is often the case, when people quit obeying the Lord and focus on their own comforts and ease, the opposition of the enemy dies down. But, for the Jews, it did not bring the satisfaction that they expected:

> *"You looked for much, but indeed it came to little; and when you brought it home, I blew it away. Why?" says the Lord of hosts, "Because of My house that is in ruins, while every one of you runs to his own house."* Haggai 1:9

Shortly after King Darius I (522-486 B.C.) began his reign, God sent Haggai and Zechariah to prophesy to the Jews in Jerusalem and Judah. You see, God still sought primacy in His people's hearts. It wasn't that He selfishly wanted His house built before theirs, but that He knew if they did not serve Him first, they would be drawn away again into idolatry and rebellion. So, with great love and mercy, He got their attention through the prophets, who told the people in no uncertain terms to recognize that they had neglected God's temple. Zerubbabel and Joshua, the high priest, immediately responded to the Lord in obedience, and the people followed. From 520 until 515 B.C., they labored to finish what they had begun, hopeful because God had promised them they would succeed:

> *"The hands of Zerubbabel have laid the foundation of this temple; his hands shall also **finish** it. Then you will know that the Lord of hosts has sent Me to you. For who has despised the day of small things?...* Zechariah 4:9-10

As soon as the Jews restarted their work on the temple, the appointed Persian governor of that satrapy, or region, wrote to King Darius I to let him know what was going on in Jerusalem, and to ask whether or not King Cyrus had actually made a proclamation for the rebuilding of the temple. This is part of King Darius I's reply:

"Now therefore, Tattenai, governor of the region beyond the River, and Shethar-Boznai, and your companions the Persians who are beyond the River, keep yourselves far from there. Let the work of this house of God alone; let the governor of the Jews and the elders of the Jews build this house of God on its site. Moreover I issue a decree as to what you shall do for the elders of these Jews, for the building of this house of God: Let the cost be paid at the king's expense from taxes on the region beyond the River; this is to be given immediately to these men, so that they are not hindered…Also I issue a decree that whoever alters this edict, let a timber be pulled from his house and erected, and let him be hanged on it; and let his house be made a refuse heap because of this. And may the God who causes His name to dwell there destroy any king or people who put their hand to alter it, or to destroy this house of God which is in Jerusalem. I Darius issue the decree; let it be done diligently." Ezra 6:6-8,11-12

Isn't that just like God? Not only does He end the opposition of their enemies, but He sets it up so that the work is paid for with money collected by and under the control of these same enemies! And, in the Persian Empire, there was no arguing with the decision of the king. His decree was law. Disobedience meant death.

King Darius I not only solved this problem for the Jews, he solved a major problem within his far-flung empire: how to communicate quickly and efficiently with all of his governors (and spies) from India to Turkey and Egypt to the Caspian Sea. He built and maintained roads, including the 1500 mile "Royal Road" from Sardis to Susa, which had road stations to provide fresh horses for the king's messengers—a system of communication much like the Pony Express riders of the mid-1800's in America! Herodotus, the Greek historian, actually traveled on this road, saying, *"At intervals all along the road are recognized stations, with excellent inns, and the road itself is safe to travel by, as it never leaves inhabited country…The total number of stations on the road from Sardis to Susa is 111…Traveling at the rate of 150 furlongs (18 miles) a day, a man will take just ninety days to make the journey."*

Not content with the size of his empire, Darius made his first strike at Europe in 512 B.C., easily conquering Thrace at the northern rim of the Aegean Sea. He continued on to the steppes of southern Russia, seeking, without success, to defeat the Scythians. After much frustration in not conquering their armies, he returned to Persia. When the Greeks in the Persian Empire (from the Ionian coastline) saw that the mighty Persian Empire was not invincible, they took great hope that they might be able to throw off the Persian yoke. In 499 B.C., the Greeks of Ionia began to rebel against Darius, with the pledged support of Athens behind them. They actually set the Persian city of Sardis (in Lydia) ablaze, an act of aggression which made the proud Darius more than willing for retaliation and retribution. He carefully prepared his army for war, and set out to teach the rebels (and their supporters) a lesson.

Thus the stage is set for the Battle of Marathon. Though Darius was able to easily recapture the Ionian cities through the sheer might of numbers, this formula did not work when it came to the Athenians. As the Persian army of 45,000 soldiers landed on the plain of Marathon, they were confronted with a Greek army of less than ten thousand. To the amazement of the Persians, this small group of fierce Greek warriors was able to wreak havoc and destruction on the much larger Persian army. As the Persians began to flee from the battle, the Greeks chased them, capturing seven ships before the Persians were able to escape.

This defeat only strengthened Darius' resolve to destroy Athens. Herodotus tells us that, *"without loss of time he dispatched couriers to the various states under his dominion with orders to raise an army much larger than before; and also warships, transports, horses, and grain. So the royal command went round; and all Asia was in an uproar for three years, with the best men being enrolled in the army for the invasion of Greece."*

When he died in 486 B.C., the duty of teaching Greece a lesson fell to his son, Xerxes (grandson of Cyrus the Great). As he was planning this war, Xerxes held a huge feast for all his nobles and officials that went on for six months. To finish off the celebrations, he held a seven day feast for all the people in Susa, and on the last day, called for his queen, Vashti.

"But Queen Vashti refused to come at the king's command brought by his eunuchs; therefore the king was furious, and his anger burned within him." Esther 1:12

In a moment of wrath, and with the advice of his counselors, Xerxes removed Vashti from her position, never to be seen by him again. And then he got back to his plans for punishing Greece.

The first item of business was to build a bridge across the stretch of water separating Asia from Europe—at the Hellespont. For this amazing endeavor, the engineers used boats, which were anchored both upstream and downstream and held together by taut cables of flax and papyrus. Over the cables planks were laid down, brushwood laid on top of the planks, with a layer of soil over the brushwood. This soil was packed down to solid firmness. To finish off the bridge, a fence was put up on each side of the boats, high enough to keep the horses and mules from seeing over the edge and becoming frightened by the water!

Over this bridge in 480 B.C., Xerxes marched the largest army ever assembled in antiquity. Though estimates differ, it was probably close to a million people marching to a war against several thousand Greek soldiers. Incredibly, though Xerxes was finally able to revenge the burning of Sardis by burning Athens, his huge navy lost to the Greeks in the Battle of the Bay of Salamis. Xerxes left most of his land army to continue fighting the Greeks while he returned to Susa, believing that, in time, the Greeks would certainly fall to the greater strength and numbers of the Persian army. However, within a year, the Greeks had nearly decimated the Persians. Xerxes was forced to withdraw what was left of his army and end his European campaign.

Coming home, bruised and beaten, Xerxes was in no mood for going without his beautiful queen. But the law of the Persians and the Medes was that once the king had made an edict, it could not be revoked. His counselors suggested a scheme whereby he could choose the most beautiful girl in the kingdom to become his new queen, and that is how the Jewish beauty, Esther, was set at just such a moment in a place of influence and power.

The book of Esther tells how an enemy of the Jews, Haman, sought to completely eradicate them from the face of the earth. He did not know, nor did Xerxes, that Queen Esther was Jewish, and he never imagined that there was anything or anyone who could prevent their annihilation once King Xerxes signed the edict. But God keeps watch over His people, and He powerfully turned what was intended for evil and destruction to good for the Jews. Though Esther very literally risked her life to go before Xerxes without being summoned (according to the custom of Persian kings as reported in archaeological and historical records), God gave her favor with the king, which led to the exposure of Haman's evil plan which led to a new edict by the king allowing the Jews to arm and defend themselves. The celebration of this deliverance of the Jews under Esther in 473 B.C. is called the Feast of Purim. And, for your edi-

fication, mention of Mordecai, Esther's uncle, as an official of Xerxes' government has been found in the Persian record under his Babylonian name, Marduka.

When Xerxes I died in 465 B.C., his son, Artaxerxes (465-424 B.C.) came to the throne. In his seventh year of rule, Artaxerxes wrote a royal decree for Ezra the scribe, instructing him to take all who were willing and return to Jerusalem, receiving as much money and provision from the king's treasury as was necessary for beautifying the temple of the Lord. Isn't it amazing to consider that this was the *third* ruler of the Persian Empire to both support the policy of repatriation for the Jews and supply money for their temple?

It is especially noteworthy that this same ruler had, at an earlier date, received notice from the rulers of Samaria that the Jews were trying to rebuild the city of Jerusalem, insinuating that they were planning a widespread rebellion against the king. His immediate response is found in Ezra 4:21-22:

> *"Now give the command to make these men cease, that this city may not be built until the command is given by me. Take heed now that you do not fail to do this. Why should damage increase to the hurt of the kings?"*

Yet, in spite of the devious plotting of their enemies, Ezra received the bountiful favor and supply of Artaxerxes, and was allowed to take thousands more Jews with him to Jerusalem in 457 B.C. In fact, Ezra had the opportunity to bear witness to Artaxerxes about the amazing goodness and power of God:

> *"...The hand of our God is upon all those for good who seek Him, but His power and His wrath are against all those who forsake Him."* Ezra 8:22

Thirteen years later, Artaxerxes' cupbearer came into his presence with obvious sorrow on his face. This official, with an extremely trusted and important post at the royal court, was a Jew by the name of Nehemiah. He had just learned that the walls of Jerusalem had been broken down and the gates were burned, leaving the city open to destruction at the whim of its enemies. Artaxerxes asked Nehemiah why he was so unhappy, and when he learned the reason, asked him to present his request. Nehemiah asked permission to go to Jerusalem and rebuild the walls, requesting even that the king would give letters of passage and supply. Artaxerxes readily agreed.

So in 444 B.C., Nehemiah and his Jewish compatriots went to Jerusalem, the third return of captives under the Persian kings. The story of the rebuilding of the city walls is as adventurous, dangerous and heroic as any best-selling epic novel. Nehemiah, knowing that the enemy was watching his every move, went by night to survey the damage to the city. Then he gathered the people of Jerusalem and told them his mission from God and from the king was to rebuild the walls. As they gladly began the process, the wrath of their enemies was great. Knowing that an attack could come at any time, Nehemiah instructed the builders that they should with one hand work at construction, and with the other hold a weapon. Though the enemy tried to draw Nehemiah into an ambush of assassination, he wisely stayed on the job. After fifty-two days, the wall was finished and Jerusalem was safe. Safe, but not obedient. The prophet Malachi, somewhere between 432 and 425 B.C., brought the word of the Lord to the people of Judah and Jerusalem. He revealed the coldness of their hearts, the insincerity of their worship, their unfaithfulness in marriage, and their arrogant ways. But, as always, God's word was intended to bring them to repentance and renewed right relationship with Him. His last recorded words to His people prior to John the Baptist, brought hope for their future, prophetically foretelling the coming of the One who would be the Redeemer of Israel:

"Behold, I will send you Elijah the prophet before the coming of the great and dreadful day of the Lord. And he will turn the hearts of the fathers to the children, and the hearts of the children to their fathers, lest I come and strike the earth with a curse." Malachi 4:5-6

Just as the vision of Jerusalem fades from the pages of Old Testament scripture, so fades the vision of Imperial Persia. The glory, renown, and power of Cyrus and Darius remained to Xerxes, but began to decline under the ineffectual rule of Artaxerxes. When he died, the struggle for the throne resulted in several kings being murdered shortly after taking the throne. Darius II (423-404 B.C.) was a degenerate, cruel king. When his son, Artaxerxes II, succeeded as king, the younger son, Cyrus, determined to seize the throne. Cyrus hired Greek mercenaries to supplement his own army, and in 401 B.C. marched against his brother. Shortly after the battle of Cunaxa began, Cyrus, the would-be usurper, was killed. One of the Greek mercenaries fighting for Cyrus was Xenophon, known in history for his military tactics, his horsemanship, and his writings. Once Cyrus was killed and the Greek commanders serving him were murdered, ten thousand Greek soldiers tried to find a way out of an incredibly hostile Persian countryside, back to the safety of Greece. They were successful, but that story belongs to the next chapter.

Reviewed Resources for Digging Deeper:

From Student Manual pages 194-195

Persia

The Persian Empire by Don Nardo

It is difficult to find books appropriate for children on the Persian Empire. This is the best one we have found. **UE+**

Persian Leaders

Cyrus the Persian by Sherman A. Nagel

This is a fascinating account of the life of Cyrus, written as historical fiction about the Babylonian, Persian and Biblical events. **UE+**

Behold Your Queen! by Gladys Malvern

Historical fiction concerning Esther, this wonderful book makes the details of the story of Esther come to life. **UE+**

Stories from Herodotus translated by Glanville Downey

This book is a children's version of the ancient Greek historian Herodotus. It details the invasion of Greece by the Persians in 490 B.C. and 480 B.C. We couldn't put it down. **UE+**

World Leaders Past and Present: Xerxes by Morgan Llwelyn

Written in a very interesting style, this is an excellent book about a fascinating leader! This gives a very thorough understanding of the most significant king of Persia. **MS+**

Within the Palace Gates—The King's Cupbearer by Anna P. Siviter

Originally published in 1932, it is a spellbinding story of Nehemiah, woven into the backdrop of the royal Persian Court. **UE+**

The Lion in The Gateway by Mary Renault

A fictional account for children of the Persian invasion of Greece. The battles of Marathon, Thermopylae, and Salamis are described in rich detail. You will not understand the history of Persia or Greece without understanding these battles. **UE+**

Children of the Fox by Jill Paton Walsh

This book could be read either in this unit or the unit on Greece. It is another fictionalized story of the Persians invading Greece in 480 B.C. Written as three short stories about Greek children, it includes a story about the aftermath of the invasion, which helps one understand the reason for the Peloponnesian wars between Athens and Sparta. **AA**

Exploits of Xenophon translated by Geoffrey Household

This is an incredible, riveting book! It is the true, autobiographical account of Greek mercenaries fighting for a Persian governor who wishes to usurp the throne and become king of Persia. **RA**

A Modern Day Daniel

Imprisoned in Iran by Dan Baumann

A riveting true story about a Christian in Iran sharing the love of God while imprisoned and facing the death penalty in the land of ancient Persia. From YWAM Publishing. **UE+**

For more books, use these Dewey Decimal numbers in your library:

Bible: #220

Ancient Mesopotamia and the Iranian Plateau: #935

Ancient Palestine: #933

Also, look for biographies on the key people listed.

Phase 2

➤ *Timeline*

1000 BC

Consider this for your Timeline:

- God's timing is perfect! He told Jeremiah that the time of captivity for the Jews in Babylon would last for seventy years, and the Medo-Persian army overthrew the Babylonian Empire at exactly the right moment to accomplish the release and repatriation of the Jews back to Jerusalem to begin rebuilding the Temple in 535 B.C.—which was exactly seventy years from when they were taken captive in 605 B.C. We must not grow indifferent to the remarkable faithfulness of God in the timeline of history!
- The Book of Esther gives an awe-inspiring glimpse of the importance each of our lives has in history: "*Yet who knows whether you have come to the kingdom* for such a time as this?" (Esther 4:14) What does this mean to you? Reflect and consider how perfectly God has set you into your moment in history.

750 BC

KEY DATES:

- Cyrus' proclamation

- Return of Jews (three separate dates)

- Temple rebuilt

- Battle of Marathon

- Xerxes

- Battle of Bay of Salamis

- Ezra

- Esther

- Nehemiah

- Malachi

1 BC

250 BC

500 BC

200 / Unit Six: *The Persians & Medes*

© 2004 Geography Matters

ad maiorem Dei gloriam!

The third kingdom of Daniel's vision emerges...

Article from Student Manual pages 213-224

Just before the defeat of the Babylonians at the hands of the Medo-Persian army in 539 B.C., Daniel was given another startling, prophetic vision by God. In this vision, he saw a mighty, victorious ram that conquered to the west, the north, and the south, and was so powerful that no one could withstand it. Suddenly, from the west came a fierce male goat which attacked the ram, and this furious goat trampled the ram to the ground. Daniel saw that "there was no one that could deliver the ram from his hand."

When Daniel sought the meaning of this vision, the angel Gabriel came to him and explained that, *"the ram which you saw, having the two horns—they are the kings of Media and Persia. And the male goat is the kingdom of Greece. The large horn that is between its eyes is the first king."* Daniel 8:20-21

Two hundred years before the event, God showed His people that a Greek king would topple the mighty Persian Empire. The name of this king was Alexander the Great, and he did exactly what Daniel saw in the vision. He was also the one described as "a leopard, which had on its back four wings of a bird" (Daniel 7:6), and his kingdom was the "belly and thighs of bronze" in the great statue dreamed by Nebuchadnezzar and interpreted by Daniel. But, before we study Alexander and the fruit of his conquests, we need to better understand the history of Greece prior to his advent.

A map of the terrain of Greece will show immediately that this area is rugged, mountainous and coastal (no village or city is far from the sea). Because the land is mostly mountainous with few large plains, and because the sea is such a prominent feature, the ancient people of Greece developed a different style of living than the ancient farmers of Mesopotamia, including travel by boat rather than overland, because the sea was generally easier to traverse than the land. This familiarity with sea travel would prove significant in the areas of trade, warfare, and the spread of philosophic influence throughout the history of the Greeks.

Beginning in the 1200's B.C. with the invasion of southern Greece by the warlike Dorian tribe, the people of Greece scattered throughout the land. Small communities formed in isolated places, separated from each other by the mountains. These communities eventually became city-states, which included a city with its surrounding villages, farms and countryside. These communities usually were set around a hill or rocky outcropping, and a fortress known as an *acropolis* was built at the summit which could be easily defended if attacked. The best known of these city-states were Athens and Sparta, though there were many others throughout the land.

The people of this time did not think of themselves as "Greeks," but rather as Athenians, Spartans, Thebans, Corinthians or whatever city-state they were from. This separation, which was both physical and philosophical, caused many difficulties for the Greek people and gave the Persian king, Darius, great assurance that he could pick off each querulous city-state one by one, rather than having to face a united enemy. In fact, in all of their history, it was only during periods of extreme duress, such as the Persian invasion by Xerxes, that the Greek city-states joined together to function as one group.

By the eighth century, the population was greater than this mountainous land could support, so many left to find new lands which would provide a more abundant life. These people traveled to many areas throughout the Mediterranean, including Italy, Sicily, France, north Africa, and up into the Black Sea region. Wherever they went, they set up Greek city-states similar to what they had experienced at home. These new settlements began trading with the city-states back in Greece, which brought about a tremendous influx of new resources for the Greek people. It also gave great wealth to those who controlled these resources, creating a prosperous middle class to compete with the wealthy, landowning aristocracy.

To fulfill their required duty to the city-state as soldiers, the newly enriched middle class developed weapons and armor in the seventh century B.C. which could be used very successfully by foot soldiers. A new shield, called a *hoplon*, was developed which put the weight of the shield on the soldier's shoulder rather than his wrist. Though this was an innovative and helpful design, it left the soldier's right side exposed. To protect this vulnerability, a new method of fighting was developed which placed soldiers shoulder to shoulder in a tight formation know as a *phalanx*. The soldiers in formation behind the front line, pushed together towards the front, which gave the phalanx an incredible, indefatigable momentum. Not only were their right sides protected now, the structure of the phalanx made the armies efficient and powerful fighting machines. These well-outfitted, extremely proficient soldiers, known as *hoplites*, became the backbone of the various city-states' military force. In fact, they were nearly invincible, as King Darius learned to his dismay at the battle of Marathon.

By the mid-sixth century B.C. in Athens, the extreme differences between the wealthy and the poor brought the city to the brink of revolution. Plutarch, a Greek biographer of the first century B.C., wrote about this time, "*The disparity of fortune between the rich and the poor had reached its height, so that the city seemed to be in a truly dangerous condition, and no other means for freeing it from disturbances...seemed possible but a despotic power.*" However, rather than a revolution, a ruler named Solon provided a means for escape in 549 B.C. In one move, he canceled all debt in Athens. All lands were released from mortgages, all people who had been made slaves due to debt were released, all sold into slavery abroad were brought home and freed. This one step had a remarkable effect upon Athens and its' people. Just as God had told Moses to proclaim a Year of Jubilee every fifty years for the dismissal of debt and the blessing of the people, this Greek ruler saw divine wisdom in releasing the people from bondage.

Though Solon brought reform to the people of Athens, it wasn't long after his departure from Athens that the historical struggle between the wealthy and the poor again appeared to trouble the city. This time, a man seized power and became a *tyrant*. This Greek word meaning "ruler" did not have the same connotation at that time as it has today. In fact, the period of Greek history from about 650 B.C. to about 500 B.C. was known as the "age of tyrants," because many rulers of Greek city-states during this time had come to power not by royal birth nor by the will of the people, but through military power. Some ruled well, others did not, some ruled for long periods

while others were quickly overthrown. In Athens, the man who seized control was named Pisistratus, and he basically enforced the laws of Solon. Under his rule, the Athenians became used to living with good laws, great public works (such as the building of temples and aqueducts), a powerful army which protected their peace, and economic improvement for all. As Will Durant wrote in **The Life of Greece**, "The poor were made less poor, the rich not less rich." After thirty-three years of this kind of peaceful rule, though, everything changed. The son of Pisistratus, who had ruled quietly for the previous thirteen years, suddenly changed his policies and subjected the Athenians to a reign of terror. He and his family were driven out of Athens in 510 B.C., and the city was plunged into two years of civil war. But in 508 B.C., Cleisthenes came to power. Finally, under this man *democracy*, a new form of government, was established in Athens. He demolished the power base of the aristocratic ruling families by dividing Athens into "tribes" composed of equal number of districts from the city, the coast, and the interior. This gave the new democracy a broader base of support from geographic regions. Regardless of wealth, each citizen now had the right to vote on laws, to speak at governmental assemblies, to participate in the government if they were selected, and to fulfill their duty by volunteering at times to be on a legal jury.

To be a citizen in Athens, men who were at least eighteen years old had to show that they were eligible by:

1) proving that both parents were born in Athens
2) proving that both parents were of the citizen class
3) proving that the parents were legally married.

Those who became citizens were then expected to devote their time to the affairs of the city, learning all they could about politics and the issues of the day, and serving the system as needed. They were also expected to be prepared for military service if necessary. However, doing physical labor or being involved in any form of business, apart from managing one's estate, was not considered proper for a citizen.

Those who were not citizens made up two other groups: the *metic*, who were the foreigners that traded, kept shops, made crafts, and owned ships; and the *slaves* who did the manual labor in homes, markets, workshops and the silver mines.

Shortly after this system of democracy began to function in Athens, the Persian Empire attacked the Athenians in 490 B.C. at the Plain of Marathon. Though the Persians were defeated in that battle, it was obvious to many that someday soon they would return, and they would be ready to take vengeance when they came.

While Athens was struggling through various types of rule, Sparta developed a completely unique form of government. Sparta also had citizens, but only a very few could obtain citizenship. The requirements were:

1) prove that both parents were descended from the original Dorian invaders
2) complete every stage of the Spartan school system (which had one main subject—warfare!)
3) belong to one of the military clubs, providing a certain amount of food and drink for it.

If you could meet these requirements, and were thirty years of age, you could be a citizen of Sparta. Now for the bad news: all Spartan citizens were full-time professional soldiers and were forbidden to do any other form of work from the ages of eighteen to sixty. If soldiers were not actually in battle, they were subjecting themselves to the harsh rigors of the Spartan soldier's lifestyle. They were expected to give total loyalty to the state, to obey those in authority, to prepare themselves at all times for war, and to prefer death to defeat in battle.

Those who were not citizens and yet were not slaves performed the function of craftsmen, fisherman, tradesmen, and sailors. The slaves were the conquered people from the neighboring land of Messenia which now belonged to the Spartan city-state. They had no chance for freedom unless they successfully revolted (which happened only a few times). They were forced to farm the land of Sparta and the land of Messenia for the Spartan citizens, who were given an allotment of land and a certain number of slaves by the government.

When a baby boy was born to the soldier-class in Sparta, he was examined to make sure he was not weak or blemished. If he passed inspection, he was allowed to live. When this boy was seven years old, he was taken from home to a barracks-school where he learned to fight and survive harsh treatment. When he finished school, each boy had to join the Spartan army where he would live in the austere barracks until old age. Though he was supposed to marry by age thirty, a Spartan soldier would not stay with his wife for more than a short time before going back to the barracks. This military mindset, and its efficient system of producing tough soldiers, made Sparta the

greatest military power in Greece. The Spartans rarely left home, however, since they were always concerned about the very real threat of a slave revolt on their native soil.

In 480 B.C., the Spartans were motivated to join with other Greek city-states. Why? The largest army ever assembled at that point in history was on the march against Greece. Led by the Persian king, Xerxes, this army of more than a million soldiers was threatening the Greeks with the loss of all their freedom and much-desired independence. King Leonidas of Sparta took control of the 7,000 troops at Thermopylae, a narrow pass through which Xerxe's huge army had to travel. An incredulous Xerxes watched his men suffering a tremendous defeat as they were repulsed again and again by this tiny army of Greeks. Who knows how long this would have continued if a traitor had not shown Xerxes a way to get behind the enemy position. Once Xerxes had annihilated King Leonidas and three hundred of his men (the rest being ordered by Leonidas to retreat), he marched on Athens.

The Athenians, after the Battle of Marathon, had wisely listened to the counsel of a leader named Themistocles, who encouraged the people to build a proper seaport and a large fleet of warships. So as Xerxes came to Athens, the people fled the city, boarded boats at the harbor, and were taken out of harm's way. Xerxes, as we saw in the last unit, retaliated against the Greeks for the burning of Sardis during his father's reign by burning the city of Athens. But that was not sufficient punishment for these rebellious Greeks, so, when he was told that the Greeks had warships in the Bay of Salamis, he called for the Persian fleet to annihilate them. Aeschylus, a Greek playwright who described this battle from the viewpoint of the Persians, wrote, *"A Greek ship charged first, chopped off the whole stern of a Phoenician galley. Then charge followed charge on every side. At first by its huge impetus our fleet withstood them. But soon in that narrow space, our ships were jammed in hundreds; none could help another. They rammed each other with their prows of bronze and some were stripped of every oar. Meanwhile, the enemy came around us in a ring and charged. Our vessels heeled over. The sea was carpeted with wrecks and dead men; all the shores and reefs were full of dead. Then every ship we had broke rank and rowed for life."*

The Persian fleet was soundly defeated, and Xerxes went home. Many of the Greek city-states were concerned, however, that the Persians might return yet again, so they banded together into the Delian League with a common treasury held on the island of Delos. Athens was the leader of this league, contributing ships rather than money. This gave the Athenians an edge over their allies (who lacked sea power), creating eventually an Athenian Empire. In the mid-400's B.C., the Athenian leader, Pericles, realized that the accumulated treasure of the Delian League was lying unused and relatively unprotected on Delos, and suggested that the Athenians take the money back to Athens. Any money beyond what was absolutely necessary for the defense of the League could then be used by the Athenians to rebuild and beautify their city. Quite a good idea for Athens, not as good an idea for its allies in the Delian League, but who was going to argue with them? None of their allies had the power of Athens.

The Classical Period of Greek history (480-323 B.C.), began with the defeat of Xerxes and lasted until the time of Alexander the Great. The first fifty years of this period are known as the *Golden Age*, since this was the time when the arts (such as architecture, literature, philosophy, sculpting, and theater) flourished in Athens. This is the time of Socrates, the philosopher who asked questions; Aeschylus, the founder of Greek tragedy and writer of ninety plays; Pheidias, the sculptor who created the statue of Zeus (one of the seven wonders) as well as the statue of Athene in the Parthenon; Herodotus, the Greek traveler and writer who became known as the "Father of History"; and many other influential people. However, the Golden Age came to an abrupt halt in 431 B.C. when Sparta and its allies went to war against Athens and its allies.

The war between Sparta and Athens was called the Peloponnesian War, and it lasted for twenty-seven years, devastating Greece. Since Sparta had a nearly invincible land army, and Athens had a superior navy, Sparta was able to invade the land surrounding Athens but Athens was able to import food through its ships. This prolonged the struggle for many years. There was a short time of peace after a treaty was signed in 421 B.C., but war soon broke out again. Eventually, Persia gave the Spartans a loan of money so that they were able to build a navy and destroy the Athenian fleet. This meant that Athens could no longer be resupplied with food, and in 404 B.C., the starving Athenians surrendered to the Spartans.

Though the war was over, peace was not forthcoming. The weakened city-states continued to struggle for supremacy over each other, with constant battles and small wars. During this troubled time, Xenophon and thousands of other Greek mercenaries (soldiers for hire) went to work for Cyrus, the brother of the Persian king. In the last unit, we learned that, after the death of Cyrus while in battle to usurp the throne, ten thousand Greek soldiers had to battle their way out of a hostile Persian land. They elected the Athenian cavalry officer and former student of Socrates, Xenophon, to lead them safely home. Against overwhelming odds, Xenophon and his troops battled their way along the Tigris and north to Kurdistan and Armenia, all the way to the Black Sea, a journey of two thousand miles, contested every step of the way. It was in this epic struggle that the lesson was learned that a small Greek army could successfully war against a massive Persian army on its own terrain. This lesson would be studied and applied by one who was yet to come.

In 359 B.C., Philip II came to the throne of Macedonia, an area northeast of Greece. The country was in turmoil at this point due to constant invasions and civil war. However, Philip brought a brilliant military mind and a diplomatic tongue to bear on the chaotic state, and within twenty years, he had turned Macedonia into the most powerful military state of the day. In 338 B.C., he won the battle of Chaeronea, conquering Athens, Thebes and their allies, which allowed Philip to take control of Greece. A year later, he united Greece and Macedonia by planning a joint war against Persia. Though he was assassinated soon after, the war effort was continued by his son, Alexander.

At last we have arrived at the point where we started this story! Alexander took control of his father's military forces when he became king of Macedonia in 336 B.C., and within two years subdued the entire country of Greece to his will. In 334 B.C., Alexander invaded Persia with 30,000 infantry and 5,000 cavalry, a paltry number compared to the size of army the Persians could muster. However, just as Xenophon had proved, the Greek army was more than capable of defeating the Persians. The battle of Issus in 333 B.C. was the first battle between the Greeks and Persians, and through Alexander's brilliant strategy it was won decisively. From there, Alexander turned toward Egypt, to secure his flanks. On the way, he captured and destroyed the heretofore impregnable city of Tyre. As he journeyed onward to Egypt, he came to the land of Palestine. He destroyed the recalcitrant city of Gaza, and then turned his eye toward Jerusalem. The Jewish historian, Josephus, describes what happened next:

"Now Alexander, when he had taken Gaza, made haste to go up to Jerusalem; and Jaddua the high

priest, when he heard that, was in an agony, and under terror, as not knowing how he should meet the Macedonians, since the king was displeased at his foregoing disobedience. He therefore ordained that the people should make supplications, and should join with him in offering sacrifice to God, whom he besought to protect that nation, and to deliver them from the perils that were coming upon them; whereupon God warned him in a dream, which came upon him after he had offered sacrifice, that 'he should take courage, and adorn the city, and open the gates; that the rest should appear in white garments, but that he and the priests should meet the king in the habits proper to their order, without the dread of any ill consequences, which the providence of God would prevent.' Upon which, when he rose from his sleep, he greatly rejoiced; and declared to all the warning he had received from God…And when the Phoenicians and the Chaldeans that followed him, thought they should have liberty to plunder the city, and torment the high priest to death, which the king's displeasure fairly promised them, the very reverse of it happened; for Alexander, when he saw the multitude at a distance, in white garments, while the priests stood clothed with fine linen, and the high priest in purple and scarlet clothing, with his mitre on his head, having the golden plate whereon the name of God was engraved, he approached by himself, and adored that Name, and first saluted the high priest. The Jews also did altogether, with one voice, salute Alexander, and encompass him about; whereupon the king of Syria, and the rest, were surprised at what Alexander had done, and supposed him disordered in his mind. However, Parmenio alone went up to him, and asked him, 'How it came to pass, that when all others adored him, he should adore the high priest of the Jews?' To whom he replied, 'I did not adore him, but that God who hath honored him with the high priesthood; for I saw this very person in a dream, in this very habit, when I was at Dios in Macedonia, who, when I was considering with myself how I might obtain the dominion of Asia, exhorted me to make no delay, but boldly to pass over the sea thither, for that he would conduct my army, and would give me the dominion over the Persians.'

And when the book of Daniel was shown him, wherein Daniel declared that one of the Greeks should destroy the empire of the Persians, he supposed that himself was the person intended: and as he was then glad, he dismissed the multitude for the present, but the next day he called them to him, and bade them ask what favors they pleased of him; whereupon the high priest desired that they might enjoy the laws of their forefathers, and might pay no tribute on the seventh year. He granted all they desired."

Alexander, over the next ten years, conquered every place he and his army came to, from Egypt to India. He was the first European to conquer Asia, and his empire was larger than any empire had ever been. When he died suddenly, at the age of thirty-three, his empire was forcibly broken up by four generals. By 281 B.C., the Hellenistic (or Greek) Empire of Alexander the Great was divided into three kingdoms: Egypt, ruled by the Ptolemies; Asia Minor, ruled by the Seleucids; and Macedonia and Greece ruled by the Antigonids.

Read the words of Daniel 8:8 and discover how perfectly God described Alexander and his empire:

> *"Therefore the male goat grew very great; but when he became strong, the large horn was broken, and in place of it four notable ones came up toward the four winds of heaven."*

The Hellenistic Empire brought the Greek language and culture to much of the known world. The permeating influence of Greek thought and Greek ways settled into the very fabric of most cultures from Rome to Egypt, and from Babylon to Jerusalem. Though many people welcomed what they considered the civilizing effect of the Greeks, there were some who fought to keep hellenism at bay.

Judea had been under the benevolent control of the Ptolemies for many years and given the same consideration for their religious beliefs and ceremonies as Alexander the Great had provided. However, when Antiochus Epiphanes (a Seleucid ruler) came to power in Syria, he decided that the Jews needed a good dose of hellenization in order to be freed from their ancient and obsolete religion. In 167 B.C., he sacked Jerusalem on the Sabbath, and set up a statue of Zeus in the Temple on the altar, where pigs were then offered as sacrifices. Next, he outlawed on pain of death the practice of circumcision, observing the Sabbath, or celebrating the Jewish holy days.

The country erupted into revolution when Antiochus Epiphanes' officer arrived in the village of Modin. He expected the old priest, Mattathias, to meekly cooperate with the projected program of offering a pagan sacrifice, but Mattathias refused. When another Jew willingly came forth, Mattathias was enraged and he killed both the traitor to Judaism and the king's officer, along with destroying the pagan altar. Mattathias and his five sons then fled to the hills. Many others who were committed to following the God of their fathers joined Mattathias in the hills, and began to wage guerilla warfare on both the Syrians and the Hellenistic Jews who supported them. When Mattathias died, shortly after starting this revolt, his third son, Judas was chosen to be the military leader of the guerilla army. He was given the name "Maccabee" which means "the hammer." Judas Maccabee was a good choice as he proved to be a phenomenally successful general. Both Josephus and the Book of First Maccabees in the Apocrypha describe Judas Maccabee as one who trusted in the Lord and looked to Him for deliverance of his nation. God enabled the outnumbered Maccabean army to recapture Jerusalem three years after Antiochus Epiphanes had sacked it. They purified the Temple, grinding the statue of Zeus into dust, and then celebrated with an eight-day Feast of Dedication, known as Hanukkah, the Festival of Lights.

Three empires have come and gone since Daniel's dream. One remains.

Reviewed Resources for Digging Deeper:
From Student Manual pages 227-229

Ancient Greece

The Greeks—Usborne Illustrated World History by Susan Peach and Anne Millard
> Filled with short descriptions and great pictures, this is a wonderful, concise, fact-filled book about ancient Greece. **UE+**

Ancient Greece by Pamela Bradley
> This Cambridge Junior History book is an excellent introduction to ancient Greece for pre-high school students. **UE+**

Growing Up in Ancient Greece by Chris Chelepi
> Great overview! This series really helps explain many different aspects of life in ancient times. **E+**

Focus on Ancient Greeks by Anita Ganeri Published by Aladdin Books
> If you can find it, this book is an excellent, multifaceted look at Greece. **E+**

Famous Men of Greece edited by Rob Shearer
> An excellent, brief introduction to the important historical figures of Greece, written in biographical style. **UE+**

Golden Days of Greece by Olivia Coolidge
> This is one of the best authors of short biographies that I've found. Her books are uniformly interesting and filled with the kinds of tidbits that make history memorable. **UE+**

Travelogue

Herodotus by Henry Cary
> This Greek historian was the first world traveler who kept track of the places he visited. Herodotus is one of the most important writers of antiquity, and his writings are still fascinating. **HS+**

Biographies

Alexander the Great by Robert Green

This is a wonderful, short biography of the man who conquered the known world in ten years. **UE+**

World Leaders Past and Present: Pericles by Terry Scott King

This was the Greek leader who masterminded the Golden Age of Greece after the victory over Xerxes. This series of books is absolutely fantastic reading! **MS+**

World Leaders Past and Present: Alexander the Great by Dennis Wepman

One of the most significant military leaders in world history, Alexander the Great was also a fascinating historical figure. **MS+**

World Leaders Past and Present: Judas Maccabees by E. H. Fortier

This is a riveting look at the Maccabean Revolt which occurred during the Hellenistic period. Skip Chapter Three, which deals with the history of Israel, because the author does not have a Biblical worldview. However, apart from that chapter, the book is fascinating, filled with historical details, and reads like fiction. **MS+**

In Search of Troy by Ventura and Ceserani

Piero Ventura is a masterful artist, and his books are always worth searching for. This is the intriguing story of Heinrich Schliemann, the amateur who discovered Troy. (Probably, the war between Troy and Greece took place during the time of the Mycenaeans.) **UE+**

Maccabean Revolt

Apocrypha

1 Maccabees is one of the major historical accounts of the Maccabean revolt. It, along with Josephus, contains the best record of these events. **UE+**

Josephus

Book XII, chapters V–VIII, contains the account of Antiochus Epiphanies and his desecration of the Temple in Jerusalem. The resulting rebellion on the part of the pious Jews was led first by Mattathias Maccabees and then by his son Judas. It is an incredible tale of courage, of military shrewdness, and of God's blessing. **RA**

Science and Math

Discoveries, Inventions & Ideas by Jane Shuter

This is an excellent introduction for younger students to the achievements of the Greeks, including astronomy, medicine, democracy, even the first fire engine! **E+**

Science in Ancient Greece by Kathlyn Gay

If you skip the second chapter on evolution, the remainder of the book is wonderful! Learn about many different areas of science which were "pioneered" by the Greeks. **UE+**

Make it Work! Ships by Andrew Solway

All of the books in this series are absolute wonders, especially because they truly create an environment for the whole family to discover science, history, etc. This book is great because it demonstrates the displacement of ships in water. That is the principle of buoyancy, which was discovered by Archimedes (see above book.) **AA**

Make it Work! Machines by David Glover

One more experiment to show an invention of Archimedes. He invented the water screw, which still has many functions and is used in many parts of the world. A fabulous book! **AA**

Mathematicians are People, Too by Reimer & Reimer

Three of the earliest named mathematicians in history were Greek. This fascinating book tells the story of these men as well as mathematicians from later times. **UE+**

Cooking

Greek Food and Drink by Irene Tavlarios

One of the best Greek cookbooks I've seen, this delightful book also describes some of the history of Greek cooking, lots of delectable pictures of food, and more. **UE+**

Warfare and Weaponry

The Greek Hoplite by Martin Windron

An excellent look at the Greek soldiers, who were among the best fighters of history. **UE+**

Digging Up the Past: Weapons and Warfare by Rivka Gonen

It's amazing how much we can learn about ancient cultures through their wars and weapons, both the winners and losers. **UE+**

Warfare in the Classical World by John Warry

An absolutely incredible book for those interested in following world history through warfare and weaponry. This book contains the best timeline I've ever seen for ancient civilizations. It is certainly worth the search. **MS+**

Charge! Weapons and Warfare in Ancient Times

Filled with pictures, this book also details ancient history through warfare. Excellent for the younger students interested in this aspect of history. **UE+**

Military History of the World— Volume One by J.F.C. Fuller

For those who really want to dig into this subject, this is the book to get. It includes some fascinating accounts of Alexander the Great. **HS+**

For more books, use these Dewey Decimal numbers in your library:

Ancient Greece: #938

Classical Literature: #880

Also, look for biographies on the archaeologists listed.

Phase 2

➤ *Timeline*

900 BC

Consider this for your Timeline:

- The Golden Age of Greece was very short-lived, though it's influence continues to be felt. As you look up the dates for the different time periods in ancient Greece and the Hellenistic Empire, think about God's purposes being fulfilled in history. How did He use these events and these people for His own plans for redemption?

650 BC

450 BC

KEY DATES:

- **Golden Age of Greece**

- **Socrates, Plato, Aristotle**

- **Pericles**

- **Peloponnesian wars**

- **Alexander the Great and his conquests**

- **Ptolemy II and the Septuagint**

- **Antiochus Epiphanies and the Maccabean Revolt**

- **Archimedes, Eratosthenes, Euclid**

- **The Pharos of Alexandria**

- **The Great Wall of China**

100 AD

150 BC

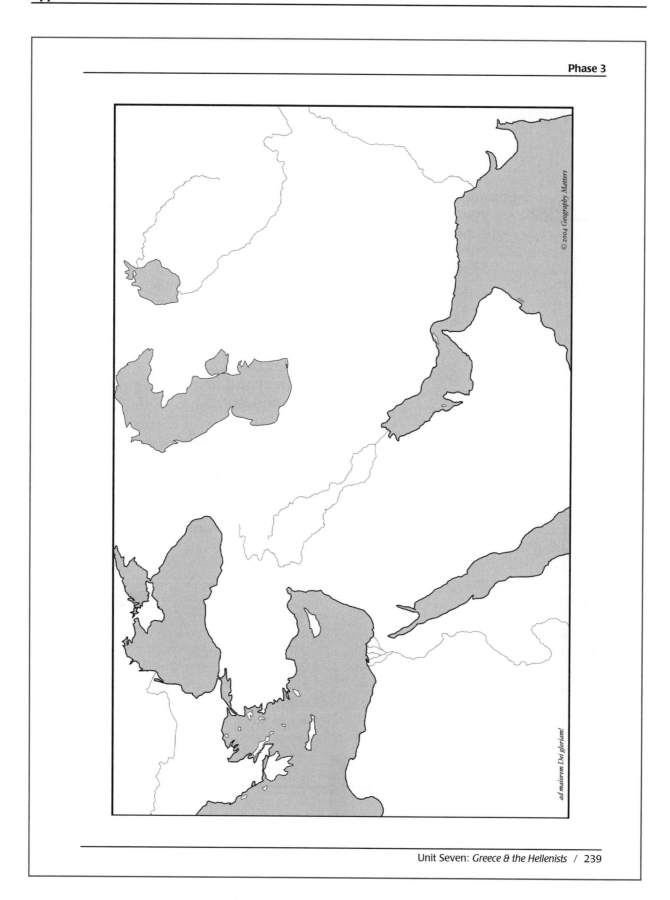

© 2004 Geography Matters

ad maiorem Dei gloriam!

The largest empire begins...
Article from Student Manual pages 251-261

"After this I saw in the night visions, and behold, a fourth beast, dreadful and terrible, exceedingly strong. It had huge iron teeth; it was devouring, breaking in pieces, and trampling the residue with its feet. It was different from all the beasts that were before it…" Daniel 7:7

Rome. The exceedingly strong country, which would swallow the kingdom of Alexander and his generals along with many far away lands, was birthed in legendary violence. The story of the beginnings of Rome tells of two brothers, Romulus and Remus, who quarreled over who should have the honor of building a city and naming it after himself. In the end, Romulus was overcome with wrath, and struck down and killed his brother. Whether this has any basis in fact or not, there was a foundation of betrayal and bloodshed, which would later be evident in Rome's history. Romulus populated his new city by inviting all of the outcasts and outlaws of the surrounding area to live in Rome. To assist him in governing the city, King Romulus decided to establish a *senate* (meaning "old man") with one hundred men whom he appointed.

Rome was located halfway up the "boot of Italy," on the fertile western side of the country. The city was built along the Tiber River, on seven hills which formed a natural fortress sixteen miles inland from the Mediterranean. Cicero, a famous Roman writer from the first century B.C. wrote, *"The site of Rome is well supplied with natural springs, and healthy, in spite of unhealthy neighboring territory. For the hills channel the breezes, and provide shade for the valley."*

The first two and a half centuries of Rome's existence were spent under the rule of seven kings, many of whom were Etruscans, the most advanced people in Italy at the time. These kings brought about great improvements in Rome, particularly the great public works projects to drain the swamps around the seven hills and build the impressive and gigantic Capitol. But the last king, Tarquinnius Superbus, was such an unbelievably cruel and wicked ruler that the people eventually banished him and his whole family. That was in the year 510 B.C., and from that point, the Roman people maintained such a continuing abhorrence for kings that, several centuries later, it would contribute to the downfall of Julius Caesar.

In place of a king, the Romans established a form of government known as a *republic* (meaning "public things"). Rather than give one ruler too much power, they preferred a multitude of government officials who had specific duties in the governing of Rome. These men were selected solely from the Senate, and their positions included: two *consuls*, who governed the military and were in charge of overseeing Rome; eight *praetors* to act as judges in the courts; four *aediles* to take care of the public buildings, as well as the public games and corn supply; and twenty *quaestors* who handled the state finances. These positions of power, and indeed all of the Senate positions, were only to be filled by those who could trace their ancestry back to the original advisors to King Romulus. These *patricians* were all wealthy landowners, who for the most part, neglected the poverty and starvation issues facing the common people. The common people, or *plebeians*, because they greatly resented the patricians controlling the government, demanded their own voice. The result was that in 494 B.C., after violent political demonstrations, the plebeians set up their own assembly, and elected ten *tribunes* to be their representatives in government. Eventually, the tribunes came to have the power to call the Senate to a meeting, to introduce laws, and to stop unjust laws passed by the Senate. The underlying struggle between patrician and plebeian would, however, continue for centuries.

This new republic was not popular with its neighbors, probably because the neighboring kings were concerned that it would give republican ideas to their own people! As they began to attack, Rome had to fight for its life. A Latin alliance of cities defeated the Romans in 496 B.C., forcing them to join the alliance. But over the next one hundred years, as they ably learned how to defend themselves, the

Romans doubled their territory and became the leading city in this alliance.

The next century was spent enlarging their territory, though it started off with disaster. In 378 B.C., a northern European tribe called the Gauls invaded and destroyed most of Rome. The devastated Romans had to both rebuild their city and then reconquer their lost lands. By the late 200's, Rome had beaten the Gauls, as well as the powerful Etruscans, and dominated all but the southern part of Italy.

You might recall from the last unit that Greek settlers in the 700's B.C. had set up Greek city-states in many areas throughout the Mediterranean, including the southern part of Italy. In 282 B.C., when one of the Greek cities asked mighty Rome for military help to protect them from a warring tribe, many others joined in the plea. However, one Greek city, Tarentum, was not pleased with the idea of Roman "barbarians" coming into their Greek area of Italy. They ended up insulting Rome and provoking a war. Since they were not personally equipped to fight against the Roman army, the people of Tarentum sought the help of a Greek king, Pyrrhus of Epirus, and his army from northern Greece. The struggle between these two armies was very costly in lives, and, though King Pyrrhus won the first few battles, he recognized that "if we win one more victory against the Romans, we shall be totally ruined." Rome pursued the war until King Pyrrhus was vanquished, and Tarentum surrendered. With this victorious conclusion, Rome became the dominant city-state in Italy with allies throughout the width and breadth of the land—allies who were increasingly Romanized in language and culture. Rome was now one of the most significant military powers in the Mediterranean.

On the coast of North Africa, about four hundred miles south across the Mediterranean from Rome, was a fabulously wealthy and powerful city-state founded by the seafaring Phoenicians somewhere between 814 B.C. (traditional date) and 750 B.C. (archaeological date). Carthage was a thriving commercial empire which had come to dominate trade in the Mediterranean, due to its massive navy and its strategic location, ever since the destruction of Tyre and Sidon by Alexander the Great. Carthage had colonized the western part of the island of Sicily in the 400's B.C. as part of its commercial empire, but when it took the Sicilian city of Messana in 264 B.C., the Romans saw this as a potential threat to their territory and gave an immediate military response. Thus began the Punic Wars, which would conclude with Carthage annihilated, and Rome standing as the greatest power in the world.

The First Punic War lasted twenty-three years. For the first eight years, Rome had the more powerful land army but virtually no navy, while Carthage ruled the seas but could not win on land. This put them into a virtual deadlock until, one earthshaking day, a Carthaginian ship was stranded on a Roman beach. Within sixty days, Rome had built a fleet of one hundred exact replicas of this ship and set to sea. Though they lost not only this fleet but the next one to the fierceness of Mediterranean storms, they eventually were able to use their third fleet of fighting ships to categorically defeat Carthage's navy in 241 B.C. and to oust them from Sicily. This ended the first war, and gave Rome the boost it needed to obtain a superior navy, which is necessary if one is to have a first-class empire.

The Second Punic War began in 218 B.C. Carthage bore a hatred toward Rome from its previous defeat, and continued to seek a way of defeating the proud Romans. Since they knew from experience that an attack on Rome from the Mediterranean side was doomed to failure, Carthage looked for another, more successful means of attack.

Unfortunately for Rome, the Carthaginian army was now commanded by one of the most brilliant generals in history, who conceived a most unexpected strategy. Hannibal, who had commanded troops in Spain, as had his father before him, took an army of 35,000 men and a secret weapon—thirty-seven war elephants—along a surprisingly unexpected route. Up to this point, the Alps mountain range across the top of Italy had been a formidable barrier for keeping out unwanted armies. Hannibal crossed them, nonetheless, in the severe cold and snow of winter. Ten thousand of his men and all but one of the elephants died, but once he entered Roman territory, his army was never defeated. For a few years, the Roman policy under Quintus Fabius was to continually harass the enemy but to avoid a major confrontation since the Roman army was not in a position to guarantee a victory against Hannibal. In 216 B.C., that policy changed and an army of 80,000 Romans—the largest ever assembled up to that time in Roman history—met the Carthaginian army at Cannae. Hannibal's shrewd tactics brought about the worst defeat the Romans ever suffered, with 50,000 men killed and 10,000 taken prisoner. It decimated the Roman army, and left the city of Rome vulnerable. Not recognizing his advantage, Hannibal did not attack the city of Rome at that vulnerable moment, since he felt it was still impregnable.

In hind sight, we know that if Hannibal had marched on Rome, he would have likely conquered the city at that point, and history would have been greatly altered.

However, as Daniel saw in his vision, Rome was destined for a much greater role on the world's stage.

Fighting for its life, Rome decided to go on the offense against Carthage in order to get Hannibal and his army out of Italy. A Roman general named Scipio took troops first to Spain to attack Carthaginian territory, then moved on to North Africa and the city of Carthage itself. The leaders of Carthage recognized the seriousness of the threat against their city-state, so recalled Hannibal from Italy. Hannibal with his army met the Roman army under Scipio in 202 B.C. at a place called Zama, and this time the Romans won. Not only did they demand a huge amount of money from the Carthaginians but also celebrated their victory by seizing Spanish territories from Carthage.

The third and final Punic War lasted three years (149-146 B.C.). The Romans discovered that Carthage, once again strong and healthy, was rearming itself for war. Determined to defeat this city once and for all, the Romans laid siege to Carthage for three years, and in the end, utterly destroyed it. All of the people of Carthage were killed, except 50,000 who were taken away to slavery. The city was set aflame, and the land itself was salted to prevent anything from ever growing there again. They devoured it, broke it in pieces, and trampled it under foot. And they gained another province, North Africa.

In that same year, the Roman army smashed a Greek uprising in the city of Corinth. The Romans had been fighting battles in Macedonia and Greece for the previous fifty years, and their military presence had increasingly infiltrated the realm of Greece. Now, with the destruction of Corinth, all of Greece came under the power of Rome, with a Roman governor ruling over them. Slowly and inexorably, Rome, with its nearly invincible army, gained control of the entire Mediterranean.

The conquering of these various lands and people caused Rome to grow in power, but it also caused increasing inequality between the rich and poor at home. As the wealthy were greatly profiting from the wars, the poor were increasingly impoverished through unemployment since more and more slaves were used for traditional jobs. Many of the soldiers of Rome were normally farmers who, during all of these wars, spent so much time away from home that their farms were ruined through neglect. Those who had profited from the conquests were then able to purchase these derelict farms, along with other lands, thereby creating huge landholdings. When the displaced farmers/soldiers went to the city to look for work, they found that most jobs were filled by slaves brought from conquered lands. An increasing number of poor people were permanently unemployed and permanently upset about it.

In 133 B.C., Tiberius Gracchus, grandson of Scipio, the conqueror of Carthage, proposed that the very wealthy give up the lands which had been unjustly taken, and that these lands be divided among the poor. This passed into law while Tiberius was a tribune, but it made the patricians and the Senate very angry. They provoked a riot in which Tiberius was killed. When his brother, Caius, also sought to help the poor stand against the rich, he too was murdered.

By 120 B.C., two political groups had emerged to deal with the tremendous tension between the rich and poor in Rome. The *optimates* believed that things should stay as they were, that the wealthy were justified in their acquisitions, and that the Senate should be firmly in control. The *populares* wanted to give the poor more land, give grain to the starving, and let the common people rise in power. Marius, one of the most powerful generals of the time, was from a plebeian family, and he came to represent the populares position. His great military success in Africa and in wars with barbarians from the Baltic Sea made him very popular with the people, who elected him as consul seven times, beginning in 107 B.C. The patricians did not dare to speak a word against him due to his popularity, but they were well aware that he was defying the law and dominating Rome in an increasingly dangerous way.

Another general, an optimate from the patrician class, was also growing in power. This man, Sulla, was elected consul in 88 B.C., and then sent by the patrician Senate to lead a Roman army against a dangerous opposing king, Mithridates, in Asia Minor. After Sulla left with his army, the plebeian Assembly decided that Marius should lead the army instead. When Marius sent word to Sulla that he was coming to take over, Sulla rallied his troops to his side and turned back toward Rome to defeat these "rebels." Marius and his troops were quickly defeated, and he was condemned to die.

Escaping from Rome, Marius fled the city and eventually landed as an exile in Africa. While Sulla went back to fighting King Mithridates, a new army of plebeians was raised to fight against the patricians for the rights of the common people. This army asked Marius to lead them and he accepted. Once on the march, he quickly conquered Rome and was elected consul yet again by the people.

Do you remember the foundation of bloodshed and betrayal in the beginning of Rome? As the Republic became more and more unstable, as armies were increasingly loyal to their generals rather than their government, as the masses of poor people were won by the politicians who provided them with gladiator contests and free food, and as the rich sought only more gain for themselves at the cost of the poor, bloodshed and betrayal would become a visible part of the political and relational structure of Rome. The Republican ideals of government by many would devolve into rule by one powerful leader, and this would eventually destroy the Republic.

When Marius was firmly in control as consul, he turned vengeful eyes on the patricians, those who had driven him into exile. He personally led his murderous guards throughout Rome, killing all of Sulla's supporters. Hundreds of the most noble men of Rome were slain, until no one who had supported Sulla was left. Two weeks later, after his unappeasable fury had spent itself, Marius died.

When Sulla returned victorious from his war in Asia, he learned of Maurius' hateful vengeance. Not only did he learn what had happened, he learned the lesson of striking terror into the hearts of anyone who disagreed with the ruler. When he became a dictator from 82-80 B.C., Sulla's focus and purpose was patrician revenge. He ordered all the followers of Marius to be executed, and when this was finished and the intimidated people of Rome thought peace would follow, he confounded them all. Not content with the destruction of his obvious enemies, Sulla brutally continued to order the seemingly random executions of thousands of people, both rich and poor, throughout Rome and Italy. After this year long reign of terror, he gathered the stunned people of Rome together for a parade of triumph, where he showed off riches and captured treasures from his military conquests in Asia Minor. Can you imagine how absolutely *surreal* this parade must have seemed, and how the terrified people must have clapped and cheered in order to avoid being the next victim? After accomplishing his revenge and his triumphant war display, Sulla retired from office and died.

Next on the scene comes Pompey, another mighty military commander of Roman armies. After Pompey helped the Roman leader Marcus Crassus put down a slave rebellion, led by Spartacus in 71 B.C., he and Crassus were each made consul the following year. Pompey then went on to brilliantly defeat marauding pirates who had been terrorizing ships and coastal lands of the Mediterranean, and to continue the war against Mithridates in Asia Minor. After years of conquering not only Mithridates, but Syria and Palestine as well, Pompey returned in triumph to Rome. When the Senate would not approve the distribution of land, which he had promised to his troops for their military successes, Pompey decided to find a way around their power. In 60 B.C., this adored idol of the masses, along with Crassus and Julius Caesar (a rising star), formed an alliance, known as the First Triumvirate, in order to battle politically against the Senate. What Pompey did not realize was that Julius Caesar was going to eclipse him in power and popularity. He would pay for this oversight with his life.

Julius Caesar was born circa 100 B.C. to patrician parents, but as he came to power, he allied himself with the plebeians. He was considered one of the best orators of Roman history (second only to Cicero), a military genius, and an astute politician. Caesar was elected to a number of political positions in Rome over a ten year period, from the lowest position of quaestor all the way to top-ranking consul in 59 B.C. He was, at this time, part of the First Triumvirate, and used his position as consul to force the Senate to accept the Triumvirate's policies. After his one year term as consul, Caesar was sent on a military conquest of Gaul. For the next nine years, he performed his duties ingeniously, beating not only the Gauls but beginning the conquest of Britain, as well. In 49 B.C., the Senate, under Pompey's prompting, demanded that Caesar return to Rome without his army. Realizing that this would leave him defenseless and at the mercy of his enemies in Rome, Caesar boldly defied the Senate, entering Italy at the head of a powerful and loyal army. Pompey and the wealthy patrician senators fled Rome, and, within sixty days, Caesar stood unopposed as the sole master of the Roman Republic. When Pompey raised an army against him in Greece, Caesar took his troops to war. In 48 B.C., Pompey was defeated, and, fleeing to Egypt for protection and exile, was murdered by the Egyptian ruler.

When Julius Caesar followed Pompey to Egypt, he found more than he had been looking for. Being presented with the embalmed head of Pompey provided relief for Caesar, but meeting the mesmerizing Cleopatra provided an ongoing entrapment, which would set many influential Romans against him. Cleopatra, the last of the reigning Ptolemies of the Hellenistic empire, had been co-ruler of Egypt with her brother, but now was engaged in a struggle for sole control. Caesar helped Cleopatra in her quest to be queen, and, at the same time, fathered her child. Then leaving Egypt, Caesar continued his battle against the hastily raised armies of Pompey's supporters in Asia Minor, Africa, and Spain for two more years. Once he returned victoriously to Rome, Caesar pardoned his enemies and made senators of those who would have traditionally been ineligible. He embarked on a number of projects, like reforming the calendar and passing laws to improve the way the government operated. He also built aqueducts, monumental buildings, and a great library. Though the people loved him, to the point of carrying his statue in a procession which honored the gods, many of the ruling senators hated him, convinced that Caesar was on the verge of making himself king. Not only did they fear his becoming king, they also saw that, once this position was obtained, Caesar would rule much of the earth with his Egyptian queen. This would end the republic, and these republicans were ready to do anything to make sure this did not happen. So, on the Ides of March (March 15), they attacked him in the Senate and assassinated him at the feet of the statue of Pompey. How ironic that the one who was responsible for Pompey's death was now dead at his statue's feet.

Julius Caesar's will designated his great-nephew, Octavius, as his heir and adopted son. Opposing this was Caesar's lieutenant, Mark Antony, who jealously believed that he should have been the heir of Caesar. Along with the disdainful antagonism of Antony, Octavius faced the daunting prospect of fighting two of Caesar's assassins, Cassius and Brutus, along with the army they had raised to defend the Republic. Antony and Octavius put their differences momentarily behind them in order to fight Cassius and Brutus in Macedonia. When this was successfully accomplished, Octavius, Antony, and a third ruler, Lepidus, drew up a list of 2,300 people who were considered powerful enemies. These 2,300 men were executed, their land and wealth confiscated and given to Roman soldiers. Eventually, Antony left Rome to deal with problems in the East while Octavius took care of the issues at home and Lepidus dropped out of sight. Antony, while soldiering in Turkey, met Cleopatra and, losing sight of everything else, spent all his energies to court her. Octavius, on the other hand, patiently and unerringly courted the favor of the Senate and restored peaceful order to Rome and Italy.

As each of these men pursued their objectives, their differences became more and more obvious to the Roman people. Antony was hated by one and all in Rome because of his illegal marriage to Cleopatra, and because he had then given Roman territory to her and her children. Octavius, the rightful heir of Caesar, was seen as a respecter of the Republic and an able leader. At last, these differences erupted into war. At the Battle of Actium, in 31 B.C., Octavius defeated the combined armed forces of Mark Antony and Cleopatra. After conquering Egypt and making it another Roman province, Octavius went back to Rome as the unchallenged ruler of the entire empire. In 27 B.C., he was given the name "Augustus" indicating an almost superhuman status. From that point, he was known as Augustus Caesar, the First Citizen, and, in effect, the first Roman emperor.

At this point in history, Rome was the center of the largest empire the world had ever known. Through the might of its well-trained and well-disciplined armies, Rome had marched against countries and city-states throughout the western part of Europe, North Africa, Egypt, Syria, Palestine, Greece, Macedonia, and Asia Minor, relentlessly devouring one after another, turning them into Roman provinces under the rule of a Roman governor.

"And the fourth kingdom shall be as strong as iron, inasmuch as iron breaks in pieces and shatters all things; and like iron that crushes, that kingdom will break in pieces and crush all the others." Daniel 2:40

The stage has been set for the final part of Daniel's vision:

"And in the days of these kings the God of heaven will set up a kingdom which shall never be destroyed; and the kingdom shall not be left to other people; it shall break in pieces and consume all these kingdoms, and it shall stand forever." Daniel 2:44

The best is now to come.

Reviewed Resources for Digging Deeper:

From Student Manual pages 264-267

Biographies

Plutarch—Lives of Noble Romans edited by Fuller

Plutarch was one of the earliest biographers in history! All the plays William Shakespeare wrote about the Romans were derived from Plutarch's biographies. Difficult reading, but some might enjoy it. Plutarch compared Roman leaders with Greek leaders. **HS+**

Famous Men of Rome edited by Rob Shearer

A much gentler version of the following book, it gives a good introduction to the most important men of this empire. **E+**

Lives of Famous Romans by Olivia Coolidge

Any set of biographies on the Romans is bound to be distasteful to some extent, since so many of the ruling Romans (especially of the Empire) were given over to utter immorality. My suggestion is to read these biographies in light of Daniel 2, and the perspective given in the gospels and Acts. **HS+**

World Leaders Past and Present: Cleopatra by Hoobler and Hoobler

This book takes a sympathetic look at the last reigning Ptolemy in Egypt. Cleopatra was revered by the Egyptians, loved by Caesar and Antony, and hated by the Romans. Learn why in this intriguing book. **MS+**

Cleopatra by Robert Green

This is a good, short biography of the last reigning Ptolemy, the woman who conquered both Julius Caesar and Mark Antony. **UE+**

Hannibal by Robert Green

Another short biography, this is an excellent introduction to Carthage's greatest general and Rome's greatest fear. **UE+**

Architecture

City by David Macauley

Mr. Macauley helps us to see the incredible cultural dynamic of architecture. Learn how a Roman city was designed and built, in this fascinating book. **UE+**

Julius Caesar

Caesar's Gallic War translated, edited by Olivia Coolidge

This version of Julius Caesar's autobiographical account of the Gallic War is fabulous! Olivia Coolidge has added enough "color" that it draws the reader in to the story. I absolutely recommend it! **MS+**

Julius Caesar by William Shakespeare

One of Shakespeare's most famous plays. **MS+**

World Leaders Past and Present: Julius Caesar by Roger Bruns

An excellent book in this excellent series! I preferred this book to the one about Mark Antony, and much of the same time period and material is covered. After reading Caesar's Gallic Wars, this book will fill in the gaps. **MS+**

Ancient Rome

The Romans—Usborne Illustrated World History by Anthony Marks and Graham Tingay

Filled with short descriptions and great pictures, this is a wonderful, concise, fact-filled book about ancient Rome. **UE+**

The Romans—Life in the Empire by Charles Guittard and Annie-Claude Martin

This is a birds-eye look at the culture and everyday life of the Roman people. Helpful for understanding the times. **UE+**

Ancient Rome by Philippa Medcalf and Jan Rolph

This Cambridge Junior History book is an excellent introduction to ancient Rome for pre-high school students. **UE+**

Augustus Caesar's World by Genevieve Foster

A fascinating book for all ages which tells the story of Augustus Caesar, describing the world in which he lived. **E+**

Growing Up in Ancient Rome by Mike Corbishley

Another book in the series, this is one of the best books I know for introducing the lifestyle and culture of ancient Rome. Excellent overview for children. **E+**

Make it Work! The Roman Empire by Peter Chrisp

This is a hands-on approach to learning history! Filled with ideas for Roman clothing, art, architecture, weaponry, and more, it certainly has enough ideas to keep everyone happy. **E+**

Archaeology

The Lost Wreck of the Isis by Robert D. Ballard

Learn about underwater archaeology while reading a fictional tale of a ship lost at sea during Roman times. Very interesting. **UE+**

Sunk! Exploring Underwater Archaeology

This is a fascinating book showing how archaeologists discover new aspects of history and ancient cultures under the water. **UE+**

Piece by Piece! Mosaics of the Ancient World

A wonderful look at this art form, this book is filled with pictures and the stories mosaics have "told" to archaeologists. **E+**

Science

Science in Ancient Rome by Jacqueline Harris

This is an excellent introduction to the scientific achievements of the Romans, perfect for younger students. **UE+**

Roman Roads and Aqueducts by Don Nardo

One of the titles in the Building History series, this is a fascinating look at how Rome was able to build such long-lasting, efficient roads and aqueducts. **MS+**

Bridges: A Project Book by Anne & Scott MacGregor

If you can find the book, there is a wonderful project for building a Roman-arch bridge. **E+**

Make it Work! Building by David Glover

Another book from this fantastic series, this one shows two different projects for the family to do: a keystone bridge and an aqueduct. **E+**

Punic Wars

The Young Carthaginian by G.A. Henty

Henty's fictional story of Hannibal's war against Rome, told from the perspective of Hannibal's young cousin, is a fantastic way to learn about this important moment in history. Highly recommended! **UE+**

Hannibal's Elephants by Alfred Powers

A fictionalized account of the mighty Hannibal, general of Carthage. It is told from the perspective of a boy who helps care for the war elephants during the Second Punic War with Rome. It is very interesting, especially for boys. **UE+**

Military View

Life of a Roman Soldier by Don Nardo

Rome was able to conquer because her soldiers were tireless, fearless, well-trained, well-organized and nearly invincible. Learn fascinating details about the Roman military in this excellent book. **MS+**

For more books, use these Dewey Decimal numbers in your library:

Ancient Rome: #937

Also, look for biographies on the key people listed.

Phase 2

➢ *Timeline*

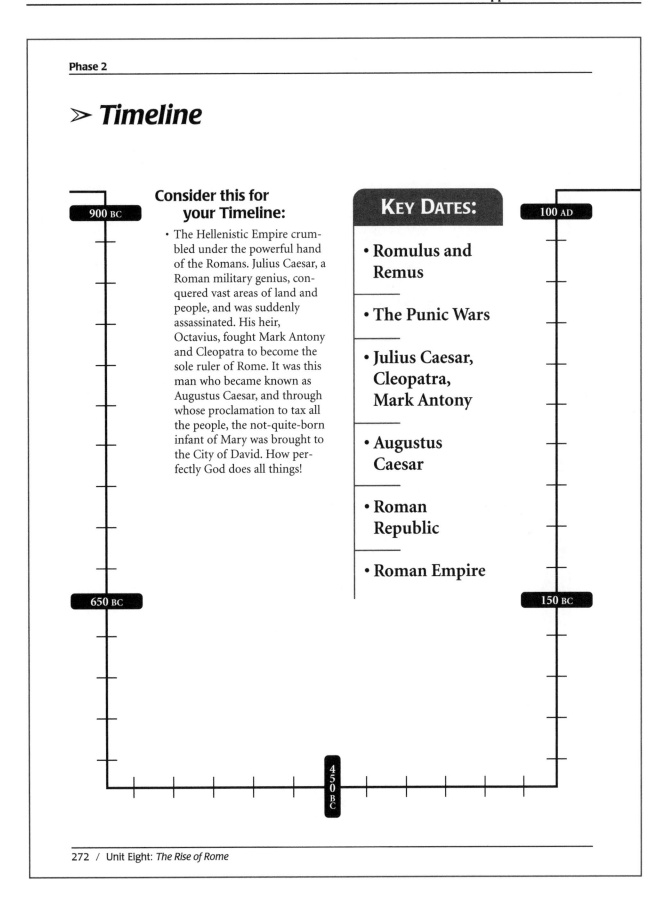

Consider this for your Timeline:

- The Hellenistic Empire crumbled under the powerful hand of the Romans. Julius Caesar, a Roman military genius, conquered vast areas of land and people, and was suddenly assassinated. His heir, Octavius, fought Mark Antony and Cleopatra to become the sole ruler of Rome. It was this man who became known as Augustus Caesar, and through whose proclamation to tax all the people, the not-quite-born infant of Mary was brought to the City of David. How perfectly God does all things!

KEY DATES:

- **Romulus and Remus**
- **The Punic Wars**
- **Julius Caesar, Cleopatra, Mark Antony**
- **Augustus Caesar**
- **Roman Republic**
- **Roman Empire**

900 BC

650 BC

100 AD

150 BC

450 BC

272 / Unit Eight: *The Rise of Rome*

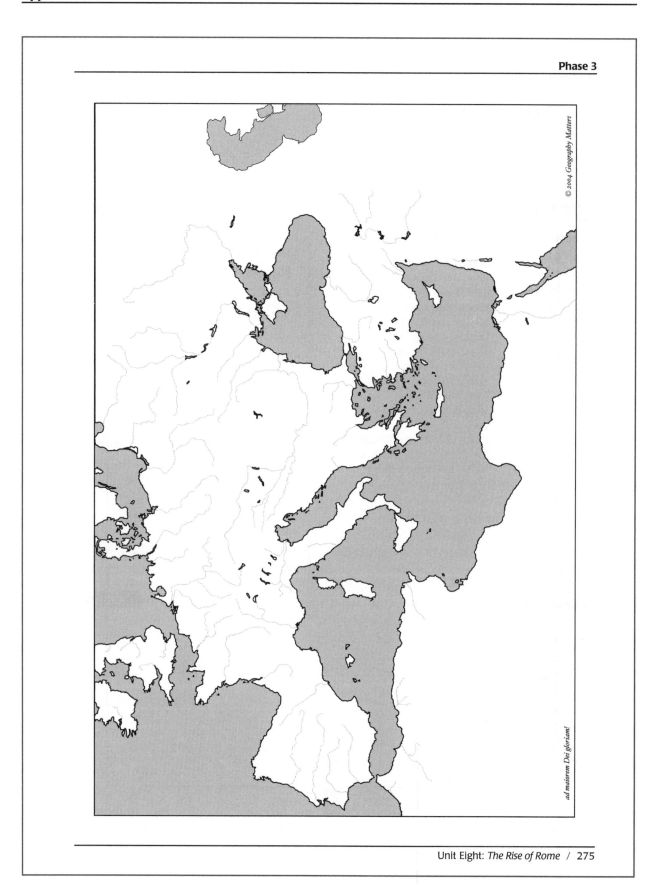

© 2004 Geography Matters

ad maiorem Dei gloriam!

Unit Eight: *The Rise of Rome* / 275

The Promised One has come...

Article from Student Manual pages 285-291

*"For unto us a Child is born, unto us a Son is
given;
And the government shall be upon His shoulder.
And His name will be called Wonderful,
Counselor,
Mighty God, Everlasting Father, Prince of Peace.
Of the increase of His government and peace
there will be no end.
Upon the throne of David and over His kingdom,
To order it and establish it with judgment and
justice
From that time forward, even forever.
The zeal of the Lord of hosts will perform this."*
Isaiah 9:6-7

All of man's history from Adam and Eve to the Roman Empire had been leading up to this moment in history. The scarlet thread of redemption, which God had been mercifully weaving through the lives of people and nations, was now to become fully visible, in vibrant living color, clothed in the robes of frail humanity. The Promised One, the Messiah, Jesus of Nazareth, was to enter our world at a precise moment known to us as "the fulness of time" (Galatians 4:4).

Since Jesus would come as a baby to a specific family (the tribe of Judah, the family of David) in a specific geographic location (Palestine) at a specific time (during the fourth kingdom of Daniel's vision), it would do well for us to understand what Palestine was like for the Jews in this time period, and how they had come to have a king over them who was not of the royal lineage of David.

After the Temple was cleansed and rededicated to the Lord in 165 B.C., Judas Maccabees continued to lead his troops against the Syrians and eventually died in battle. His brother, Jonathan, then became the leader of the Maccabean revolt from 160-143 B.C.. Jonathan was remarkably adept at diplomacy, which resulted in his signing a treaty with Rome against Syria. Jonathan then used his diplomatic skills with the rulers of Syria to gain the posts of High Priest over the Jews and political governor over Judea. Oddly enough, Jonathan was even made one of the Syrian nobility!

When Jonathan died, his brother, Simon, succeeded to the position of High Priest and political ruler over Judea (143-135 B.C.). Israel attained its longed-for independence when Simon, through the means of diplomacy, ended the taxation imposed on Israel by the Syrians. For this stupendous endeavor, the Jewish leaders gave Simon the name, "leader and High Priest for ever, until there shall arise a faithful prophet." This was the beginning of the Hasmonaean dynasty (from the line of Mattathias), which would continue until the reign of Herod (37-4 B.C.). Isn't it interesting to consider that the family of Mattathias was neither in the line of Aaron the first High Priest, nor David the king whom God had promised would have a descendant on the throne forever? This means that the selection of Simon's family to rule and reign was a man-made decision, with political foundations. And, as we shall see, leaving God out of the equation resulted in a Godless rulership of His chosen people.

Israel's independence would last for only eighty years, until Pompey and his Roman army invaded Jerusalem in 63 B.C. These eighty years were filled with Greek tragedy, as the increasingly Hellenized Hasmonaean rulers of Israel murdered their siblings for the throne, acquired the Hellenistic propensity for expanding their boundaries militarily, and grew as far from orthodox Judaism as the east is from the west. On the eve of civil war between Hyrcanus II and Aristobulus II, two Hasmonaean brothers who each laid claim to the throne, Pompey came from Syria to subdue this Jewish strife. In his coming—which was justified because of Jonathan's treaty with Rome in 160 B.C.—he laid siege to Jerusalem for three months and, when he had gained the city, proceeded to execute twelve thousand Jews. Israel was then forcibly brought into the Roman fold, as part of the Roman Province of Syria.

By Rome's authority, Hyrcanus II was made governor of Judea and High Priest, though the man behind the scenes, who really controlled the throne, was a non-Jew by the name of Antipater. Before Pompey's invasion, Antipater had been the governor of a land conquered and Judaized by the Hasmonaeans. Antipater, both cunning and politically savvy, was well aware that Rome was the emerging power to be reckoned with in the Middle East. Necessity forced him to become very adept at changing loyalties in order to stay on the winning side. As you may remember from the last unit, Pompey was defeated by Julius Caesar, which did not bode well for those who had gained their power through Pompey. However, Antipater jumped sides and brought much-needed assistance to Julius Caesar in Egypt. For this, he was given the title and political position of Procurator of Judea, while Hyrcanus continued as High Priest. After Julius Caesar's assassination, Antipater and his sons quickly welcomed Cassius, one of Caesar's assassins, who had come to the area with his newly raised army. Further, Antipater took the initiative to provide to Cassius the tribute taxes belonging to Rome. When Cassius and Brutus were defeated by Mark Antony, Antipater's sons changed sides once again (Antipater having been murdered by a rival). Antipater's son, Herod, went in person to meet with Mark Antony. Convincing Antony of his family's loyalty with a generous amount of money, Herod and his brother, Phasaelus, were now made Tetrarchs of Judea.

When the Parthians from the East invaded Jerusalem in 40 B.C., Phasaelus died a prisoner, and Herod, who barely escaped with his life, fled to the safety of Rome. Antony introduced Herod to Octavius, heir of Julius Caesar—a most fortuitous meeting for Herod. Through the influence of Mark Antony and Octavius, the Roman Senate voted Herod, "King of the Jews." This was most likely a political prize to motivate Herod to rid Palestine of the Parthians, who had never been defeated by Rome, but what it did, in effect, was link Herod's rule of Judea to the military might of Rome. From that point on, anyone who wanted to mess with King Herod would have to deal with the Roman Empire. It took a few years and a large Roman army to accomplish the defeat of the Parthians, but by 37 B.C., Herod was on his throne. Can you imagine? The ruler designated by Rome to be "King of the Jews" was not even Jewish! This was utterly abhorrent, especially to the growing nationalistic movement and to those who still clung to the Jewish faith.

There were at this time four main groups or *sects* within Judaism. The Sadducees were the aristocracy of Jerusalem and the administrators of the Temple, including the high priesthood. To be a Sadducee, one had to be born a Sadducee, as membership to this aristocratic and wealthy group was restricted to those whose families already belonged. Essenes, the second group, were a mostly monastic group who lived in strict, isolated religious communities of the desert. They conducted their religious worship services in their desert communities, refusing to offer sacrifices in Jerusalem, since the worldly Sadducees were in charge of the Temple. The third group was the Pharisees, or *separated ones*, who held to orthodox Judaism. They considered the oral traditions of Judaism to be of the same importance, however, as the written Law, or *Torah*. These oral traditions had originally been delivered by influential rabbis over a period of time in an attempt to deal with the increasing complexities of living out the Law in a Greek world. But, by the time of Jesus, the strict observance of these traditions had become more important and far more legalistic than God's Law. The fourth group were the Zealots, the fiercely nationalistic movement to free Israel from hated Roman rule. Herod, when he had earlier ruled in Galilee, tried to brutally suppress this movement by executing a Zealot leader and many of his followers, but they continued to foment violent opposition to Rome and to seek Israel's independence. Though they seem to have headquartered in Galilee, their influence was felt throughout the land. Eventually, the Zealots' passion to overthrow Roman authority would bring about the destruction of Jerusalem in 70 A.D.

Now the stage is set. The place is Palestine, in the Roman Province of Syria. The date is approximately 4 B.C.

"And it came to pass in those days that a decree went out from Caesar Augustus that all the world should be registered." Luke 2:1

In a tiny corner of the Roman Empire, far from the centers of political power and influential wealth, a young couple traveled sixty miles from their poor home in Nazareth of Galilee to Bethlehem in Judea. Joseph, of the house of David, had to return with his wife to their ancestral home in order to be registered. This young wife, Mary, carried her soon-to-be-born infant. Her God-given pregnant condition was both miraculous and prophetic.

"Therefore the Lord Himself will give you a sign: Behold, the virgin shall conceive and bear a Son, and shall call His name Immanuel." Isaiah 7:14

Immanuel. It means, "God with us." No longer would we be alone and hopeless. God Himself would be *with* us...with us in our humanity because He would become human. We would be able to walk with Him in an intimacy of relationship we had not known since the Garden of Eden. The distance between the Creator and the created would change to closeness as the Creator became Immanuel, God with us.

And now, at one of the most dark and helpless times in Israel's history, a child, who was the Son of God, grew inside this Jewish girl's womb. Beyond our ability to fully comprehend, He was conceived by the Holy Spirit, and was fully God and fully man. God the Son—the second person of the Trinity—humbled Himself to become one of us...in order to be with us.

"Let this mind be in you which was also in Christ Jesus, who, being in the form of God, did not consider it robbery to be equal with God, but made Himself of no reputation, taking the form of a servant, and coming in the likeness of men."
Philippians 2:5-7

This humbling of Himself did not end with His willingness to become a human baby. God had very precisely and specifically chosen the one who would be the mother of Immanuel. But, though Mary and Joseph were both of the royal lineage of David, they were poor. Jesus, the Son of God, entered the world He had created, not in the luxury, beauty and comfort of a royal palace fit for a king, but rather in a smelly, dirty animal stable. You see, there was no room for His human parents at the travelers' inn.

God with us, Immanuel, entered the world surrounded by all the trappings of poverty in all its hopelessness.

"For you know the grace of our Lord Jesus Christ, that though He was rich, yet for your sakes He became poor, that you through His poverty might become rich." 2 Corinthians 8:9

He did it for us. And He did it in a way that no one would expect. That is part of who God is and who we are

not. He sees things from a perspective we would never perceive and He does things we can not imagine doing:

"'For My thoughts are not your thoughts, nor are your ways My ways,' says the Lord. 'For as the heavens are higher than the earth, so are My ways higher than your ways, and My thoughts than your thoughts.'" Isaiah 55:8-9

Everything about Jesus—the manner of His birth, the hiddenness of his youth (apart from one notable exception), the style of His ministry, the shame of His death, the shock of His resurrection—is so different than the way we would have written the story. His convention-breaking conversation with the loose-living Samaritan woman totally confounded His own disciples; His simple answer to the politically explosive question, "Is it lawful to pay taxes to Caesar, or not?" muzzled his opponents; His wisdom-beyond-Solomon's judgment of the woman caught in the act of adultery revealed the hearts of her accusers; His reputation of being a drunkard and a glutton destroyed any hope of seeming sufficiently religious. How could He have walked so differently than we do? How could He have so totally ignored the social and religious norms of His day? How could He love the ones no one liked, even a money-grubbing tax collector, and a friend who would betray Him? How could He resist the instant popularity of the mob by telling them they would need to eat His body and drink His blood? Beyond all this, how could He willingly offer His life as a sacrifice in order to save us? The answers all reside in who God is. We can not understand Jesus unless we recognize that He is God. God with us.

Jesus did not come to be a religious icon. He did not come to be a word in our vocabulary or a theological concept in our doctrines. He did not come to be a movie star, nor a fund-raising method, nor the origin for popular jewelry. He came for one purpose: to restore us to relationship with Himself.

This is all about Jesus. History shows us our desperate need and God's divine rescue. It is not an academic subject—it is a means of pointing us to Jesus. And He, Immanuel, came to be with us. We are back where we started in Unit One: "He made us for relationship, deeper and more satisfying than anything we have ever imagined."

Are you willing? The way back to God has been made for you, and His name is Jesus.

Reviewed Resources for Digging Deeper:

From Student Manual pages 295-296

Apologetics

Evidence that Demands a Verdict by Josh McDowell

This is not a book to sit down and read, it is a book to study. It will teach you the historical evidences for the Christian faith. (A term often used for this is "apologetics.") Filled with historical, archaeological, medical, legal references, this book will give you a very firm foundation for the defense of Biblical Christianity. **MS+**

Mere Christianity by C.S. Lewis

One of the classics of Christian apologetics, this considers the issue of whether Jesus was a liar, a lunatic, or Lord, as well as many other concepts. **HS**

Historical Fiction

Titus: A Comrade of the Cross by Florence Kingsley

A classic, this book helps make the events of the Gospel come to life. **MS+**

The Bronze Bow by Elizabeth Speare

Written for children, this is an absorbing tale about a young Jewish boy who struggles with his hatred for the conquering Romans. A very good insight into the mood of the times. **E+**

The Runaway by Patricia St. John

A very good story about a Phoenician boy whose sister is demon-possessed. The Scriptures come to life as you see the boy encounter many different people who have met Jesus. Our family couldn't put it down! **RA**

Ben Hur by Lew Wallace

This classic is written from the perspective of a prince of Judah who is thrown into Roman slavery. When he regains his freedom, he joins the guerrilla fighters who want a political Messiah. Having watched the movie and also read the book, I would highly recommend the book as it contains far more understanding of the culture, the times, the thoughts of the people. **MS+**

Ben Hur edited by Kottmeyer

If reading the original is beyond your students, you may want to consider getting a younger version. **E+**

Vinegar Boy by Alberta Hawse

This is the story of the boy assigned to bring vinegar to those who were crucified. It is a story of the bitterness of defeat being turned into the joy of victory **UE+**

The Robe by Lloyd Douglas

This is an excellent look at Roman ways and their conflict with Christianity. **MS+**

Biographies

Pontius Pilate by Paul Maier

> Historical fiction, the events of this book are based entirely on historic documentation. It is a fascinating look at this historic person. (There is one scene I would avoid, when Salome dances for King Herod.) **MS+**

The Jesus Story retold from the Bible by Mary Batchelor

> Though I prefer to have the actual story directly from Scripture, this is an excellent adaptation of the life of Jesus for younger students. **RA E+**

For more books, use these Dewey Decimal numbers in your library:

Bible: #220

Ancient Palestine: #933

New Testament: #225

Gospels & Acts: #226

Jesus Christ: #232

Also, look for biographies on the key people listed.

Phase 2

≫ *Timeline*

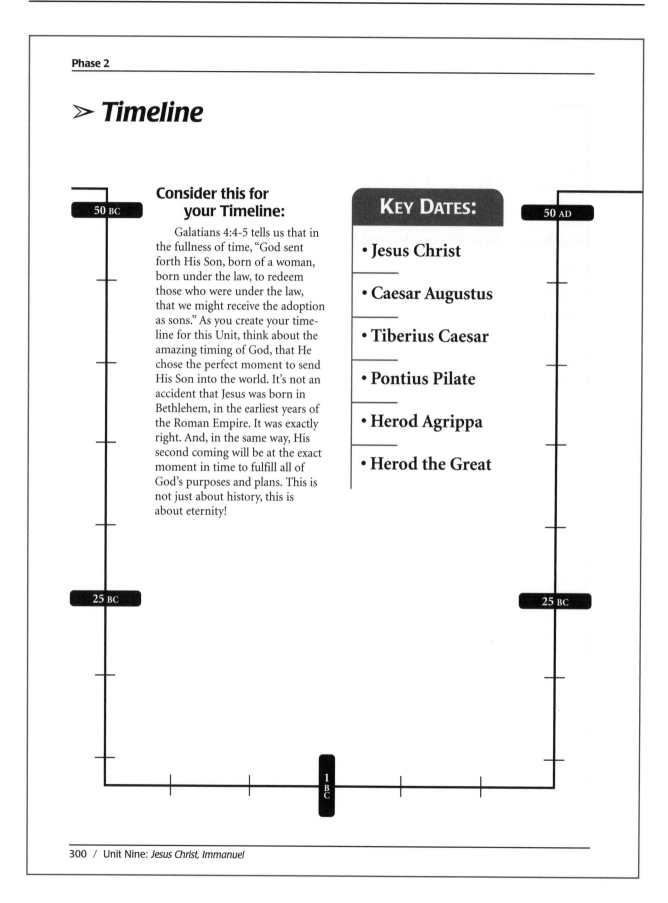

Consider this for your Timeline:

Galatians 4:4-5 tells us that in the fullness of time, "God sent forth His Son, born of a woman, born under the law, to redeem those who were under the law, that we might receive the adoption as sons." As you create your timeline for this Unit, think about the amazing timing of God, that He chose the perfect moment to send His Son into the world. It's not an accident that Jesus was born in Bethlehem, in the earliest years of the Roman Empire. It was exactly right. And, in the same way, His second coming will be at the exact moment in time to fulfill all of God's purposes and plans. This is not just about history, this is about eternity!

KEY DATES:

• **Jesus Christ**

• **Caesar Augustus**

• **Tiberius Caesar**

• **Pontius Pilate**

• **Herod Agrippa**

• **Herod the Great**

50 BC

25 BC

1 BC

50 AD

25 BC

300 / Unit Nine: *Jesus Christ, Immanuel*

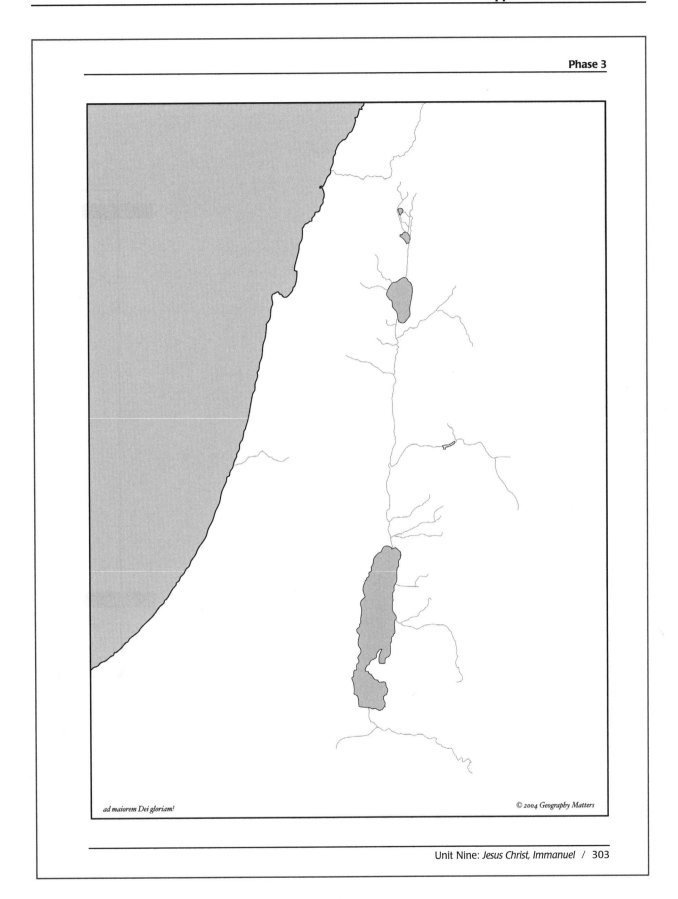

ad maiorem Dei gloriam!

© 2004 *Geography Matters*

ABOUT THE AUTHOR

Diana Waring has been fascinated by history since she was old enough to discover that World War II had ended ten years prior to her birth in Germany. As a child, she always wanted to understand the chronological march of kings, the connection between momentous events—epecially wars—and the international tapestry of fascinating people throughout the ages. The first glimmers of understanding came in a rapid-fire African history course at university, but the full explosion of light dawned when she began teaching world history side by side with the Bible to her three children. It was at that point, with the research required to answer their innumerable questions, that all the pieces began to fall in place. The contagious excitement of discovery led to her speaking and writing about history.

Mrs. Waring lives in a small town in the Black Hills of South Dakota with her husband and dog, when she is not visiting her adult children or traveling around the world to educate teachers and parents on the wonders of learning.